WOODY GUTHRIE
(*Robin Carson Photo*)

Woody Guthrie
Bound for Glory

Illustrated with sketches by the author
WITH AN INTRODUCTION BY STUDS TERKEL

E. P. DUTTON & CO., INC. | NEW YORK | 1976

770643

Introduction copyright © 1961, 1973 by Studs Terkel
This edition of *Bound for Glory* first published 1976 by
E. P. Dutton & Co., Inc.

Copyright 1943 by E. P. Dutton & Co., Inc.
Copyright renewed 1971 by Marjorie M. Guthrie
All rights reserved. Printed in the U.S.A.

10 9 8 7 6 5 4 3 2 1

No part of this publication may be reproduced or transmitted in any
form or by any means, electronic or mechanical, including photocopy,
recording, or any information storage and retrieval system now known
or to be invented, without permission in writing from the publisher,
except by a reviewer who wishes to quote brief passages in connection
with a review written for inclusion in a magazine, newspaper
or broadcast.

Published simultaneously in Canada by Clarke, Irwin &
Company Limited, Toronto and Vancouver

ISBN: 0-525-07025-7
Library of Congress Catalog Card Number: 68-28884

CONTENTS

CONTENTS

INTRODUCTION
by Studs Terkel

WOODY GUTHRIE, a tough, skinny, russety, wind-blown curly-head. A little piece of leather. A dirt road, hard pavement, dank boxcar, ship galley, cold city, hot desert, coast-to-coast poet and minstrel. The champion of all American ballad writers.

Plus newsboy, shoeshine boy, spittoon washer, hoer of fields, picker of mustang grapes, carpenter's helper, well-driller's assistant, sign painter, street singer.

Woody Guthrie died, at the age of fifty-five, in a Brooklyn hospital, after suffering for fifteen years from an ailment for which no cure has yet been found. Age fifty-five, and he had lived the lives of a dozen men.

In 1912, the *Titanic* sank. In 1912, Woodrow Wilson Guthrie was born. Fate sings its own kind of poetry. The day was July 14. Bastille Day in Paris, France. Woody's Day in Okemah, Oklahoma.

> This land is your land, this land is my land
> From California to the New York island.
> From the Redwood Forest to the Gulf Stream waters
> This land was made for you and me.

Nobody knows the exact number of songs written by Woody. Take a thousand, a good round conservative figure. The odds are better than even that there were more, many more. Written on the spot, any old spot. The wayside inn, the gas station, the greasy spoon, the Ma and Pa tavern, the hamburger heaven, the subway bench, the jungle camp, the friendly davenport. Been-here-and-gone pieces. How many of these were lost, bartered for a pint of "musky" or casually flipped away, not even Woody had the faintest idea.

I remember the summer of '41. Woody and three singing colleagues were in transit and spent a few days and nights in our jam-packed Chicago flat. At four in the morning, my dream was interrupted by the click-click of my Royal portable. It was Woody, who had just ambled home, touch-typing like crazy. I turned over and slept dreamlessly. A few hours later, as Woody snored softly and innocently in the adjoining room, I was picking sheets of paper from out the waste basket. There must have been at least thirty pages, single-spaced. Verse, prose, fragments of song; impressions, wild and vivid images of his night at a South Side tavern. They danced off the pages. The remembered words of barflies, their lost-in-the-fog look and a cock-eyed, tangential wisdom poured forth from the mumbo-jumbo of beer, the whisky shot in the false-bottom glass and the wino's muscatel.

Dust bowl songs, hobo songs, children's songs, work songs, loafing songs, war songs, peace songs, union songs, river and dam songs, lonesome turtle dove songs, *gemütlich* bear-hug songs, songs infinite in their variety celebrating the wonder of Man. For what is Man to Woody? "Just a hoping machine, a working machine. . . . The human race is a pretty old place."

> Now, as I look around
> It's mighty plain to see
> This wide and wicked world

Is a funny place to be.
The gambling man is rich and the working man is poor
And I ain't got no home in this world anymore.

"I hate a song that makes you think that you're not any
good. I hate a song that makes you think you are just born
to lose. No good to nobody. No good for nothing. Because
you are either too old or too young or too fat or too slim
or too ugly or too this or too that. Songs that run you down
or songs that poke fun at you on account of your bad luck
or hard traveling." Woody talking. "I am out to sing songs
that will prove to you that this is your world and that if it
has hit you pretty hard and knocked you for a dozen loops,
no matter how hard it's run you down and rolled over
you, no matter what color you are, what size you are, how
you are built, I am out to sing the songs that make you take
pride in yourself and in your work."

On up the river is Grand Coulee Dam,
The biggest thing built by the hand of man
To run the great factories and water the land.
Roll on, Columbia, roll on!

The men of the Bonneville Power Administration sensed
the strength and poetry of Woody's way. They commis-
sioned him in 1941 to write songs celebrating the building
of the Coulee and Bonneville Dams, of the Columbia River
project that was changing the whole face of our Northwest.
With pencil stub, pen, battered portable or whatever he
could lay his hands on, he wrote twenty-six such ballads
in thirty days. The impact of these rolling, sweeping songs
on all who heard was inestimable. A Washington state
senator is reputed to have said that any one of these Woody
works was worth a dozen legislative speeches in getting
things done.

Getting things done. Affecting people, touching them where they live, moving them up a little higher. This was Woody.

> There's a better world a-comin',
> I'll tell you why, why, why;
> There's a better world a-comin',
> I'll tell you why . . .

Yes, and disturbing them, too; shaking them out of their magnolias, interrupting their pipe dreams; jabbing as a stubborn surgeon jabs at sores, carbuncles and cankers.

> Now as through this world I ramble
> I see lots of funny men.
> Some will rob you with a sixgun
> And some with a fountain pen.

"He's always spoken the truth as he saw it," said cowboy Jack Elliott, who traveled a ways with Woody, who in his own singing of songs has been deeply affected by the man from Oklahoma, his manner, his speech, his nuances, his thoughts. Though Elliott is his own man—and Woody would want it no other way, celebrating as he has done, with Walt Whitman, the uniqueness of each individual— Jack's inner as well as outer self has been molded by his acquaintance with the bard. And so, too, has Pete Seeger, perhaps the most fulfilled as well as fulfilling of all our singers of folk song. And so, too, has Lee Hays, senior member of The Weavers. And so, too, the gentle Cisco Houston.

Cisco in the last days of his life talked and wrote at length of his friendship with Guthrie: of their travels and travails around the country in Woody's 1927 Chevrolet "whose four wheels all went in different directions. You had to turn the steering wheel several times around before you got any response from the front wheels, which on occasion came perilously close to being too late"; of saloon and street-corner singing; of shows and skits staged for the migratory workers of the Southwest in the company of Will Geer, of later renown as Jeeter Lester in the play, *Tobacco Road;* of their adventures as merchant mariners, twice torpedoed, during World War II. Cisco tells it: "I can remember Woody coming aboard ship looking like a walking pawn shop window, with guitars, mandolins and fiddles hanging all over him. We took the instruments with us everywhere we went, and we sang and played all over Sicily, Africa and the United Kingdom. And when the ship didn't sink too fast we would get the whole crew to join in the singing of the '*Reuben James.*' "

> Have you heard of a ship
> Called the good *Reuben James?*
> Manned by hard fighting men
> Both of honor and fame?
> She flew the Stars and Stripes
> Of this land of the free
> But tonight she's in her grave
> On the bottom of the sea.
>
> Tell me what were their names,
> Tell me what were their names.
> Did you have a friend
> On that good *Reuben James?*

It's no accident, the universal appeal of Woody's songs. Cisco recalled his trip to India, under the auspices of the State Department: how Woody's songs, especially his children's tunes, were so well received. And in England and Scotland, the groundswell of interest in the man and his music. We ourselves have been singing some of his songs, hearing them played and replayed on jumbo jukeboxes, without knowing the identity of the writer.

> So long, it's been good to know you,
> So long, it's been good to know you,
> So long, it's been good to know you.
> This dusty old dust is getting my home
> And I've got to be drifting along.

Who is Woody Guthrie? Man, child, fighting game-cock, towering giant?

He was a child, that's certain. And never had he lost the free, imaginative, uninhibited way of the child. Nor his understanding of children. Beatrice Landeck, New York educator, wrote in the introduction to his *Songs to Grow On:* "Woody Guthrie has an understanding of children that is a source of unceasing joy to all who have the good fortune to know him either personally or through his recordings."

"Watch the kids," advised Woody. "Do like they do. Act like they act. Yell like they yell. Dance the way you see them dance. Sing like they sing. Work and rest the way the kids do. You'll be healthier. You'll feel wiser. You'll go higher, do better and live longer here amongst us, if you'll just only jump in here and swim around in these songs like the kids do. I don't want the kids to be grownup. I want to see the grown folks be kids."

He remembered his mother playfully crying out. He remembered so many things, so graphically, and so clearly recorded them in this autobiography, *Bound for Glory.*

"We chased all around over the front room and back through the kitchen. She grabbed me up off the floor and swung me around and around till my feet stuck straight out. She was laughing and I felt hot tears salty on the side of her face. When she let me down on the floor, she knelt down on her knees and held me up real warm, and I said, 'Mama, I'll tell ya. I like to have ya chase me. Play. Stuff like that. Talk ta each other. Hug each other. But I don't like fer ya to call me secha little boy all th' time.' "

What Lougherne, Wales, was to Dylan Thomas, what Chicago has been to Nelson Algren, Okemah was to Woody Guthrie. The idyll forest of the poet, where the lost, dead child springs to life, is reborn and yells again, where the small boy climbs the fence, jumps down, howls with glee, and, on stubborn occasion bites his tongue to keep from crying. Never in all the years that follow will there ever be such a place as this. Not for the poet.

"Okemah was one of the singingest, square dancingest, drinkingest, yellingest, preachingest, walkingest, talkingest, laughingest, cryingest, shootingest, fistfightingest, bleedingest, gamblingest, gun- club-and razor-carryingest of our ranch and farm towns, because it blossomed out into one of our first Oil Boom towns."

It was a nasal, dragged-out way Woody had of telling a tale. The seemingly undramatic pause, followed by what *seemed* to be a reluctantly drawled out punchline. In retrospect, we recognize the consummate artistry, the comic-tale craftiness of a Twain and, to a lesser extent because his targets were less formidable, the approach of his fellow Oklahoman, Will Rogers.

The small boy on the front porch sang out to the grass, the flowers, and the picket fence:

> Listen to the music
> Music, music,
> Listen to the music
> Music band.

It was his first composition and came quite naturally to him. For didn't his mother, Nora, with the blood of olden Scots in her, sing him all variety of gay song and sad ballad, mixed with the Mexican and Spanish as well? It was later, with one misfortune banging upon another, that she "commenced to sing the sadder songs in a loster voice, to gaze out our window and to follow her songs out and up and over and away from it all, away over yonder in the minor keys."

> Have you forsaken your house and home?
> Have you forsaken your baby?
> Have you forsaken your husband dear
> To go with the Gypsy Davy
> And to sing with the Gypsy Davy
> That song of the Gypsy Davy?

As for his father, Charlie, he had his kind of music and his kind of life. "From a shirt-tearing boy, Papa had grown up to a straight-talking man, a trained fistfighter in the days when Jess Willard and Jack Dempsey were sung like songs. Charlie grew up to be as clever a trader as he was a fighter. He stepped out from back of his store counter and hung out his sign as a Real Estate Dealer. Land Leases. Royalties. Deeds and Titles. He was a clerk of the county court for several years and our house was full of the smells of big leather law books, and the poems of pomp and dignity that he memorized and performed over for us with the same wild outdoor chant as he sang his Negro and Indian square dances and blueses. He was a guitar and banjo picker with a cowboy band or two, then hung up his deviled strings for domestic reasons."

> I'll tell you my story of Billy the Kid,
> I'll tell you of some of the things that he did

Way out in the West when our country was young,
When your gun was the law and your law was your gun.

How did the troubles set in? How did this summer idyll
end? One piece of bad luck upon another ruined Charlie
Guthrie. It was his rueful brag that he was the only man
in the world that lost a farm a day for thirty days. And to
put him in the same league with Job, there was a series
of fires. In the life of Woody Guthrie, there were many
fires.

It was the first that brought to an end Woody's age of
innocence. It was the lovely house that went up in smoke.
Nobody knows how it happened. It just happened. Those
"hot tears salty on the side of her face" as his mother held
him close that chasey afternoon came more often from that
day hence.

In listening to Woody in later years intone the hymn,
"Sowing on the Mountain," a listener was impressed by
the tragic irony of circumstance as he came to the line
"It won't be water but fire next time." He had been child
to fire all his life, it seemed. His sister, Clara, was killed by
an explosion of a coal oil stove. The ugly shack his mother
hated also burned down. The first tragedy sent his mother
to the state asylum; the second sent his father to the sick
bed. But the most tragic conflagration in Woody's life was
to come years later.

His daughter, Cathy Ann—Miss Stackabones, he called
her—the inspiration for the best and most carefree of his
children's songs, perished in a flame. She had just about
made kindergarten when it happened. In his notes to the
album, *Songs to Grow On,* her father wrote, hot with
the flush of creativity: "Stackabones likes her songs and
stories best of all when her mommy and her pappy sing,
talk, listen and dance with her. She joins in lots quicker

and louder and freer when all of us lay down our books, papers, our knitting, twitting and our heavy spirits and all get going together on our story, our song, or dance. We beat on books, boxes, on tin cans and floors. We rattle spoons, shakers and bells, and we jump around in a long trot, a rig-a-jig-jig, a crazy lope, gallop or wild jump. We settle down then and tell some real quiet story in a whisper. We make up a new story if we forget our old ones. I've been making songs and playing and singing them now for nearly twenty years and Cathy at nearly four years can out-rhyme, out-play me, out-sing me any old day."

> You get a hammer and I'll get a nail,
> You catch a bird and I'll catch a snail,
> You bring a board and I'll bring a saw
> And we'll build a house for the babyo.

But Woody, despite brutal circumstances, refused to be Saturday's Child. Life was too much with him; always he was in the midst of it. Curious. Probing. Stubborn. Fighting back. In the long, long ago, back in Okemah, he showed the first signs of it. His mother's younger brother, Leonard, was walloping the bejeepers out of him for no reason at all. The little gamecock was pecking back, kicking, clawing, slobbering angrily as the strap descended on him again and again. "Your old blisters won't hurt me. Your old stropping belt won't hurt long. Your old arm will give out. You don't know. You think you're scaring me. You think you're takin' some of my fight out of me. You'll whip me now, and I'll look like I'm cryin', but I won't really be cryin'. I'll be havin' tears in my eyes because I'm mad at you."

The songs Woody sang and wrote all his life were inexorably bound to his own being. Though his sharecropper songs deal with sharecroppers, they deal with the poet himself; though his dust bowl ballads deal with other Okies, they deal with this Okie.

> That old dust storm killed my baby
> But it can't kill me, Lord,
> It can't kill me.

> That old dust storm killed my family
> But it can't kill me, Lord,
> It can't kill me.

It was in the blood of Charlie Guthrie. The never-give-up streak, the spitting in the wind of adversity. When that Sooner cyclone hit and blew everything down and high and way up in the crazy sky, Charlie held little Woody against him in the open field and hollered out, challenging the elements: "Let's let the wind get harder! Let's let the straw and the feathers fly! Let that old wind go crazy and pound us over the head! And when the straight winds pass over and the twisting winds crawl in the air like a rattlesnake in boiling water, let's you and me holler back at it and laugh it back to where it come from! Let's stand up on our hind legs, and shake our fists back into the whole crazy mess and holler and cuss and rave and laugh and say, 'Old Cyclone, go ahead! Beat your bloody brains out on my old tough hide! Rave on! Blow! Beat! Go crazy, Cyclone! You and I are friends! Good old Cyclone!' "

Among many peoples, thirteen is the age a boy becomes a man. At thirteen, with his family now scattered, splintered, exploded, Woody was on his own. He hit the Texas trail: Galveston, the Gulf, the Panhandle, Pampa. He blew a self-taught harmonica in barbershops, around poolhalls, at shoe stands—wherever the big, horny-handed men assembled. He jig-danced on the streets, he rattled the bones. As he put it, he learned all the tricks of the strings; chording a battered guitar, bowing a squawling panther fiddle. As he played and sang and sign-painted, he listened and looked—and he who ran was reading. Appropriately enough, he called this chapter "Boy in Search of Something."

He played at carnivals, rodeos, centennials, fairs, parties, any old place there were people tied down long enough to listen. "Some people liked me, hated me, walked with me, walked over me, jeered me, cheered me, rooted me and hooted me, and before long I was invited in and booted out of every public place of entertainment in that country. . . . I made up songs telling what I thought was wrong and how to make it right, songs that said what everybody in that country was thinking.

"And this has held me ever since."

It's a mighty hard road that my poor hands has hoed
And my poor feet has traveled a hot dusty road.
Out of your dust bowl and westward we rolled
Lord, your mountains are hot and your desert is cold.

I work in your orchards of peaches and prunes
And I sleep on the ground 'neath the light of your moon.
On the edge of your city you'll see us and then
We come with the dust and we go with the wind.

The time was ripe for the man and the man was ripe for the time. When the Big Bust came on Black October of '29 and Men of Substance threw themselves out of windows, a folk poet was growing up. The creative juices in him were fermenting. The sights, the sounds, the buried memories dug up: a father who had it and lost it, a mother who almost had it and lost it, a family that almost was. An idea was coming to Woody as now—in the '30s—he saw hundreds of thousands of the stranded, broke and hungry lining up the highways. And so many from his home state, fleeing the dust, heading for the land of milk and honey, California.

> California is a Garden of Eden,
> A paradise to live in or see,
> But believe it or not,
>   you won't find it so hot
> If you ain't got the Do Re Mi.

Woody's album for Victor, "Dust Bowl Ballads," released in 1940, brought him to the attention of thousands and, like Steinbeck's novel, helped focus attention on the plight of the Okies, the people who lost all their worldly goods during the great dust storms. Like *Grapes of Wrath*, Woody's songs were a furious holler against national callousness.

> I'm a dust bowl refugee,
> Just a dust bowl refugee
> From that dust bowl to the peach bowl
> Now the peaches is killing me.
> 'Cross the mountains to the sea
> Come the wife and kids and me.
> It's a hard old dusty highway
> For a dust bowl refugee.

There were the boxcar days. Young Woody, guitar slung around his back, jam-packed with desperate, weary, dusty 'boes. All, in one way or another, heading somewhere on a rough, bumpy, flatwheeler.

> This train don't carry no gamblers,
> Liars, thieves and big shot ramblers.

This train is bound for glory,
This train!

Some glory. It was a world in itself, full of men, good, bad and indifferent. Woody, being an excellent journalist, described not a world as it *might* be but as it *was*. There is a flavor of Algren in his work as he tells of Cripple Whitey, the Fight Spotter. He was a spotter all right. If there was no fight, he'd find some way to start it himself. As other poets saw sermons in stones and running brooks, Woody saw parables in that boxcar. Who can tell where a running thought begins and how it ends?

In that bumpy, rough-riding, rough-talking boxcar, the fights that broke out were beyond reality. A wild, terrible surrealism. And the scrawny bag of bones of an Orpheus, with his lyre slung over his back, his lyre that was no more than a half-busted cheap guitar, had a vision. It was the Apocalypse. "Men fighting against men. Color against color. Kin against kin. Race pushing against race. And all of us battling against the wind and the rain and that bright crackling lightning that booms and zooms, that bathes his eyes in the white sky, wrestles a river to a standstill, and spends the night drunk in a whorehouse."

This train don't carry no smoker,
Lyin' tongues or two-bit jokers.
This train is bound for glory,
This train!

Everyone has his favorite from Woody's capacious bag of songs. Some will say "This Land Is Your Land." Others will choose "Roll On, Columbia." To many it's "Tom Joad." Jack Elliott says: "Whenever I'm at a party and I'm singing songs and it's very late, sometimes I fall asleep while I'm singing. Sometimes it's loud applause that wakes me up. Then I know I've been singing 'Tom Joad.' "

Just as he remembered the cyclone his father defied, so he remembered the dust storms of later years. "I've lived these dust storms all my life. I met millions of good folks trying to hang on, trying to stay alive, with the dust cutting down every hope. So black you can't see your hands before your eyes, or the light in your room, or the dollar in your pocket, or the meal on your table. That's what the kids grown and married can't see through."

Sweethearts sat in the
Dark and sparked,
They hugged and kissed
In that dusty old dark.

They sighed and cried
And hugged and kissed,
Instead of marriage
They talked like this . . .

So long, it's been good to know you
So long, it's been good to know you
So long, it's been good to know you
This dusty old dust is getting my home
And I've got to be drifting along.

Traveling. Hard traveling. As the Joad family piled all into their creaking, puffing, panting jalopy, so did thousands of others from about sixteen Midwestern states, the rootless and the roofless. So, too, did Woody Guthrie.

Keeping a weather-eye peeled for the tough railroad bulls, the town cops, guardians of the Garden of Eden. They spotted the tart-tongued little guy with the guitar as a troublemaker. Not that he was saying anything particularly explosive. He just didn't know enough to keep his mouth shut. He was just too undefeated for a bedraggled vagrant, who should, by all signs and portents, be thoroughly defeated and ask no questions when told to move on. After all, it was Authority speaking, badge on shirt and gun on hip.

> Well, what is a Vigilante man?
> Tell me what is a Vigilante man?
> Has he got a gun and a club in his hand?
> Is that a Vigilante man?

He saw the sign: "Fruit—beat it." Another: "Fruit—see, but don't pick." And a third in bold, no-fooling-around print: "Trespassers prosecuted. Keep out. Get away from here." This threw him because he also saw fruit rotting on the ground and hungry mouths all around. And he wasn't feeling any too full either. So he paused. Courting trouble. Was a song taking shape in his mind?

> Rainy night, down in the engine house,
> Sleepin' just as still as a mouse.
> Man come along and chased us out in the rain.
> Was that a Vigilante man?

"Keep walkin' down that highway and don't look back. Just keep travelin'."

Mumbled the thoroughly drenched poet: "I was born travelin'. Good-bye."

> I've been havin' some hard travelin',
> I thought you know'd.
> I've been havin' some hard travelin'
> Way down the road.

I've been havin' some hard travelin', hard
    ramblin', hard gamblin',
I've been havin' some hard travelin', Lord.

I've been ridin' them fast rattlers,
I thought you know'd.
I've been ridin' them flat-wheelers
Way down the road.
I've been ridin' them dead-enders, flyin'
    passengers, pickin' up cinders,
I've been havin' some hard travelin', Lord.

Well, I been walkin' that Lincoln Highway,
I thought you know'd.
I been hittin' that Sixty-Six
Way down that road.
Heavy load and a worried mind, lookin' for
    a woman that's hard to find,
I've been havin' some hard travelin', Lord.

A traveling man, Woody found out, riding old shanks'
mare when the flat-wheeler goes by too fast, makes all sorts
of discoveries. The respectable part of the town will slam
the door in your face when they read "hand-out" on your
mind. But try the seamy side and you more often than not
get some sort of break. Consider the time Woody shook the
Los Angeles dust off his feet and came to a rundown shack
some miles to the north. An old couple was listening on a
loop-legged radio to a sermon by Aimee Semple McPher-
son ("Aimee Semple Temple," Woody called her). They
fed him a chicken dinner; the old lady surreptitiously
shoved a paper bag full of food at him, cautioning him not
to tell the old man; the old man shoved a quarter at him,
cautioning him not to tell the old lady. Billie Holiday sang,
"Them that has, got." Woody discovered "them that has
not, give."

It had been ever so with Woody. Even back in those early days when singing over radio station KFVD, Los Angeles. It was a fifteen-minute show, yet it pulled down 20,000 pieces of mail in two years. Woody and his partner, Lefty Lou from Old Mizoo. Lou Crissman was a tall, skinny Missouri farm girl with a rough, husky voice. The songs they sang were not manufactured in Tin Pan Alley. They came off no commercial assembly line; they were all handmade pieces. Out of the lives and experiences of the performers. And it was their own kind who sent in all those letters.

> Well, I'm a goin' down this old dusty road,
> Yes, I'm goin' down this old dusty road,
> Yes, I'm goin' down this old dusty road,
> And I ain't gonna be treated this a way.

All the songs were simple and direct as the very lives which inspired them were simple and direct. Woody always maintained anyone could write a song. There was no magic formula involved. "You just use your ears to remember what you hear. You sort of write down a bunch of sounds somewhere in your head and save them for future use. Sometimes you hear a tune and catch some of the words and for a time you go around with it roaring through your head like a lost steamboat."

Sometimes, if you're Woody Guthrie, you write a whole song on the spot. There was the time the hitchhiker-poet was picked up by a 1929 sedan. Bang! The tire blew. Write a song about *that*, one of his fellow passengers challenged. The bard stuck his tailor-made behind his ear, swung his guitar around and improvised:

> Tell me, mamma, is your tread thin as mine?
> Hey! Hey! Woman, is your tread thin as mine?

Work and roll, is your tread thin as mine?
Every old tire's gonna blow its side sometime.

"Wheel 'em an' deal 'em!" Woody recalls the driver
laughing out.

Say, Godamighty, roll them wheels around!
Hey! Good gal, you gotta roll them wheels around!
Workin' woman, roll your wheels around!
I'll find me a job or roll California down!

"I know my voice is not one of the smooth-riding kind,
because I don't want it to sound smooth. None of the folks
that I know have got smooth voices like dew dripping off
the petal of a morning violet, and still they can sing louder,
longer and with more guts than any smooth voice I ever
heard." The man had always been partial toward the on-
the-street, on-the-job, at-the-bar kind of voice. Just as he
felt anybody could write a song, so he felt anybody could
sing one. Let the spirit do the moving. As in the case of
those two young girls in that jungle camp near Redding,
California, where the Sacramento bends—
"Girls," said their father as he puckered up his face and
sprayed a tree with tobacco juice. "Go in the house and
get your music box, and set there on the bed and play with
the baby, so's he won't fall off."
The girls began to sing and every soul in that wretched
camp was listening. As Woody recalled, they "kept as still
as daylight . . ."

Takes a worried man to sing a worried song
Takes a worried man to sing a worried song
Takes a worried man to sing a worried song
I'm worried now
But I won't be worried long.

It was a world of such open faces in sharp contrast to the one of "darkling glasses"—Hollywood drinking parties to which this "colorful character" was invited at a later date. Woody was keenly aware of the con in the daily lives of these pros. To them, he was a fashion as mah jong was a fashion. Knowing this, he rationed his patience and heisted a trinket, moving on with a "So long, it's been good to know you . . ."

He tried all of New York for size, living in the comfortable apartment of a friend one day and holing up in the Bowery the next. He performed on popular radio network programs, ranging from Norman Corwin's "Pursuit of Happiness" to "Cavalcade of America." When radio censors tried his patience, he fled South and West.

Just as Woody recognized our natural wonders and our man-made ones, so he was recognized. One of the first to sense the importance of his gifts was Alan Lomax, the most perceptive of all our musicologists. In 1940, he persuaded Woody to record several hours of talk and song for the Library of Congress. From this session there came the commercial recordings, including the memorable Victor set, "Dust Bowl Ballads." And it was Moe Asch of Folkways Records, and long before that on other labels, who did most in capturing the art and truth of Woody Guthrie on recordings. It was Lomax who first described Woody as "our greatest contemporary folk poet" and Asch who followed through in seeing to it that the poet would be heard wherever there was a plain or fancy phonograph.

Though Guthrie may be best remembered for the songs he wrote, let us remember the way he sang. It was a particular kind of bite to his voice, a particular kind of drama to his cadence. It was not pretty as a girl on a billboard is pretty. Nor was it as forgettable. It was harsh as life is harsh; it was casually tender as life is casually tender. There is a frontier ballad called "Buffalo Skinners." Carl Sandburg has described it not as a song but as a saga. Many have sung it. Yet Woody's manner with it was *the way*. Don't ask me how I know; I just know. From the first chord sounded on his guitar, you sense the impending tragedy of the skinners on their way to a double-cross. And the brutal denouement as offered by Woody is as inexorable and deadly and true as a pair of snake eyes.

The same kind of truth found its way into his singing of union songs around the country. He joined Pete Seeger, whom he described as "a long tall string-bean kid"; Lee Hays, "Arkansaw Hard-Luck Lee"; and writer Millard Lampell. They were known as the Almanac Singers. Traveling the land in a tired jalopy, they wrote, concocted, conjured up all kinds of songs that in one way or another preached Casey's credo: "Boys, Organize!"

There was humor, bite, anger and the all-around surge of life in their songs and fashion. Though their message was twentieth-century, their tradition was as old as busking. Buskers in all lands and all times were the traveling minstrels, who, picking up a stray piece of change here and there, would in Woody's words say: "Well, it's getting a bit dead around here. Let's find a livelier place."

With the oncoming of the war, Woody put his attention to anti-Hitler songs. His Oklahoma twang was heard by soldiers overseas via OWI broadcasts. Songs of all variety, serious, stirring, comical: "Folks, I'm gonna tell you about the kickingest mule in any man's army. Her name was Maggie. We spent more time chasing and fighting with old Maggie than we did with the Nazis or the Fascists either one."

> She kicked the lieutenant over a fence,
> Tee roodle tee roodle over a fence.

We ain't never seen the lieutenant since,
Tee roodle tee roodle that lieutenant since.

With Cisco and another friend, he shipped out as a member of the merchant marine. "We played our guitars, and I took along a fiddle and a mandolin. Our first boat was torpedoed off the coast of Sicily, and we got to visit the old bombed-out town of 400,000 souls, Palermo." It would be stretching a point to describe Woody as an able-bodied seaman, yet what he did was equally important as anybody on board. "I fed fifty gun-boys, washed their dirty dishes, scrubbed their greasy messroom, and never graduated up and down in my whole eleven months." And he sang songs to and about them, this scullery boy.

Doorbell rang and in come a man.
I signed my name and git a telegram.
Said, "If you want to take a vacation trip
Got a dishwashin' job on a Liberty ship."
     Woman a-cryin' . . . me a-flyin' . . . out the
door and down the line.

The dish-washing minstrel caught a Liberty ship back to the States and shipped out again, this time to North Africa. Here, his roving, compassionate eye lit upon the wretched Arab villages, even more miserable than the jungle camps of recent memory. He "saw whole swarms of people race out of their rock and mud huts and fight like cats and dogs over a hunk of soap, and then run away when the soap was torn into a hundred pieces. We heard these people pound on their native skin drums and sing some of the saddest and prettiest music I have ever heard anywhere."

They drafted him into the army on May 8. On that very day Hitler surrendered. "I don't know if it was me or that big Red Army or those few million Yanks there across his fence that caused him to give in." The chances are it was the impact of all three elements. Undeniably, the fighting men had a good deal to do with it. But the minstrel boy who to the war had gone, he hurt Hitler, too. So it has been all through Man's checkered history: not the gun alone has spoken but the song of the boy with the wild harp slung behind him.

"Let me be known as just the man who told you something you already knew," wrote Woody. Maybe so, maybe so. But it is his telling and re-telling that may in some small way help make us better men than we have been.

> Bound for glory? This train? Ha!
> I wonder just where in the hell we're bound.
> Rain on, little rain, rain on!
> Blow on, little wind, keep blowin'!
> Cause them guys is singin' that this train is bound
>   for glory, an' I'm gonna hug her breast till I find
>   out where she's bound.

Chapter I

SOLDIERS IN THE DUST

❖

I could see men of all colors bouncing along in the box-car. We stood up. We laid down. We piled around on each other. We used each other for pillows. I could smell the sour and bitter sweat soaking through my own khaki shirt and britches, and the work clothes, overhauls and saggy, dirty suits of the other guys. My mouth was full of some kind of gray mineral dust that was about an inch deep all over the floor. We looked like a gang of lost corpses heading back to the boneyard. Hot in the September heat, tired, mean and mad, cussing and sweating, raving and preaching. Part of us waved our hands in the cloud of dust and hollered out to the whole crowd. Others was too weak, too sick, too hungry or too drunk even to stand up. The train was a highball and had the right of way. Our car was a rough rider, called by hoboes a "flat wheeler." I was riding in the tail end where I got more dust, but less heat. The wheels were clipping it off at sixty miles an hour. About all I could hear above the raving and cussing and the roar of the car was the jingle and clink on the under side every time the wheels went over a rail joint.

I guess ten or fifteen of us guys was singing:

> This train don't carry no gamblers,
> Liars, thieves and big-shot ramblers;
> This train is bound for glory,
> This train!

9

"We would hafta git th' only goddam flat wheeler on th' whole dam train!" A heavy-set boy with a big-city accent was rocking along beside me and fishing through his overhauls for his tobacco sack.

"Beats walkin'!" I was setting down beside him. "Bother you fer my guitar handle ta stick up here in yer face?"

"Naw. Just long as yuh keep up th' music. Kinda songs ya sing? Juke-box stuff?"

"Much oblige, just smoked." I shook my head. "No. I'm 'fraid that there soap-box music ain't th' kind ta win a war on!"

"Little too sissy?" He licked up the side of his cigaret. "Wisecracky, huh?"

"Hell yes." I pulled my guitar up on my lap and told him, "Gonna take somethin' more'n a dam bunch of silly wisecracks ta ever win this war! Gonna take work!"

"You don't look like you ever broke your neck at no work, bud!" He snorted some fumes out of his nose and mashed the match down into the dust with his foot. "What th' hell do you know 'bout work?"

"By God, mister, I work just as hard as you er th' next guy!" I held the ends of my fingers up in his face. "An' I got th' blisters ta prove it!"

"How come you ain't drafted?"

"I never did get by those medical gents. Doctors and me don't see eye to eye."

A blond-headed man about forty nudged me in the ribs with his elbow on my left side and said, "You boys talkin' about a war. I got a feelin' you're goin' to see a little spell of war right here in just a few minutes."

"Makes ya think so?" I looked around all over the car.

"Boy!" He stretched out his feet to prop his self back up against the wall and I noticed he was wearing an iron brace on his leg. "They call me Cripple Whitey, th' Fight Spotter!"

"Fight spotter?"

"Yeah. I can spot a fist fight on the streets three blocks before I come to it. I can spot a gang fight an hour before it breaks out. I tip off the boys. Then they know how to lay their bets."

"Ya got a fight spotted now?"

"I smell a big one. One hell of a big one. Be some blood spilt. Be about ten minutes yet."

"Hey! Heavy!" I elbowed the big boy on my right. "Whitey here says he smells a big fight cookin'!"

"Awwww. Don't pay no 'tention to that crippled rat. He's just full of paregoric. In Chicago we call 'im 'P. G. Whitey'! I don't know what they call him here in Minnesota!"

"You're a goddam lyin' rat!" The cripple got up and swayed around on the floor in front of us. "Get up! I'll cave your lousy dam head in! I'll throw you inta one of these lakes!"

"Easy, boy, easy." Heavy put the sole of his shoe in Whitey's belly and held him back. "I don't wanta hit no cripple!"

"You guys watch out! Don't you stumble an' fall on my guitar!" I eased over a little. "Yeah! You're some fight spotter! If you spot a fight an' then it don't happen just when you said, why, you just pitch in and start one yer self!"

"I'll crack that box over your dam curly head!" The cripple made a step toward me, laughing and smearing cement dust down across his face. Then he sneered and told me, "Goddam right! Hell yes! I'm a bum! I gotta right ta be. Look at that gone leg. Withered away! You're too dam low down an' sneakin' to make an honest livin' by hard work. Sonofabitch. So you go into a saloon where th' workin' stiffs hang out, an' you put down your kitty box an' play for your dam tips!"

I told him, "Go jump in one of these lakes!"

"I'm settin' right there!" He pointed at my guitar in my lap. "Right, by God, on top of you!"

I grabbed my guitar and rolled over three or four other fellows' feet and got out of Whitey's way just as he turned around and piled down backwards yelling and screaming at the top of his lungs. I stumbled through the car trying to keep my balance and hold onto my guitar. I fell up against an old man slumped with his face rubbing up against the wall. I heard him groan and say, "This is th' roughest bastardly boxcar that I ever swung into."

"Why doncha lay down?" I had to lean up against the wall to keep from falling. "How come ya standin' up this a way?"

"Rupture. It rides a little easier standin' up."

Five or six guys dressed like timberjacks brushed past us cussing and raving. "I can't stand this dust no longer!" "Out of our way, men!" "Let us by! We want to get to the other end of the car!"

"You birds won't be no better off in th' other end!" I hollered at them. The dust stung the roof of my mouth. "I tried it!"

A big husky gent with high boots and red wool socks rolled back on a pair of logger's britches stopped and looked me over and asked me, "Who in the hell are you? Don't you think I know how to ride a boxcar, sonny? I'm gettin' out of this wind!"

"Go ahead on, mister, but I'm tellin' ya, ya'll burn up back in that other end!" I turned again to the old man and asked him, "Anything I can do ta help ya?"

"Guess not, son." I could see by the look on his face that the rupture was tying him up in knots. "I was hopin' ta ride this freight on in home tonight. Chicago. Plumber there. But looks like I'll have ta get off at the next stop an' hit the highway."

"Purty bad. Well, it ain't a dam bit lonesome in here, is it?"

"I counted sixty-nine men in this car." He squinted his eyes and gritted his teeth and doubled over a little farther. "Might be, I counted wrong. Missed some of th' ones layin' down or counted some of them twice. Pretty close ta sixty-nine though."

"Jest like a car load of sheep headed fer th' packin' house." I let my knees bend in the joints a little bit to keep the car from shaking me to jelly.

A long tall Negro boy walked up and asked us, "You men know what's makin' our noses burn?" He was wearing a pair of work shoes that looked like they had seen Civil War service. "Eyes, too?"

"What?" I asked him.

"Cement dust. This heah cah wuz loaded down wid sack cement!"

"Shore 'nuff?"

"I bet I done sucked in three sacks of th' damn stuff!" He screwed his face up and mopped across his lips with his hands.

"I've breathed in more'n that! Hell, friend! You're talkin' to a livin', breathin' stretch of concrete highway!"

"Close as we is jammed an' packed in heah, we'z all gonna be stuck 'n' cemented together time we git outta dis hot box."

"Boys," the old man told both of us, "I hope we don't have no trouble while I'm in here. If somebody was ta fall on me or push me around, this rupture, I know, it would kill me."

"I'll he'p see to it dat nobody don' push nobody on toppa you, mistah."

"I'll break 'em of th' habit," I told both of them.

"What time of day is it? Must be fightin' time?" I looked around at the two.

"Mus' be 'roun' about two or three o'clock," the Negro boy told me, "jedgin' from that sun shinin' in th' door. Say! What's them two boys doin' yondah?" He craned his neck.

"Pourin' somethin' out of a bottle," I said, "right by that old colored man's feet. What is it?"

"Wettin' th' cement dust wid it. Strikin' a match now."

"Gasoline!"

"Ol' man's 'sleep. They's givin' 'im de hot foot!"

The flame rose up and burned in a little spot about the size of a silver dollar. In a few seconds the old man clawed at the strings of his bundle where he was resting his head. He kicked his feet in the dust and knocked little balls of fire onto two or three other men playing some poker along the back wall. They fought the fire off their clothes and laughed and bawled the kids and the old man both out.

"Hey! You old bastard! Quit bustin' up our card game!"

I saw one of the men draw back to hit the old man. Another player was grinning and laughing out to the whole crowd, "That wuz th' funniest dam sight I ever seen!"

The two boys, both dressed in overhalls, walked back through the crowd, one holding out the half-pint bottle. "Drinka likker, men? Who wantsa drinka good likker?" The boy with the bottle shoved it up under my nose saying, "Here, mister music man! Take a little snort! Then play somethin' good an' hot!"

"I been a needin' a little drink ta ease me on down ta Chicago." I wiped my hand across my face and smiled around at everybody. "I shore thank ya fer thinkin' 'bout me." I took the bottle and smelled of the gasoline. Then I sailed the bottle over a dozen men's heads and out of the door.

"Say, stud! Who daya t'ink youse are? Dat bottle was mine, see?" He was a boy about twenty-five, wearing a flop hat soaked through with some kind of dime-store hair oil. He braced his self on his feet in front of me and said again, "Dat bottle was mine!"

"Go git it." I looked him straight in the eye.

"Whattaya tryin' ta pull?"

"Well, since yer so interested, I'll jest tell ya. See, I might wanta lay down after while an' git a little sleep. I don't wanta wake up with my feet blistered. 'Cause then, dam yer hide, I'd hafta throw ya outta this door!"

"We was gonna use dat gas ta start a fire ta cook wid."

"Ya mean ta git us all in jail with."

"I said cook an' I mean cook!"

Then my colored friend looked the two boys over and said, "You boys, how long you been goin' 'roun' cookin' people's feet?"

"Keep outta dis! Stepinfetchit!"

"You cain't call me dat an' git by wid it, white boy!"

I put my shoulder against the colored boy and my hand against the white boy's arm, and told them, "Listen, guys! Goddamit! No matter who's mad at who, we jest cain't start a fight of no kind on this freight! These big Burlington dicks'll jail th' whole bunch of us!"

"Yaaa. Skeerd!"

"You're a dam liar! I ain't afraid of you ner twenty more like ya! But do you know what would of happened if these railroad bulls shook us down ta look at our draft cards, an' found you with that bottle of gasoline on ya? It'd be th' lockup fer you an' me an' all of th' rest of us!"

The old man with the rupture bit his lips and asked me, "Son, do you suppose you could get one of the men to move up out of the door and let me try to get a little breath of that fresh air? I feel like I've just got to get a little air."

The colored boy held the old man up while I walked over to the door and tapped a nice healthy-looking boy on the back. "Would you mind lettin' this old man ride in yer place there in th' door fer a little while? Sick. Rupture trouble."

"Not at all." The boy got up and set down back where the old man had been standing. He acted friendly and hollered at us, "I think it's about time we took turns ridin' in the doors. Let everybody have a whiff of that fresh air!"

Almost everybody in the car rolled over or stood up and yelled, "Hell yes!" "Turn about!" "I'm ready." "Too late, boys, I been dead an' buried in solid cement for two hours!" "Gimme air!" "Trot out yer frash airr!" Everybody mumbled and talked, and fifteen or twenty men pushed their way through the others to stand close to the doors, hoping to be first.

Heavy walked through a bunch of them saying, "Watch out. Men, let this Negro boy through with this old man. He's sick. He's needin' air. Back up a little. Make room."

"Who'n th' hell are you? Tubba lard! Dictater 'round here?" one old boy popped off.

Heavy started for the man, but he slipped back in through the crowd. "All of you men get up! Let a new bunch get cooled off! Where's the old man that the boys put the hot foot on a few minutes ago? There you are! Hey! Come on! Grab yourself a hunk of this nice, fresh, cool climate! Set right there! Now, who's to be next?"

A red-eyed vino drunkard took a man by the feet and pulled him along the deck to the door. "My buddy. Ain't said a word since I loaded 'im in last night in Duluth. Bummed th' main stem fer two bits, then he scooped his flue."

A Mexican boy rubbed his head and got up from somewhere along the wall. He drank half of a quart vinegar jug of water and then sailed the bottle out the door. Then he set down and hung his feet out the door and rode along holding his head in his hands vomiting into the wind. In each door there was room for five men. The first ten being sick and weakly, we let them ride for about half an hour. Then they got up and ten more men took their seat for only fifteen minutes.

I was watching a bunch of men hold their fingers to their lips and shush each other to keep quiet. Every one of them haw-hawing and tittering under their breath and pointing to a kid asleep on the floor. He was about twenty. Little white cap from the ten-cent store, a pair of old blue washed-out pants, shirt to match, a set of dirty heels caked over with the dust of many railroads, and a run-over pair of low-cut shoes. He was hugging his bed roll and moving his lips against the wool blanket. I saw him dig his toes in the dust and kiss the bundle.

I walked over and put my foot in the middle of his back and said, "Wake up, stranger. Git ya some fresh air there in th' door!"

The men cackled and rolled in the dirt. They rared back and forth slapping their hands against their legs. "Ddrrreeeeeeeeaaaammmming of youuuu with your eyes so bluue!" One man was grinning like an ape and singing worse than that.

"What's th' boy dreamin' about so purty, music man?"

another big guy asked me with his tongue in his cheek and
eyes rolling.

"Leave th' boy alone," I told him back. "What th' hell
do you dream about, freight trains?"

I set down with my back against the wall looking all
through the troubled, tangled, messed-up men. Traveling
the hard way. Dressed the hard way. Hitting the long old
lonesome go.

Rougher than a cob. Wilder than a woodchuck. Hotter than a depot stove. Madder than nine hundred dollars. Arguing worse than a tree full of crows. Messed up. Mixed-up, screwed-up people. A crazy boxcar on a wild track. Headed sixty miles an hour in a big cloud of poison dust due straight to nowhere.

I saw ten men getting up out of the door and I took my guitar over and set down and stuck my feet out. The cold air felt good whipping up my pants leg. I pulled my shirt open to cool off across my waist and chest. My Negro friend took a seat by my side and told me, "I reckon we's 'bout due some frash air, looks like."

"Jest be careful ya don't use it all up," I kidded back at him.

I held my head in the wind and looked out along the lake shoreline with my ear cocked listening to the men in the car.

"You're a lyin' skunk!" one was saying. "I'm just as hard a worker as you are, any old day!"

"You're a big slobbery loafin' heel!"

"I'm th' best dadgum blacksmith in Logan County!"

"You mean you use ta was! You look like a lousy tramp ta me!"

"I c'n put out more manly labor in a minnit then you kin in a month!"

"Hay, there, you sot! Quit spittin' on my bed roll!"

"Yeah! Yeah! I know! I'm a woikin' stiff, too, see? But I ain't no good here! Yeah! I woiked thirteen years in th' same weave room! Breakout fixer on th' looms! Poil Harbor comes along. Big comp'ny gits alla de war orders. My place is a little place, so what happens? Just like dat! She closes down. An' I'm out on de freights. But I ain't nuttin' when I hit th' freights. Takes it all outta me. Nuttin'. But a lousy, dirty tramp!"

19

"If you're such a good weaver, mister, you can come back here and sew up my drawers! Ha! Ha! Ha!"

"Fancy pants! Whoooeee!"

"I plowed th' straightest row of corn in Missouri three year ago!"

"Yaaa! But, mister big shot, dey don't grow no corn in dese here boxcars, see! Yaaa! Dat's de last bitta woik yez ever done!"

"No Swede cut much timber as me, Big Swede! I cutta 'nuff of that white pine ta build up da whole town!"

"Quiet down! You dam bunch of liars, you! Blowin' off at yer head what all you can do! I hear this talk all up and down these railroads! You had a good job somewhere once or twice in your life, then you go around blabbin' off at your mouth for fifteen years! Tellin' people what all kinds of wonders you done! Look at you! Look at your clothes! All of the clothes in this car ain't worth three dollars! Look at your hands! Look at your faces! Drunk! Sick! Hungry! Dirty! Mean! Onery! I won't lie like you rats! An' I got on the best suit of clothes in this car! Work? Me work? Hell, no! I see somethin' I want, an' I just up an' take it!"

Looking back over my shoulder, I saw a little man, skinny, puny, shaking like he had a machine gun in his hands, raise up on his knees from the other end of the car and sail a brown quart bottle through the air. Glass shattered against the back of the well-dressed man's head. Red port wine rained all over me and my guitar and twenty other men that tried to duck. The man in the suit of clothes keeled over and hit the floor like a dead cow.

"I got my papers! I got my job already signed up!" The guy that slung the bottle was tromping through the car patting his chest and preaching. "I had a brother in Pearl Harbor! I'm on my way right this minute to Chicago to go to work rollin' steel to lick this Hitler bunch! I hope the gent with the nice suit on is restin' comfortable! But I ain't apologizing to none of you! I throwed that bottle! Want to make anythin' out of it?" He shook both fists and stood there looking at all of us.

I wiped my hands around over me where the wine was spilled. I saw everybody else was picking chips of glass out of their clothes and mumbling amongst themselves. "Crazy lunatic." "Hadn't ought ta done that." "Might of missed 'im, hit one of us."

The mumble got loud and broke into a crack like zigzag lightning. Little bunches of men circled around arguing. A few guys walked from bunch to bunch preaching over other fellows' shoulders. At the side of me a husky-looking man got up and said, "What all he says about Pearl Harbor and all is okay, men, but still he hadn't ought to have thrown that wine bottle. I'm going to walk back there and kick his rear good and proper just to teach him a lesson!"

Then from somewhere at my back a half-breed Indian boy dove out and tackled the husky man around the ankles and they tangled into a knot and rolled around over the floor, beating, scratching, and clawing. Their feet kicked other men in the face and other men kicked them back and jumped into the fight.

"You're not gonna hurt that little fella!"

"I'll kill you, Indian!"

"Hey! Watch who th' hell you're kickin'!"

Heavy split through the car knocking men out of his way hollering, "Hey! Cut it! Cut!"

"You fat pimp, keep outta dis!" A dirty-looking, dark-complected man was pulling a little oily cap down over his eyes and making for Heavy.

Heavy grabbed him by the throat and busted the back

of his head up against the wall about a dozen times cussing, "I'll teach you that you cain't call no decent man a pimp! You snaky-looking hustler!"

All down the line it started and spread. "You said I wouldn't work fer my livin', huh? I'll bat your eyes out!"

"Who wuz it yez called da loafer?"

Shirts and pants ripped and it sounded like everybody was getting their duds tore off them.

"I didn't lak ya dam looks frum da very start!"

Five and then ten other couples dove in.

"Where's that low-life bastid that called me a bum?"

Men walked up and down the car pushing other men off of their feet, heaving others to one side, looking at the few that was still riding along on the floor.

"They're goin' an' blowin'!"

"There ye air, ye foul-mouth cur, you!"

I saw six or eight reaching down and grabbing others by their shirt collars, jerking them to the middle of the floor. Fists sailing in the air so fast I couldn't see which fist was whose.

"I knowed you was nuthin' but a lousy chiselin' snake when I first seen yuh climb on this train! Fight! Goddam yuh! Fight!"

Shoe soles cracked all around over the car and heads banged against the walls. Dust flew up in the air as if somebody was dumping it in with trucks.

"I'm a tramp, am I?"

Men's heads bobbed around in the dust like balloons floating on the ocean. Most everybody shut their eyes and gritted their teeth and swung wild haymakers up from the cement and men flattened out on the floor. Water bottles flew through the air and I could see a few flashes that I knew was pocketknife blades. Lots of the men jerked other men's coats up over their heads to where they couldn't see nor use their arms, and they fought the air like windmills, blind as bats. A hard fist knocked a fellow stumbling through the dust. He waved his hands trying to keep balanced, then fell, spilling all kinds of junk and trash out of his pockets over five or six other men trying to keep out of the fight. For every man who got knocked down, three more jumped up and roared through the mob taking sidelicks at any head that popped up.

"Boy!" My colored friend was shaking his head and looking worried. "You sho' as hell bettah not git yo' music box mixed up in dis!"

"I've got kicked in th' back about nine times. 'Nother good poke an' I'll sail plumb out this door inta one of them there lakes!" I was fighting to get myself braced again. "Here, let's me an' you hook our arms together so we can hold each other in th' dam car!" I clamped my hands together in front of me holding the guitar on my lap. "Be hell of a thing if a feller was ta git knocked outta this dern boxcar goin' this pace, wouldn't it? Roll a week. Hey! Look! Train's slowin' down."

"Believe she is at that." He squinted his eyes up and looked down the track. "She's slowin' down ta make a switch."

"I been lookin' fer you, mister music maker!" I heard somebody talking behind me. I felt a knee poking me in my back, each time hard enough to scoot me a little more out the door. "So ya thought I'd forgot about da bottla gas, huh? I t'ink I'll jist boot yez offa dis train!"

I tried to hold onto the colored boy's arm. "Watch out there, ya silly dam fool! What're ya tryin' ta do? Kick me out? I'll git up from here an' frail yore knob! Don't ya kick me again!"

He put his foot flat up against my shoulder blade and kicked me out the door. I swung onto the Negro's arms with both hands, and the leather strap of my guitar slipped out of my hold. I was holding both feet clear of the cinders down on the ground. When my guitar fell, I had to turn loose with one hand and grab it by the handle. The Negro had to hold onto the side of the door to hold his own self in the car. I seen him bend backwards as far as he could and lay down flat on the floor. This pulled me up within an inch or so of the edge of the door again, and I was about to get one arm inside. I knew he could pull me back in if I could make it that far. I looked down at the ground going past under me. The train was slowing down. The Negro and me made one more hard pull together to swing me back inside the door. "Hol' on! Boy!" he was grunting.

"No ya don't!" The young fellow bent down into a squatting position, heaving at the Negro's shoulders with both hands. "I'll jist kick da pair of yez out!"

The colored man yelled and screamed, "Hhhaaaayyy! Hheeelllpp!"

"Goddam it, donnn't!" I was about to lose all of my strength in the left arm locked around the Negro's, which was the only thing between me and the six-by-three grave.

"Dis is where da both of yez hits de cinders! Good-bye! An' go ta hell!" He stuck his tongue out between his teeth and throwed every ounce of his weight against the colored man's shoulders.

Slowing down, the train jammed its air brakes and jarred every man in the boxcar off his feet. Men stumbled against each other, missed their licks, clawing and swinging their fists through the air. Two dozen hit the floor and knocked hide and hair and all off each other's heads. Blood flew and spattered everybody. Splinters dug into hands and faces of men tromped on the floor. Guys dove on their faces on top of strangers and grabbed handfuls of loose skin in their fingernails, and twisted until the blood caked into the dust.

They rolled across the floor and busted their heads against the walls, knocked blind by the jar, with lungs and eyes and ears and teeth full of the cement. They stepped on the sick ones, ruptured the brave ones, walked on top of each other with loggers' and railroaders' spike shoes. I felt myself falling out of the Negro's hand hold.

Another tap on the brakes jerked a kink in the train and knocked the boy loose from his hold on the Negro's shoulders. The jar sent him jumping like a frog from where he was squatting, over me and the Negro both, and over the slope of the steep cinder grading, rolling, knocking and plowing cinders twenty feet to each side till like a wild, rolling truck tire he chugged into the water of the lake.

I pulled the Negro friend over the edge with me and both of us lit running with our feet on the cinders. I stumbled and took a little spill, but the colored boy run and managed to stay on his feet.

I made a run for the door of the same boxcar again, and put my hand down on an iron bolt and tried to run along with the train and swing myself up again. Men's hands reached out the door trying to grab me and help me in, but my guitar was going wild and I had to drop my hold on the bolt and trot off to the edge of the cinders. I was giving up all hopes of getting back in, when I looked behind me and saw my colored partner gripping onto the iron ladder on the end of the car. Holding the ladder with one hand, he was waving his other one in the air and yelling, "Pass me yo' guitah!"

As he went by me I got a running start on the cinders and held the guitar up to him. He caught it by the neck and clumb up onto the roof of the car. I swung the ladder and went over the top just at his heels.

"Hurry on up heah! You wanta see dat fella in th' lake?"

He pointed back down along the string of cars picking up

speed again. "Off at d' side of dat little clump of trees there, there! Wadin' out yondah? See 'im? See! Boy, I bet you dat dip sobered 'im up!"

Both of us was standing side by side propping each other up. The roof of the car moved and bounced rougher than the floor inside.

The Negro friend grinned over at me with the sun in his eyes. He still hadn't lost his little greasy brown cap and was holding it down on his head while the wind made a few grabs at it. "Whoooee! Dat wuz a close one! Boy, you set fo' a good fas' ride on top? Sho' ain't no way gettin' back down inside dat cah when this roller gits ridin' ag'in!"

I squatted down cross-legged and took hold of the boards on the runwalk on top of the car. He laid down with his hands folded back of his head. We laughed at the way our faces looked with the cement all over them, and our eyes watering. The black coal dust from the locomotive made us look like white ghosts with black eyes. Lips chapped and cracked from the long ride in the hot sun and hard wind.

"Smell dat cool aih?"

"Smells clean. Don't it? Healthy!"

"Me 'n' you's sho' in fo' a soakin', ourselves!"

"Makes ya think?"

"I knows. Boy, up heah in dis lake country, it c'n cloud up an' rain in two seconds flush!"

"Ain't no rain cloud I can see!"

"Funny thing 'bout dese Minnesoty rain clouds. Evah cloud's a rain cloud!"

"Gonna go hard on my guitar." I played a few little notes without really noticing what I was doing. The air turned off cooler as we rolled along. A second later I looked up and saw two kids crawl from an open-top car just behind us: a tall skinny one about fifteen, and a little scrawny runt that couldn't be over ten or eleven. They had on Boy Scout looking clothes. The older one carried a pack on his back, and the little kid had a sweater with the sleeves tied together slung around his neck.

"Hiyez, men?" The tall one saluted and dumped his pack down a couple of feet from us.

The little feller hunched down and set picking his teeth with a rusty pocket knife, talking, "Been wid 'er long?"

I'd seen a thousand kids just like them. They seem to come from homes somewhere that they've run away from. They seem to come to take the place of the old stiffs that slip on a wet board, miss a ladder, fall out a door, or just dry up and shrivel away riding the mean freights; the old souls that groan somewhere in the darkest corner of a boxcar, moan about a twisted life half lived and nine tenths wasted, cry as their souls hit the highball for heaven, die and pass out of this world like the echo of a foggy whistle.

"Evenin', gentulmen, evenin'." The Negro boy raised up to a sitting position. "You gents is a little shade yo'ng t' be out siftin' th' cinders, ain't you?"

"C'n we help how old we are?" The biggest kid spit away into the wind without even looking where it would land.

"Me ole man's fault. Oughtta been bornt sooner," the little runt piped up.

The big one didn't change the expression on his face, because if he'd of looked any tougher, something would have busted. "Pipe down, squoit!" He turned toward us. "Yez hittin' fer de slaughter-house er Wall Street?"

"I don't git ya." I looked over at him.

"Chi? Er N'Yok?"

I tried to keep from busting out laughing in the kid's face. And I could see the colored boy turning his head the other way to hide a snicker. "Me," I answered the kid, "me, I'm headed fer Wall Street, I reckin." Then I thought for a minute and asked him, " 'Bouts you boys goin'?"

"Chi."

"On da fly."

"Kin ya really beat it out on dat jitter box dere, mister?"

"I make a rattlin' noise."

"Sing on toppa dat?"

"No. Not on top of it. I stand up and hold it with this leather strap around my shoulder, or else I set down and play it in my lap like this, see?"

"Make anyt'ing wid it?"

"I've come purty close ta starvin' a couple of times, boys, but never faded plumb out of th' picture yet so far."

"Yeah?"

"Dat's bad."

I come down on some running notes and threw in a few sliding blues notes, and the kids stuck their ears almost down to the sound-hole, listening.

"Say ya hit da boog on dere, don'tcha?"

"Better boog all yez wants, sarg," the older kid said. "I dunno how dat box'll sound fulla wadder, but we gon'ta be swimmin' on toppa dis train here in about a minnit."

The Negro boy turned his head around toward the engine and whiffed of the damp air. "About one minnit's right!"

"Will it wreck dat music box?" The biggest kid stood up and threw his pack on his back. The coal dust had covered his face over in the days when this railroad was first laid, and a few drops of the spit and moisture from the lower streets of a lot of towns had been smeared like brushmarks in every direction around his mouth, nose and eyes. Water and sweat had run down his neck and dried there in long strings. He said it again: "Will de rain wreck dat rackit box?"

I stood up and looked ahead at the black smoke rolling out of the engine. The air was cool and heavy and held the big coil of smoke low to the ground along the side of the train. It boiled and turned, mixed in with the patches of heavy fog, and spun into all kinds of shapes. The picture in the weeds and bushes alongside the tracks was like ten thousand drunkards rolling in the weeds with the bellyache. When the first three or four splats of rain hit me in the face I said to the kids, "This water won't exactly do this guitar any good!"

"Take dis ole sweater," the smallest kid yelled at me. " 'S all I got! Wrap it aroun' yer music! Help a little!" I blinked the water out of my eyes and waited a jiffy for him to pull the sweater from around his neck where he had tied the sleeves. His face looked like a quick little picture, blackish tobacco brown colors, that somebody was wiping from a window glass with a dirty rag.

"Yeah," I told him, "much oblige! Keep out a few drops, won't it?" I slipped the sweater over the guitar like a man putting clothes on a dummy in a window. Then I skint out of my new khaki shirt and put it on the guitar, and buttoned the buttons up, and tied the sleeves around the neck. Everybody laughed. Then we all squatted down in a little half circle with our backs to the rain and wind. "I don't give a dam how drippin' I git, boys, but I gotta keep my meal ticket dry!"

The wind struck against our boxcar and the rain beat itself to pieces and blew over our heads like a spray from a fire hose shooting sixty miles an hour. Every drop that blew against my skin stung and burned.

The colored rider was laughing and saying, "Man! Man! When th' good Lord was workin' makin' Minnesoty, He couldn' make up His mind whethah ta make anothah ocean or some mo' land, so He just got 'bout half done an' then He quit an' went home! Wowie!" He ducked his head and shook it and kept laughing, and at the same time, almost without me noticing what he was doing, he had slipped his blue work shirt off and jammed it over into my hands. "One mo' shirt might keep yo' meal ticket a little bettah!"

"Don't you need a shirt to keep dry?"

I don't know why I asked him that. I was already dressing the guitar up in the shirt. He squared his shoulders back into the wind and rubbed the palms of his hands across his chest and shoulders, still laughing and talking, "You think dat little ole two-bit shirt's gonna keep out this cloudbu'st?"

When I looked back around at my guitar on my lap, I seen one more little filthy shirt piled up on top of it. I don't know exactly how I felt when my hands come down and touched this shirt. I looked around at the little tough guys and saw them humped up with their naked backs splitting the wind and the rain glancing six feet in the air off their shoulders. I didn't say a word. The little kid pooched his lips out so the water would run down into his mouth like a trough, and every little bit he'd save up a mouthful and spit it out in a long thin spray between his teeth. When he saw that I was keeping my eyes nailed on him, he spit the last of his rainwater out and said, "I ain't t'oisty."

"I'll wrap this one around the handle an' the strings will keep dry that way. If they get wet, you know, they rust out." I wound the last shirt around and around the neck of the guitar handle. Then I pulled the guitar over to where I was laying down. I tied the leather strap around a plank in the boardwalk, ducked my head down behind the guitar and tapped the runty kid on the shoulder.

"Hey, squirt!"

"Whaddaya want?"

"Not much of a windbreak, but it at least knocks a little of th' blister out of that rain! Roll yer head over here an' keep it ducked down behind this music box!"

"Yeeehh." He flipped over like a little frog and smiled

all over his face and said, "Music's good fer somethin', ain't it?"

Both of us stretched out full length. I was laying on my back looking straight up into the sky all gray and tormented and blowing with low clouds that whined when they got sucked under the wheels. The wind whistled funeral songs for the railroad riders. Lightning struck and crackled in the air and sparks of electricity done little dances for us on the iron beams and fixtures. The flash of the lightning knocked the clouds full of holes and the rain hit down on us harder than before. "On th' desert, I use this here guitar fer a sun shade! Now I'm usin' th' dam thing fer a umbreller!"

"T'ink I could eva' play one uv dem?" The little kid was shaking and trembling all over, and I could hear his lips and nose blow the rain away, and his teeth chatter like a jackhammer. He scooted his body closer to me, and I laid an arm down so he could rest his head. I asked him, "How's that fer a pillow?"

"Dat's betta." He trembled all over and moved a time or two. Then he got still and I didn't hear him say anything else. Both of us were soaked to the skin a hundred times. The wind and the rain was running a race to see which could whip us the hardest. I felt the roof of the car pounding me in the back of the head. I could stand a little of it, but not long at a time. The guitar hit against the raindrops and sounded like a nest of machine guns spitting out lead.

The force of the wind pushed the sound box against the tops of our heads, and the car jerked and buckled through the clouds like a coffin over a cliff.

I looked at the runt's head resting on my arm, and thought to myself, "Yeah, that's a little better."

My own head ached and pained inside. My brain felt like a crazy cloud of grasshoppers jumping over one another across a field. I held my neck stiff so my head was about two inches clear of the roof; but that didn't work. I got cold and cramped and a dozen kinks tied my whole body in a knot. The only way I could rest was to let my head and neck go limp; and when I did this, the jolt of the roof pounded the back of my head. The cloudbursts got madder and splashed through all of the lakes, laughing and singing, and then a wail in the wind would get a low start and cry in the timber like the cry for freedom of a conquered people.

Through the roof, down inside the car, I heard the voices of the sixty-six hoboes. There had been sixty-nine, the old man said, if he counted right. One threw his own self into the lake. He pushed two more out the door with him, but they lit easy and caught onto the ladder again. Then the two little windburnt, sunbaked brats had mounted the top of our car and were caught in the cloudburst like drowned rats. Men fighting against men. Color against color. Kin against kin. Race pushing against race. And all of us battling against the wind and the rain and that bright crackling lightning that booms and zooms, that bathes his eyes in the white sky, wrestles a river to a standstill, and spends the night drunk in a whorehouse.

What's that hitting me on the back of the head? Just bumping my head against the roof of the car. Hey! Goddam you! Who th' hell do you think you're a hittin', mister? What are you, anyhow, a dam bully? You cain't push that woman around! What's all of these folks in jail for? Believing in people? Where'd all of us come from? What did we do wrong? You low-down cur, if you hit me again, I'll tear your head off!

My eyes closed tight, quivering till they exploded like the rain when the lightning dumped a truckload of thunder down along the train. I was whirling and floating and hugging the little runt around the belly, and my brain felt

like a pot of hot lead bubbling over a flame. Who's all of
these crazy men down there howling out at each other like
hyenas? Are these men? Who am I? How come them here?
How the hell come me here? What am I supposed to do
here?

My ear flat against the tin roof soaked up some music and
singing coming from down inside of the car:

> This train don't carry no rustlers,
> Whores, pimps, or side-street hustlers;
> This train is bound for glory,
> This train.

Can I remember? Remember back to where I was this
morning? St. Paul. Yes. The morning before? Bismarck,
North Dakota. And the morning before that? Miles City,
Montana. Week ago, I was a piano player in Seattle.

Who's this kid? Where's he from, and where's he headed
for? Will he be me when he grows up? Was I like him when
I was just his size? Let me remember. Let me go back. Let
me get up and walk back down the road I come. This old
hard rambling and hard graveling. This old chuck-luck
traveling. My head ain't working right.

Where was I?

Where in the hell was I?

Where was I when I was a kid? Just as far, far, far back,
on back, as I can remember?

Strike, lightning, strike!

Strike, Goddam you, strike!

There's lots of folks that you cain't hurt!

Strike, lightning!

See if I care!

Roar and rumble, twist and turn, the sky ain't never as
crazy as the world.

Bound for glory? This train? Ha!
I wonder just where in the hell we're bound.
Rain on, little rain, rain on!
Blow on, little wind, keep blowin'!
'Cause them guys is a singin' that this train is bound for glory, an' I'm gonna hug her breast till I find out where she's bound.

Chapter II

EMPTY SNUFF CANS

◈

Okemah, in Creek Indian, means "Town on a Hill," but our busiest hill was our Graveyard Hill, and just about the only hill in the country that you could rest on. West of town, the wagon roads petered themselves out chasing through some brushy sand hills. Then south, the country just slipped away and turned into a lot of hard-hit farms, trying to make an honest living in amongst the scatterings of scrub oak, black jack, sumac, sycamore, and cottonwood that lay on the edges of the tough hay meadows and stickery pasture lands.

Okemah was an Oklahoma farming town since the early days, and it had about an equal number of Indians, Negroes, and Whites doing their trading there. It had a railroad called the Fort Smith and Western—and there was no guarantee that you'd get any certain place any certain time by riding it. Our most famous railroad man was called "Boomer Swenson," and every time Boomer come to a spot along the rails where he'd run over somebody, he'd pull down on his whistle cord and blow the longest, moaningest, saddest whistle that ever blew on any man's railroad.

Ours was just another one of those little towns, I guess, about a thousand or so people, where everybody knows everybody else; and on your way to the post office, you'd nod and speak to so many friends that your neck would be rubbed raw when you went in to get your mail if there was any. It took you just about an hour to get up through town, say hello, talk over the late news, family gossip, sickness, weather, crops and lousy politics. Everybody had something to say about something, or somebody, and you usually knew almost word for word what it was going to be about before you heard them say it, as we had well-known and highly expert talkers on all subjects in and out of this world.

Old Windy Tom usually shot off at his mouth about the weather. He not only could tell you the exact break in the exact cloud, but just when and where it would rain, blow, sleet or snow; and for yesterday, today, and tomorrow, by recalling to your mind the very least and finest details of the weather for these very days last year, two years, or forty years ago. When Windy Tom got to blowing it covered more square blocks than any one single cyclone. But he was our most hard-working weather man—Okemah's Prophet—and we would of fought to back him up.

I was what you'd call just a home-town kid and carved my initials on most everything that would stand still and let me. W. G. Okemah Boy. Born 1912. That was the year, I think, when Woodrow Wilson was named to be the president and my papa and mama got all worked up about good and bad politics and named me Woodrow Wilson too. I don't remember this any too clear.

I wasn't much more than two years old when we built our seven-room house over in the good part of Okemah. This was our new house, and Mama was awful glad and proud of it. I remember a bright yellow outside—a blurred haze of a dark inside—some vines looking in through windows.

Sometimes, I seem to remember trying to follow my big sister off to school. I'd gather up all of the loose books I could find around the house and start out through the gate and down the sidewalk, going to get myself a schoolhouse education, but Mama would run out and catch me and drag me back into the house kicking and bawling. When Mama would hide the books I'd walk back to the front porch, afraid to run away, but I'd use the porch for my stage, and the grass, flowers, and pickets along our fence would be my crowd of people; and I made up my first song right there:

> Listen to the music,
> Music, music;
> Listen to the music,
> Music band.

These days our family seemed to be getting along all right. People rode down our street in buggies and sarries, all dressed up, and they'd look over at our house and say, "Charlie and Nora Guthrie's place." "Right new."

Clara was somewhere between nine and ten, but she seemed like an awful big sister to me. She was always bending and whirling around, dancing away to school and singing her way back home; and she had long curls that swung in the wind and brushed in my face when she wrestled me across the floor.

Roy was along in there between seven and eight. Quiet about everything. Walked so slow and thought so deep that I always wondered what was going on in his head. I watched him biff the tough kids on the noodle over the fence, and then he would just come on in home, and think and think about it. I wondered how he could fight so good and keep so quiet.

I guess I was going on three then.

Peace, pretty weather. Spring turning things green. Summer staining it all brown. Fall made everything redder, browner, and brittler. And winter was white and gray and the color of bare trees. Papa went to town and made real-estate deals with other people, and he brought their money home. Mama could sign a check for any amount, buy every little thing that her eyes liked the looks of. Roy and Clara could stop off in any store in Okemah and buy new clothes to fit the weather, new things to eat to make you healthy, and Papa was proud because we could all have anything we saw. Our house was packed full of things Mama liked, Roy liked, Clara liked, and that was what Papa liked. I remember his leather law books, Blackstone and others. He smoked a pipe and good tobacco and I wondered if this helped him to stretch out in his big easy-riding chair and try to think up some kind of a deal or swap to get some more money.

But those were fighting days in Oklahoma. If even the little newskids fought along the streets for corroded pennies, it's not hard to see that Papa had to outwit, outsmart, and outrun a pretty long string of people to have everything so nice. It kept Mama scared and nervous. She always had been a serious person with deep-running thoughts in her head; and the old songs and ballads that she sung over and over every day told me just about what she was thinking about. And they told Papa, but he didn't listen. She used to say to us kids, "We love your Papa, and if anything tries to hurt him and make him bad and mean, we'll fight it, won't we?" And Roy would jump up and pound his fist on his chest and say, "I'll fight!" Mama knew how dangerous the land-trading business was, and she wanted Papa to drop out of the fighting and the pushing, and settle down to some kind of a better life of growing things and helping other people to grow. But Papa was a man of brimstone and hot fire, in his mind and in his fists, and was known all over that section of the state as the champion of all the fist fighters. He used his fists on sharks and fakers, and all to give his family nice things. Mama was that kind of a woman who always looked at a pretty thing and wondered, "Who had to work to make it? Who owned it and loved it before?"

So our family was sort of divided up into two sides: Mama taught us kids to sing the old songs and told us long stories about each ballad; and in her own way she told us over and over to always try and see the world from the other fellow's side. Meanwhile Papa bought us all kinds of exercising rods and stretchers, and kept piles of kids boxing and wrestling out in the front yard; and taught us never and never to allow any earthly human to scare us, bully us, or run it over us.

Then more settlers trickled West, they said in search of elbow room on the ground, room to farm the rich topsoil; but, hushed and quiet, they dug into the private heart of the earth to find the lead, the soft coal, the good zinc. While the town of people only seventeen miles east of us danced on their roped-off streets and held solid weeks of loud celebrating called the King Koal Karnival, only the early roadrunners, the smart oil men, knew that in a year or two King Koal would die and his body would be burned to ashes and his long twisting grave would be left dank and dark and empty under the ground—that a new King would be dancing into the sky, gushing and spraying the entire country around with the slick black blood of industry's veins, the oil—King Oil—a hundred times more powerful and wild and rich and fiery than King Timber, King Steel, King Cotton, or even King Koal.

The wise traders come to our town first, and they were the traders who had won their prizes at out-trading thousands of others back where they come from: oil slickers, oil fakers, oil stakers, and oil takers. Papa met them. He stood up and swapped and traded, bought and sold, got bigger, spread out, and made more money.

And this was to get us the nice things. And we all liked the prettiest and best things in the store windows, and anything in the store was Clara's just for signing her name, Roy's just for signing his name, or Mama's just for signing her name—and I knew how proud I felt of our name, that just to write it on a piece of paper would bring more good things home to us. This wasn't because there was oil in the wind, nor gushers thrashing against the sky, no—it was because my dad was the man that owned the land—and whatever was under that land was ours. The oil was a whisper in the dark, a rumor, a gamble. No derricks standing up for your eye to see. It was a whole bunch of people chasing a year or two ahead of a wild dream. Oil was the thing that made other people treat you like a human, like a burro, or like a dog.

Mama thought we had enough to buy a farm and work it ourselves, or at least get into some kind of a business that was a little quieter. Almost every day when Papa rode home he showed the signs and bruises of a new fist fight, and Mama seemed to get quieter than any of us had ever seen her. She laid in the bedroom and I watched her cry on her pillow.

And all of this had give us our nice seven-room house.

One day, nobody ever knew how or why, a fire broke out somewhere in the house. Neighbors packed water. Everybody made a run to help. But the flames outsmarted the people, and all that we had left, in an hour or two, was a cement foundation piled full of red-hot ashes and cinders.

How did it break out? Where'bouts did it get started? Anybody know? Hey, did they tell you anything? Me? No. I don't know. Hey, John, did you happen to see how it got on afire? No, not me. Nobody seems to know. Where was Charlie Guthrie? Out trading? Kids at school? Where was Mrs. Guthrie and the baby? Nobody knows a thing. It just busted loose and it jumped all through the bedrooms and the dining room and the front room—nobody knows a thing.

Where's th' Guthrie folks at? Neighbors' house? All of them all right? None hurt. Wonder what'll happen to 'em now? Oh, Charlie Guthrie will jist go out here an' make about two swaps some mornin' before breakfast an' he'll make enough money to build a whole lot better place than that. . . . No insurance . . . . They say this broke him flat . . . . Well, I'm waitin' ta see where they'll move to next.

I remember our next house pretty plain. We called it the old London House, because a family named London used to live there. The walls were built up out of square sandstone rocks. The two big rooms on the ground floor were dug into the side of a rocky hill. The walls inside felt cold, like a cellar, and holes were dug out between the rocks big enough to put your two hands in. And the old empty snuff cans of the London family were lined up in rows along the rafters.

I liked the high porch along the top story, for it was the highest porch in all of the whole town. Some kids lived in houses back along the top of the hill, but they had thick trees all around their back porches, and couldn't stand there and look way out across the first street at the bottom of the hill, across the second road about a quarter on east, out over the willow trees that grew along a sewer creek, to see the white strings of new cotton bales and a whole lot of men and women and kids riding into town on wagons piled double-sideboard-full of cotton, driving under the funny shed at the gin, driving back home again on loads of cotton seed.

I stood there looking at all of this, which was just the tail-end section of Okemah. And then, I remember, there was a long train blew a wild-sounding whistle and throwed a cloud of steam out on both sides of its engine wheels, and lots of black smoke come jumping out of the smokestack. The train pulled a long string of boxcars along behind it, and when it got to the depot it cut its engine loose from the rest of the cars, and the engine trotted all around up and down the railroad tracks, grabbing onto cars and tugging them here and yonder, taking some and leaving some. But I was tickled best when I saw the engine take a car and run and run till it got up the right speed, and then stop and let the car go coasting and rolling all by its own self, down where the man wanted it to be. I knew I could go and get in good with any bunch of kids in the neighborhood just by telling them about my big high lookout porch, and all of the horses and cotton wagons, and the trains.

Papa hired a man and a truck to haul some more furniture over to our old London House; and Roy and Clara carried all kinds of heavy things, bedsteads, springs, bed irons, parts for stoves, some chairs, quilts that didn't smell right to me, tables and extra leaves, a boxful of silverware which I was glad to see was the same set we had always used. A few of the things had come out of the other house before the fire got out of hand. The rest of the furniture was all funny looking. Somebody else had used it in their house, and Papa had bought it second hand.

Clara would say, "I'll be glad when we get to live in another house that we own; then Mama can get a lot of new things."

Roy talked the same way. "Yeah, this stuff is so old and ugly, it'll scare me just to have to eat, and sleep, and live around it."

"It won't be like our good house, Roy," Clara said. "I liked for kids to come over and play in our yard then, and drink out of our pretty water glasses and see our pretty flower beds, but I'm gonna just run any kid off that comes to see us now, 'cause I don't want anybody to think that anybody has got to live with such old mean, ugly chairs, and cook on an old nasty stove, and even to sleep on these filthy beds, and . . . ." Then Clara set down a chair she was carrying inside of the kitchen and looked all around at the cold concrete walls, and down at the rock floor. She picked up a water glass that was spun half full of fine spider webs with a couple of flies wrapped like mummies and she said, ". . . And ask anybody to drink out of these old spidery glasses."

Roy and Clara cooked the first meal on the rusty stove. It was a good meal of beefsteak, thickened flour gravy, okra rolled in corn meal and fried in hot grease, hot biscuits with plenty of butter melted in between, and at the last, Clara danced around over the floor, grabbed a can opener out of the cupboard drawer, and cut a can of sliced peaches open for us. The weather outside was the early part of fall, and there was a good wood-smoke smell in the air along towards sundown and supper time, and families everywhere were warming up a little. The big stove heated the rock walls and Papa asked Mama, "Well, Nora, how do you like your new house?"

She had her back to the cook stove and faced the east window, and looked out over Papa's shoulder, and not in his face, and held a hot cup of coffee in both of her hands, and everybody got quiet. But for a long time she didn't answer. Then she finally said, "I guess it's all right. I guess it'll have to do till we can get a better place. I guess we won't be here very long." She run her fingers through her hair, set her coffee down to cool, and the look on her face twisted and trembled and it scared everybody. Her eyes didn't look to see anything or anybody in that house, but she had pretty dark eyes and the gray light from the east window was about all that was shining in her mind.

"How long we gonna stay, I mean live here, Papa?" Roy spoke up.

Papa looked around at everybody at the table and then he said, "You mean you don't like it here?" His face looked funny and his eyes run around over the kitchen.

Clara cleared away a handful of dirty plates off of the table and said, "Are we supposed to like it here?"

"Where it's so dirty," Roy went on to say, "an' spooky lookin' you can't even bring any kids around your own home?"

Mama didn't say a word.

"Why," Papa told Roy, "this is a good house, solid rock all over, good new shingle roof, new rafters. Go take a look at that upper attic. Lots of room up there where you can store trunks and things. You can fix a nice playhouse up in that attic and invite all of the kids in the whole country to come down here on cold winter days, and play dolls, and all kinds of games up in there. You kids just don't know a good house when you see one. And, one thing, it won't ever catch afire and burn down."

Roy just ducked his head and looked down at his plate and didn't say any more. Mama's cup of hot coffee had turned cold. Clara poured a dishpan of hot water, slushed her finger around to whip up the suds, cooled it down just right with a dipper of cold water, and told Papa, "As for me, I don't like this old nasty place. 'Cause it's got old cold dingy walls, that's why. 'Cause I don't like to sleep up there in that old stinky bedroom where you can smell the snuff spit of the London family for the last nine kids. 'Cause you know what kinds of stories everybody tells about this old house, you know as well as I know. Kids swelled up in that old bedroom and died. Broke out all over with old yellow, running sores. Not a kid, not in this whole town, not a single girl I used to play with will ever, ever play with me again as long as we live in this town, if we let them find out we've got the London House seven-year itch!" Clara turned her head away from the rest of us.

Papa wasn't saying much, just sipped his coffee and listened to the others talk. Then he said, "I've got something to tell you all. I don't know, I don't know how you're going to take it. Well, I'm afraid we're going to have to live in this house for a long time. I bought this place for a thousand dollars yesterday."

"You mean . . ." Mama talked up. "Charlie, are you trying to sit there and tell me that you actually . . . ?"

". . . Bought this place?" Clara said.

"A thousan' dollars for this old dump?" Roy asked him.

"I'm afraid so." Papa went ahead drinking his coffee and leaving the rest of his dinner setting in front of him to get cold. "We'll pitch in and fix it all up real nice, new plaster, and cement all inside. New paint all over the woodwork."

Clara dried her hands on her apron and then pushed her curls back out of her face and stepped over to the west back door, opened the door and walked out onto the hill.

Roy got up and pushed the door shut behind her.

Papa said, "Tell your sister to come on in here out of this night air, she'll take down sick after standing over that hot stove."

And Roy said, "Th' hot stove an' th' night air don't hurt us as . . . ."

"Bad as what?" Papa asked Roy. And Roy said, "Bad's what Clara was tellin' you about, that's what."

"Roy, you mind what I tell you to do! I told you to open up that door and call Clara back in this house. You do it!" Papa gave his orders, and his voice was half rough and tough, but halfway hurt.

"Call 'er in if you want 'er in," Roy told Papa, and then Roy made a run around Papa's elbow and through the front room, and he mounted the stairs outside and chased up to his bedroom and pulled the covers all up over his head.

Papa rose up from his chair and walked over and opened up the kitchen door and walked out to find Clara. He called her name a few times and she didn't answer back. But somewhere he could hear her crying and he called her again, "Clara, Clara! Where are you? Talk!"

"I'm over here," Clara spoke up, and when Papa turned around he saw that he had walked right past her skirt on his way out the door. She was leaning back against the wall of the house.

"You know your old Papa don't want anything to happen to you, because, well, I get mean sometimes, and I treat all of you bad, but sometimes it's just because I want to treat you so good that I'd . . . . Come on, let me carry you back in the house. I'm your old mean Papa. You can call me that if you want to." He reached down and took Clara by the arm, and gave her a little pull. She let her body just go limp and limber, and kept crying for a minute.

Then Papa went on talking, "I might be mean. I guess I am. I might not stop often enough trying to work and make a lot of money to buy all of you some nice things. Maybe I've got to be so mean trading, and trying to make the money, that I don't know how to quit when I come in home where you are, where Roy is, and where Mama's at."

Clara snubbed a little, folded her arm over her face, and then she wiped the tears away from her eyes with the wrong end of her fist and said, "Not either."

"Not either, what?" Papa asked her.

"Not mean."

"Why? I thought I was."

"Not either."

"Why ain't I?"

"It's something else that's mean."

"What else?"

"I don't know."

"What is it that's mean to my little girl? You just tell me what it is that's even one little frog hair mean to my little girl, and your old mean dad'll roll up his sleeves, and double up his fists and go and knock the sound out of somebody."

"This old house is mean."

"House?"

"It's mean."

"How can a house be mean?"

"It's mean to be in it."

"Oh," Papa told Clara, "now, I see what you're driving at. You know how mean I am?"

"Not mean."

"I'm just big and mean enough to pick you up just like a big sack of sugar and put on my shoulder, like this, and like this, and then like this, and . . . see . . . I can carry you all of the way in through this back door, and all of the way in through this big, nice, warm kitchen, and all of the way. . . ." Papa carried Clara laughing and giggling under her curly hair back into the kitchen. When he was even with the stove, he looked up and saw Mama washing the dishes and piling them on a little oilcloth table to drain.

Clara kicked in the air and said, "Oh! Let me down! Let me down! I'm not crying now! And besides, look what's happening! Look!" She squirmed out of Papa's hold around her, and slid to the floor, and she sailed over into a corner, brought out a mop, and started mopping up all around Mama's feet, talking a blue streak.

"Mama, look! You're draining the dishes without a drain pan! The water's dripping like a great big . . . river . . . down. . . ."

And then Clara looked over the hot-water reservoir on the wood stove and nobody in the house saw what she saw.

Her eyes flared open when she seen that her mama wasn't listening, just washing the dishes clean in the scalding water; and when her mama set still another plate on its edge on the little table, Clara kept quiet, and Papa took a deep breath, and bit his lip, and turned around and walked away into the front room.

I found a new way to spend my time these days. I went across the alley on top of the hill and strutted up and down in front of a bunch of kids that spent most of their time making up games to play on top of their cellars. Almost every house up and down the street had a dugout of some kind or another full of fresh canned fruit, string beans, pickled beets, onions. I snuck into one cellar after another with one kid after another, and saw how dark, how chilly and damp it was down in there. I smelled the cankery dank rotten logs along the ceiling of one cellar, and the hemmed-up feeling made me want to get back out into the open air again, but the good denned-up feeling sort of made me want to stay down in there.

The kid next door had a cellar full of jars and the jars were full of pickled beets, long green cucumbers, and big round slices of onions and peaches as big as your hat. So we pulled us up a wooden box, and took down a big fruit jar of peaches. I twisted the lid. The other kid took a twist. But the jar was sealed too tight. We commenced getting hungry. "Ain't that juice larepin'?" "Yeah, boy, it is," I told him, "but what's larepin'?" So he says, "Anything you like real good an' ain't got fer a long time, an' then you git it, that's larepin'."

All of our hard wrestling and cussing didn't coax the lid off. So we sneaked over behind the barn. The other kid squeezed his self in between a couple of loose boards, stayed in the barn a minute, and came back out with a claw hammer and a two-gallon feed bucket. "Good bucket," he told me. I glanced into it, seen a few loose horse hairs, but he must have had a pretty hungry horse, because the bucket had been licked as clean as a new dime.

I held the jar as tight as I could over the bucket, and he took a few little love taps on the shoulder of the jar with his hammer. He saw he wasn't hitting the glass hard enough, so he got a little harder each lick. Then he come down a good one on it, and the glass broke into a thousand pieces; the pewter lid and the red rubber seal fell first, then a whole big goo of loose peaches, skinned and cut in halves slopped out into the bottom of the bucket; and then the neck of the jar with a lot of mean-looking jagged edges sticking up, and the bottom of the jar that scared us to look at it.

"Good peaches," he told me.

"Good juice," I told him.

We fingered in around the slivers of glass and looked each peach over good before we downed it, pushing little sharp chips off through the oozy juice; and the warm sun made the specks of glass shine up like diamonds.

"Reckon how much a really diamond sparks?" he said to me.

"I don't know," I said to him.

Then he said, "My mama's got one she wears on her finger."

And I said, "My mama ain't . . . jest a big wide gold'un. Some glass on yer peach, flip it."

"Funny 'bout yer mama not havin' 'cept jest one ring. Need a diamond one too ta be really, really married ta each other."

"What makes that?"

"Diamonds is what ya put in a ring, an' when ya see a

girl ya jest put th' diamond ring on 'er finger; an' then next ya git a gold ring, an ya put th' gold one on 'er finger; an' next—well, then ya c'n kiss 'er all ya want to."

"Perty good."

"Know what else ya c'n do?"

"Huh uh, what?"

"Sleep with her."

"Sleep?"

"Yes sir, sleep right with 'er, under th' cover."

"She sleep, too?"

"I don't know. I never put no diamond on no girl."

"Me neither."

"Never did sleep with no girl, 'cept my cousin."

"She sleep, too?" I asked.

"Shore. Cousins they jest mostly sleep. We told crazy stories an' laffed so loud my dad whopped us ta git us ta go ta sleep."

"What makes yore dad wanta sleep unner th' covers with a diamond ring an' a gold one on yer mama's hand?"

"That's what mamas an' daddies are for."

"Is it?"

"'At's what makes a mama a mama, an' a papa a papa."

"What about workin' together, like cleanin' up around th' yard, an' cleanin' up th' house, an' eatin' together; how about talkin' together, an' goin' off somewheres together, don't that make nobody a mama an' a papa?"

"Naww, might help some."

"'S awful funny, ain't it?"

"My mama an' dad won't tell me nothin' about what makes you a dad or a mama," he told me.

"They won't?"

"Naww. Sceered. But, I keep my eyes open wide, wide open; an' I stay awake on my bed, an' I listen over onto their bed. An' I know one thing."

"Yeah?"

"Yeah."

"What?"

"I know one main thing."

"What main thing?"

"That's where little babies come from."

"From mamas an' papas?"

"Yep."

"Ain't no way they could."

"Yes they is."

"You got to go somewhere to a store, or down to see a doctor, or make a doctor come an' bring a little baby."

"No, 'tain't ever' time that way. I hear my mama an' I hear my dad, an' they said they slept together too much, an' got too many kids out from under th' cover."

"You don't find little babies under covers."

"Yes you do. Once in a while you find one, an' he's a little boy or a little girl. Then this little baby grows up big, an' you find another'n."

"What's the next one?"

"Like you, or like me."

"I ain't no little baby."

"You ain't but four years old."

"But I ain't no little cryin' baby."

"No, but you was when they first found you."

"Heck."

"'S purty bad, all right, but maybe that's why my mama or dad won't tell me nothin' about th' covers. 'Fraid I might find some more little babies in under there, an' mama cries a lot an' says we done already got too many."

"If your mama didn't want 'em, why don't she just put 'em back in under th' sheet?"

"Naww, I don't know, I don't think you can put 'em back."

"How come your papa don't want so many?"

"Cain't feed an' clothes us."

"That's bad. I'll get you somethin' to eat over at my house. We ain't got so many covers, I mean, so many kids as you got."

"You know th' reason, don't you?"

"No, why?"

"Jest 'cause your mama ain't got no two rings, one gold one, an' one diamond one."

"Maybe she did used to have a diamunt ring; an' maybe she got it burnt up when our pretty big house caught afire an' burnt down."

"I remember about that. I seen th' people runnin' up that way that day. I seen th' smoke. How big was you then?"

"I was just fresh out from under th' cover."

"Say, if I ask you a favor, will you tell me it?"

"Might, what?"

"Kids say your mama got mad an' set her brand-new house on fire, an' burnt ever'thin' plumb up. Did she?"

I didn't say anything back to him. I sat there up against the warm barn for about a minute, hung my head down a little, and then I reached out and kicked his bucket as far as I could kick it; and a million flies that had been eating the peachy juice, flew out of the bucket, and wondered what had hit them. I jumped up, and started to throw a handful of manure on him, but then I let my fingers go limber, and the manure fell to the ground. I didn't look him in the face. I didn't look anywhere special. I didn't want him to see my face, so I turned my head the other way, and walked past the pile of manure.

I played around our yard some and talked to the fence posts, sung songs and made the weeds sing, and found all of the snuff cans the London folks had throwed out into the high weeds around the house for the last ten or fifteen years. I found a flat board, and loaded the cans onto it, and crawled on my hands and knees, pushing it like a big wagon, in and out and all along under the weeds, and it made a road everywhere it went. I come to deep sandy places where the horses had to pull hard and I cussed out, "Hit 'em up, Judie! Git in there, Rhodie! Judie! Dam yore muley hide! Hit 'em in easy! Now take it together! Judie! Rhodie!" I was the world's best team skinner with the world's best team and the world's best wagon.

Then I made out like I delivered my load, got my money, turned all of my horses and mules out onto their pasture, and was going to see some of my people. I slipped on loose rocks lying around the corner of our house, made the white dust foam up when I stomped through our ash pile, and when I got to the top of the hill, I saw the boy next door standing on top of his manure pile watching more flies get fat on the slice of peach. When he seen me he made a hard run down off of the pile, jumped up onto a sawhorse and yelled, "This is my army horse!"

I clumb up in a broke-down wheelbarrow and hollered back at him, "This is my big war tank!"

Then he sailed down off his sawhorse and tore up on top of his manure pile, and said, "This is my big battleship!"

"War tanks can whip ole battleships!" I told him. "War tanks has got fast, fast machine guns! Battleships cain't go 'less they're in water! I can chase Germans on land!"

"But you cain't shoot but just a hunderd Germans! Yer ol' war tank ain't got as many bullets as my big battleship!"

"I can hide in my war tank, behind a rock, an' when ya start ta git off of yore ship, I can kill ya, an' ya'll die!"

He ripped down off of the manure pile, darted behind his barn, and after a little while, he poked his head out of the hayloading door up in the top door. Then he hollered, "This is my big fort! I got my cannons an' my ship tied up down here under me! Yer ol' war tank cain't even hurt me! Ya! Ya!"

"Ya! Yerself! Yer ole fort ain't nothin'!" I pulled myself up out of the wheelbarrow and clumb up onto the first limb of a big walnut tree. "Now I got my airplane, an' ya don't even know what I can do to ya!"

"Cain't do nuthin'! Yore ol' airplane ain't even as high as my fort!"

"I can git up higher!"

"I'm still higher in my fort than yore ol' airplane! Cain't drop no bumbs on me!"

I looked up above me and saw that I'd come to the high top of the tree. The limbs was already swaying around so much that the ground below me seemed like it was a rough ocean. But I had to get up higher. "I c'n git up as high as I wanta! Then I c'n dump out a big bomb on toppa yer ol' crazy fort, an' it'll blow ya all ta pieces, knock yer head off, an' yer arms off, an' yer both legs off, an' ya'll be dead!"

The few limbs in the top of the tree weren't as big as a broomstick, and the wind was whirling me around up there like I was the last big walnut of the season.

Mama slammed our back door and I kept real quiet so she wouldn't see me up in the tree. The kid's mama walked out of her back door with a bushel basket full of old cans and papers, and my mama said, "Say, wonder where our little stray youngins are?"

And his mama said, "I heard them hollering just a minute ago!"

They stood under my tree and asked each other little questions. "Ain't these brats a fright?"

"I tell you, it's a shame to the dogs the way a woman's got to run and chase and wear her wits out to keep a big long string of kids from starving to death."

I looked down through the shady limbs and seen the tops

of the women's heads, one tying a hair ribbon a little tighter in the wind, the other one holding her hair by the big handfuls. The sun shot down through my tree, the light places hit down the back and shoulders of my mama, and the forehead and dress of his mama, and the whole thing was traveling. I felt the sun humming down hot and heavy on my head. It was a crazy feeling. The thing was whirling, moving all around, and I couldn't get it to slow down or stop. I grabbed a better grip on the little limber limbs, and ducked my head down and closed my eyes as tight as I could, and I bit my tongue and lip to keep from crying out loud. It was dark all over then, but my head was splitting open, and everything in me was jumping and pounding like wild horses running away with a big wagon with only one or two loose potatoes rumbling around in it.

I yowled out, "Mama!" She looked all around over the lot. "Where 'bouts are you?"

"Up here. Up in th' tree."

Both of the women caught their breath and I heard them say, "Oh! For heaven's sakes! Hurry! Run! Go get somebody! Get somebody to do something!"

"Can't you just climb down?" Mama asked me.

"No," I told her. "I'm sick."

"Sick? For God's sake! Hold on tight!" Mama got up on the wheelbarrow and tried to climb up to the first limb. She couldn't make it any higher. She looked up where I was sticking like a 'possum in the forks, and said, "It's a good twenty-five feet up to where he is! Oh, Lord, goodness, God, I wish somebody would come along! Wait! There's a bunch of kids yonder along the road at the bottom of the hill! You stay here and talk to him. Tell him anything, anything, but don't let him get scared. Just talk. Hey! You kids down there! Wait a minute! Yes, you! Come here! Want a dime each one of you?"

Five or six mixed colors of kids run up the hill to meet her, and every kid was saying, "Dime? Golly, gosh, yes! Whataya want done? Work? Whole dime?"

"I'll show you, here, down this alley. Now, I wanta know something. Do you see that little boy hanging up yonder in the top of that tall tree?"

"Yeh."

"Gosh."

"Shoot a monkey!"

"Cain't he get back down?"

"No," my mama told them, "he's hung up there or something. He's getting sicker and sicker, and is going to fall any minute, unless we do something to get him down."

"I can climb that tree after him."

"Me, too."

"Yeah, but you can't do no good; them little old weak limbs won't hold nobody else."

Mama was pulling her hair. "You see, you see, you kids, don't you? You see how much gray hairs and worry you pile on to your old mothers' backs! Don't you ever sneak off and pull no such a stunt as this!"

"No ma'am."

"No'm."

"Yes'm."

"I wouldn't."

"I never would chase my folks up no tree."

"Shut up, ijiot, she didn't say that."

"Shh. What'd she say?"

"She said don't get hung up in no tree."

"I been hung up in every tree in this end of town."

"Shut up, she don't know that."

"Hey, guys! These lowest limbs is stout enough to hold us up! See here! You just got to watch out and keep your

feet in real close to th' top of th' tree, an' not out on the
limbs when you hit a fork! Okay, Slew, you're the littlest,
skin up in there far's you can; climb right up next to him!
Sawdust, you're next littlest! Flag it up in there and stop
right under Slew!"

Slew and Sawdust skint up into that tree. The little one's
head was up as high as my belly, and the next kid was right
under him.

"We're up here! Whatta you wanta do next?"

"Buckeye, you got long arms and legs; you stand yonder
a-straddle of them two wide limbs!"

"I'm here 'fore you got it said."

"Thug, you set yourself down right here low to the
ground. All of you watch; maybe if he falls, you can at least
make a grab and try to ketch him'."

"What's th' rest of us gonna do?"

"Rabbit, an' you, Star Navy, you too, Jake—you three
run yonder to that lady's wellhouse, an' take yer pockitknife an' cut that rope, an' git back here in nuthin' flat!"

Three kids aired out over the hill, come out lugging a long
piece of rope.

"Okay, here, Thug, you hand this on up to Buckeye.
Buck, you shoot it on up to Saw, an' Sawdust, you wheel'er
on in to Slew! Got a good holt on 'er, Slew?"

"Yeah! Whattaya want me ta do with it? Tie it around
his belly?"

"Yeah! But, first, you'd better'd put the end, th' knot end,
up over that fork there where he's hung! That's her! Throw
a loop around his belly now!"

"Okay! He's looped so's he never could git loose, even
if he's ta try!"

Then the main foreman of the gang took off a little dirty
white flour-sack cap, and rubbed the dirt and sweat back

off of his head and told Mama and the other lady, "All right, ladies. Yore worryin' days is over. Keep yer britches on. That kid'll live ta be a flat hunderd."

"The rope won't slip or break?" Mama asked him.

"Good wet rope." The kid was watching every move that the other kids made.

"Okay! We're all set!" one kid yelled down out of the tree.

"We're ridin' high, an' settin' purty!" another one talked up.

Then the ramrod said, "Rabbit, Star, Jake, you three guys take th' tail end of this rope, an' back off out across down th' hill yonder with it. Pull it good an' straight. 'At's her. Okay!"

"She's straighter'n a preacher's dream."

"Thug, you, up there! Hold onto th' main rope! You grab 'er, Saw, you too, Slew! Now, let me git a grip on 'er down here on th' ground! You three kids down the hill there brace yer feet, dig yer heels, dig 'em in! You wimmen folks jist rare back, take a big dip of snuff, an' tell some funny stories! We ain't never dropped a kid yit, an' this is th' first time we ever got paid a dime fer not droppin' one!"

"Look what you're doing."

"Okay! Worry Wart, you, Slew! Now! Lift his legs up loose from the forks! Hey, help, make him help you. Lift 'im plumb up! 'At'saboy! Jist let 'im hang down there!"

"Man's unhung much's he can be unhung!"

"You guys down th' hill! His weight's on this rope now! You let it git tight, real slow, then as I feed th' rope through my hands, why, you three birds come a-walkin' up th' hill, see? Like this, see, an' she slips a little, an' you walk a little, an' she oozes a little bit more, an' you walk up a little closter!"

"We're wheelin'!"

"An' a-dealin'!"

"Just walk along slow, keep a tight rope, take it easy. Okay, Slew, he's down out of yore reach! Sawdust, keep th' rope stretched under th' pit of yore one arm, an' guide th' gent down past you with the other arm!"

"He's slidin'! Easy ridin'!"

"Keep 'im slidin'! Easy on th' ridin'! Guide 'im on down ta where we git th' six dimes! You ladies can be goin' to th' house ta git out yore pockitbooks."

Mama said, "No, thank you, sir, I'll stay right here, if you don't mind, and see to it that you get him down right. Are they hurting you, Woody?"

"Not me!" I told her back. "This is lotsa fun. Got lotsa kids ta play with now!"

"You hold on tight to that rope, mister fun-haver!" the other lady was saying.

"I will!" I said to her. "Mama, do I get a dime, too?"

I come down past the last kid on the last limb and when I got both feet on the ground, I forgot all about my headache and sun-stroke. I laughed and talked with everybody like I was a famous sailor just back from sea. "'At wuz fun! Hey! I wanta do it all over agin'!"

Mama grabbed me by the shirt collar and pulled me home. I was fighting every step of the way and yelling back, "Hey! Kids! Come an' play with me! Come an' see my wagon road! I wanta dime, too, Mama!"

"I'll dime you!" she told me. "You kids wait right there. I'll get your six dimes for you."

"I wanta dime! I want some candy!" I was letting it out.

"We'll save ya a piece out of our candy an' stuff!" the head captain of the kids yelled. "An' we'll bring it over in a sack all by itself, first thing in th' mornin'!"

Another kid said, "It was yore tree!"

"It's yore yard!"

"Yeah, an' it was even yer mama's dimes!"

And just as our back door flew shut with me halfway caught with my neck sticking out, Mama grabbed a better handful of me, and I yelled, "It was my sore head, it was my dizzy head!" And Mama jammed the door shut, and I didn't see any more of the big bunch of awful good smart kids. Regular tree unhangers.

Mama took my shirt and overhalls off, stripped me down to my bare hide and spent about an hour giving me a bath.

"Come on, young sprout, I'm putting you off to bed. Come on."

"I'm comin'; I feel good an' warm in my new clean unnerwear."

"Do you?"

"You know, Mama, I never do like for you ta do anything to me, like make me mind, or make me stay home, or make me drink milk, or take a bath, but I hate most of all to have you put a new pair of unnerwear on me. Then, after ya do it, I like you a whole lot better."

"Mama knows every little thing that's taking place in that little old curly head of yours. You're my newest, and my hardest-headed youngin."

"Mama, what's a hard head?"

"It means you go and do what you want to."

"Is my head a hard one?"

"You bet it is."

"What's a youngin?" I asked Mama. "Am I a youngin?"

And Mama told me, "Well, it means you're not very old."

She pulled the covers up around my neck and tucked me down into the bed good.

"When I get up to be real big, will I still be a youngin?"

"No. You'll be a big man then."

"Are you a youngin?"

"No, I'm a big woman. I'm a grown lady. I'm your

mama." I started getting drowsy and my eyes felt like they was both full of dry dirt.

I asked Mama, "Wuz you good when you wuz first a little baby?"

And she rubbed my face with the palm of her hand and said, "I was pretty good. I believe I minded my mama better than you mind yours."

"Wuz you just a little tiny baby, this big?"

"Just about."

"An' Gramma an' Grampa found you in under their covers?"

Mama's face looked like she was trying to figure out a hard puzzle of some kind. "Covers?"

"That boy that clumb up on his barn door, he tol' me all about married rings, an' all about where you go an' find little babies. Youngins."

"What did you say?"

"All 'bout married rings."

"This ring is pure gold," Mama told me, holding up her hand for me to see it. "See these little flower buds? They were real plain when your papa and me first got married. . . . But why don't you ever go to sleep, little feller?"

"You know who I'd marry if I wuz gonna marry, Mama?"

"I haven't got the least inkling," she said. "Who?"

"You."

"Me?"

"Uh huh."

"You couldn't marry me if you wanted to. I'm already married to your papa."

"Cain't I marry you, too?"

"Certainly not."

"Why?"

"I told you why. You can't marry your own mama. You'll just have to look around for another girl, young man."

"Mama."

"Yes."

"Mama."

"Yes."

"Mama, do you know somethin'?"

"No, what?"

"Well, like, say, like what that little ole mean kid acrost th' alley asked me?"

"What?"

"Well, he asked me how many married rings you had on."

"And then?"

"So I told him, told him you didn't have but one gold one. No diamunt glass one."

"And?"

"And he said ever'body in town would git awful, awful mad at you for losin' yore diamunt 'un."

"Did he?"

"An' he said, 'Where did you lose yore diamunt 'un at?' An' so, I told him maybe it got lost in our big house fire."

Mama just kept listening and didn't say a word.

Then I went on, "An' he asked me how come it, our big perty house got burnt up. An' then he asked me if—if you struck a match an' set it on fire. . . ."

Mama didn't answer me. She just looked up away from me. She looked a hole through the wall, and then she looked out through my bedroom window up over the hill. She rubbed my forehead with her fingers and then she got up off the edge of my bed, and walked out into the kitchen. I laid there listening. I could hear her feet walking around over the kitchen floor. I could hear the water splash in the drinking dipper. I heard everything get quiet. Then I drifted off to sleep, and didn't hear a sound.

Chapter III

I AIN'T MAD AT NOBODY

❖

It was an Indian summer morning and it was crispy and clear, and I stuck my nose up into the air and whiffed my lungs full of good weather. I stood on the side of the street in the alley crossing and saw Clara drift almost out of sight toward the schoolhouse. I turned around and ran like a herd of wild buffaloes back down the hill, around the house, and come to our front yard, skidding to a stop. I hollered in at the window to where Mama was finishing up the breakfast dishes and said, "Where's Gramma at?"

Mama slid the window up and looked out at me and said, "This is Grandma's day to come all right, how'd you know?"

"Clara told me," I told Mama.

"And why're you so fussed up about Grandma coming, young sprout?" Mama said to me.

"Clara said Gramma'd take me with her to trade her eggs."

"Who is she, might I ask you?"

"She's my big sister. She's bigga 'nuff ta tell me where all I can go, ain't she?"

"And I'm your Mama. Could you tell me what I'm suppose to be able to tell you?"

"You can tell me I can go with Gramma, too."

"Oh! Well, I'll tell you, you've been having a hard time getting used to living in this old house. So I'll tell you what.

63

If you'll come in and wash your face and neck and ears real good, and get both of your hands clean enough for Grandma to see your skin, maybe I'll be right real good to you and let you go out and stay a few days with her! Hurry!"

"Is my ears clean?"

Mama took a good look at both of my ears and told me, "This first one will do in a pinch."

"How long's Gramma been yore wife?" I asked Mama.

"I told you a thousand times Grandma is not my wife. She's your Grandpa's wife."

"Has Grampa gotta husban', too?"

"No. No. No. Grandpa is a husband already, Grandma's husband."

"Nobody ain't my husban', is there?" I asked her.

Mama grabbed the washrag away from me and rubbed my hide to a cherry red. "Listen, you little question box, don't ask me anything else about who is kin to who; you've absolutely got my head whirling around like a windmill."

"Mama. Know somethin'?"

"What?"

"I ain't never gonna git real mad at you."

"Well, that is good news. Why? Whatever made you say that?"

"I jist ain't."

"You're being awful, awful good for some reason or another. Nickel. Dime. What?"

"Not really, really mad."

"You certainly will have to change your ways a lot. You get mad at your old mama just about every day about something. You get awful riled up sometimes."

"That ain't worst mad."

"What kind of mad do you mean?"

"Mad that stays mad. 'At's th' kind I'm tellin' ya about.

You won't ever git mad at me if I won't ever git mad at you, will ya?"

"Never in your whole life, young feller." Mama patted my naked hide where the cakes of dirt had just been washed off and told me, "That's the best thing that could ever happen to all of us. Your little old head has got it all thrashed out."

"Thrashed where? What's thrashed mean?"

"Thrash. Thrash. Means when you whip something and beat it, and well, like Grandpa does his oats."

"I got oats in my head! Oats in my head! Yumpity yay! Yumpity yay! I got oats in my head! Git outta my way! Git outta my way!" I made a hard run around the kitchen.

"You crazy little monkey. Go ahead, have a good time. Just go ahead and tear this old house down. You're my littlest baby. You're going out and stay a long, long time with your grandma, and I won't have no little boy to drive me crazy! Have a good time. Let's see you! Run! Holler! Loud! I'm gonna gitcha! Gonna gitcha! Run!"

We chased all around over the front room and back through the kitchen. She grabbed me up off the floor and swung me around and around till my feet stuck straight out. She was laughing and I felt hot tears salty on the side of her face. When she let me down on the floor, she knelt down on her knees and held me up real warm, and I said, "Mama, I'll tell ya. I like ta have ya chase me. Play. Stuff like that. Talk ta each other. Hug on each other. But I don't like fer ya ta call me secha little boy all th' time."

"Oh, I thought so. I was looking for you to say that most any day now," she told me, holding me off at arm's length and looking me up and down. "You're getting to be a mighty awful big man."

"Bigger'n I usta wuz?"

"Bigger than you used to be."

"Usta wuz. Cain't stay still."

"I know," Mama said to me, and she set down on the floor and pulled me down in her lap. "You grow."

"Up."

"Up this way. Out this way. Across this way."

"Big."

"You can't stay still," she went on.

"Gotta hurry. Grow."

"Tell me, mister grower, this. Now, when you was just a little boy with curly hair a little over four years old, you said to me that you never would get mad and stay mad at me anymore. Will you still say that while you're growing up so big so fast?"

"Fast as I grow a little, I'll tell you it again."

"You promise? You cross your heart and hope to die?"

"Cross. Double cross."

"Fine. Now look right out through that window there and tell me what you see coming down the road?"

"Gra-mma!"

"Grandma's right!"

"Hey! Hey! Gramma! Gramma!"

I snorted out the front door running to meet the buggy, waving my hands about my head like I was signaling a battleship. When I got about halfway down the hill, I struck my big toe against a sharp rock, and it tumbled me so bad the tears started down my cheeks; but I started running that much faster, for my only chance to get a free ride was to catch the buggy while she was on the level, because once she got headed up the steep hill to our house she wouldn't stop to pick me up.

I had tears on my face and dirt on the tears when I got to the road, but I was there ahead of the buggy. I jumped up and down at the side of the road and I made all kinds of signals with my hands, but Grandma just kept looking straight ahead. I yelled, "Gramma! Hey! Gramma!" But she didn't even as much as glance over my way.

I trotted along a ragweed ditch full of fine washed sand, and kept hollering, "It's me! Hey! It's me! Gramma! Me!" And she just kept old White Tom and Red Bess trotting right along, throwing more dust, straw, and chalky manure dirt back in my face.

About six foot this side of where the level road took off up the hill toward our house, the buggy stopped, and I made one long, sailing jump, in between the wheels, and up into the seat beside Grandma, and she was bouncing the whole buggy up and down laughing and saying, "Why, was that you? Back yonder? I saw a little old dirty-faced boy standing back there, and I says to myself, 'No, that's not Woody, not my Woodsaw.' "

Sweat was in little bumps on Grandma's face, because she was so hot, and her whole face was bouncing with the buggy because she was so fat. A black hat with some flowers on top and a big pin that always made me wonder if it wasn't sticking right on through her hair and head from one ear to the other. Gray hair commencing to make a stand that had come from hoeing and working a crop of worries for about fifty years.

"I was clean when I seen ya comin'. Then I started a runnin', an' stumped my big toe on an ol' rock. Hurt. Real bad. Gimme th' lines."

She put one arm around me and handed me the long leather reins, and told me, "Yes, you look like my little grandson now. I can tell by the shape of your head that's my Woodchuck."

I stood up on the floorboards and held both of the big reins in one hand. It was more than a handful, but I managed to wave at Mama. "Hi! Hi! I got 'em! I got 'em! Hi! Lookit me! See me drive?"

I jumped out of the buggy in front of our house and Grandma met me coming around the horses. She put both of her hands on her hips and straightened her corsets up a little and smiled at me, and said, "Well, you are a smart feller. Already know how to tie a slipknot on a buggy wheel."

I spent the next few minutes looking at the knot I'd tied on the buggy spoke, tracing the reins up over the horses' backs, and up to the bits in their mouths. I handled the loose bits and the steel shined in the sun. When I rubbed Tom's bald spot between his eyes, Bess looked over at me kind of lonesome like, so I rubbed her, too. I walked around and around the buggy, and it smelled like strong paint and hot leather. At the back were seven or eight gallon buckets, all full of milk and cream and clabber to take around to folks in town.

I could hear Mama and Grandma talking through the kitchen window.

Grandma was saying, "You're not looking any too good, Nora. You're working too hard. Straining yourself. Something. I don't know. What is it?"

"Why, I feel all right; do I look bad? Just everyday housework. Nothing else."

"Something else, too, young lady. Something else. This old house. That's what it is. This old house is so old and rotten and so awful hard to keep clean."

Grandma was leaning back in a big wide chair that just about fit her, sizing Mama up and down. A few gray hairs had got loose from her hairpins, and she was pressing them back with her hands, and pinning them down where they belonged.

"We're about to get all straight again," Mama said.

"Here. Something's wrong around here. Tell me the truth before I go. I just got to know."

Mama rubbed her hair back out of her eyes and said, "I feel good, I feel good all over. I work hard and feel good, but I don't know. Just seems like right in through my head some way or another, something. Little dizzy spells."

"I thought so," Grandma told her, "I thought so. I could tell. You can't fool an old fooler, you know. Might fool your own self a little. But not me. Not your old Mama. If it was one of your own kids sick, you'd be able to tell it a mile away. I'm the same way about my flock of kids. I know when one of them is out of kilter. I put diapers on you and I washed your ears a million times and I sent you off to school in dresses we made together, and if you just so much as blink one eye crossways, I can tell it. You promise to get the doctor down here and let him look you over!"

"Milk will sour in the buggy."

"Oh, to the dickens with milk and butter, Nora! I'm talking sense. Promise me you'll get the doctor down. Have him come down every few days for a while. He can keep up with you, and do you some good."

"Your eggs will hatch out. Well, all right, all right. I'll get the doctor. Here, kiss me good-bye." Mama kissed Grandma on the forehead.

Grandma crawled back into the buggy seat and found me perched up beside her. "What about this young jaybird going home with me? Is it all right with you? Will you miss his hard-working hands around the place here?"

Mama was standing in the yard waving. "I will! 'Bye! I'll tell Papa you're gone. He'll miss you!"

The team knocked dust up between their legs and it was good because the little biting flies couldn't bother their ankles. Grandma was letting me hold the reins.

She told me, "Stop here a minute or two." I pulled the team to a stop. "Get three pounds of butter out of the back and take it up to Mrs. Tatum's door. Get the money. Don't squeeze the butter too hard, it'll have your finger marks on it."

I knocked on the door and handed a lady three pounds of butter and got a dollar bill and a twenty-five-cent piece in the palm of my hand. It felt like some kind of magic sheet of paper and a magic piece of silver. I handed it up to Grandma and she yelled, "Thank you, Mrs. Tatum! Mighty fine weather! Thank you!" And Mrs. Tatum yelled back, "I can just smell a blue norther on top of these pretty days!"

We drifted on down the road a few more blocks, passing a lot of scattered houses, and I held the reins again, being awful careful to hold them up plenty high in the air so the people all along the road could see I was ramrodding this driving business. Grandma just sort of smiled and said, "Turn here to your right. Which a way's my right? North. Cold up there. Hurry and make your turn. Stop over there in front of that little white house. Get out and take Mrs. Warner three pounds of butter. Then come back and take three buckets of milk. That family of hers is getting bigger and hungrier all of the time. I don't think her boy is working anymore down at the gin."

"Howdy do," I said to Mrs. Warner, and she said, "Why, Mrs. Tanner's got a mighty good little boy working for her now. Isn't three big heavy pounds of butter a little too heavy for you?"

"Nope." I ran back to the buggy and piled in again.

"Now, do you see that little old broke-down shack over there in under that black walnut tree?"

"Yeah, I see it. Say, Gramma, why didn't Mrs. Warner gimme no dollar an' no quarter? I see th' shack."

"Mrs. Warner does a charge account with me. Sews. Fixes clothes for my whole family. Now this next lady's name is Mrs. Walters. Take two pounds of butter to her. Then come back and take three buckets of milk."

I walked up to the little shack and tried to keep my feet on a rotten plank that was used as a boardwalk. It was too rickety and caused me to lose my balance. I stumbled and dropped one of the pound squares of butter and I felt like one of Oklahoma's worst outlaws when I saw the wet cloth unroll, and the butter roll out across the ground, picking up little dark rocks and a solid coat of hard dust. I was standing there with tears in my eyes, and more coming all of the time, when I heard somebody talking in my ear.

"I was watchin' you frum th' kitchen window. My, my. What a nice little boy yo' gran'ma's got to go 'roun' an' carry her buttah an' milk. I oughtta knowed you couldn' make it ovah that ol' trippy boardwalk. Lordy, me! Jes' lookit that nice big yeller poun' o' buttah all layin' theah in my ol' dirty, filthy yard! Oh, well, don' you git no gray head 'bout it, little 'livery man. I can use it all right. See heah? I can jes' scrape, scrape, scrape, an' then they won' be too much wasted."

I finally got up strength enough to mumble out, "Stumped my toe agin'."

"Is he all right, Matilda?"

"Sho', sho'! He's all right. Jes' a little toe stump. Shoot a 'possum, I goes 'roun' heah all barefoot jes' like you do. See my ol' bare foot, how tuff 'tis? Come right on in through th' front room heah, that's right. I bet you this is th' firs' time you evah wuz in a black niggah's house. Is it?"

"Yes ma'am."

"I don' hafta tell you no mo' than what yo' eyes can already see, do I?"

"No ma'am."

"You leas'ways sez, yas ma'am an' no ma'am, don' you?"

"Yes'm."

"An' me jes' an ol' black niggah. Hmmm. Sho' do soun' good."

"Are you a nigger lady?"

"Whatta I look like, honey?"

"Are you a nigger 'cause you're black?"

"What folks all says."

"What do people call you a nigger for?"

" 'Cause they jes' don' know no bettah. Don' know what 'niggah' means. Don' know how bad makes ya feel."

"You called your own self that," I told her.

"When I calls my own se'f a niggah, I knows I don' mean it. An' even anothah niggah calls me a 'niggah,' I don' min', 'cause I knows it's most jes' fun. But when a white pusson calls me 'niggah,' it's like a whip cuts through my ol' hide."

"I gotta go bring you in some milk," I told Matilda.

"Did you speak 'milk'?" She got a big smile all over her face.

"My gramma's got you three buckets."

"Some weeks it's buttah. Some weeks eggs. An' now you speaks out somethin' 'bout milk. Lawd God, little rattle-snakes! C'mon, I'll he'p you."

I went running through the house chasing her and said, "I'm driver 'n d'livery boy!"

We got back to the buggy and Grandma said, "Did you tell the lady you were sorry that you dropped her butter?"

I looked down at the dusty road and didn't say anything.

Matilda cut in and said, "Missy Tanner, any little boy that does work fo' you's jes' mortally gotta be good. You gives me th' buttah an' th' sweet milk, an' he 'livers it to me. My ol' man's a-gonna chomp down on that same ol' co'nbread, an' 'stead o' it a-bein' all so dry an' gritty it sticks in yo' throat an' cuts through yo' belly, it's a-gonna be all slick an' greasy with good ol' runnin' buttah. An' it'll go down his oozle magoozler so slick an' easy it won't have time ta scrape his neck 'er belly neither one. An' my kids'll git greasy all over an' wipe it off on their ovahalls, but po' little fellas, I ain't even a-gonna cuss 'em out 'bout it if they do; 'cause they'll be jes' like me, so hongery fo' buttah on co'nbread, an' sweet milk, they'll jes' think they's oozin' ovah inta th' sho' 'nuff promised lan'."

Grandma said, "I try not to ever just clean forget you."

"I knows ya do," Matilda told Grandma.

"I just wish it could be more of it more often," Grandma went on to say.

"I wishes I could he'p you out mo' an' mo' often, too. You knows that, don't ya, Missy Tanner?" When she looked in under the back lid of the buggy, Matilda went on, "I'll see if I can see any of mah own kids aroun'. Pack in two of these heah big gallion buckets. Tuckah! Tuckah!"

"Yes'm. Heah I is! Watcha wan'?"

"Undo yo'self, Tuckah Boy, undo yo'self! Come out heah an' see with yo' own big eyes what all's a-gonna grease dat belly o' yo's! Sweet milk! 'Nuff ta fatten an' raise fo' hogs ta butchah!"

Tucker flew out from behind a patch of weeds, and then I saw three or four other little heads shoot out and stand up and look and think and listen.

Grandma smiled and said, "Hi, Tuck! Still playing in that old patch of gimpson weeds, I see."

"Howdy do, Miss Tanner."

Matilda handed me a gallon bucket and then she handed Tuck one. Then she said, "Tuck, this is Mistah Woodpile. Mistah Woodpile, dis heah is my boy, Tuckah."

I shook hands with Tuck and we said, "Glad ta know ya."

Then he laughed at the top of his voice and grabbed a

bucket of milk between his two hands, bent over it with his face almost touching the top of the milk, his breath blowing rings out across it, saying, "Good ol', good ol', good ol' milk! Good ol', good ol', good ol' milk!"

For the first two or three miles we just trotted along west down the Ozark Trail. Half a mile west past the Buckeye schoolhouse, we saw two saddle horses tied to the fence, the Black Joker, wild and mean, that Grandma's oldest boy, Warren, rode; and an old tame family horse that the two younger kids, Lawrence and Leonard, rode double.

"I see Warren's sneaked out that Black Joker horse and rode him to school again. That fool horse is loco."

I set there in the seat all loose and limber, both knees under my chin, sort of thinking, and then I told Grandma, "Mama'll need me home."

Grandma looked down at me and she put her arm around me and pulled me over close to her in the buggy seat, and I held one rein in each hand and let both hands fall down across her lap. "You're worried, too. You're a worried little man, that's what you are, a worried little man."

"Gramma."

"Yes."

"You know somethin', Gramma? My mama don't never go out an' visit th' other people acrost th' alley."

"Why not?"

"She jest stays an' stays an' stays home in that ole Lon'on House."

"Do any of the neighbor ladies ever come around to visit and talk with Nora?" Grandma asked me.

"Huh uh. Never nobody."

"What does she do? Read a book?"

"Jest sets. Looks. Holds a book in 'er lap mosta th' time, but she don't look where th' book's at. Jest out across th' whole room, an' whole house an' ever'wheres."

"Is that right?"

"If Papa tells Mama somethin' she forgot, she gits so mad she goes off up in th' top bedroom an' cries an' cries all day long. What makes it?" I asked Grandma.

"Your mama is awful bad sick, Woody, awful bad. And she knows she's awful bad sick. And it's so bad that she don't want any of you to know about it . . . because it's going to get a whole lot worse."

It was a minute or two that Grandma didn't say a word, and neither did I. I stared along the side of the little old road. The rain had come and the waters had run, and the road had wrinkled up like an old man's skin. Over across the tops of the weeds I saw Grandma's big high cornfield.

"Gramma," I finally spoke up, "is Tom an' Bess trottin' fast 'cause they wanta git home quicker?"

She didn't move or change the blank look on her face much. She said, "I suppose they do."

"Is one horse a girl?"

"Bess."

"One's a boy horse?"

"Tom."

"They live together, don't they?"

"Same barn, yes. Same pasture. I don't know just exactly what you're getting at."

"Can horses marry each other?"

"Can they do what?"

"Horses marry?"

"Well, now there you go again with your dang fool infernal questions. I don't know whether horses get married or not."

"I wuz jest askin' ya."

"You're always asking, asking, asking something. And half of the time I can't tell you the answer."

"Horses work, don't they?"

"You know they work. I wouldn't even have a cat or a dog or a chicken on my place that didn't do his share of the work. Yes, even my old cat does a lot of work. That reminds me, you know old Maltese Mother?"

"Ol', ol' one? Yeah. She knows me, too. Ever' time she sees me, she comes over to where I am."

"She's got a whole bunch, seven of the nicest soft, fuzzy little kittens that you ever saw."

"Seven? How many fingers is seven?"

"Like this. Here. All of the fingers on this hand and two fingers on this hand. That's right."

"Are they good little kittens?"

"Now, what could a little kitten do, anyway, to be mean? They're the best little fellers you ever saw. Sleepers. You never saw anything sleep like these little baby cats."

"Where did ole Mother Maltese go to to come back with this many little baby kittens?"

"Out in the trees somewhere, somewhere out in the grass. She found one little kitten here, and one little kitten over there, and one or two back across yonder, and that's how she got all seven."

"Is it?"

"Certainly is."

"Why couldn't old Mama Maltese go and find all seven of 'em in jes' one place?"

"Listen, young man, you'll just have to ask the mama cat. Watch your horses there, straighten yourself up. You remember we're coming to the gate? You jump out and open it."

I saw the old barb-wire gate coming and said, "Me?

Shore! Shore! I know ever'thing ya gotta do ta open a gate!"

The gate was tough. I put one arm around the post that was set in the ground, and the other arm around the loose gatepole, and got sort of a headlock on them both. I heard Grandma holler out, "I see the boys riding down the road yonder! Come on!"

Then I heard a bunch of horses' hoofs coming down the road, and I looked up and saw just a big white-looking cloud of dust coming at me. Out of the dust I could hear the three boys whooping and barking, "Wwaaahoooo! Yip! Yip! Yyyyyiiipppeee! Looky ooouuuttt! Woodrow! Looky outttt!" The thought of getting tromped under the horses' feet caused my eyes to fly open like a goggle-eyed bee, and my two ears stood straight out from the sides of my head.

My first thought was to drop the gatepole and run off into the weeds to get clear of the horses. The boys were still coming straight at me and yelling, "Gonna git run oovver! Run overr! Looky outtt, Woodrow! Gonna git run over an' killed!"

The boys and the horses were within ten foot of me, when I decided that I'd just hold the gate shut. I happened to take one last look back at the little wire loop on top, and it had slipped into the notch where I'd been trying to put it. The gate was shut good as she ever was. I fell down off of the brace post backwards and scrambled up to my feet again, and made the worst face I could, and yelled back at the boys, "Ya! Ya! Ya! Thought you wuz smart! Thought you'z smart!"

Both horses run keeeblamm into the gate. Warren, riding the Black Joker, was traveling too fast to turn or stop, or even slow down. Lawrence and Leonard had figured on the gate being open, and their own dust had blinded them.

Their horse stopped so quick that the boys slid right about a couple of feet up onto the horse's neck; the horse waved his head a time or two and threw both kids down amongst the wires where Warren was rolling around.

All of this time I mostly just run about three times as fast as the wild horses, till I come to Grandma's buggy. I mounted the back of it, set there all humped up, and watched the crazy rodeo back at the gate. There was the Black Joker stamping around still crying and squeeling a little, over yonder in the west corner of the cotton field; and over there in the east corner, in a few wild weeds, just on the edge of the cotton patch, there was the horse without a name; and yonder in the middle of the whole thing there was a cloud of Oklahoma's very best dust, that looked about like where you'd heaved a hand grenade; you might not believe it to stand back off and look at it, but somewhere in that dust I knowed there was three awful tough boys. You couldn't see the boys. Just the dust fogging up. But you could see a few slivers of barb wire wiggling in the sun.

"Warren! Lawrence! Leonard!" Grandma was just about to yell her yeller out. "You boys! Where! Wait! Are you hurt!"

She waded into the dust and was fanning both arms, reaching in around the loose wires and fishing for mean boys. Then all I saw was her hat bobbing up and down as she bent over and stood up, and bent over again, hunting for kids. In a few minutes the dust crawled off of its own accord, like a big animal of some kind, away from the gate, across the little rutty road.

"Pore ol' Gran'ma! Leonard's got killed, an' Warren's got killed, an' Lawrence got killed." I was setting on the back end of the buggy, looking. Tears the size of teacups was oozing down my cheeks and I could taste the slick salt when the tears run down to the corner of my mouth.

"Warren! Warren!" Grandma called. "What are you doing over here in this old ditch? Are you hurt bad?"

Warren got up and tried to brush the dirt off of his self; but his school clothes was so full of holes and rips that every time he brushed, he tore a bigger hole somewhere. He was sobbing and his whole body was jerking, and he told Grandma, "It was that little ornery runt, Woodrow, done it! I'm gonna cave his head in for 'im!"

"Now, you just hold yourself, Mister Rough Rider," Grandma told Warren. "Woodrow was doing the best he could. He was closing that gate for me. You bigger boys had no reason to come ridin' down the road yelling and trying to scare a little kid to death. I don't care if it did skin you up a little, you need it." Then she got to looking around for another boy, and she found one laying flat of his belly out in a clump of sumac bushes, and it was Leonard puffing and blowing like he'd been shell-shocked in four wars.

"Leonard! You dead?" Grandma said to him.

Leonard jumped up so quick that it would have made a mountain lion look slow, and he started running toward the buggy as hard as he could tear, squawling out, "I'm goin' ta beat that little skunk inta th' ground. Goin' ta tear him up just like he tore me up!" And he kept coming for the buggy.

I was breathing pretty hard, and sometimes not at all. I knew what he'd do. I let myself just sort of slide over the back of the buggy seat and down onto the cushion, and held the reins as tight as I could and bit my tongue, and looked out over the horses' backs toward the house.

Grandma found Lawrence in the same patch of weeds, skint up just about like the other two, some hide and some duds and some hair missing. Leonard was climbing up on the buggy seat beside me. He drew his hand back and made a pass at my head, and I ducked to one side and let the lick fly past. He hit the back of the buggy seat with his hand and that made him a whole lot madder. The next lick he swung, he caught me square on the side of the head, and my ears rung like a steam calliope. I fell down on the seat with my hands covering my head, and he rung two or three harder ones around over my skull. I squeezed out of his grip, but I banged my head on the sharp corner of a heavy wooden box in the bottom of the buggy, and when I touched my hand to the knot that raised up just above my ear, and seen blood all over my fingers, I let out a scream that rattled pecans in trees for a mile around.

The horses heard me, and jumped like they'd been blistered with a lightning whip. They jerked the loose reins out of my hand. Tom made a lunge in his harness, a leather strap broke; then Bess got scared and jumped sideways, and snapped a hitching chain; and then both horses started snorting, laying their ears back, and running for the barn just like a cyclone. Leonard fell back on the cushion of the buggy seat. I was still doubled up in a ball rolling around with the wooden box on the floor boards. Neither of us could get a chance to jump. The horses kept loping faster and after they got the buggy in motion, they broke out into their hardest run. Leonard got madder than ever, and every time the horses' hoofs hit the ground, or the wheels went around, he would give me a good kick in the back. He was barefooted and he didn't hurt me much, but when he saw he wasn't, he decided just to put both of his feet on my neck and try to choke me. The buggy wheels bounced against rocks, hit roots, and jolted both of us out of our wits.

Grandma was within three feet of the buggy when the horses broke and run away, and I could hear her hollering, "Whoa! Whoa! Tom! Bess! Stop them horses! God

Amighty! There's a hundred sticks of dynamite in that buggy!"

I heard the horses grunt, and heard the water in their bellies jostle around, heard the air snorting through their nostrils, and their hoofs beating against the ground.

"That box you're leanin' up against is fulla dynamite!" Leonard hollered.

"I don't care!" I yelled at him.

"If this buggy turns over, we're gonners!" he told me.

I told him, "I cain't stop 'em!"

"I'm goin' t' jump! Leave you with it!" he bellered.

"Jump! See if I care!" I told him.

Leonard got up and stood with his feet in the seat, and the first time he got his chance, he piled over the side, and hit rolling through a patch of bullhead sticker weeds. All I saw was the seat of his britches as he flew over the wheels. And that left me banging all around over the floor of the buggy with nothing but a box of dynamite, and TNT caps, to keep me company. The post of the gate swung past, and I let out my breath when we missed it by about an inch; but I looked ahead of the horses and saw that the whole barn lot was standing full of things that we couldn't miss. Straight ahead was a steam tractor, and beside that was a couple of wagons with their tongues propped up on their singletrees. Here was a hog-oiling machine. A pile of corn cobs was in our path. I could picture Grandpa's barn, barn lot, all of his plows, tools, and machinery, blowing up over the tree tops; but the old horses knew more about this place than I did, and they made a big horseshoe bend around the thrasher, cut in real quick to shave the tractor, sidestepped a little to pass the pile of cobs, and then curved wide again. But when they made a run for the barn door, I told myself good-bye. The whole barn was stacked full of more wagons, machinery and plows, and there was a concrete slab running across the ground just as you went in the door, which I knew was enough of a hump to throw that box of dynamite plumb out of the buggy. With my ear against the box, I could hear the big sticks thumping about inside.

But, all at once, the horses come to the door. They wheeled sideways again and stopped; horses aiming one direction, and the buggy another.

For a minute I just laid there hugging the box. Then I made a quick high dive over the seat, and lit on the ground. Warren and Leonard come riding up and jumped off of their horse.

"You little devil, you! You've caused us enough trouble!"

Warren made a run and grabbed me by the neck. "Come on, Leonard! I got 'im for ya! Here th' little bastard is! Beat th' livin' hell out of 'im!"

"Hold 'im!" Leonard was saying. "Hold 'im till I can get my belt loose! I'm gonna whop blisters on yore little hide that a dollar bill won't cover! Yore whole dam family ain't nuthin' but bad luck! Hold 'im, Warren!"

Leonard took a few seconds to unloose his belt buckle and get it pulled out of the loops. I was kicking and crying, not loud. I didn't want Grandma to think I was bellering so's she could hear me; but I was fighting. I was using every cuss word that ever was or ever will be.

Your old blisters won't hurt me. Your old stropping belt won't hurt long. Your old arm will give out. You don't know. You think you're scaring me. You think you're takin' some of my fight out of me. You'll whip me now, and I'll look like I'm cryin', but I won't really be cryin'. I'll be havin' tears in my eyes because I'm mad at you. My family can't help what happened to them. My mama can't help what happened.

You used to be friendly and nice to my mama when she was pretty and healthy, and people was nice to you because you was my mama's brothers. But then, when she had some bad things happen to her, and lost her pretty house, and got sick, and needed you to treat her nice, you stand off and howl and bark like a crazy bunch of coyotes, and laugh and poke fun at us. It makes me tough enough to stand here and let you whack me acrost the back and the neck and ears, and blister my shoulders with that little old flimsy leather strop, and I don't even feel it.

I was thinking these things, but I only said, "Cowards! Two on one!"

"Here's one across yer bare legs, you little runt, just to remember that you caused us a lot of trouble!" And Leonard wrapped the belt around my legs.

"Hurts, don't it? I want yuh to feel it plumb down to yer bones! I want it to hurt! Does it?"

"Don't," I told him.

"What? You mean I ain't comin' down hard enough on this here belt?" Leonard doubled the strap up in his hands and said, "I can make you say, 'hurt'! I'll give it to you doubled up an' double hard! I'll make you crawl up to me on yer hands and knees and say, 'hurt'!" He was beating me one lick after another one, all over my body, stinging, raising ridges, making bruises and welts. I was fighting Warren, trying to get loose from his grip.

"Lemme loose! I want loose! I'll stand right here!" I told him.

"Say, 'hurt'!" Leonard brought down another hard one around my bare legs.

"Turn me loose! I won't run!" I told them.

And then Warren loosened his hold on my arms, and said, "I'll just see if you've got nerve enough to stand up like a man and take your beatin'!" He let go of me, and I stood there looking at Leonard while he drew back to give me some more of the strap.

"Say it hurts!" Leonard said. "I want to know I ain't been wastin' my time! Say it hurts!"

Warren warned me from behind, "Better say what he wants you to say. It'll be over quicker. Go ahead. Say it's hurtin'!"

"Won't," I said back at him.

"You little hard-headed, hard-luck sonofabitch! I'll make you say what I want, or I'll beat you into the ground!" Leonard started striking first from one side, and then the other, without even taking time to say a word or to breathe in between. "Talk like I tell yuh ta talk!"

"Ain't," I told him.

Then Grandma spoke up right behind Leonard's back and said, "No, you don't, you young Kaiser Bill! You're too dang mean to be a living son of mine! Give it here!" Almost before he knew it, she yanked the belt out of his hand, and Leonard ran about twenty feet away and stood there shivering. He knew that Grandma was hell on wheels when she got her dander riled up.

Warren was talking up for Leonard. "That dam little old stinkin' Woodrow was the cause of the whole thing, Ma."

"Hush your trap!" Grandma turned to Warren and said, "You're just as much in on this as your mean brother is! And you're running your old ma crazy, both of you to-gether!" She wadded the belt up into a little ball in her two hands. Lawrence stood beside Grandma, not saying much, just looking at first one of us and then the other.

"I don't know," she said, standing there with big tears rolling down her cheeks, "I don't know what to do. I just don't know what to try next!"

The three boys were wiggling their feet and toes around, ducking their heads, looking at the ground, but not saying a word.

"Any of you young studs got anything to say for yourselves?"

Leonard talked out and said, "What good's he doin' us by comin' around? We don't wanta hafta play with 'im. We ain't a-gonna let 'im foller us! He's just ol' Nora's little ol' sickly runt. I don't like 'im, an' I hate his guts!"

Grandma made about four quick steps and grabbed Leonard by the shirt collar. She wound her hand around a time or two in his shirt till she had a good hold on him, and then she started pushing him backwards, taking big long steps, and he was falling back, listening to her say, "I've told you this a dozen times before, young buck! Nora is just as much my little girl as you are my little boy, get that? Nora's dad was just as good, and some ways a whole lot better than your dad! He was my first husband! Nora was our only child!" She jammed him back up against the side of the barn and every time she'd tell him a word, she'd push him back a little harder, trying to jar him into thinking. "No. Nora's not like you. No. I remember how Nora was, even away back when she was just your age. She went to my little schoolhouse where I taught, over on the Deep Fork River, and she read her books and got her lessons, and she helped me mark and grade the papers. She liked pretty music and she sung songs and played her own chords on the piano; and she learned just about everthing pretty that she got a half a chance, just half a chance to! She made herself at home everywhere she went, and people liked her; and I was always proud of her because . . . she . . ." and Grandma turned her head away from the boy up against the barn; and her hand fell open and the belt fell down onto the ground, and she said, "Leonard, there's your belt. There.

Laying on the ground, there. Pick it up. Put it back in your britches. They're falling off. Come on. Come over here by the wagon. I'm going to set myself down there on the tongue. Here, now, come on over here, all of you boys, and your ma's going to hug all of you. And I want you to put your arms around me, too, just like you always did. Just like everything was all right."

Grandma rested herself by sitting down on the wagon tongue, and the boys looked out of the corners of their eyes at each other, and walked over, a little slow, but they walked, and put their arms around her; loose at first, and she used her own hands to take hold of their arms and make them tighter around her neck and shoulders. When she did, the boys hugged her tighter, and she closed her eyes, and moved her head from one side to the other, first brushing the bosom of one kid, and then the shirt, and the shoulder of another.

She kept her eyes closed and said, "Woodrow, don't stand away over there by yourself. You belong in my lap here. Come on and crawl up. That's it. You belong with your little old curly head snuggled right close up, just like that. God, this is good! Yes, all of you are my boys, doing the best you've been taught. All of you will make mistakes, but, Lord, I can't make any difference between you!"

There wasn't a sound out of any of the boys. I was holding my head up under Grandma's mouth, listening to her talk real slow and long and soft; and my eyes dripped tears down across the front of her bosom and faded her town dress. The other three boys moved their heads, kept their eyes down.

"I'm sorry, Ma."

"Me, too, Ma."

"Don't cry, Maw."

"Gramma, I ain't mad at nobody."

Chapter IV

NEW KITTENS

❖

Up at the house an hour later, Warren and Leonard had poured water and washed their cuts clean, and drifted off into the house getting on some clean clothes. Grandma talked a little to herself, getting some coffee ground for supper. Lawrence trotted out into the yard in a few minutes and I set on the stone steps of the porch and watched him. He pranked around under the two big oak trees and then walked around the corner of the house.

I followed him. He was the littlest one of Grandma's boys. He was more my size. I was about five and he was eight. I followed him back to a rosebush where he pointed to old Mother Maltese and her new little bunch of kittens. He was telling me all there is to know about cats.

First, we just rubbed the old mama cat on the head, and he told me she was older than either one of us. "Cat's been here longer'n me even."

"How old is ol' mama cat?" I asked Lawrence.

"Ten."

"An' you're jest eight?" I said.

"Yeah."

"She's all ten fingers old. You ain't but jest this many fingers old," I went on.

"She's two older'n me," he said.

"Wonder how come you th' biggest?"

"Cause, crazy, I'm a boy, an' she's a cat!"

"Feel how warm an' smooth she is," I told him.

"Yeah," he said, "perty slick, all right; but th' little 'uns is th' slickest. But ol' mama cat don't like for strangers ta come out here an' stick yore han' down in her box an' feel on her little babies."

"I been out her 'fore this," I told him, "so that makes me not no stranger."

"Yeah," he told me back, "I know that; but then, you went back ta town ag'in, see, an' course, that makes you part of a stranger."

"How much stranger am I? I ain't no plumb whole stranger; mama cat knowed me when I wuz jest a little teeny weeny baby; jest this long; an' my mama had ta keep me all nice an' warm jest like them little baby cats, so's I wouldn't freeze, so's nuthin' wouldn't git me." I was still stroking the old cat's head, and feeling of her with my fingers.

She was holding her eyes shut real tight, and purring almost loud enough for Grandma to hear her in the house. Lawrence and me kept watching and listening. The old mama cat purred louder and louder.

Then I asked Lawrence, "What makes 'er sound that a-way in 'er head?"

And he told me, "Purrin', that's what she's doin'."

"Makes 'er purr?" I asked him.

"She does it 'way back inside 'er head some way," Lawrence was telling me.

"Sounds like a car motor," I said.

"She ain't got no car motor in 'er," he said.

"Might," I said.

"I don't much think she has, though."

"Might have a little 'un, kinda like a cat motor; I mean a reg'ler little motor fer cats," I said.

"What'd she be wantin' with a cat motor?"

"Lotsa things is got motors in 'em. Motors is engines. Engines makes things go. Makes noise jest like ol' mama cat. Motor makes wheels go 'round, so cats might have a real little motor ta make legs go, an' tail go, an' feet move, an' nose go, an' ears wiggle, an' eyes go 'round, an' mouth fly open, an' mebbe her stomack is 'er gas tank." I was running my hand along over the old mama cat's fur, feeling of each part as I talked, head, tail, legs, mouth, eyes, and stomach; and the old cat had a big smile on her face.

"Wanta see if she's really got a motor inside of 'er? I'll go an' git Ma's butcher knife, an' you hold 'er legs, an' I'll cut 'er belly open; an' if she's got a motor in 'er, by jacks, I wanta see it! Want me to?" Lawrence asked me.

"Cut 'er belly open?" I asked him. "Ya might'n find 'er motor when ya got cut in there!"

"I c'n find it, if she's got one down in there! I helped Pa cut rabbits an' squirrels an' fishes open, an' I never did see no motor in them!"

"No, but did you ever hear a rabbit er a squirrel either one, or a fish make a noise like mama cat makes?"

"No. Never did."

"Well, mebbe that's why they ain't got no motor. Mebbe they gotta differnt kinda motor. Don't make no kind of a noise."

"Might be. An' some of th' time mama cat don't make no noise either; 'cause some of th' time ya cain't even hear no motor in 'er belly. What then?"

"Maybe she's just got th' key turned off!"

"Turned off?" Lawrence asked me.

"Might be. My papa's gotta car. His car's gotta key. Ya turn th' key on, an' th' car goes like a cat. Ya turn th' key off, an' it quits."

"There yore hand goes ag'in! Didn' I tell you not ta touch them little baby kittens? They ain't got no eyes open

ta see with yet; you cain't put yore hands on' em!" He cut
his eyes around at me.

"Ohhhhhppppp! All right. I'm awful, awful sorry, mama
cat; an' I'm awful, awful sorry, little baby cats!" And I let
my hand fall back down on the old mama cat's back.

"That's all right ta pat 'er all you want, but she'll reach
up an' take 'er claws, an' rip yore hand plumb wide open
if you make one of her little cats cry!" he told me.

"Know somethin', Lawrence, know somethin'?"

"What about?" he asked me.

"People says when I wuz a baby, jest like one of these
here little baby cats, only a little bit bigger, mebbe, my
mama got awful bad sick when I wuz borned under th'
covers."

"I heard Ma an' them talk about her," he told me.

"What did they talk about?" I asked him.

"Oohhh, I dunno, she wuz purty bad off."

"What made 'er bad off?"

"Yer dad."

"My papa did?"

"What people says."

"He's good ta me. Good ta my mama. What makes people
say he made my mama git sick?"

"Politics."

"What's them?"

"I dunno what politics is. Just a good way ta make some
money. But you always have troubles. Have fights. Carry
two guns ever' day. Yore dad likes lots of money. So he
got some people ta vote fer 'im, so then he got 'im two
guns an' went around c'lectin' money. Yore ma didn't like
yore dad ta always be pokin' guns, shootin', fightin', an' so,
well, she just worried an' worried, till she got sick at it—an'
that was when you was borned a baby not much bigger'n
one of these here little cats, I reckon." Lawrence was digging

his fingernails into the soft white pine of the box, looking at the nest of cats. "Funny thing 'bout cats. All of 'em's got one ma, an' all of 'em's differnt colors. Which is yore pet color? Mine's this 'un, an' this 'un, an' this 'un."

"I like all colors cats. Say, Lawrence, what does crazy mean?"

"Means you ain't got good sense."

"Worried?"

"Crazy's more'n just worry."

"Worse'n worryin'?"

"Shore. Worry starts, an' you do that fer a long, long time, an' then maybe you git sick 'er somethin', an' ya go all, well, you just git all mixed up 'bout ever'thing."

"Is ever'body sick like my mama?"

"I don't guess."

"Reckin could all of our folks cure my mama?"

"Might. Wonder how?"

"If ever single livin' one of 'em would all git together an' git rid of them ol' mean, bad politics, they'd all feel lots better, an' wouldn't fight each other so much, an' that'd make my mama feel better."

Lawrence looked out through the leaves of the bushes. "Wonder where Warren's headin', goin' off down toward th' barn? Be right still; he's walkin' past us. He'll hear us talkin'."

I whispered real low and asked Lawrence, "Whatcha bein' so still for? 'Fraida Warren?"

And Lawrence told me, "Hushhh. Naw. 'Fraid fer th' cats."

"Why 'bout th' cats?"

"Warren don't like cats."

"Why?" I was still whispering.

"Just don't. Be still. Ssshhh."

"Why?" I went on.

"Sez cats ain't no good. Warren kills all th' new little baby cats that gits born'd on th' place. I had these hid out under th' barn. Don't let 'im know we're here. . . ."

Warren got within about twenty feet of us, and we could see his long shadow falling over our rosebush; and then for a little time we couldn't see him, and the rosebush blocked out of sight of him. Still, we could hear his new sharp-toed leather shoes screaking every time he took a step. Lawrence tapped me on the shoulder. I looked around and he was motioning for me to grab up one side of the white pine box. I got a hold and he grabbed the other side. We skidded the box up close to the rock foundation of the house, and partly in behind the rosebush.

Lawrence held his breath and I held my hand over my mouth. Warren's screaky shoes was the only sound I could hear. Lawrence laid his body down over the box of cats. I laid down to hide the other half of the box, and the screak, screak, screak got louder. I whiffed my nose and smelled the loud whang of hair tonic on Warren's hair. His white silk shirt threw flashes of white light through the limbs of the roses, and Lawrence moved his lips so as to barely say, "Montgomery girl." I didn't catch him the first time, so he puckered his lips to tell me again, and when he bent over my way, he stuck a thorn into his shoulder, and talked out too loud:

"Montgomery—"

The screak of Warren's shoes stopped by the side of the bush. He looked all around, and took a step back, then one forward. And he had us trapped.

I didn't have the guts to look up at him. I heard his shoes screak and I knew that he was rocking from one foot to the other one, standing with his hands on his hips, looking down on the ground at Lawrence and me. I shivered and could feel Lawrence quiver under his shirt. Then I turned my head over and looked out from under Lawrence's arm, both of us still hugging the box, and heard Warren say, "What was that you boys was a-sayin'?"

"Tellin' Woody about somebody," Lawrence told Warren.

"Somebody? Who?" Warren didn't seem to be in any big rush.

"Somebody. Somebody you know," Lawrence said.

"Who do I know?" Warren asked him.

"Th' Mon'gom'ry folks," Lawrence said.

"You're a couple of dirty little low-down liars! All you know how to do is to hide off in under some Goddamed bush, an' say silly things about other decent people!" Warren told us.

"We wuzn't makin' no fun, swear ta God," Lawrence told him.

"What in the hell was you layin' under there talkin' about? Somethin' your're tryin' to hide! Talk out!"

"I seen you was all nice an' warshed up clean, an' told Woody you was goin' over ta Mon'gom'ry's place."

"What else?"

"Nuthin' else. 'At's all I said, swear ta God, all I told you, wasn't it, Woody?"

"'S all I heard ya say," I told him.

"Now ain't you a pair of little old yappin' pups? You know dam good an' well you was teasin' me from behind 'bout Lola Montgomery! How come you two hidin' here in th' first place? Just to see me walk past you with all of my clean clothes on? See them new low-cut shoes? See how sharp th' toes are? Feel with your finger, both of you, feel! That's it! See how sharp? I'd ought to just take that sharp toe and kick both of your little rears."

"Quit! Quit that pushin' me!" Lawrence was yelling as loud as he could, hoping Grandma would hear. Warren pushed him on the shoulder with the bottom of his shoe, and tried to roll Lawrence over across the ground. Lawrence swung onto his box of cats so tight that Warren had to kick as hard as he could, and push Lawrence off the box.

The only thing I could think of to do was jump on top of the box and cover it up. Lawrence was yelling as loud as he could yell. Warren was laughing. I wasn't saying anything.

"Whut's that box you're a holdin' onto there so tight?" Warren asked me.

"Jest a plain ol' box!" Lawrence was crying and talking.

"Jest a plain wooden box," I told Warren.

"What's on th' inside of it, runts?"

"Nuthin's in it!"

"Jist a ol' empty one!"

And Warren put his shoe sole on my back and pushed me over beside Lawrence. "I'll just take me a look! You two seems mighty interested in what's inside of that box!"

"You ol' mean outfit, you! God, I hate you! You go on over an' see yore ol' 'Gomery girl, an' leave us alone! We ain't a-hurtin' you!" Lawrence was jumping up. He started to draw back and fight Warren, but Warren just took his open hand and pushed Lawrence about fifteen feet backwards, and he fell flat, screaming.

Warren put his foot on my shoulder and give me another shove. I went about three feet. I tried to hold onto the box, but the whole works turned over. The old mama cat jumped out and made a circle around us, meowing first at Warren, and then at me and the little baby kittens cried in the split cotton seed.

"Cat lovers!" Warren told us.

"You g'wan, an' let us be! Don't you tech them cats! Ma! Ma! Warr'n's gonna hurt our cats!" Lawrence squawled out.

Warren kicked the loose cotton seed apart. "Just like tearin' up a bird's nest!" he said. He put the sharp toe of his shoe under the belly of the first little cat, and threw it up against the rock foundation. "Meoww! Meoww! You little chicken killers! Egg stealers!" He picked the second kitten up in the grip of his hand, and squeezed till his muscles bulged up. He swung the kitten around and around, something like a Ferris wheel, as fast as he could turn his arm, and the blood and entrails of the kitten splashed across the ground, and the side of the house. Then he held the little body out toward Lawrence and me. We looked at it, and it was just like an empty hide. He threw it away out over the fence.

Warren took the second kitten, squeezed it, swung it over his head and over the top wire of the fence. The third, fourth, fifth, sixth, and seventh.

The poor old mama cat was running backwards, cross-ways, and all around over the yard with her back humped up, begging against Warren's legs, and trying to jump up and climb up his body to help her babies. He boxed her away and she came back. He kicked her thirty feet. She moaned along the rocks, smelling of her babies' blood and insides. She scratched dirt and dug grass roots; then she made a screaming noise that chilled my blood and jumped six feet, clawing at Warren's arm. He kicked her in the air and her sides were broke and caved in. He booted her up against the side of the house, and she laid there wagging her tail and meowing; and Warren grabbed the box and splintered it against the rocks and the mama cat's head. He grabbed up two rocks and hit her in the stomach both shots. He looked at me and Lawrence, spit on us, threw the loose cotton seed into our faces, and said, "Cat-lovin' bastards!" And he started walking on away toward the barn.

"You ain't no flesh an' blood of mine!" Lawrence cried after him.

"Hell with you, baby britches! Hell with you. I don't even want to be yore dam brother!" Warren said over his shoulder.

"You ain't my uncle, neither," I told him, "not even my mama's half brother! You ain't even nobody's halfway brother! I'm glad my mama ain't no kin ta you! I'm glad I ain't!" I told him.

"Awwww. Whattaya know, whattaya know, you half-starved little runt?" Warren was turned around, standing in the late sun with his shirt white and pretty in the wind. "You done run yore mama crazy just bein' born! You little old hard-luck bringer! You dam little old insane-asylum baby!" And Warren walked away on down to the barn.

Then Lawrence rolled up onto his feet off of the grass and

tore around the side of the house hollering and telling Grandma what all Warren had done to the cats.

I scrambled up over the fence and dropped down into the short-weed patch. The old mama cat was twisting and moaning and squeezing through at the bottom of the wire, and making her way out where Warren had slung her little babies.

I saw the old mama walk around and around her first kitten in the weeds, and sniffle, and smell, and lick the little hairs; then she took the dead baby in her teeth, carried it through the weeds, the rag weeds, gypsums, and cuckle burrs that are a part of all of Oklahoma.

She laid the baby down when she come to the edge of a little trickling creek, and held up her own broken feet when she walked around the kitten again, circling, looking down at it, and back up at me.

I got down on my hands and knees and tried to reach out and pet her. She was so broke up and hurting that she couldn't stand still, and she pounded the damp ground there with her tail as she walked a whole circle all around me. I took my hand and dug a little hole in the sandy creek bank and laid the dead baby in, and covered it up with a mound like a grave.

When I seen the old Mama Maltese holding her eyes shut with the lids quivering and smell away into the air, I knew she was on the scent of her second one.

When she brought it in, I dug the second little grave.

I was listening to her moan and choke in the weeds, dragging her belly along the ground, with her two back legs limber behind her, pulling her body with her front feet, and throwing her head first to one side and then to the other.

And I was thinking: Is that what crazy is?

97

Chapter V

MISTER CYCLOME

◈

"Here I am, Papa!" I ripped out the east door and went running down to where Papa was. "Here I am! I wanta help shoot!"

"Get back away from that hole! Dynamite!" He hadn't noticed me as I trotted out.

"Where 'bouts?" I was standing not more than three feet away from the hole he'd been drilling through a rock. "Where?"

"Run! This way!" He grabbed me in his arms, covered me over with his jacket and fell down flat against the ground. "Lay still! Down!"

The whole hill jarred. Rocks howled out over our heads.

"I wanna see!" I was trying to fight my way out from under him. "Lemme out!"

"Keep down!" He hugged his jacket around me that much tighter. "Those rocks just went up. They'll be down in a jiffy!"

I felt him duck his head down against mine. The rocks thumped all around us and several peppered the jacket. The cloth was stretched tight. It sounded like a war drum. "Wowie!" I said to Papa.

"You'll think, Wowie!" Papa laughed when he got up. He brushed his clothes off good. "One of those rocks hit you on the head, and you wouldn't think anything for a long time!"

"Le's go blow another'n up!" I was pacing around like a cat wanting milk.

"All right! Come on! You can take the little hoe and dig a nice ten-foot hole!"

"Goshamighty! How deep?"

"'Teen feet."

"Lickety split! Lickety split!" I was chopping out a hole with the little hoe. "Is this 'teen feet deep?"

"Keep on with your work!" Papa acted like a chaingang boss. "Whew! I don't believe I ever did see it get so hot this late in the summer. But I guess we'll have to keep digging without air! We've just got to get this old London Place fixed up. Then we can sell it to somebody and get some money and buy us another better place. You like that?"

"I don't like nuthin' bad. I wanta move. Mama wants ta move, too. So does Roy an' Clara, an' ever'body else."

"Yes, little boy, I know, I know." Papa knocked the blue rock smoke out of the hole every time his crowbar come down. "I like everything that's good, don't you?"

"Mama had a piano an' lotsa good things when she was a little kid, didn't she?" I kept leaning on the handle of my hoe. "An' now she ain't got no nice things."

"Yes. She always loved the good things." Papa pulled a red bandana out of his hip pocket and wiped the sweat from his face. "You know, Woody boy, I'm afraid."

"'Fraida what?"

"This infernal heat. It's got me guessing." Papa looked all around in every direction, sniffed in the air. "Don't know exactly. But it feels like to me there's not a single breath of air stirring."

"Purty still, all right. I'm sweatin'!"

"Not a leaf. Not a blade of grass. Not a feather. Not a

spider-web stirring." He turned his face away to the north. A quick, fast breath of cool air drifted across the hill.

"Good ol' cool wind!" I was puffing my lungs full of the new air stirring. "Good ol', good ol', cool, cool wind!"

"Yes, I feel the cool wind." He stayed down on his hands, looking eyerywhere, listening to every little sound. "And I don't like it!" He yelled at me. "And you hadn't ought to say that you like it, either!"

"Papa, what'sa matter, huh?" I laid on my belly as close up beside Papa as I could get, and looked everywhere that he did. "Papers an' leafs an' feathers blowin'. You ain't really scared, are ya, Papa?"

Papa's voice sounded shaky and worried. "What do you know about cyclones? You've never even seen one yet! Quit popping off at your mouth! Everything that I've been working and fighting for in my whole life is tied up right here in this old London Place!"

I never thought that I would see my dad so afraid of anything.

"'Tain't no good!"

"Shut your little mouth before I shut it for you!"

"'Tain't no good!"

"Don't you dare talk back to your papa!"

"'Tain't no good!"

"Woody, I'll split you hide!" Then he let his head drop down till his chin touched the bib of his overhalls and his tears wet the watch pocket. "What makes you say it's not any good, Woody?"

"Mama said it." I rolled a foot or two away from him. "An' Mama cries alla th' time, too!"

The wind rustled against the limbs of the locust trees across the road running up the hill. The walnut trees frisked their heads in the air and snorted at the wind getting harder.

I heard a low whining sound everywhere in the air as the spider webs, feathers, old flying papers, and dark clouds swept along the ground, picking up the dust, and blocking out the sky. Everything fought and pushed against the wind, and the wind fought everything in its way.

"Woody, little boy, come over here."

"I'm a-gonna run." I stood up and looked toward the house.

"No, don't run." I had to stand extra still and quiet to hear Papa talk in the wind. "Don't run. Don't ever run. Come on over here and let me hold you on my lap."

I felt a feeling of some kind come over me like the chilly winds coming over the hot hill. I turned nervous and scared and almost sick inside. I fell down into Papa's lap, hugging him around the neck so tight his whiskers rubbed my face nearly raw. I could feel his heart beating fast and I knew he was afraid.

"Le's run!"

"You know, I'm not ever going to run any more, Woody. Not from people. Not from my own self. Not from a cyclone."

"Not even from a lightnin' rod?"

"You mean a bolt of lightning? No. Not even from a streak of lightning!"

"Thunner? 'Tater wagon?"

"Not from thunder. Not from my own fear."

"Skeerd?"

"Yes. I'm scared. I'm shaking right this minute."

"I felt ya shakin' when th' cyclome first come."

"Cyclone may miss us, little curly block. Then again, it may hit right square on top of us. I just want to ask you a question. What if this cyclone was to reach down with its mean tail and suck away everything we've got here on this hill? Would you still like your old Papa? Would you still come over and sit on my lap and hold me this tight around the neck?"

"I'd hug tighter."

"That's all I want to know." He straightened up a little and put both arms around me so that when the wind blew colder I felt warmer. "Let's let the wind get harder. Let's let the straw and the feathers fly! Let the old wind go crazy and pound us over the head! And when the straight winds pass over and the twisting winds crawl in the air like a rattlesnake in boiling water, let's you and me holler back at it and laugh it back to where it come from! Let's stand up on our hind legs, and shake our fists back into the whole crazy mess, and holler and cuss and rave and laugh and say, 'Old Cyclone, go ahead! Beat your bloody brains out against my old tough hide! Rave on! Blow! Beat! Go crazy! Cyclone! You and I are friends! Good old Cyclone!'"

I jumped up to my feet and hollered, "Blow! Ha! Ha! Blow, wind! Blow! I'm a Cyclome! Ha! I'm a Cyclome!"

Papa jumped up and danced in the dirt. He circled his pile of tools, patted me on the head, and laughed out, "Come on, Cyclone, let 'er ripple!"

"Chhaaarrrliee!" Mama's voice cut through all of the laughing and dancing and the howling of the wind across the whole hill. "Where are you?"

"We're down here fighting with a Cyclone!"

"Chasin' storms an' hittin' 'em!" I put in.

"Whhaaattt?"

Papa and me snickered at each other.

"Wrestling a Cyclone!"

"Tell 'er I am, too," I told Papa.

Grandma and Mama walked through the trash blowing in

the wind and found me and Papa patting our hands together
and dancing all around the dynamite and tools. "What on
earth has come over you two?"

"Huh?"

"You're crazy!" Grandma looked around her.

The wind was filling the whole sky with a blur of dry
grass, tumbling weeds, and scooting gravel, fine dust, and
sailing leaves. Hot rain began to whip us.

"We're heading for a storm cellar, and you're coming
with us. Here's a raincoat."

"Who will carry this Sawhorse?" Papa asked them.

"I wanta wade th' water!" I said.

"No you won't. I'll carry you myself!" Mama said.

"Give him to me!" Papa joked at Mama. "Put him right
up here on my shoulders! Now the raincoat around him.
We'll splash every mudhole dry between here and Oklahoma City! We're Cyclone Fighters! Did you know that,
Nora?"

The wind staggered Papa along the path. Grandma
grunted and throwed her weight against the storm. Mama
was buttoning up a slicker and bogging in the slick clay
in the path.

"This rain is like a river cutting loose!" Papa was saying
under my coat. He poked his face out between two buttons
and took two steps up and slid one step back.

At the top of the hill the water was deeper, and in the
clear alley the wind hit us harder.

"Charlie! Help Grandma, there! She's fell down!" Mama
said.

Papa turned around and took Grandma by the hand and
pulled her to her feet. "I'm all right! Now! Head on for the
cellar!"

I felt the wind drive against me so hard that I had to hug

onto Papa's neck as tight as I could. The wind hit us again and drove us twenty feet down the alley in the wrong direction. Papa's shoes went over their tops in mud and he stood spraddle-legged and panted for air. "You're choking my wind off! Hold on around my head!"

The wind rolled tubs and spun planks of ripped lumber through the air. Trash piles and bushel baskets sailed against clothes-line. Barn doors banged open and shut and splintered into a hundred pieces. Rain shot like a solid wall of water and Papa braced his feet in the soggy manure, and yelled, "You all right, Wood?" I told him, "I'm all right! You?"

A wild push of wind whined for a minute like a puppy under a box and then roared down the alley, squealing like a hundred mad elephants. My coat ripped apart and turned wrongside out over my head and I grabbed a tight hold around Papa's forehead. We staggered twenty or thirty more feet down the alley and fell flat in some deep cow tracks behind a chicken pen.

"Charlie! Are you and Woodrow all right?" I heard Mama yelling down the alley. I couldn't see ten feet in her direction.

"You take Grandma on to the cellar!" Papa was yelling out from under the rubber raincoat. "We'll be there in a minute! Go on! Get in!"

I was laying at first with my feet in a hole of manurey water, but I twisted and squirmed and finally got my head above it. "Lemme loose!"

"You keep your head down!" Papa ducked me again in the hole of watery manure. "Stay where you are!"

"Yer drownin' me in cow manure!" I finally managed to gurgle.

"Keep down there!"

"Papa?"

"Yes. What?" He was choking for air.

"Are you and me still Cyclome Fighters?"

"We lost this first round, didn't we?" Papa laughed under the raincoat till cellars heard him ten blocks around. "But we'll make it! Just as soon's I get a little whiff of fresh air. We'll make 'er here in a minute! Won't we, manure head?"

"Mama an' Grandma's better Cyclome Fighters than we are!" I laughed and snorted into the slush pool under my nose. "They done got to th' storm cellar, an' left us in a 'nure hole! Ha!"

Phone wires whistled and went with the wind. Packing boxes from the stores down in town raised from their alleys and flew above the trees. Timbers from barns and houses clattered through windows, and cows bawled and mooed in the yards, tangled their horns in chicken-wire fences and clotheslines. Soggy dogs streaked and beat it for home. Ditches and streets turned into rivers and backyards into lakes. Bales of hay splitting apart blew through the sky like pop-corn sacks. The rain burned hot. Everything in the world was fighting against everything in the sky. This was the hard straight pushing that levels the towns before it and lays the path low for the twisting, sucking, whirling tail of the cyclone to rip to shreds.

Papa wrapped me in the raincoat and hugged me as tight as he could. We crawled behind a cow barn to duck the wind, but the cow barn screamed like a woman run down in the streets, tumbled over on its side, and the first whisk of the wind caught the open underside and booted the whole barn fifty feet in the air. We fell six feet forward. I hugged around Papa's neck. He turned me loose with both hands and swung onto a clothesline, slipping his hands along the wires, pushing off sacks, mops, hay and rubbish of all kinds till we got to the back of the first house. He edged his way to the next house and felt along their clothes-line. In a minute or two we come to within fifteen feet of the cellar door where Grandma and Mama had gone with the neighbors. Papa crawled along the ground, dragging me underneath him.

"Nora! Nora!" Papa banged against the slanting cellar door with his fists hard enough to compete with the twister. "Let us in! It's Charlie!"

"An' meee!" I let out from under the coat.

The door opened and Papa wedged his shoulder against it. Five or six neighbor men and women heaved against the door to push it back against the wind.

I was just as wet as any catfish in any creek ever was or ever will be when Papa finally got into the cellar.

Mama grabbed me up into her lap where she was setting down on a case of canned fruit. A lantern or two shot a little gleam of light through the shadows of ten or fifteen people packed into the cellar.

"Boy! You know, Mama, me an' Papa is really Cyclome Fighters!" I jabbered off and shook my head around at everybody.

"How's your papa? Charlie! Are you all right?"

"Just wet with cow manure!"

Everybody laughed and hollered under the ground.

"Sing to me," I whispered to Mama.

She had already been rocking me back and forth, humming the tune to an old song. "What do you want me to sing?"

"That. That song."

"The name of that song is 'The Sherman Cyclone.'"

"Sing that."

And so she sang it:

You could see the storm approaching
And its cloud looked deathlike black
And it was through
Our little city
That it left
Its deathly track.

And I drifted off to sleep thinking about all of the people in the world that have worked hard and had somebody else come along and take their life away from them.

The door was opened back and the man in a slicker was saying, "The worst of it's gone!"

Papa yelled up the steps, "How do things look out there?"

"Pretty bad! Done a lot of damage!" I could see the man's big pair of rubber boots sogging around in the mudhole by the door. "She passed off to the south yonder! Hurry out, and you can still see the tail whipping!"

I jumped loose from Mama and slid down off her lap. "I'm a-gonna see it gitt a-whippin'!" I was talking to Papa and following him out the door.

"Out south yonder. See?" The man pointed. "Still whipping!"

"I see it! I see it! That big ole long whip! I see it!" I waded out into the holes of water barefooted and squirted mud between my toes. "I hate you, ol' Cyclome! Git outta here!"

The clouds in the west rolled away to the south and the sun struck down like a clear Sunday morning across town. Screen doors slammed and cellar doors swung open. People walked out in little lines like the Lord had rung a dinner bell. A high wind still whipped across the town. Wet hunks of trash waved on telephone poles and wires. Scattered hay and junk of every calibre covered the ground for as far as my eyes could travel. Kids tore out looking for treasures.

Boys and girls loped across yards and pointed and screamed at the barns and houses wrecked. Ladies in cotton dresses splashed across little roads to kiss each other. I watched for a block or two around and listened to some people laugh and some people cry.

Mama walked along in front of Grandma. She didn't say much. "I'm anxious to see over the rim of that hill," she told us.

"What's over it?" I asked her.

"Nora! Grandma! Hur y up!" Papa waved from the alley where we had been blown off of our feet in the storm. "Here comes Roy and Clara!"

"Roy and Clara!" Grandma hustled up a little faster. "Where have they been during all of this?"

"In th' school cellar, I suppose." Mama looked up the alley and seen them splashing mudholes dry coming toward us.

"Why did ya stay in that ol' school cellar?" I bawled them out when they walked up. "Me an' Papa had a fight with a cyclome twister all by ourselfs! Ya!"

"Nora." Papa talked the quietest I had ever heard him. "Grandma. Come here. Look. Look at the house."

We walked in a little bunch to the top rim of the hill. He pointed down the clay path we had come up to the cellar. The sun made everything as clear as a crystal. The air had been thrashed and had a good bath in the rain. There we saw our old London House. Papa almost whispered, "What's left of it."

The London House stood there without a roof. It looked like a fort that had lost a hard battle. Rock walls partly caved in by flying wreckage and by the push of the twister. Our back screen door jerked off of its hinges and wrapped around the trunk of my walnut tree.

Papa got to the back door first and busted into the kitchen.

"Hello, kitchen." Mama shook her head and looked all around. "Well, we've got a nice large sky for a roof, anyway." She saw very little of her own furniture in the kitchen. Every single window glass was gone. Water and mud on the floor come above our shoe tops. She turned around and picked me up and lifted me up on the eating table, telling me, "You stay up here, little waterbug."

"I wanta wade in th' water!" I was setting on the edge of the table kicking my bare feet at the water in the floor. "I wanta git my feet wet!"

"There's all kinds of glass and sharp things on this floor. You might cut your feet. Just look at that cupboard!" Mama waded across the kitchen. The cupboard was face down and half under water. Dishes smashed in a thousand pieces laid all around. Joints of stove pipe, brooms, mops, flour sacks half full, aprons, coats, and pots, and pans, hay, weeds, roots, bark, bowls with a few bites of food still in them. She pointed to a big blue speckled pot and said, "Mister cyclone didn't wash my pots any too clean."

"You don't seem to care much." Papa was nervous and breathing hard. He sloshed all around the room, touching everything with his fingers and caressing the mess of wet trash like it was a prize-winning bull, sick and down with the colic. "Jesus! Look at everything! Look! This is the last straw. This is our good-bye!"

"Good-bye to what?" Mama kept her eyes looking around over the house. "What?"

Clara backed up to the eating table. "Hey, Woodblock," she said, "climb up on my back. I'll take you for a horseback ride to the front room!"

"You children hadn't ought to be joking and playing

around, not at a time like this!" Papa cried and the tears wet his face like a baby.

"Gitty up!" I kicked Clara easy with my heels and waved my hands in the air above her head. "Swim this big ol' kinoodlin' river! Gitty up!" I hugged on around her neck as tight as I could while she pitched a few times and splashed her feet in the water. Then I yelled back, "C'mon, Papa! Let's swim th' big river, an' fight th' mean ol' hoodlum leeegion!"

"I'm coming to help fight! Wait for me!" Mama cut in splashing the water ahead of us. She jumped up and down and splattered slush and wet flour and mud and sooty water all over her dress and two feet or three up on the rock walls of the kitchen. "Splash across the river! Whoopie! Splash across the quicksand! Here we come! All of us movie stars, to fight the crooks and stealers! Whoopie!"

"Ha! Ha! Look at Mama fightin'!" I hollered at everybody.

"Mama's a good Cyclone Fighter, too, ha?" Clara was laughing and kicking slushy filth all over the place. "Come on, Papa! We got to go and keep fighting this cyclone!"

Mama slid her feet through the water, sending long ripples and waves busting against the walls. "Charlie, come on here! Look at this next room!"

Clara rode me on her back once around the whole front room. Sofa upside down in the middle of the floor, its hair and springs scattered for fifty feet out the south window. Papers, envelopes, pencils floated on top of the water on the floor. The big easy chair in the corner was dropped on its side like a fighter stopped in his tracks. Big square sandrocks from the tops of the four walls had crashed through the upper ceiling and smashed Mama's sewing machine against the wall. Spools of colored thread bobbed around on top of the water like barrels and cables on the ocean.

"It didn't miss anything." Grandma looked the room over. "I know an Indian, Billy Bear, that swears a cyclone stole his best work horse while he was plowing his field. He walked home mad and swearing at the world. And when he got home, he found the cyclone had been so good as to leave the harness, $6.50, and a gallon crock jug of whiskey on his front doorstep!"

Everybody busted out laughing, but Papa kept quiet. "Nora, I can't stand this any longer!" he yelled out all at once. "This funny business! This tee-heeing. This joking! Why do all of you have to turn against me like a pack of hounds? Isn't this, this wrecked home, this home turned into a pile of slush and filth, this home wiped out, isn't this enough to bring you to your senses?"

"Yes," Mama was talking low and quiet, "it has brought me to my senses."

"You don't seem to be sorry to see the place go!"

"I'm glad." Mama stood in her tracks and breathed the fresh air down deep in her lungs. "Yes, I feel like a new baby."

"Hey, ever'body! Ever'body! C'mere!" I walked out a bare window and stood on the ground pointing up into the air.

"What is it?" Mama was the only one to follow me out into the yard. "What are you pointing at?"

"Mister Cyclome broke th' top outta my walnut tree!"

"That's the one you got hung up in." Mama patted me on the head. "I think old Mister Cyclone broke the top out of that walnut tree so you won't get hung up there any more!"

And I held onto Mama's hand, looking at her gold wed-

ding ring, and telling her, "Ha! I think ol' Mister Cyclome tore down this ol' mean Lon'on House ta keep it from hurtin' my mama!"

woody Guthrie

Chapter VI

BOOMCHASERS

❖

We picked up and moved across town to a lot better house in a nice neighborhood on North Ninth Street, and Papa got to buying and selling all kinds of lands and property and making good money.

People had been slinking around corners and ducking behind bushes, whispering and talking, and running like wild to swap and trade for land—because tests had showed that there was a whole big ocean of oil laying under our country. And then, one day, almost out of a clear sky, it broke. A car shot dust in the air along the Ozark Trail. A man piled out and waved his hands up and down Main Street running for the land office. "Oil! She's blowed 'er top! Gusher!" And then, before long—there was a black hot fever hit our town—and it brought with it several whole armies, each running the streets, and each hollering, "Oil! Flipped 'er lid! Gusher!"

They found more oil around town along the river and the creek bottoms, and oil derricks jumped up like new groves of tall timber. Thick and black and flying with steam, in the pastures, and above the trees, and standing in the slushy mud of the boggy rivers, and on the rocky sides of the useless hills, oil derricks, the wood legs and braces gummed and soaked with dusty black blood.

Pretty soon the creeks around Okemah was filled with black scum, and the rivers flowed with it, so that it looked like a stream of rainbow-colored gold drifting hot along the waters. The oily film looked pretty from the river banks and from on the bridges, and I was a right young kid, but I remember how it came in whirls and currents, and swelled up as it slid along down the river. It reflected every color when the sun hit just right on it, and in the hot dry weather that is called Dog Days the fumes rose up and you could smell them for miles and miles in every direction. It was something big and it sort of give you a good feeling. You felt like it was bringing some work, and some trade, and some money to everybody, and that people everywhere, even way back up in the Eastern States was using that oil and that gas.

Oil laid tight and close on the top of the water, and the fish couldn't get the air they needed. They died by the wagon loads along the banks. The weeds turned gray and tan, and never growed there any more. The tender weeds and grass went away and all that you could see for several feet around the edge of the oily water hole was the red dirt. The tough iron weeds and the hard woodbrush stayed longer. They were there for several years, dead, just standing there like they was trying to hold their breath and tough it out till the river would get pure again, and the oil would go, and things could breathe again. But the oil didn't go. It stayed. The grass and the trees and the tanglewood died. The wild grape vine shriveled up and its tree died, and the farmers pulled it down.

The Negro sharecroppers went out with their bread balls and liver for bait. You saw them setting around the banks and on the tangled drifts, in the middle of the day, or along about sundown—great big bunches of Negro farmers trying to get a nibble. They worked hard. But the oil had come, and it looked like the fish had gone. It had been an even swap.

Trains whistled into our town a hundred coaches long. Men drove their heavy wagons by the score down to pull up alongside of the cars, and skidded the big engines, the thick-painted, new and shiny machinery, and some old and rusty machines from other oil fields. They unloaded the railroad cars, and loaded and tugged a blue jillion different kinds of funny-looking gadgets out into the fields. And then it seemed like all on one day, the solid-tired trucks come into the country, making such a roar that it made your back teeth rattle. Everybody was holding down one awful hard job and two or three ordinary ones.

People told jokes:

Birds flew into town by the big long clouds, lasting two or three hours at a time, because it was rumored around up in the sky that you could wallow in the dust of the oiled roads and it would kill all kinds of flees and body lice.

Dogs cured their mange, or else got it worse. Oil on their hair made them hotter in hot weather and colder in cold weather.

Ants dug their holes deeper, but wouldn't talk any secrets about the oil formation under the ground.

Snakes and lizards complained that wiggling through so many oil pools made the hot sun blister their backs worse. But on the other hand they could slide on their belly through the grass a lot easier. So it come out about even.

Oil was more than gold ever was or ever will be, because you can't make any hair salve or perfume, TNT, or roofing material or drive a car with just gold. You can't pipe that gold back East and run them big factories, either.

The religion of the oil field, guys said, was to get all you can, and spend all you can as quick as you can, and then end up in the can.

I'd go down to the yards and climb around over the cars loaded down with more tools. And the sun was peppering down on all of the steel so hot, it kept me prancing along the loads like a football player running. I heard the tough men cuss and swear and learned more good cuss words to use to get work done.

My head was full of pictures like a movie—different from movies I'd been sneaking into. The faked ones about outlaws, rich girls, playboys, cowboys and Indians, and shooting scrapes, killings, and a pretty man kissing a pretty girl on a pretty spot on a pretty day. It takes a lot more guts, I thought, to work and heave and cuss and sweat and laugh and talk like the oil field workers. Every man gritted every tooth in his head, and stretched every muscle in his whole body—not trying to get rich or rare back and loaf, because I'd hear one beller out, "Okay, you dam guys, hit 'er up, or else git down out of a workin' man's way, an' let me put in a Goddam oil field!"

A block and tackle man showed me how to lift all kinds of heavy stuff with the double pulleys, "Ride 'em down! Grab 'em down! When th' chain goes 'round, somethin's leavin' th' ground!" There was a twenty-foot slush bucket used for getting mud and slush out of the hole, and it looked so heavy in a railroad car that you never could lift it out; but you'd hear a man on a handle of a crank yell out, "Tong bucker, tong bucker! Mister hooker man! Grab a root, boy! Grab a root!" The man on the hooks would yell back, "Gimme slack! Gimme slack!" Some of the cable men would guide the big hook over to the hooker man and yell out, "Give 'im slack! Give 'im slack!" "Take it back! Take it back! Won't do one thing you don't like!" "Take yer slack! Bring it back!" "Ridin' with ya! Got yer grab!" "Got my grab!" "Grab a root an' growl! Grab a root an' growl!" "Take yore grab! Take 'er home!" The men took in all of the slack on the chain or cable and it would get as tight as a fiddle string, and the joint of bailing bucket would raise up off of the floor of the car and one man would yell, "She was a good gal, but she lost her footin'!"

I piled on top a wagon every day and set on a gunny sack stuck full of hay, by the side of a teamskinner that told me all kinds of tales and yarns about the other ten dozen oil fields he, personally, had put down. I picked up five or ten books full of the cuss words the mule drivers use to talk to each other, which are somewhat worse than the ones they use to cuss their teams into pulling harder.

Out in the fields, I walked from derrick to derrick through the trees, and hung around each place till the driller or the tool dresser would spot me and yell, "Git th' hell outta here, son! Too dangerous!" The bull wheels spun and the cable unrolled as they dropped the mud buckets down into the hole; the boiler shot steam and danced on its foundation; the derrick shook and trembled, and strained every nail and every joint when the mud bucket, full again, would stick in the bottom of the hole, and the cable would pull as tight as it possibly could, trying to pull the bucket out. The rig and derrick would creak and crack, and whole swarms of men would work like ants. The slush ponds were full of the gray-looking shale and a film of slick oil reflected the clouds and the sky, and lots of times I'd take a stick and reach out and fish out some kind of a bird that had mistook the oil pool for the real sky, and flew into the slush. The whole country was alive with men working, men running, men sweating, and signs everywhere saying: Men Wanted. I felt good to think that some day I'd grow up and be a man wanted; but I was a kid—and I had to go around asking the men for a job, and then hear them say, "Git th' hell outta here! Too dangerous!"

The first people to hit town was the rig builders, cement men, carpenters, teamskinners, wild tribes of horse traders and gypsy wagons loaded full, and wheels breaking down;

crooked gamblers, pimps, whores, dope fiends, and peddlers, stray musicians and street singers, preachers cussing about love and begging for tips on the street corners, Indians in dirty loud clothes chanting along the sidewalks with their kids crawling and playing in the filth and grime underfoot. People elbowed up and down the streets like a flood on the Canadian, and us kids would run and jump right in big middle of the crowds, and let them just sort of push us along a block or so, and play like we was floating down stream. Thousands of folks come to town to work, eat, sleep, celebrate, pray, cry, sing, talk, argue, and fight with the old settlers.

And this was a pretty mixed-up mess, but it was always three or four times worse on election day. I used to follow the different speakers around and see who got beat up for voting for who. I would stay out late at night to see the election returns come in, and see them count the votes. Lots of kids stayed out that night. They knew that it wasn't any too safe down on the streets on account of the men fighting and throwing bottles and stuff—so we would climb up the cast-iron sewer pipes, up to the tops of buildings, and we'd watch the votes counted from up there.

A board was all lit up, and the different names of the men that was running for office was painted on it. One column would be, say, "Frank Smith for Sheriff," and the next, "John Wilkes." One column would say, "Fist Fights," and another column would read, "Gangfights." A man would come out every hour during the night and write: "Precinct Number Two, for Sheriff, Frank Smith, three votes, Johnny Wilkes, four. Fist fights four. Gangfights, none."

In another hour he'd come out with his rag and chalk, and write, "Precinct Number Three just heard from. For Sheriff, Frank Smith, Seven votes, John Wilkes, Nine; Fist fights: Four. Gangfights, Three." Wilkes won the Sheriff's office by eleven odd votes. The fights added up: Fist Fights, Thirteen. Gangfights, Five.

I remember one particular gangfight. The men had banged into one another and was really going at it. They spent as much time getting up and down as they had working on their pieces of land for the past three months. Some swung, missed, and fell. They each brought down two more. Others got knocked down and only brung down one or so. Others just naturally went down and stayed down. I got interested in one big old boy from out around Sand

Creek; he was in there for all it was worth, and I wanted to crawl down off of the building and ooze in a little closer to where he was standing fighting. I edged through the crowd with fists of all sorts and sizes going past my head, barely missing, and I got right up behind him. He took pretty good aim at a cotton farmer from Slick City, drawed back with his fist, hit me under the chin with his elbow, hit the cotton farmer from Slick City, on the chin with his fist, knocked me a double handspring backwards one direction, and the cotton farmer from Slick City a twin loop the other.

I was down on my hands and knees, and all of the well-known feet in that county was in the small of my back. Men fell over me, and got mad at me for tripping them. Every time I started to get up, they would all push in my direction, and down I'd go again. My head was in the dirt. I had mud in my teeth, oil in my hair, and water on the brain.

Right after the oil boom got under way, I found me a job walking the streets and selling newspapers. I stuck my head into every door, not so much to sell a paper, but to just try to figure out where in the devil so many loud-yelling people had struck from. The tough kids, one or two of them new in town, had glommed onto the very best-selling corners, and so I walked from building to building, because I knew most of the landlords and the other kids didn't.

Our Main Street was about eight blocks long. And Saturday was the day that all of the farmers come to town to jump in with the several thousand rambling, gambling oil field chasers. Folks called them boom chasers. A great big rolling army of hard-hitting men and their hard-hitting families. Stores throwed their keys away and stayed open twenty-four hours a day. When one army jumped out of bed another army jumped in. When one army marched out of a café, another one marched in. As fast as one army went broke at the slot machines in the girly houses, it was pushed out and another army pushed in.

I walked into a pool hall and poker room that had big pictures of naked women hung along the walls. Every table was going with from two to six men yelling, jumping up and down, whooping around worse than wild Indians, cussing the jinx and praying to the god of good luck. Cue balls jumped tables and shot like cannon balls across the hall. Eight tables in line and a whole pow-wow and war dance going on around each table. "Watch out fer yer Goddam elbow, there, brother!"

Poker tables wheeling and dealing. Five or six little oil-cloth tables, five or six mulers, hustlers, lead men, standing around winking and making signs in back of every table. And behind them, five or six more hard-working onlookers, laughing and watching five or six of the boys with a new paysack getting the screws and trimmings put to them. A guy or two slamming in and out through the back door, picking pints of rotgut liquor out of trash piles, and sliding them out of their shirts to the boys losing their money around the tables. "Whitey's gettin' perty well stewed. Gonna bet wild here in a minute, an' lose his hat."

Along the sides of the walls was mostly where the old and the sick would come to set for a few hours and keep track of the robbing and the fights; the old bleary-eyed bar-flies and drunks that rattled in the lungs with asthma and TB and coughed corruption all day and seldom hit a cuspidor on the floor. I walked around saying, "Paper, mister? Five cents." But kids like me wasn't allowed on the inside of dives like this, unless we knew the boss, and then the bouncer kept his eye peeled on me and seen to it that I kept moving.

"Boys! That gal there on th' Goddam wall has got breasts

like a feather pillow! Nipples like a little red cherry! Th' day I run onto somethin' like that, I'm gonna give up my good ol' ruff an' rowdy ways! Whooooeee!" "Ya dam sex-minded roustabout, you, c'mon, it's yore next shot!"

I very seldom sold a paper in the joints like this. The men were too wild. Too worked up. Too hot under the collar to read a paper and think about it. The old dice, the cards, the dominoes, the steer men for the pimps and gamblers, the drinking and climbing the old spitty steps that lead to the girly houses, maybe the wild spinning of all of these things had the men whipped up to a fever heat, jumpy, jittery, wild and reckless. A two-hundred pounder would raise up from a poker table broke, and stumble through the crowd yelling, "You think I'm down! You think you got me down! You think I'm drunk! Well, maybe I am drunk. Maybe I am drunk. But I'll tell you low-life cheating rats one thing for sure! You never did hit an honest days work in your whole life! You follow the boom towns around! I've seen you! Seen your faces in a thousand towns. Cards. Dice. Dominoes. Snooker. Pool. Flabbery ass whores. Rollers. I'm an honest hard-working man! I help put up every oil field from Wheeler Ridge to Smackover! What the hell have you done? Rob. Roll. Steal. Beat. Kill. Your kind is coming to a bad end! Do you hear me? All of you! Listen!"

"Little too much noise there, buddy," a cop would walk up and take the man by the arm. "Walk along with me till you cool off."

In front of the picture show a handful of old batty electric lights hit down on a couple of hundred men, women and kids, everybody blocking the sidewalks, pushing, talking, arguing, and trying to read what was on at the show. Wax dummies in steel cages showed "The Cruel And Terrible Facts Of The Two Most Famous Outlaws In The

History Of The Human Race, Billy The Kid, and Jesse James. And Also The Doomed Life Of The Most Famous Lady Outlaw Of All Time, The One And Only Belle Starr. See Why Crime Does Not Pay On Our Screen. Today. Adults Fifty Cents. Children Ten Cents. Please Do Not Spit On The Floor. To Do So May Spread Disease."

I sauntered along singing out, "Read all about it! Late night paper. Ten men drowned in a dust storm!"

"Can't read, sonny, sorry, I've got horseshoe nails in my eyes! Ha! Ha! Ha!" A whole circle of men would bust out laughing at me. And another one would smile at me and pat me on the head and say, "Here, Sonny Boy. You ain't nobody's fool. I cain't read yer paper, neither, but here's a dime."

I watched the crowds sweat and mop their faces walking along, the young boys and girls all dressed up in shirts and dresses as clean as the morning sky.

"The day of th' comin' of th' Lord is near! Jesus Christ of Nazareth will come down out of the clouds in all of His purity, all of His glory, and all of His power! Are you ready, brother and sister? Are you saved and sanctified and baptized in the spirit of the Holy Ghost? Are your garments spotless? Is your soul as white as the drifted snow?"

I leaned back against the bank window and listened to the people talk as they walked along. "Is your snow spotless?" "Souls saved. Two bits a lick." "I ain't wantin' t' be saved if it makes ye stand around th' street corners an' rave like a dam maniac!" "Yes, I'm goin' to join th' church one of these days before I die." "Me too, but I wanta have some fun an' live first!"

I walked across the street in the dark in front of the drugstore and found a drunk man coming out. "Hey, mister, wanta good job?"

"Yeah. Where'sh a job at?"

"Sellin' papers. Make a lotta money."

"How'sh it done?"

"You gimme a nickel apiece fer these twenty papers. You walk up an' down th' streets yellin' about th' headlines. Then you sell all of th' papers, see, an' you git yer money all back."

"Ish that th' truth? Here'sh a doller. Gimme th' papersh. Shay. What doesh th' headlines shay?"

" 'Corn liquor found to be good medicine!' "

"Corn likker ish found t' be good medishin."

"Yeah. Got that?"

"Yesh. But, hell fire, shonny, if I wash t' holler that, th' bootleggersh would kill me."

"Why would they kill ya?"

"Cause. Jusht would. Ever'body'd quit drinkin' 'fore mornin'!"

"Just holler, 'Paper! Latest tissue!' "

" 'Latest tissue!' Okay! Here I go! Mucha 'blige." And he walked off down the street yelling, "Papersh! Latest tissue!"

I spent sixty cents for twenty more papers at the drugstore. "Listen," the paper man was telling me, "th' sheriff is gettin' mighty sore at you. Every night there's three or four drunks walkin' up and down th' streets with about twenty papers yelling out some goofy headline!"

"Business is business."

I hopped up on top of a big high load of oil-field pipe and rode along listening to the teamskinner rave and cuss. He didn't even know I was on his load. I looked up the street and seen twenty other wagons oozing along in the dark with men cracking their twenty-foot leather reins like shotguns in the night, knocking blisters on the hips of their tired horses. Cars, buggies and wagons full of people waiting their chance to pull out between the big wagons loaded down with machinery.

So this is my old Okemah. All of this fast pushing and loud talking and cussing. Yonder's twenty men piling onto the bed of a big truck waving their gloves and lunch pails in the air and yelling, "Trot out yer oil field that needs buildin'!" "See ya later, wimmen, when I git my bank roll!" "You be careful out there on that night shift in that timber!" a woman called out at her man. "I'll take care of myself!" Men riding along by the truckloads. Pounding each other on the backs, swaying and talking so fast and so loud you could hear them for a mile and a quarter.

I like all of this crowd running and working and making a racket. Old Okemah is getting built up. Yonder's a crowd around a fist fight in front of the pawnshop. Papa beat a man up there at that café last night for charging him ninety cents for a forty-cent steak.

I never did think I'd see no such a mob on the streets of this town. The whole air is just sort of full of a roar and a buzz and a feeling that runs up and down your back and makes the roots of your hair tingle. Like electricity of some kind.

Yonder is the bus caller. "It's a fine ride in a fine roller! Th' quickest, easiest, most comfortable way to the fields! Get your bus tickets here to all points! Sand Springs. Slick City. Oilton. Bow Legs. Coyote Hill. Cromwell. Bearden. A big easy ride with a whiskey driver!"

"You write 'em up! An' sign 'em up! Best wages paid! Hey, men! It's men wanted here! Skilled and unskilled! Killed and unkilled! Brain jobs! Desk jobs! Settin'-down jobs! Jobs standing up! Jobs bending over! Jobs for the drunk men, jobs for the sober! Oil field workers wanted! You sign a card and hit it hard! Pay and a half for overtime! Double on Sunday! Right here! Fifteen thousand men wanted! Roughnecks! Roustabouts! Tong buckers! Boiler men! Dirt movers! Horse and mule drivers! Let's go! Men! Work cards right here!"

There was old Riley the auctioneer standing in front of his hiring office, pointing in at the door with a walking cane. Gangs of men pushing in and out, signing up for field work. "Rig builders! It's carpenters! We need your manly strength, your broad shoulders, and your big broad smiles, men, to get this oil field built! Anything from nail drivers, screw drivers, truck drivers, to slave drivers! Wimmen! Drive your husbands here! Yes, madame, we'll sober him up, wash him up, clean him up, feed him up, fill him up, rest him up, build him up, and straighten him up! You'll have a big fat bank roll and a new man when we send him back off of this job! Write your name and win your fame! Men wanted!"

An old timer was preaching from the other side in front of a grocery store, "These here dern wild boom chasers is tearin' our whole town down! They don't no more pay 'tention to th' law than if we didn't have laws!"

"You're a damned old liar! You old miserly crab!" a lady yelled out from the crowd around him. "We're a-buildin' this town up ten dozen times more'n you ever could of! We do more actual work in a minute than you do settin' on yore rear a year!"

"If you wuzn't a lady, I'd resent that!"

"Don't let that hold you back, brother!" She knocked four or five toughs out of her way getting to him. "As far as these laws go, who made them up? You! And three or four more about like you! We come to this town to work an' build up an oil field an' make it worth something! Maybe these boys are a little wild and woolly. You've got to be to work like we work, an' travel like we travel, an' live like we live!"

I laid down on the load of pipe and stretched my feet out

and looked up where the stars was. My ears still heard the babbling, yelping, swushing along the streets, wheels rolling, horses straining, kids chasing and babies screaming. The big trucks tooted their horns in the dark. I wanted to ride there with my eyes closed, listening. I wanted to ride past the picture show, gambling hall, whore house, drug store, church house, court house, and the jail house and just listen to old Okemah growing up.

Okemah. She's a going, blowing oil boom town.

In the summer I played with other kids in the gang house. Our gang house was built by a week's hard work of about a dozen kids of most every sort, size, color, brand, trade mark, and style. It started when an old lady told us a big long story, all about the howls and laughs you could hear if you went very close to the old haunted house of the Bolewares. So I figured my whole gang had ought to go spend a night in the old haunted house. I rounded up about the whole dozen and over we went after it got dark. Nothing but a stray goat come across the yard and some bats flew in and out of a few broke windows. Right then we decided to haunt the house our own selves, and we all moaned and groaned and tromped around in the dark, choking and gurgling like we was being lynched, and stomping down with all of our weight on the loose boards of the floor and the attic.

Next, one of us got the bright idea of carrying the loose boards across town to an old sawed-down peach orchard on a side of the schoolhouse hill, and put up a gang house to haunt. Every night we'd sneak out from home after supper, some of us going to bed, creeping out from under covers and out of windows to get away from our folks. Howls and screams from the Boleware house caused neighbors to lock and bar their doors and windows; women stayed in houses in bunches and sewed or knitted all night. As we kept haunting the old house, rent come down to less than half what it had been on this street. Dogs hung along under porches and whined with their tails pulled up real tight between their hind legs. And then nothing but the very worst old rotten boards were left on the outside of the house, and we'd hauled away all of the nice inside boards. They went up like a big toadstool on schoolhouse hill, and neighbors wondered what the hell. Last of all, we wrote a sign with dim paint that we hung on the front side of the old Boleware hull: "Haunted House. Stay Out." I heard two ladies walk past it a month or so later and read the sign. My ears was like an old hound dog's, and I heard one lady say, "See the sign on the front? 'Haunted House. Stay Out'?" The other one said, "That landlord is a smart man. Doing that to scare the kids away." And I thought, "Bull."

Pretty soon we had a regular early Oklahoma township a-going right there on the lot around that old gang house. It was our City Hall, mail box, court house, jail, picture show, saloon, gambling hall, church, land office, restaurant, hotel and general store.

That shack was busier than our town depot. Each kid had a bin. In that bin he kept his junk, whatever that might run into. Most of the kids would take a gunny sack and go "junking" about twice or three times a week. They would come carrying in big sacks full of rubber inner tubes, brass faucets, copper wire, light brass gadgets, aluminum pots and pans beat up into a tight little ball. The city junk man bought them. That was money in our pocket. We packed those sacks more than we did school books. We also gathered up scrap iron, lead, zinc, rags, bottles, hoofs, horns, and old bones, and you could put your own stuff in your own bin without being afraid of somebody a-stealing it. We thought it was a mighty bad thing to steal something somebody else had already stolen.

We had gang money made out of sheets of paper. Every time you brung in a certain amount of junk, it was judged to be worth so much. You could go to the bank and the banker would hand you out a school tablet or two cut up in squares like dollar bills, and a few fancy marks around the edge, and signed by the captain of the gang. Fifty cents worth of junk was worth Five Thousand Dollars. You could cash your gang money in any time you wanted to, and pack your junk down to the city junk yard and sell it for real money.

A kid named Bud run the gambling wheel. It was an old lopsided bicycle wheel that he had found in the dumps and tried to even up. He paid you ten to one if you called off the right spoke it would stop on. But there was sixty spokes.

We rode stick horses, and some of the kids had nine, and all of the nags named according to how fast they could run. Like if you was riding Old Bay Tom, and Rex took in after you with a red handkerchief tied over his face, why you'd switch horses right in the big middle of the road—and get off of Old Bay Tom, and yell, "Giddyap, Lightnin'!"

We made horse-wrangling trips to the river and back, and gathered the best of our stick horses, the long, keen straight and springy ones with lots of fiery sap in them, and worth several hundred dollars each in gang money. I jig-trotted the seven miles back from the river, with a big bundle of wild broomtail Indian ponies tied up on both arms; and there was always such a showing and swapping and training of horses on the side of that hill as would out-class any horse-trading lot in the State of Oklahoma. A kid buying a horse would first, of course, want him broke to saddle; and there was four or five kids that made their whole living by busting bad ponies at ten dollars a head. Two or three kids grabbed the horse's head and blinded his eyes while the rider mounted to the saddle, and then would holler, "Fan 'im!" The rider and the horse broke away,

bucked and jumped all over the place, beating the weeds to a frazzle, snorting, and nickering, and humping into the air. Pounding and spurring the bronco, the kid frogged over sticker patches, whammed through can piles, flounced down the hillside and sidestepped rocks and roots and stumps. Since a horse was worth more if he was a wild one to break, the buyer would tip you an extra fifty or maybe even a hundred, if you showed all of the other kids that this was the snuffiest horse in the whole history of the hill. With always two or three or four hoss tamers out there busting a mount at the same time, you can just picture in your own mind how our hill looked—each kid trying and straining every gut to out-buck, and out-nicker, and out-ride the others. And then, to make a horse really in the dollar-a-year class, you had to ride him till he quit bucking, and then run him through all of his gaits; through the hard ones and easy ones, running as fast as he could tear, till he slowed into a fast rough gallop, and then down to a slow easy lope, pace him down the foot path, single-foot across the gang house yard, fox trot up to the door, and then walk as nice and as easy as an old member of the family till he was tied at the hitch rack, eating apples and sugar out of everybody's hand. And then you got your pay-off and somebody was the proud owner of another pureblood. And not only did the horse get a good proud name, and pedigree, and papers, but every little habit, onery streak, nervous spell, and fear, along with all of his likes and dislikes, was known by his owner, and there struck up between that stick horse and that kid a friendship, partnership, and love. Lots of kids had rode their horses, talked their troubles, winnings and losings, sick spells, and streaks of good luck, over and over a thousand times—for two or three years.

In a patch of big high weeds, near the gang house, was an old oat binder. We used it one hour for an airplane, and the next for a submarine. The World War was on over in France, and the Americans had gone in. We played war, war, war. We shot down weeds and trampled them into the dust, and we licked the same weed army every day. We grabbed up sticks, and waded out into the high weeds, fighting them hand to hand, cussing, sweating, hacking them down. They surrendered every few minutes. Then they'd do something mean to us again, and we'd get out and frail them back into the notion of surrendering all over again. We'd walk up and grab each individual weed by the coat collar, throw off his helmet, search him for Lugers, chuck away his rifle, and say, "Surren'er?"

"Surren'er!"

In the fall, when our school started, the kids got more excited about fighting than about books. New kids had to fight to find their place on the grounds, and the old bullies had new fights to settle who was still who. Fights had a funny way of always ringing me in. If it was between two kids that I didn't even know, whoever won, some smart aleck kids would holler, "Yeah, yeah, I bet ya cain't lick ol' Woody Guthrie." And before long I'd be somewhere out across the playgrounds whaling away and getting whaled, mostly over something I didn't know a thing about. I went around with some part of me puffed up all of the time, and the other parts just going down.

There was four of us that more or less respected each other, because we was the fightingest four around there, not because we wanted to fight, not because we was brave, or had it in for anybody, but just because the kids in school had us picked out to entertain them with our broke fists and noses, and they would carry tales and lies and cuss words back and forth like a messenger service just to keep the old fires going and the pot boiling and the skin a-flying.

But Big Jim Robins and Little Jim Whitt was the only two of the round-town four that fought amongst their selves. They beat half of the weed patches back into a cloud of hot, white, cement-looking dust, every school season, and the kids would all gang up and foller Big Jim and Little Jim home every afternoon when school was out, just to get them to fighting, which wasn't a hard job, since they never could agree just who'd got the best of it. Big Jim was a head taller than Little Jim. I was about the same size as Little Jim. Big Jim was red-headed, speckle-faced, snaggle-toothed, and broad through the shoulders, with great big flat feet. His hands was like hog quarters, and his arms was six inches longer than anybody else's in school, and he walked around in a hunch, slouched down careless, and he picked up snipes. He was the big Luis Firpo around that schoolhouse, and depended alone on his main strength and awkwardness to keep him in the Round Town Four Fist Fighting Association. His dad was a carpenter, his brother a grocery man. But Big Jim was the toast of the town, the natural-born comic, the loud-mouth insulter, and yelled at everybody that come along. His great big size scared the living daylights right out of most of the little kids. When it come to a fight, Big Jim seldom won, but he roared so loud, snorted so big, and kicked up so much dust and fine splinters that the kids would holler and laugh, and cheer for him, because wherever Big Jim had a fight, there you saw a complete two-feature show with two comedies and short subjects added on.

Little Jim was mostly the opposite. Light whitish hair that looked like frog fuzz, a slim, scary face and eyes that blinked and batted at everything that rustled in the wind. He was famous for going around dirty and slouchy, and when the kids would tease him, he would blow between his teeth like a train starting, and kick back dirt with his toes. Little Jim was quiet when he was left alone, and would walk ten blocks out of his way to keep out of a fight; but the kids liked to watch him sneer and blow, and so they headed him off across vacant lots, and pushed him into fights.

One day it was Trades Day, with sermons on the streets, singers in the saloons, and plotters and politicians lying on every corner. The town was alive, booming with the mixed voices of Negro farmers, the broke-down, hungry, dirt farmers, and the talking of the Indians that sometimes took on a high note, when some buck pointed away out yonder with his hand, and made a big curving motion, so that you could tell that he was talking about the whole country, the whole thing, the whole problem and, probably, the whole people. The white folks talked of this and that, hogs, horses, shoes, hats, whiskey, dances, women, politics, land, crops, weather and money. Everybody stood around with a long string of red tickets, for one of the merchants was aiming to give a new buggy away. It was a-standing out yonder in the middle of the street right where everybody could see her set there in the dusty sun and try her best to shine a little. Kids of all three colors, and an occasional mixture of each, crawled, walked, run, chased loose chickens, took in after cur dogs, clumb poles, fell across wagon tongues, and slipped down on the sidewalk with a brand-new pair of shoes on. Ice cream cones was waving around up and down the streets.

Down about the middle part of town, Big Jim and Little Jim was playing marbles on a flat, dusty place by the side of the drug store. Already they had attracted a couple of hundred folks down there to see the big Dominecker Rooster and the right little Game Cock commence kicking the pants off of each other.

The crowd mumbled, laughed, roared, and talked, some taking sides with Big Jim, and some with Little Jim. It was a game of agates up. Agates up was about as high as you could get in Okfuskee County politics without being an adult.

Little Jim was shooting, Big Jim watching him like a hawk, and both hollered every five seconds, "Dobbs!" "Venture Dubbs!" "You go ta hell, you bastard, you!"

When the fight started, even the few idle wanderers who had tried for the buggy soon come running down the street to see what was going on. They spied the big noisy crowd, and they knew it must be an awful good fight. The dust flew, and the skin, too, and you could see Big Jim's red head bobbing and weaving in the middle of the crowd. He was taking long haymaker swings at Little Jim's blond, silken-haired head, and hitting about once out of every nine swings. Little Jim was faster and surer. He laid it into Big Jim like a young mule kicking a clumsy old cow, and his fists seldom hit out without landing in the neighborhood of Big Jim's nose.

He hit straight. But time was passing. Months rolling by. Big Jim was getting bigger and bigger. He had completely outgrown Little Jim. Head and shoulders he raised up above his little opponent, and lumbered down like thunder and slow lightning, crushing when he landed a blow. Little Jim fought faster. He fought much better. Barefooted in the hot dirty ring, he pranced around, punching the big hulk of Big Jim, but just naturally not doing one ounce of damage. He fought long. He got tired. Dust choked him down. It choked Big Jim and the whole crowd, but Big Jim wasn't having to spend his energy. It looked as if he couldn't decide what he wanted to do, so he just made his hands sail around in the air to put on a show for the people. But after a while, he wore Little Jim down, and gave him the best beating that he had ever laid onto anybody. He brought blood running out of Little Jim's nose, thumped his head and ears till they swelled and stung. Beat his cheeks till you could see blue spots and red bruises. Little Jim Whitt lost his standing in the fist-fighting game that day, right then and there.

The town went wild. A decision had been reached. Little Jim had lost. Two other fights as to which kid had won started out in the crowd among men betting. But Big Jim was the stud buzzard in our town that day.

The school kids yelled when the fight was over. Their

voices hummed so fast that it sounded like a chant, like a
wave swelling out across the ocean.

"Where's Woody?" "Betcha cain't lick ol' Woody!"
"Woody ain't here! Where's Woody? He was down here
in town early this mornin'—he's gone!"

Kids took out down the road like traveling preachers, by
ones and twos, and the others lit out through streets and
alleys like a couple of dozen little Paul Reveres. Grown
men even strolled off up the hill to hunt me up, and to give
Big Jim time to rest up, and to rig us into a fist fight. Bets
mounted high. The crowd moved around like a big bunch
of bugs on top of a hole of water. It always stayed together, but it moved.

I was across town. I was up on Main Street, climbing
the rafters and braces of a big sign just across the street from
the jail house. When a couple of kids seen me climbing up
on top of that signboard, they hollered, "Hey, here he is!
Here he is! Here's Woody! Bring on Big Jim!"

Oklahoma has had runs. Land runs and whiskey runs.
But that crowd took out in such a hard run up that hill that
they jammed the streets where they crossed, shoved each
other down the boardwalks, skint their shins on the concrete curbs, tore off the wooden corner posts of grocery
stores, pushed over stacks of chicken coops, turned the
chickens loose, made the feathers fly, slipped and fell across
sacks of horse and mule feed, crawled over wagons and
buggies parked in the road, made the hay fly, lost their
kids, dropped plugs of tobacco, laughed, yelled, whooped,
and caused teams to break and run away.

Like I said, I was getting closer and closer to the top of
that sign-board, and when I heard that big crowd coming
up the steep street raising so much cain, I didn't know
what the devil was going to happen. They was yelling my
name, and running full blast. I hit the top of the signboard,

and throwed one leg across, just as the crowd scraped a coat of old paint off of the corner of the court house, crowding past it, to gather all around the signboard and yell all kinds of things, like: "Come on down! Lick Big Jim!" "Little Jim just got beat up!" "Whataya say, boy? Coward?" "Git 'im, Yallerback!" "Come on down offa there! You aint' no dam eagle!"

Well, I just hunkered over and made myself right real comfortable and set up there. I knew then what it was all about. Just another one of them dam fool fights all rigged up and fixed up before you know what it's all about. I knew how tired Big Jim must be. Just had one fight. Now they wanted to sic him onto me and see another one. I must of killed a full five minutes just setting up there. They tried every kind of a trick to get me down. Kids and men clumb halfway up to where I was. They lured me and baited me. They promised me dimes. But I didn't come down. Then they fell back onto the one and only dare that I couldn't stand. They yelled, "Old man Charlie Guthrie's a fighter! Old Charlie Guthrie would come down to fight!"

Something inside of me went out and something come in. I set there about two or three seconds, my face went sort of blank, and I gritted my teeth; and then I slid down off of the frame of the sign, and clumb like a monkey down through the braces, and the crowd was in an uproar.

The crowd got around me. There was so much noise I couldn't do nothing. It was just some kind of a roaring ocean rising and falling in my head. I couldn't see Jim. It was too crowded. I saw every kind of a face but that big speckled one. The crowd squared off, and they cleared out the usual three-foot hole in the middle, which was big enough for two kids to knock off twenty-five square foot of hair and hide in. I couldn't see Jim.

Something hit me right square between the horns. It was

a big outfit of some kind, a team of wild bay mares, or a wagon load of cotton seed—anyway, it knocked me blind. I shook my head, but I couldn't see. After a minute it hit me again, Kkkkkkkeeeeeeebbllllloooooooom!!!!!!

Sometimes, you know, when you're fighting, it's a funny thing, one lick will knock you blind, and the next one will knock you to where you can see again. I could see Big Jim right there in front of me. I was tired and my head was like a bread pan full of dry dough. I was sick. Couldn't get my breath good. My face was all numb. I never had been hit that hard. I didn't know how to fight this way. But I was in a good spot to learn. I didn't know of but one way to beat Big Jim. I knew that he was tired. He was big and he was slow. But many more of them piledrivers, and I'd be slower than that. I'd been still. Big Jim couldn't fight a running fight. I was bigger than Little Jim, by a pound or two, but not near as big as Big Jim. I had to bust loose with everything that I ever had or ever hoped to borrow. I had to beat my fists to pieces over his big red head. I didn't know why. Just had to. Jim had busted me twice in the face. He didn't know why. Just done it.

I started. I started walking, swinging, ducking, dodging. I couldn't even quit, not one split second. He wasn't used to that kind of fighting. Kids usually danced and wasted a little time. Some of them waste all of the time. I had fought that way some, it was all right then, but it wouldn't work now. I kept my fists sailing to and from Jim's head without even a letup. It was a fistic sweatshop. And with low pay. I wasn't mad at Jim. I was mad at this kind of stuff. Mad at the men that started the fight. At the kids that had been taught to yell for it. At the women that gossiped about it, and spread lies about it. I hated fighting my home-town kids. I was throwing my fists at Big Jim, but I was really fighting these crazy notions that folks get and keep in their heads.

Jim was going backwards. He didn't have time to haul off and wind up. He didn't have time to get his big feet to working. He just didn't have time to do anything. He rained big haymakers down across my back and over my head, and it was like beating me up with a fire hose. I wasn't doing so good myself. I fired away like sixty. I got in close, inside Jim's big arms, inside his reach, and fought like a wild dog drunk on slaughterhouse blood. I only wanted it to be over.

Jim was stumbling backwards trying to get balanced long enough to break my whole body with one of his fire-engine arms and fists, but it didn't work. He stumbled over a wagon tongue. He got up and fell over it again. He raised up and fell back against the front wheel, and braced his self by holding onto the spokes.

He was just standing there using one arm to sort of wave and push me aside with, but I couldn't let him stand there and get his breath and get the dust wiped out of his eyes, and get rested up. Then he would take good aim and knock my head to rolling down Main Street. I hit him as fast as I could and as hard. I really didn't think I had that much power. He caved in a couple of times, and he laid back against the wagon wheel. He propped his big shoulders up against the rim. He couldn't fall. He plowed into my face. I felt it turn numb. My whole jaw was just hanging there. It didn't know why. All at once and for no good reason that the crowd could see, Big Jim stopped fighting, he held up both hands. He quit.

I said, "Ya done?"

Jim said, "—can't go."

"Gotta 'nuff?"

"—reckon so—gotta stop."

The crowd hollered and jumped and screeched like a bunch of maniacs.

"Big Jim's hollered calf-rope!"

"He's all in an' down!"

"Downed 'im three times!"

"Whoopee!"

"Tough titty!"

Jim let his body sink down a little bit, rubbed his hair and forehead with one hand and propped his self up on the wheel with the other. He set there for a few minutes, but the crowd wouldn't let him rest. I stepped in close beside him and said once more to make double sure, "Gotta 'nuff, Red?"

"I said I had ta quit. I'll see you later—"

"I don't want it ta be later. I want it ta be settled right here once an' fer all. I don't want it ta hafta take place ever' Goddam day. You wanta go some more— —er say, let this be th' end of it fer me an' you both?"

"All right—this ends it."

Poor old Jim was fagged completely out, and so was I. "I'm—I've gotta 'nuff," he said.

And I sort of whispered in his ear, "So've I."

Men handed me dimes. Others slipped me two-bits pieces. I got over a dollar. I run down the street to where Jim was walking along. He looked bad. I said, "Ice-cream cone, Jim?"

"Naww. You git yore own self one."

"How 'bout you one, too?"

"Naww."

" 'C'mon. T' hell with all of 'em. We ain't mad at no-body—nobody but them dam guys that keeps us a-fightin' amongst ourselfs."

"Bastards."

"Cream cone, Jim?"

"Yeahhh—might."

What kind did he want.

"Strawberry," he told me, "how much ya git?"

"Lemme see, dollar, fifteen, twenty-five."

He handed me a dime. This wasn't a new thing. We done it everytime we'd fought before. Split up the money or part of it. He'd raked in a dollar and a half.

"How much ya got now?" Jim asked me.

"Dollar thirty-five."

"I gotta nickel more'n you."

" 'At's all right."

He held the new-looking buffalo nickel out in the palm of his hand and the sun hit down against it, and Jim was setting down and thinking on the ground.

"Know who I'm gonna give that exter nickel to?"

"Huh uh." I shook my head.

"Little Jim."

The fire whistle moaned out across the town like a panther moaning in a canyon. Dogs whined and run tuck-tail. The whistle kept blowing and every time it went low and high I counted the wards on my fingers so I would know which part of town to run to and see the fire.

That's a funny fire whistle. It just keeps blowing. Okemah hasn't got that many wards. It's still blowing. Fifteen. Sixteen. Seventeen times.

Looks like everybody is running up South Third Street there. Wagons. Cars. Buggies. People on horseback. I'll run with this bunch of kids coming here. "Hey! Where's th' fire at?"

"Foller us!"

"We'll show ya!"

"I don't see no flare in th' sky!"

"It ain't here in town! Look over south yonder, way out of town. See all of that red?"

"Oil field fire?"

"Yeah! Whole town!"

"Which one?"

"Cromwell! We can see it when we hit th' top of th' hill there!"

Several hundred people crowded up the hill talking and gasping, short of wind. Little bunches of men and women trotted along and talked. Horses snorted and jumped all over the road. Dogs barked at weeds and pieces of paper blowing in the dark. All along in under the locust trees people tore as hard as they could run.

"There she is!" I heard some guy talking and pointing.

"Whew! Plain as day! That's a mean-lookin' fire!" I was saying to some kids along the top of the hill.

"Seventeen miles away."

"Flames jumpin' up higher th'n th' tops of th' trees!"

"I know how high them trees is!"

"Me too. I been there a lot of times!"

"Yeah, me, too. I go a-swimmin' right in this side of there all th' time. Them Cromwell kids is really tough. Wonder how much of th' town's on fire?"

"Plenty of it," a man was saying.

"Five or six houses all at once, huh?"

"About a hunder houses all at once," the man said.

"Them old flames is really clawin' an' scratchin', ain't they?" Another man talked up.

"I know a lot of people are clawing and scratching, try-ing to get out of there."

"Them little old tar-paper shacks burn up just like paper!" an Indian kid was saying.

I walked along the hill listening to the people talk.

"Is it th' oil wells er th' houses?"

"Some of both, I would guess."

"I reckon there are already a couple of hundred people on their way from Okemah out there to help fight the fire."

"I hope there is. That's a bad blaze."

"Spreading all in through the timber there. Lots of folks losing their houses in that fire tonight."

"All of their belongings."

"But th' people!" A lady spoke out. "It's the' little kids, an' th' mothers, an' people sleepin' an' sick people in bed, an' everything else in those shacktowns. I've got a feeling that lots of people are just caught like moths in a bonfire."

I laid down on the grass and listened to folks talk for an hour or so. Then, by families, and little bunches, and one at a time, they took their last long look at the flames and turned around walking and talking and going home to bed.

I laid there by myself for about another hour. Cromwell was one of the biggest oil field towns in the whole country. I've seen the boxcar shacks stripped over with tar paper lots of times, the oak trees and the sandy land and the fishing creeks and swimming holes.

That night Okemah watched Cromwell crackle and roar and dance in the wind and fall into a flat bed of red-hot cinders.

Fire is a funny thing. It helps you and it hurts you. It builds a town up and it eats it down.

What could be left of those little old lumber houses with all of the boards as dry as powder and running full of rosin?

What could be left of a family caught asleep and choked down in the smoke? What could be left of a man that lost his family there?

I forgot all about the cold dew and went to sleep on the top rim of the hill just thinking about it.

Chapter VII

CAIN'T NO GANG WHIP US NOW

❖

A new tribe of boomchasers hit town every day, families with kids, kids looking for work and play. The gang-house kids made a law that new kids coming in couldn't have any say-so in how the gang was run, so the new kids got mad and moved a little farther on down the hill. I was sore at the old gang and went and hooked up with the new one. And trouble had got so hot between the two gangs that it looked awful dark.

"Woody, did you write that war letter, like we said last night?" The captain of our new gang was saluting and nodding to several kids as they come out for the day's playing.

I read out:

To the Members of the Old Gang:
Dear Captain and Leaders and Members:

We told you why we are fighting this war. It is because of your leaders mostly. Most of us kids is new here in town and we ain't got no other place to play except at your gang house. You made us work but you didn't let us vote or nothing like that when it was time.

The only way out is to let all of us kids own the gang house together. We was always fighting the other way. One gang against the other one. It will always be this a-way unless we change it, and you don't want us to change it, but we aim to anyhow. Both gangs has got to join up together and be one gang.

We will come to see you at eight o'clock, and if you still try to keep us split up, we will start a war.

It will not be a play war. It will take place with sling shots and flint rocks. It will be a real war and it will last till one side or the other wins out on top.

> The Boom Town Kids,
> Thug Warner, Chief.
> Woody Guthrie, Messenger.

"Sounds okay."

"Purty fair letter."

"It'll do." Our captain pulled a big dollar watch out of his overalls pocket. "Fifteen minnits, then war's on!" Then he said, "Okay, go on, read 'em th' letter."

"Yessir." I touched the bill of my corduroy hunting cap I always wore in a hard fight. I put a white handkerchief on my arm and went to the old gang house.

"Git back thar, trater!" I heard a couple of highway flints zoom past my ears.

"Quit shootin'! I'm a mess'nger! Ya c'n see this white rag on my arm!"

The door opened up and Colonel and Rex stepped out into the open. Colonel had his early morning chew of scrap tobacco pretty well limbered up, and spit three or four long squirts while he gritted his teeth and read the letter.

Rex read over Colonel's shoulder, "A real war . . . till one side or the other wins out on top." He flipped his lip with his fingers and looked up across the hill. "What chance you fools think you got 'ginst our gang house shootin' with flint-rock sling shots?"

"You'll see." I turned my corduroy hat around so the bill protected the back of my head and neck. "You guys has seen me wear this cap backwards before, haven't ya? Ya know that means fight, don't ya? I don't feel funny fightin' on th' new kids' side, 'cause, ya see, men, I jes' happen ta believe they're right an' you're wrong."

"You an' yore letter, an' yore pack of mangy curs! Boom town rats!" Colonel tore the war letter up into a hundred little pieces and slung them into my face like a quick snow.

Rex shut the door and latched it. "Okay, fellas," I heard him tell his fighters inside, "it's war! Everybody ready? Rocks easy to reach? Keep out of shootin' range of these open windows!" Then he stuck his head out the window that had been the jail and yelled at me, "You yeller-bellied quitter! Git movin'!"

I expected a rock to whack me in the back any time as I run back up the hill, but nothing hit me. "I guess you seen what happened ta our letter!" I told the captain.

"Three minnits, boys. Then she's war!" Thug turned to me and winked and said, "Round up th' men. Bring all of 'em right here in th' alley."

I whistled through my teeth and waved my hand in the air as a signal for all of the kids on our side to follow me. Everybody stood in the alley above the trash pile at the top of the hill.

"You four go with Slew." Thug pointed out the squads. "You four foller Woody through the trash pile. You three fight here in the middle with me. Git to yer places!"

"Fire away, boys!" some kid yelled out.

"Hold yer fire!" Thug bawled him out. "If we shoot one second ahead of eight o'clock, they'll go aroun' lyin' that we sneaked up on 'em, an' didn't give 'em a chance!"

"How long, Thug?"

" 'Bout ten secinds!"

"Places ever'bodyyyy! Gitt reaeeeedyyy!"

We ripped and tore and yelled on our way to our places. Three kids pulled homemade coaster wagons loaded to the hub with good shaped sling-shot rocks. The gang house was built on a flat place dug out of the hill. A patch of weeds about three foot high run along the upper part where we stood and was the only thing that would hide us from the rock fire of the fighters in the house. Kids eyed one another, patted the old trusty stocks and rubbers of their sling shots. Then all eyes centered on Thug.

He looked at his big dollar watch and hollered, "Chaaarrge!"

"Down on yer bellies!" Slew yelled out to the whole line. He was as good a fighting captain any old day as Thug. "Crawl inta these weeds! Save your rocks! Keep crawlin' down th' hill! Let's put that guy in th' lookout tower out of order first!"

Thug was standing on the north end of our line. He

drawed back his rubbers so tight they sung a bugle call in the hard wind, and whizzed a rock through the jail-house window. Inside some kid with the first punk knot of the war, hollered, "Ooohhhh!"

Trick doors the size of a cigar box slid open, first here, then there, all over the front side of the house. Hands of a dozen kids stuck from underneath and around the edges of the windows, rubbers stretched, and rocks howled through the air.

"Hot rocks! Red hot! Feel that!" Claude was cussing next to me, touching the end of his finger to an agate-looking flint that had dug the grass roots a couple of inches from his head. "Heatin' 'em on that dam stove they got inside!"

I bit my bottom lip and pasted one into the lookout nest that splintered a sliding trap door to shavings. A red-hot rock flew back out of the tower and glanced off of my shoulder blade, leaving a burnt red welt, about six inches long. Claude heard the thump and felt me roll over against him moaning.

"Looky here!" Claude pointed to the rock laying between us in the grass. "Simmerin'. Scorchin' th' grass!" He tried to pick it up and load it into his sling, but jerked his fingers back saying, "Wowie! Boy! Howdy! Hotter'n a bitch!"

I put my hand up to my mouth and ducked low and yelled back at our bunch, "Hot rocks! Watch out! Hot rocks!"

I seen Thug crawling through the weeds toward me, wearing a flop felt hat a couple of sizes too big, folded full of newspapers, for a helmet. He jumped to this feet and run through the weeds, pointing at a couple of kids in charge of our ammunition wagons. "Hey! You two! Git plenty of good firewood! Them birds'll be awful sorry they ever started this hot-rock fightin'!"

Before many minutes a new fire was crackling on the side of the hill behind our lines. The two kids lifted tin buckets from a wagon, each bucket piled brim full of round flints, and set on a two-foot sheet of corrugated roofing tin. Papers, sticks, and weed stalks blazed underneath. The fire got hotter and, before long, there was a tin bucket of the hot rocks within easy reach of every kid on our side.

"How'dya take a-holt of 'em ta shoot, without blistering yer hands?" I asked a kid when he set a bucket down between Claude and me. I could feel the heat from the bucket of rocks striking my skin from two feet away. "Red-hot mommers!"

The ammunition boy grinned at me and said, "Gotta par o' gloves on ya?"

"I ain't got none here." I dodged a foot to one side and seen a rock knock a hole the size of a horseshoe track. It buried itself a good inch in the grass roots and shot sizzling hot steam from the damp ground under the dead grass. "Kill a man if it'd hit 'im jest right."

"We got two pairs o' gloves fer our whole bunch. Thirteen of us. So, here, here's a left-handed glove. Ya gotta load an' shoot real quick, so's ya don't git burnt." He dropped a glove between me and Claude.

I pulled on the glove, fished a nice juicy roasted rock out of the bucket, slipped it into the leather of my sling shot, stretched the rubbers as far as they would go, and felt the heat of the rock burning the tips of my fingers when I let go. The shot knocked a handful of splinters off of the side of the house. "Trouble is, ya don't shoot as straight with a glove on."

"Clumsy. Yeah." He finished digging his little hole. "Think we might oughtta switch back to just plain rocks, an' shoot straighter? More of 'em?"

"We gotta use 'em hot. See, them guys in th' house

knows that we cain't crawl around on our bellies if they lay a lot of heated rocks all over this weed patch. One of these here rocks'll stay hot fifteen 'er twenty minnits. Step on 'er, lay down on one, or come down on one with your knee, boy, it'd dam near it put ya outta commish'n!"

"Halfa our kids is goin' barefooted, too." Claude squinted his eyes up and said, "See that little window up yonder in that there lookout tower? Watch it."

"Got 'er kivvered." I heard Claude's rubbers sing like a big airplane motor. "Like a bat goin' home ta roost," I laughed when the rock clattered inside the crow's-nest window.

Zuuumm. Another kid from the weeds played a nice little tune in the wind. Then Zinnng. Sswwiiissshh. Rocks flew like geese headed south in the winter, lined up in good order, spaced well apart, each man sending his shot when it come his time, and not one second before. Hot flints in the wind as heavy as .45 bullets. Thug trotted wide around our lines telling everybody, "Take yer time, boys. Don't git excited. Shoot when yer time comes." Just then his head jerked back and his hand flew up to his forehead. He dropped his sling shot to the ground and staggered across the hill.

"Thug! They cracked 'im!" I could hear one kid yelling.

"Thug. Watch out where you're goin' there! You're gettin' too close to th' fort!" Ray was Claude's little runt of a brother, the cussingest and runningest kid in our outfit. He darted from his hideout in the weeds and made a bee line for Thug. "Thug! Open yore eyes! Watch out!"

Several secret shooting doors slid open on the south side of the house, and Thug was walking blind within twenty-five foot of them. He made a face when a rock caught him on the backbone. He stood up and stiffened his muscles all over as another one glanced off the side of his neck. Blood splashed on his jaw and he covered his face and eyes with both hands.

"Take my hand!" little runty Ray was telling him. Thug ducked his head in the palms of his hands and shook the blood all over his shirt. "C'mon! Back this a-way!" Ray pulled Thug by the arms and pushed him along the ground. Ray got hit all over his body trying to get Thug back behind our lines. "Okay!" he told Thug when they'd moved out of range. "Set down over here out of th' way. I'll run over th' hill an' git a bucket o' water an' wet a rag!"

"Thug! Need some help?" I yelled up over the weeds.

"Yeah. Best kinda help you c'n gimme is ta keep on puttin' th' hot pepper inta that lookout!"

"Gotcha, Cap!" I rolled back over in the weeds and laughed at Claude and raised up on my knees long enough to lay a nice one right in through the middle of the window. "Bull's-eye!" I yelled at the rest of the kids.

I heard a loud mouth blurt out from up in the piano-box lookout. "Here's yore answer!" The ground about an inch from my nose popped open and the damp dirt sizzed against the sides of a slick one. I heard another whine in the air and felt my ankle crack and sting just above my shoe top. I tried to wiggle my foot, but it wouldn't work. A cutting pain felt like it was burning all the way up my leg to my hip bone. "Mmmooohhhhh!" I grunted and rolled through the grass, grabbing my ankle and rubbing it as hard as I could.

"Gitcha ag'in'?" Claude looked over at me. "Better stay laid down, boy, low! Leave your head stickin' up above th' weeds like that, an' them boys'll chop you down just like you was a weed!"

Little Ray trotted down the path by the chicken house, and carried the water over to where Thug was humped up holding his head in his hands. He puffed and blowed and pulled out a rag. "Here. Good 'n' wet. Hold still!"

Thug grabbed the rag away from Ray and told him, "I'll wipe off my own blood. You skat back ta yer own place an' keep sailin' 'em."

Ray didn't argue with the captain. He tore out across the hill toward his fighting partner hid in the grass and yelled what Thug had told him, "Keep 'em sailin'! Boys! Hot rocks hailin'! Give that buncha gang house crooks a good, good frailin'!"

A big heavy one whirled through the wind humming and knocked little Ray's feet up into the air, laying him flat on his back. He didn't say a word or make a sound.

"Ray went down!" Claude punched me in the ribs. "See?"

"Keep down!" I held Claude by the arms. I happened to be watching the smoke rolling out of the gang house stove pipe. "Boy, they're really throwin' th' wood ta that baby, ain't they?"

"You know, a feller could go up there and stick a hat or a gunny sack or somethin' down in th' end of that stove pipe an' really smoke them birds outta there!"

"Make their eyes so watery they couldn't see ta shoot straight!" I told him. "But that lookout . . . them kids up there'd drill ten holes in yer skull while ya was stuffin' th' pipe."

"Hey! Look!" Claude nudged me with his elbow. "What in th' dern livin' hell is that?"

"Hey, men!" I yelled back to the kids in our line. "Front door! Look!"

That front door was coming open. "Okay! Men! Charge!" The gang house captain bawled out from inside.

A big wooden barrel with a hole sawed out in front with

a square piece of heavy-duty screen wire tacked over a peek hole, lumbered out through the door. Our boys peppered more sizzlers into the open door.

"That's good, men!" Thug was yelling at us, wiping the cut places on his face and neck. "Shoot inside th' house! Not at th' barrel!" So thirteen more rocks clattered in at the door.

Inside there was cussing, sniffing, squawling as the hot rocks bounced against kids and kids stepped on the scorching floor. "Lay 'em in! Keep 'em sailin'!" Thug was trotting around back of us, wiping his face with his wet rag. "Pour it on 'em! That war tank they've invented, hell with it, we can take care of that later! Blast away! Right on through th' door!"

"Charge!" The gang house captain yelled again. A second double-size barrel waddled out into the yard with a kid walking under it. Thirteen more cooked rocks flew to roost through the door, and thirteen more cuss words, both imported and homemade, roared back at us.

"Charge! Tanks!" The captain of the shack yelled the third time, and the third barrel tank waddled out onto the battlefield.

Already the first tank had come to a bad end. The barefooted kid humped under it had stepped down on a rock hot enough to cook hot cakes on, and had squealed like a pig with his head caught in a slop bucket, turned his barrel over upside down against the house, and run like a wild man across the hill.

Tank number two had shoes on. Pretty tough. His screenwire peek hole was fixed so he could shoot his sling shot and a pair of springs pulled his screen shield shut before we had a chance to put a rock inside. We bounced all kinds of rocks off of it, but he kept coming. He come to a standstill just about five or six feet from where Claude and me

was bellied down. A rock sung out from the barrel and
stung Claude on the shoulder. Another one caught him on
the back of the leg. I got hit in the back of the hand. We
jumped up and beat it back through the weeds.

"What's a feller gonna do up aginst a dam reg'ler war
tank?" Claude was rubbing his stings and blowing through
his nose.

Tank number three had shoes on, too. He oozed up to
the two guys next in our line. Three or four hot shots spit
out from the barrel. Two more of our men jumped up out
of the weeds and come limping into the alley. Tank number
two went to work on our next two men, and they crippled
away through the weeds.

"Run fer th' alley, fellers!" Thug was ordering the men

facing the tanks. "No use ta git shot 'less ya c'n make it pay!"

The gang house roared and cheered. The whole little house shook with cries and yelps of victory. Dancing jarred the whole side of the hill. A chant floated through the walls of the fort:

> Hooray fer th' tanks!
> Hooray fer th' tanks!
> That'll teach a lesson
> To th' boom town rats!

"Whattaya wanta do? What's best?" Thug was holding the wet cloth to the back of his neck to make the blood quit dripping. "Whattaya say?"

"I say fight!"

"Fight!"

"Charge 'em!"

"Okay, boys! Here she comes! Git 'em! By God, charge!" He led the way, running fast and jumping through the weeds. "Knock hell outta them tanks, boys, no matter if ya hafta do it with yer head!"

"Ain't no tank hard as my head!" I was laughing and trying to keep up with Thug.

"I'll tear that barrel apart, stave from stave!" Claude was running faster on his club foot than any of the rest of us. He passed me up, and then went past Thug. "Clear outta my way!"

"Yyyaaaayyyyy-hoooo!"

"Circle 'em, men!"

"Knock 'em out!"

"Hit 'em with yer shoulder!"

About ten or twelve feet before he got to the tank, Claude took good aim. The last five feet he cleared in one long kick, swatting the side of the barrel with the triple sole of his crippled foot. There was a cuss from Claude and a squawl from the barrel. Then the barrel, kid, rocks, sling shot, and the whole works rolled away, and we all pointed down the hill and laughed at the kid's feet turning around and around in the open end of the rolling barrel. It busted in a hundred staves against a rock.

We charged tank number three, and in a few seconds it had got the same dose as the one before. We joked and laughed, "I'd hate ta be that tank driver!" "Boys, look at his feet flyin' around! Look like an airplane perpeller in th' end of that barrel a rollin'!"

Tank number one got straighted up again. It scooted in after us as we hid around at our old places in the weeds, and a kid in the barrel yelled out, "This is ou'rn now! We captur'd it! Don't shoot! Jist gimme a bucket of them hot rocks, boys, an' I'll roll up an' bounce 'em in at that window so fast they'll think it's snowin' hot rocks! Ha! Yo!" He got his rocks. The barrel moved up within five feet of the window and settled down to a spell of fast, steady shooting.

"Armored soldiers, charge!" We all heard the captain holler in the house. Out of the door pushed three kids with heavy overcoats and mackinaws on, thick gloves, and a broom handle apiece. We spotted all of our shots on the open door again and heard our rocks bouncing from wall to wall. Inside kids raved and foamed. The first armored man was loaded heavy and wrapped pretty good, a mackinaw coat on backwards, and the big sheep-skin collar turned up to hide his face. This made him a dangerous man. He could just walk up and push our tank over and frail the knob of the driver. Our rocks rained all around him, hitting his thick coat and he laughed because they couldn't hurt him. He took just one step toward our tank. But, right off the bat, the armored man had trouble. A good stingeree bounced and fell down inside the collar of the thick mackinaw and come to rest against the skin of his neck. Other kids had buttoned him into the coat. We last seen him airing it out down the hill, slinging a glove here, and one yonder, slinging cuss words and tears at the whole human race.

The second armored man walked within five foot of us, and our rocks bounced off of his overcoat padded with a couple of flannel blankets underneath. He was out to rush the tank, push it over, beat the driver up with a broom handle, and capture the whole shebang. As long as he was walking, he was mean and dangerous. He sneaked up out of range of the tank and stopped. The tank turned toward him. He moved around. The tank turned toward him. He moved a step or two in a circle. It looked like a bird fighting a rattlesnake. The kid in the barrel was sweating. His breathing, even ten or fifteen feet away, sounded like a steam engine. He shot a rock out with enough power to down a Jersey bull. It cracked the armored kid on the shin, and he hopped down the hill rubbing and cussing, his broom handle laying where he'd been standing. Slew chased out, tackled him while he was hopping on one foot, and marched the prisoner back of our lines.

In a jiffy or two Slew was strutting up and down, wearing the blankets, overcoat, a fur hunting cap on backwards with the earflaps down all the way around, laughing and joking with the kids in the house, and following their third armored man around and around the house. They went out of sight. Then armored unit number three backed into plain sight again around the corner with both hands up in the air. He was wrapped about six times around with gunny sacking tied around his chest, neck, belly and legs with cotton rope. Slew ordered the prisoner to keep backing up. When they got to our lines, the knots in the rope was untied, gunny sacking rolled off, and rolled back onto another one of our men.

"Hold 'er down a few minnits," I told Claude next to me. "Gonna see if I know them two kids."

I run a wide bend back of our men and come to the place where little Ray had went down in the weeds a few minutes ago. Ronald Horton, who was the best whittler in that whole end of town, had stuck right in the weeds with Ray even when the rest of us had retreated from the tanks. "How's Ray?" I ducked down in the weeds close to Ronald. "Hurt bad?"

"He bats his eyes a little," Ron told me. "But then he ain't plumb woke up yet." Ron held his hand out and I looked down and seen a steel ball-bearing the size of the end of your finger.

"You ain't aimin' ta shoot that!" I grabbed his wrist and took the steely.

"Somebody in that shack plugged Little Ray with it!" Ron got down more on his belly. "Better'd duck low, boy, might be more steel balls where that'n come from."

"I'm goin' over here ta see if I know who these two strange kids is." I was walking away, hunched down like a monkey dragging his arms in the dirt. "I'm wonderin' where so many strange kids is comin' from outta that house."

"Bring me back that bucket of water, if Thug's done with it. We need a Red Cross gal aroun' here." Ron rolled to one side to dodge a rock. "I wanta wet a rag an' put it on Little Ray's face."

"Okay." And then I circled through the weeds till I got to where Slew and his four men was strung out.

I asked one of the prisoners, "You ain't no member of th' gang here at th' house, are ya?"

"Hell, no." The kid wasn't very scared of us. "I ain't been livin' in this town but three days. Folks follers th' oil field work."

"How come ya fightin' us kids?"

"Gimme two bits. Cap'n uv that gang house."

"Two bits? You jest a soldier that goes aroun' hirin' out ta fight fer money, huh?" I looked his old dirty clothes over.

"They said they wuz th' oldist gang in this town. Best fighters." He rested back on his hands. Wasn't afraid of nobody.

"I'll tell ya one thing, stranger, whoever ya are, th' oldist bunch ain't always th' best fighters!"

"Which bunch is you guys?" he asked us.

"Most of us is new here in town," Slew spoke up.

"Who's them ginks in th' shack?" he kept asking.

"Home-town kids, biggest part," I told him. "Like me. Born an' raised here."

"How come you fightin' on th' new side then?" The prisoner give me a good looking over, with a wise tough look on his face.

"I didn't like th' old laws. Newcomers didn't have no say-so in how th' joint wuz run." I heard a couple of dozen rocks humming around over the hill. "Old bunch booted me out. So I went in with the new kids."

"Maybe ya got somethin' there, fellas." He stood back up on his feet and stuck out his hand. "Here. Put 'er there. Could you sorter count me in on yore new side?"

"Honist? Fight?" Slew doubted him a little.

He smiled at both of us. Then he looked back over our shoulders at the gang house. "I won't charge you guys no two bits."

"Did they pay ya yer two bits already?" I asked him.

"Nawww. They c'n keep their ol' two bits." He didn't take his eyes off of the gang house. He whistled the first note of a little tune and went on saying, "We'll take th' whole works."

I shook hands with the prisoner and said, "I think this man'll make us a good captain one of these days."

"Janiter by trade." The kid shook my hand and told us.

"I'm runnin' fer scavenger nex' 'lection." Slew stuck out his hand. They shook on the deal. "Gonna clean out this place from th' bottom up."

I reached inside my shirt and offered the kid a sling shot.

"Nawww. That's too sissy fer me. You guys wanta win this war in a hurry?"

"How?"

"See that ol' stumpy tree up yonder?"

"With th' few old limbs. That 'un?"

"Well, now, boys, if you was ta run home an' git a handsaw, an' if you was ta saw off that first limb stickin' up, an' that lower limb stickin' acrost, what would ya have left?"

"It'd be a stump shaped like a V!"

"A V with a handle on it makes what?" he went on.

"A big sling-shot stock!"

"Cannon!"

"Take a whole inner tube! We can git that in two minnits!"

"Some bailin' wire aroun' th' tops!"

"Just take yer pockitknife an' split yore inner tube, see? Rope th' ends onto th' forks of th' stump. Blim. Blam. Blooey!"

Slew's face lit up like the rising sun. "Rocks this big! We can shoot rocks as big as yer head!" He started backing away saying, "See you birds in about two minnits flat!"

He struck across the hill, jumped a deep clay ditch, and was almost out of sight before I could ask the new kid, "What's your name? Mine's Woody."

"My name's Andy."

"Okay, Andy. Yonder's our captain. Thug. Le's go tell 'im about th' cannon."

Thug met us, saying, "You fellers look awful friendly fer one of ya ta be a pris'ner."

"Andy's on our side now," I told Thug.

"Yeah. I changed uniforms," Andy laughed.

"Andy jus' now told us how ta saw th' extry forks off of that there old peach tree stump up yonder. Make a cannon."

"Ya figgered that up, Andy?" Thug started smiling.

"I want th' new side ta come winner on top!" Andy had a look in his eyes like a trained bulldog itching for a fight.

"Slew's comin' yonder with th' saw an' inner tube! Come on, Andy," I said. "We'll fix this cannon in about forty-four flat, an' about three good solid licks will settle this war once and fer all!"

"Pour it on their ol' sore backs! After we win, Andy, maybe you'll be capt'in in my place!" Thug went away waving his hands in the air, making all kinds of motions at our boys fighting. "Double yer fire, men! Shovel them rocks onta that house! Pepper it on 'em! Don't give 'em a chance ta breathe! Shoot th' buckets at 'em if ya run shorta rocks! Wow! Wow!" He was bending and grunting through the weeds, counting slow like a string of jail birds chopping on a logging gang. "One! Two! Wow! Wow! Fire! Load! Aim! Fire!"

The dribble of rocks doubled and got twice as loud against the house. I'd been inside that little old house through a lot of wars and a lot of hailstorms. I know how it sounded inside now. It was loud, and as mean, only a hell of a lot hotter than three years of rough weather all added up.

"Tied all right?" I asked Slew and Andy.

"My end's hot an' ready ta ramble!" Slew jerked the last knot in his rope.

"My fork's sizzlin'!"

"Gonna take two guys!" I couldn't stretch the big inner tube much by myself. I dug my heels into the hill and throwed my weight against it, heaving backwards, but it was too tough. "Go gitta couple of kids outta our lines. Put 'em ta packin' rocks."

Claude come over bringing four or five rocks about the size of brick bats.

"Keep 'em hailin'!" I was yelling back along our string of kids. I turned back to Claude and said, "Go take a look at yer bruther Ray, that's him they're pourin' water yonder in them weeds. Didn't no ice-cream cone knock 'im out, either! Hell, no! A steely ball!" I turned away from Claude and said to Andy, "Load 'er up!"

"She's loaded fer war!" Andy hollered. "Let's pull 'er back!"

Andy and me pulled the rock back in the 1000-gauge sling shot. It was all we could do to stretch it back. "One! Two! Three! Fire!" We both turned loose.

The new hum of the big rock in the air brought a big loud whoop and holler from up and down our string of kids. "Loooky! Cannon! Hooray fer th' cannon!"

Everybody watched the big rock.

A low shot. It hit the ground about fifteen feet this side of the fort. It plowed a bucketful of loose rock and dirt when it hit, and went rolling into the side of the house. A board screaked and split and the gang house got as still as a feather floating.

"What th' hell wuz that?" their captain yelled at us.

"It wasn't no steel ball!" Claude hollered from over where they was pouring water on Little Ray. "It was a cannon!"

"Cannon?" Their captain sounded a little shaky in the throat.

"Yes, cannon! Here she comes ag'in!" I hollered out.

"What kinda cannon?" another kid hollered out from in the house.

"Cannon cannon!" Andy put in.

"No fair usin' cannons!" a kid barked from the house.

"No fair usin' a dam fort! Ha!" one of ours laughed back. I waited a second or two, then asked, "Like ta give up?"

"Hell, no!"

"Okay, Andy! Load 'er up ag'in! Let's pull 'er back! One! Two! Three! Fire!"

A zoom in the air like a covey of quails, or like the wind whistling through an airplane's wings. A bigger board split into forty-nine little shavers and three or four flew in every direction. We could see the kids' feet and legs through the hole in the house. Hunkered on boxes, beer cases, rolls of gunny sacks, and old rags, fidgeting and traipsing the floor, and standing then as still as a deer.

"Surrender?" our captain yelled again.

"Hell, no!" the gang-house boss howled at us. "What's more, I'll shoot th' first man in this house that surrenders! I'll shoot you in th' back of th' head! You hired out to fight till this war is over! I'm th' boss till it's over! See!"

Claude caught all of the kids inside looking in the direction of the cannon. He sneaked up under the eaves of the house and took off his padded hat and jammed it into the end of the stove pipe.

"Sneak!" The man in the lookout tower drew aim and shot square down on top of Claude's head. We seen him stumble over against the side of the house, then slip to the ground. "That'll teach ya ta sneak!" the lookout man laughed back at all of us.

"Load 'er up, Andy! Pull 'er back! One! Two! Three! Fire!" I watched the rock leave the sling. We had pulled it back a little harder this time, and learned how to aim it better.

The lookout tower swayed in the middle, screeched like pulling a hundred rusty nails, and boards shattered apart, sailing in every direction and leaving a hole several feet around tore out of one side of the piano box.

"No more! Don't! God! Surren'er! Stop!" The lookout man jumped down off of the roof and started walking toward our men with his hands in the air, snubbing and crying, jerking his head and squawling, "I'm done! I'm done!"

He keeled over to the ground with a little groan.

"You dam right you're done!" The captain of the shack was looking out the window, putting a new rock into his sling shot. "Well!" He ducked inside and cussed at all of his kids, "Whattaya standin' there gawkin' at me for? You cowardly dam snakes! I got lots more rocks where that'n come from!"

"You kids inside! Surren'er?" I asked them again.

No sound. Only the captain sniffing and crying and breathing hard. The smoke was filling the whole house full of red-eyed, snorting and hissing kids. Claude's old hat was still in the stove pipe. Two kids took him out into the weeds where they had just woke his brother up with a bucket of water. Ray blinked when he seen them carry Claude in. "Had his hat off. Nicked 'im in th' toppa th' head," they told him.

"Load 'er up!"

Little Ray looked over our way and asked the boys, "Load what up?"

"Cannon."

"Hahhh! Funny's hell! I wuz jis' dreamin' somp'in' 'bout a cannon!"

"Run gitta bucket a water fresh fer Claude's head."

"That ain't no dream, though!" Little Ray's eyes smiled as he trotted up the hill past the cannon. "Knock 'em plumb offa th' hill! I'll be right back with Claude's water!"

"Andy! Got 'er loaded?"

"She's jam up!"

Smoke rolled out of the house. Sneezing. Coughing. Snorting of noses. Mad, fist-slinging kids. The house was darker than night inside. Cusses. Insults. Bad names. Poking. Everybody cutting back at everybody else. The captain stood on a chair inside and kept his sling shot drawed on the whole pack.

"Pull 'er back! Andy, boy!"

"She's back, bruther cap'n!"

"One! Two! Three!"

Then I said, "Wait! Listen!"

The house roared and pitched. Howls and cries of all kinds flew through the windows and cannon holes. The grumbling, scraping of lots of feet, grunting and straining, heads and tail ends whamming against the board walls. House quivering. Fists and feet thumping against kids' heads. Dragging sounds and the breaking of sticks, old boards, clubs, and clothing zipped and ripped open. A loud wrestling and clattering at the door. A heavy board cracked. All got quiet and still. The door came open.

"Don't shoot us!" The first kid stepped out with his hands in the air, waving a bloody hunk of white cloth.

"We surren'er!"

"I didn' wanta fight you guys in th' first place."

"Whatcha gon'ta do ta us?"

The kids walked out, one by one. Then every gang-house fighter was searched. They wiped their faces and pinched their toes where the hot rocks had blistered them. One by one, our captain sent them over to set down on the ground.

"What'll we do now, Thug? I don't mean about th' men. I mean about th' house here," I was saying at his shoulder.

"House? We'll fix it back better'n th' dam thing ever was. We'll have a votin' match to see who's captain."

Thug looked around at everybody. He thought a minute and then said, "Well, men. Alla my men. Stand around. What're we gonna do ta these here guys?"

"Take over!"

"No use ta hurt 'em!"

"Give 'em all a job!"

"Let ever'body have a vote. Say-so."

Thug laughed at the ground covered with rocks still cooling. "Naw. We ain't gonna beat nobody up." He kept talking along the ground. "You men wanta be in on th' new gang? If ya don't, why, git up, an' beat it ta hell offa this hill, an' stay off."

The captain of the gang house got up, rubbing dirty tears back across his face and walked up over the rim of the hill.

"Anybody else wanta leave?" Thug took a seat on the ground and leaned back up against the side of the house, putting his sling shot in his hip pocket. Every little ear and every little dirty eye and every little skint face was soaking in what Thug was saying. "Well, ain't much use ta make a big speech. Both gangs is one now. That was what we was fightin' for."

He grinned up into space and wind blew dirt across the blood drying on his face when he said, "Cain't no gang whip us now."

Chapter VIII

FIRE EXTINGUISHERS

❖

One day about three in the afternoon when I was playing out on Grandma's farm, I heard a long, lonesome whistle blow. It was the fire whistle. I'd heard it before. It always made me feel funny, wondering where fire had struck this time, whose new house it was turning into ashes. In about an hour a car pulled in off the main road in a big fog of dust, and rolled on up to the house. It was my brother, Roy, looking for me. He was with another man or two. They said it was our house.

But first they said, ". . . it's Clara."

"She's burnt awful bad . . . might not live . . . doctor come . . . said for everybody to get ready. . . ."

They throwed me into the car like a shepherd dog, and I stood up all the way home, stretching my neck in that direction. I wanted to see if I could see any sign of the fire away down the road and up on the hills. We got home and I saw a big crowd around the house. We went in. Everybody was crying and sobbing. The house smelled full of smoke. It had caught fire and the fire wagon had come. It was wet here and there, but not much.

Clara had caught fire. She had been ironing that day on an old kerosene stove, and it had blowed up. She'd filled it with coal oil and cleaned it—it was on her apron. Then it got to smoking, wouldn't burn, so she opened the wick to look in, and when the air hit the chamber full of thick oily smoke, it caught fire, blowed up all over her. She

flamed up to the ceiling, and run through the house screaming, out into the yard and around the house twice, before
she thought to roll in the tall green grass at the side of the
house and smother her clothing out. A boy from the next
house saw her and chased her down. He helped to smother
the flying blaze. He carried her into the house and laid her
on her bed. She was laying there when I walked in through
the big crowd of crying friends and kinfolks.

Papa was setting in the front room with his head in his
hands, not saying very much, just once in a while, "Poor
little Clara," and his face was wet and red from crying.

The men and women standing around would tell good
things about her.

"She cleaned my house better than I could have. . . ."

"Smart in her books, too."

"She made my little boy a shirt."

"She caught the measles by going to bed with my
daughter."

Her school teacher was there. Clara had stayed out of
school to do the ironing. Mama and her had quarreled a
little about it. Mama felt sick. Clara wanted to get ready for
her exams. The school teacher tried to cheer Mama up by
telling her how Clara led the class.

I went in and looked over where Clara was on the bed.
She was the happiest one in the bunch. She called me over
to her bed and said, "Hello there, old Mister Woodly." She
always called me that when she wanted to make me smile.

I said, "Hello."

"Everybody's cryin', Woodly. Papa's in there with his
head down crying. . . ."

"Uhh huhh."

"Mama's in the dining room, crying her eyes out."

"I know."

"Old Roy even cried, and he's just a big old tough boy."

"I seen 'im."

"Woodly, don't you cry. Promise me that you won't ever cry. It don't help, it just makes everybody feel bad, Woodly. . . ."

"I ain't a-cryin'."

"Don't do it—don't do it. I'm not bad off, Woodly; I'm gonna be up playing some more in a day or two; just burnt a little; shucks, lots of folks get hurt a little, and they don't like for everybody to go around crying about it. I'll feel good, Woodly, if you just promise that you won't cry."

"I ain't a-cryin', Sis." And I wasn't. And I didn't.

I set there on the side of her bed for a minute or two looking at her burnt, charred skin hanging in twisted, red, blistered hunks around over her body, and her face wrinkled and charred, and I felt something go away from me. But I'd told Sis I wouldn't bawl about it, so I patted her on the hand, and smiled at her, and got up and said, "You'll be all right, Sis; don't pay no 'tention to 'em. They don't know. You'll be all right."

I got up and walked out real easy, and went out on the porch. Papa got up and walked out behind me. He followed me over to a big rocking chair that was out there, and he set down and called me over to him. He took me up in his lap and told me over and over how good all of us kids was, and how mean he had treated us, and that he was going to be good to all of us. This wasn't true. He had always been good to his kids.

I was out in the yard a few minutes later and cut my hand pretty bad with an old rusty knife. It bled a lot. Scared me a little. Papa grabbed me and doctored me all up. He poured it full of iodine. That burnt. I squinched my face around. Wished he hadn't put it on there. But I'd told Clara I wouldn't ever cry no more. She laughed when the school teacher told her about it.

I walked back into the bedroom after a while with my hand all done up in a big white rag, and we talked a little more. Then Clara turned over to her school teacher and sort of smiled, and said, "I missed class today, didn't I, Mrs. Johnston?"

The teacher tried to smile and said, "Yes, but you still get the prize for being the most regular pupil. Never late, never tardy and never absent."

"But I know my lesson awful good," Clara said.

"You always know your lessons," Mrs. Johnston answered.

"Do you—think—I'll—pass?" And Clara's eyes shut like she was half asleep, dreaming about everything good. She breathed two or three long, deep breaths of air, and I saw her whole body get limber and her head fall a little to one side on her pillow.

The school teacher touched the tips of her fingers to Clara's eyes, held them closed for a minute, and said, "Yes, you'll pass."

For a while it looked like trouble had made us closer friends with everybody, had drawn our whole family together and made us know each other better. But before long it was plainer than ever that it had been the breaking point for my mother. She got worse, and lost control of the muscles in her body; and two or three times a day she would have bad spells of epileptics, first getting angry at things in the house, then arguing at every stick of furniture in every room until she would be talking so loud that all of the neighbors heard and wondered about it. I noticed that every day she would spend a minute or two staring at a lump of melted glass crystals, a door stop about as big as your two fists, and she told me, "Before our new six-room house burned down, this was a twenty-dollar cut-glass casserole. It was a present, and it was as pretty as I used to be. But now look how it looks, all crazy, all out of shape. It don't reflect pretty colors any more like it used to—it's all twisted, like everything pretty gets twisted, like my whole life is twisted. God, I want to die! I want to die! Now! Now! Now! Now!"

And she broke furniture and dishes to pieces.

She had always been one of the prettiest women in our part of the country: long black wavy hair that she combed and brushed for several minutes twice or three times a day, medium weight, round and healthy face and big dark eyes. She rode a one-hundred-dollar sidesaddle on a fast-stepping black horse; and Papa would ride along beside her on a light-foot pacing white mare. People said, "In them days your pa and ma made a mighty pretty picture," but there was a look in people's eyes like they was just talking about a pretty movie that come through town.

Mama had things on her mind. Troubles. She thought about them too much, or didn't fight back. Maybe she didn't know. Maybe she had faith in something that you can't see, something that would cause it all to come back, the house, the lands, the good furniture, the part-time maid, and the car to drive around the country. She concentrated on her worries until it got the best of her. The doctor said it would. He said for her to get up and run away, for us to take her to a place, a land somewhere where there wouldn't be any worries. She got to where she would shriek at the top of her voice and talk for hours on end about things that had went wrong. She didn't know where to put the blame. She turned on Papa. She thought he was to blame.

The whole town knew about her. She got careless with her appearance. She let herself run down. She walked around over the town, looking and thinking and crying. The doctor called it insanity and let it go at that. She lost control of the muscles of her face. Us kids would stand around in the house lost in silence, not saying a word for hours, and ashamed, somehow, to go out down the street and play with the kids, and wanting to stay there and see how long her spell would last, and if we could help her. She couldn't control her arms, nor her legs, nor the muscles in her body, and she would go into spasms and fall on the floor, and wallow around through the house, and ruin her clothes, and yell till people blocks up the street could hear her.

She would be all right for a while and treat us kids as good as any mother, and all at once it would start in—something bad and awful—something would start coming over her, and it come by slow degrees. Her face would twitch and her lips would snarl and her teeth would show. Spit would run out of her mouth and she would start out in a low grumbling voice and gradually get to talking as loud as her throat could stand it; and her arms would draw up at her sides, then behind her back, and swing in all kinds of curves. Her stomach would draw up into a hard ball, and she would double over into a terrible-looking hunch—and turn into another person, it looked like, standing right there before Roy and me.

I used to go to sleep at night and have dreams; it seemed like I dreamed the whole thing out. I dreamed that my mama was just like anybody else's. I saw her talking, smiling, and working just like other kids' mamas. But when I woke up it would still be all wrong, all twisted out of shape, helter-skelter, let go, the house not kept, the cooking skipped, the dishes not washed. Oh, Roy and me tried, I guess. We would take spells of working the house over, but I was only about nine years old, Roy about fifteen. Other things, things that kids of that age do, games they play, places they go, swimming holes, playing, running, laughing—we drifted into those things just to try to forget for a minute that a cyclone had hit our home, and how it was ripping and tearing away our family, and scattering it in the wind.

I hate a hundred times more to describe my own mother in any such words as these. You hate to read about a mother described in any such words as these. I know. I understand you. I hope you can understand me, for it must be broke down and said.

We had to move out of the house. Papa didn't have no money, so he couldn't pay the rent. He went down fighting, but he went right on down. He was a lost man in a lost world. Lost everything. Lost every cent. Owed ten times more than he could ever pay. Never could get caught up again, and get strung out down the road to success. He didn't know that. He still believed that he could start out on a peanut hull and fight his way back into the ten-thousand-dollar oil deals, the farms, and ranchlands, the royalties, and the leases, changing hands every day. I'll cut it short by saying that he fought back, but he didn't make the grade. He was down and out. No good to them. The big boys. They wouldn't back him. He went down and he stayed down.

We didn't want to send Mama away. It would be better some other place. We'd go off and start all over. So in 1923 we packed up and moved away to Oklahoma City. We moved in an old T Model truck. Didn't take much stuff along. Just wanted to get away somewhere—where we didn't know anybody, and see if that wouldn't make her better. She was better when we got gone. When we moved into an old house out there on Twenty-eighth Street, she felt better. She cooked. It tasted good. She talked. It sure sounded good. She would go for days and days and not have one of her spells. That looked like the front door of heaven to all of us. We didn't care about our selfs so much— it was her that we wanted to see get better. She swept the old house and put out washings, and she even stuck a few little flower seeds down in the ground and she watched them grow. She tied twine string up to the window screens, and the sweet peas come up and looked at her in through the window.

Papa got some fire extinguishers and tried to sell them around at the big buildings. But people thought they had enough stuff to keep them from burning down, so he didn't sell many. They was one of the best kind on the market. He had to pay for the ones that he used as samples. He sold about one a month and made about six dollars off of every sale. He walked his self to a frazzle. We didn't have but one or two sticks of furniture in the house. An old monkey heater with room for two small pots, one beans, one coffee; and we fried corn-meal mush and lived mostly on that when we could get it. Papa gave up the fire-putter-outters because he wasn't a good enough salesman, didn't look so pretty and nice. Clothes wore out. Shoes run down. He put new soles on them two or three times, but he walked them right off again. I guess he was thinking about Clara, and our first house that burned up, and all, when he would lug those fire extinguishers around over the big hot city. And the big cold town.

Papa visited a grocery store and got some food stuffs on credit. They gave him a job working in the store, helping out around, and driving the delivery wagon. He got a dollar a day. I carried milk to the store for a lady that had a cow. She gave me a dollar a week.

But Papa's hands was all busted and broken from the years of fist fighting. Now somehow or other the muscles in his fingers and hands started drawing together. They got tighter every day and pulled his fingers down so that he couldn't open his hands. He had to go to a doctor and have the little finger on his left hand cut off, because the muscles drawed it down so hard against the palm of his hand that the fingernail cut a big hole into his flesh. The rest of the fingers tightened worse than ever. They hurt him every hour of the day, but he went on working, carrying the trays and baskets and boxes and sacks of big groceries for the people that had money to buy at the store. He used to come in for his meals and fall across his bed fagged out, and

I'd see him working his hands together, and nearly crying with the pain. I would go over and rub them for him. My hands was young, and I could work with the hard, crackling muscles that had lost all of their limberness, and were losing all of their use. Big knots on every joint. Hard like gristle. His palms were long, stringy sinews, standing way up out of the skin, pulled as tight as they could be. His fist fights had done most of it. His bones broke easy. When he hit he hit hard. It shattered his fingers. And now it was the grocery-store work—it looked like that he got the worst job that he could get for hands like that. But he couldn't think much about his hands. He was a-thinking about Mama and us kids. He was going to have them cut again, the muscles cut into, cut loose, so that he could relax them, so that they wouldn't pull down any more. You could see by looking at them that they hurt awful bad.

At night he'd lie awake and call over to me, "Rub them, Woody. Rub them. I can't go to sleep unless you rub them."

I'd hold both of his hands under the covers and rub them, and feel the gristle on his knuckles, swelled up four times natural size, and the cemented muscles under each finger, drawing his fists together so tight that they would never come open again. I forgot how to cry. I wanted to cry and do a lot of it, but I wanted him to talk on and on.

So I'd keep quiet and he'd say, "What do you want to do when you grow up to be a big man?"

"Just like you, a good, good fighter."

"Not bad and mean and wrong like me—not a wrong fighter. I've always lost out—won the little street fights but always lost the big fights."

I'd rub his hands some more, and say, "You done good, Papa. You decided what was good and you fought every day for it."

We'd been in Oklahoma City almost a year when Leonard, Mama's half brother, turned up. He was a big, tall, straight, good-looking man, and always giving me nickels. He'd been in the army now, and he was an expert, among other things, at riding a motorcycle. So he'd got a good break and was given the State Agency for a Motorcycle Company which made the new, black, four-cylinder Ace.

He rode into our front yard one day on one of those black motorcycles, with a flashy side-car, all trimmed in nickel-plated steel, shining like the state capitol, and he had good news.

"Well, Charlie, I been a-hearing about your hard luck, you and Nora, and I'm gonna give you a fine job. You've always been a good office man, good hand to write letters, handle books, and take care of your business—so you're appointed the head of all of that for the Ace Motorcycle Co., in the State of Oklahoma. You'll make around two hundred dollars a month."

The world got twice as big and four times brighter. Flowers changed colors, got taller, more of them. The sun talked and the moon sung tenor. Mountains rubbed bellies, and rivers tore loose to have picnics, and the big redwood trees held dances every night. Leonard handed me nickels. Candy was good. I'd play with an orange till it got all soft and juicy, and then I'd kiss it when I was eating it. Roy smiled and told quiet jokes. Kids ganged in. I was a man of standing again. They quit jumping on me for two reasons: I'd beat the hound out of one of them, and the others wanted to ride on that motorcycle.

The big day come. Papa and Leonard got on the motorcycle and roared out down the road to go to work. A big crowd of people stood in the street and watched them. It was a pretty sight.

The next day was Sunday. We didn't have no furniture to speak of, but had been eating a little better. I don't know how far you'd have to go to find a family that was any gladder than ours that morning. We cooked and ate a nice round meal for lunch, and Papa went out and bought the ten-cent Sunday paper. He came back with a new package of cigarettes, smoking one, and when he went into the bedroom, he laid down and covered his self up, and dug into the comics part of the paper, and laughed once in a while. First he read the funnies. He read the news last.

All at once he swept all of the papers away. He jumped up and looked around sort of wild like. He had turned into the news section, page two, and something had knocked him blank like a picture show with no pictures on it. His face was just white and vacant. He got up. He walked through the house. He didn't know what to do or say. Read it to us? Keep it quiet? Forget it? Burn the paper up and throw away the ashes? Kill it? Tear the building down! Tear the whole world down! Make it over, and make it right! He couldn't talk.

Roy looked at the paper and he couldn't talk for a minute, and then Papa said, "Get your mama, get your mama!"

"Mama, come here for a minute. . . ." Roy got her to come in and set down beside Papa on the old springy bed, and Roy read sort of soft—something like this:

MOTORCYCLE ACE KILLED IN CRASH

Chicasha, Oklahoma:—Leonard Tanner, Ace Motorcyclist, was killed instantly in an accident that wrecked a car and a motorcycle at a street intersection yesterday afternoon. Tanner seemed to be driving about forty miles per hour, thus breaking the speed limit, when he crashed into the side of a 1922 model Ford sedan, fracturing his skull. Mr. Tanner was going into business for himself for the first time when disaster overtook him at the cross-roads in his life.

I walked out in the front yard and stood in the weeds in a daze, and then all at once about twenty kids chased across the street, skipping, waving at each other, and they walked up to me and quieted down.

"Hey. Where's th' motersickle ride ya said we're gonna git?" The leader of the kids was biting on a bitter stick and looking around for the big black machine.

I chewed down on my tongue. I heard others say, "We come ta ride!" "Where's th' 'cycle?" "C'mon!"

I run out through the high grass in our back yard, and when I got to the alley they followed me.

"He ain't even got no uncle what owns no motorsickle!" "Liar!" "Lyin' bastard!"

I picked up a pocketful of good rocks and sailed them into the whole crowd.

"Git outta my yard! Say gone! Who's a liar? I hadda uncle with a motorcycle! I did! But—but—"

Chapter IX

A FAST-RUNNING TRAIN WHISTLES DOWN

◆

I was standing up in the truck with my feet on our old sofa, waving both hands in the air, when we hit the city limits of Okemah. Leonard's death had tore down most of the good things growing up in Mama's mind, and we were coming home. I looked a mile away to the north and saw the old slaughter pen where wild dogs had chased me across the oat stubble. I looked to the south and seen the vacant lots I'd fought in a million times. My eyes knew everything at a glance.

When the old truck crawled past Ninth Street, Roy stuck his head out on his side of the cab and yelled, "See anything you know, Woodsaw?"

"Yeah!" I guess I sounded pretty washed out. "House where Clara burned up."

I spotted a couple of kids jumping across a plowed hill. "Hi! Matt! Nick! Hi! I'm back! See? All of us!"

"Hi! Come play with us!" "Where ya livin'?" They waved back at me.

"Old Jim Cain house! East end!"

They ducked their heads and didn't ask me to come and play with them any more.

The model-T truck almost had a runaway coming down a steep hill, frogged across the railroad tracks, and bounced me down on the bed-springs. The truck was passing the whole town by, it seemed like to me. It was passing the nice streets and the shady streets where the kids with good clothes on fought wars in the weeds and raced bareback on high-priced horses. It was headed now for the east end, where every house is a pile of junk. Rotten boards soak up good paint and just stay rotten. Rotten dogs with dishwater and grease in their hair drift across the old sandy roads. Kids with sores on their heads and snuff rotting their teeth out yip and yell and hide under mouldy floors of old crazy houses. Horses try to switch their tails hard enough to beat off the big blue flies that had got harder lickings than that when they weren't but little maggots. Dust flew up from under the truck wheels. Hot winds burned the patches of stinging weeds. But it felt good to me. It was where I come from. Okemah. To me the garbage in the alleys of my home town was better than being in a big town like Oklahoma City where my papa couldn't get a job. If he couldn't, he wasn't much use to nobody, and if he wasn't much use to nobody, we would all unload the old truck and move into the old Jim Cain house, and try to be of some use to each other.

"Okay! Work hand!" Roy backed the truck off the main highway and I piled down from the load.

"So this is it?" Mama got out of the truck and walked through the gate.

The Jim Cain house. Twenty-five years ago somebody had built it. Two rooms with a little lean-to kitchen, and a front porch. Maybe it had housed somebody, lots of people, before we come, but it never had got a coat of paint. The rain rotted the shingles and the ground rotted the bottom boards, and the middle had just warped and twisted itself into fits trying to hold together. Decaying boards of all kinds had been nailed over knotholes and cracks; tin buckets flattened out and nailed up to fight against the weather. And the whole yard was running wild with weeds and wild flowers, brittle and sticky and covered with a fine sifting dust that lifted and fell from the highway.

"This is she." Roy got out and looked over the fence. "Home sweet home."

"Gosh! Looky at them purty flowers!" I told them. "Look how thick they are. Like somebody had got out here and threw big handsful of flower seeds an' then jist let 'em grow wild!"

"Mostly hollyhocks, few zinnias," Mama said. "Just look at that honeysuckle climbing up the side of the house there."

Roy walked up onto the porch and stomped the boards with his feet. "Whole piles of dust. I never saw that much dust before."

"We can clean it out. I'm anxious to see the kitchen and the insides." Mama walked in the door.

Bedroom full of spider webs and rotten papers. Front room full of spider webs and scattered old tubs full of trash. Somehow or other I looked around and thought, maybe our old furniture would just about match this place. This is the kitchen, with the roof almost hitting me on the head and big holes with rat manure around them rotted through the floor. Dirt everywhere, a half an inch deep. It was a long, long ways across that floor.

"I smell something dead under this old soggy floor," Roy said. "I guess it's a dead cat."

"This ol' house is all haunted with dead cats," I yowled out. "I don't like this ol' dead-cat house!"

"Maybe all of the old sore-eyed cats come to this house to die." Mama laughed and took a look out the north kitchen window at the Graveyard Hill.

"All of th' glass is busted. This room. This room. This room." I was walking around with my hands stretched out dragging my fingers on th' walls. "Wallpaper all busted aloose. Dirt driftin' in through th' holes bigga 'nuff fer a dog ta trot through. What makes us hafta live in this ol' bad dead-cat house, Mama?"

"We'll get something better before long. I just know. I just know."

I carried the first load from the truck into the bedroom. "First load in our purrrty new house! Hollyhocks! Sunnyhockle vines! Buzzlin' bees! Picket fence! New wallpapers! We'll git some whitewarsh, white, white, white, whitewarsh!" I skipped all around the house. "Then we'll git some newer boards an' nail 'em up where th' ol' ones, one ones, ol' ones, ol' ones is!"

I felt the dust on the flower leaves when I walked and skipped back out to the truck.

"Give you fifty cents to help unload this thing," Roy was telling a big fat man walking along with his underwear dropped down around his belt and his chest and shoulders bare to the sun. "That all right with you?"

"Fine. Fine with me. How long you been away, say?"

"Year exactly." Roy was swinging up onto the truck and dropping a set of bedsprings over the sides.

I had another armload of loose clothes and pots and pans. "July Fourteenth is my birthday! I'm twelve! But this ol' house is seven hunderd an' twelve! We left Okemah on my birthday, an' come back on it! Today! I'm gonna plant me a big, big garden out in th' backyard! Sell cucumbers, an' green beans, an' watermelons, an' shellin' peas!"

"That's my little hard-headed brother," Roy said to the man.

"So you're our little farmer neighbor, huh?" the man asked me. "Say, where you goin' to sell all of this stuff that you grow?"

"Up in town. Lots of people."

"That's just what's got me worried." He scratched his head. "Just where you aim to find all of these people."

"Oil field folks. Gotta eat, ain't they, at grocery stores, rester'nts?"

"What few's left."

"Whattaya mean, few?"

"Have you been up on the main street today?"

"Jist got back from Oklahoma City. Ain't been on Main Street of Okemah fer a whole year!"

"You're in for a mighty big surprise."

"I c'n grow stuff."

"You're still in for a big surprise. Oil field's went dead'er than a doornail."

"I c'n work jist as much's you 'er anybody else. I know th' store men. I know th' eatin'-joint guys. They'll buy what I take 'em."

"To feed who, did you say?"

"Shucks, they's ten jillion folks runnin' aroun' needs feedin'! Streets is full of 'em. You think I don't know all of 'em? You're crazy!"

"Not so smart there, young feller," Roy cut in, "not so smart aleck."

"You hush up!"

"You can grow a garden, all right, little feller; you're as good a worker as me or your brother here, either one, any day; but when you get all of this stuff raised and everything—oh well, why should I tell you? You'll go up in town. You'll see something that will make your eyes bug out. She'd one dead town. People has ducked out just like birds in the bushes. Nobody knows where they went. Okemah's all but a ghost town."

"It ain't! It ain't!" I run past him on the porch. "You're tellin' a lie!"

I darted out the gate and headed south past piles of rotten boards called other people's houses. Mean dogs thought I was running from them and wheeled out behind my heels.

"Ain't dead! Ain't dead! Okemah ain't dead! Okemah is where I was borned at! Cain't no town die! Old Luke yonder beatin' that same little mule. I see Dad Nixon's mare had a new colt. Here she is. Good ol' Main Street. Full of people, pushing and trying to get past each other. They didn't get all of the oil out the ground. They didn't build all of this country up. They ain't done all of the work yet. They ain't run off. They're still right here working like the devil. Who said stop? Who said go? Who said let Okemah die?"

Main Street! I rounded the corner of the depot and skidded across a few cinders and my feet hit the sidewalk with me trying to come to a stop so I can look.

Main Street. Main Street? What's so quiet? Lonesome. I felt a cold bunch of goose pimples bumping up on my skin. First block nothing. All nailed up. I stood there looking at wild papers drift up and down the sidewalks and pavement like nobody tried to stop them. Snatches of grass and dirt along the concrete. A few old cars asleep, and some wired-up wagons and teams drooped along. I didn't budge from my tracks. I didn't much want to walk on up Main Street. How come them to all get up and go? It wasn't any noisier on Main Street than up on top of the Graveyard Hill.

All at once a tough-looking boy with a blue-gray shirt and pants to match, a soggy chew of tobacco punching his jaw out, somewhere in the neighborhood of fifteen, with dirty bare feet, walked out from across by the cotton yards and said, "Hey, Kid! Stranger here in town?"

"Me? I was borned here. I'm Woody Guthrie."

"I'm Coggy Sanderson. New kid comes ta town, I meet 'im. Give 'im a good welcome."

Five or six kids knocked up the dust running from in between the strings of cotton bales by the gin. "Cog's caught a new 'un!" "Le's see th' fun!" "Welcome!"

I looked around at all of them and said, "Don't none of you guys know me?"

They just stood there watching Coggy and me. Nobody said a word.

Coggy stuck his foot behind my heels and pushed me down into the dirt. I hit on my back and knocked some hide off. Then I jumped up and made a run at Coggy. He stepped to one side and took a long straight jab with his right hand and knocked my head back on my shoulders. I hit the ground again almost in the same spot. I got up and his fists met me halfway again, and I staggered about ten feet batting my eyes. He cracked one up along my temple that made my head ring like a church bell. Another left crossed over and knocked me almost down and he cut through with a right haymaker that batted me back up on my feet again. I ducked my head forward to try to cover up with my arms and he nailed a couple of uppercuts that whistled like trains right on my mouth and chin and busted my lips against my own teeth. I turned around and wiped the blood off with my hands and ducked my head with my back to him. He booted me in the rear and knocked me a yard or two, and then grabbed my shirt out of my pants and jerked the tail up over my head. I was smearing blood and sweat all over my face trying to keep out of his reach. Then he put his foot up on my hip and pushed me about fifteen feet and I plowed up the deep dirt with my face.

"Now. Yer an old-timer here." Cog turned around and dusted off his hands while the other kids laughed and danced up and down in the dust. "Welcome ta Okemah."

I pulled my shirt back down and stumbled on up the main street holding my head over and spotting the old sidewalk with big red drops of blood. I blinked my eyes and stopped over one of the squares in the sidewalk. *W.G. 1921.* And it was funny to see the blood drip from my face and blot out my own initials in the cement.

I humped along. Drug along. Maybe that old man was right. I looked in at the lobby of the Broadway Hotel. Nobody. I looked through the plate glass of Bill Bailey's pool hall. Just a long row of brass spittoons there by their self in the dark. I looked in at the Yellow Dog bootleg joint. Shelves shot all to pieces. I looked in the window of a grocery store at a clerk with glasses on playing a fast game of solitaire. Weeds and grass in the door of this garage? Always was a big bunch of men hanging around there. Nobody running in and out of the Monkey Oil Drug Store. They even took the monkey and the cage from out in front. Benches, benches, benches. All whittled and cut to pieces. Men must not have much to do but just hump around and whittle on benches. Nobody even sweeps up the shavings. Chewed matches piled along the curb. Quids of tobacco. No cars or wagons to run over you. Four dogs trotting along with their tongues dripping spit, following a little bitch that draws her back up in a knot like she's scared to death and glad of it.

I walked down the other side of the street. It was the same thing. Grass in the dirt crack along the cement. I stood there at the top of the hill in front of the court house and it looked like there never had been an Indian lose his million dollars in there. A pair of sleepy-looking mules pulled a wagon up through town. No kids. No hell-raising. No running and stumbling. No pushing and yelling. No town growing up. No houses banging with hammers all around. No guys knocked you down running late to work. No ham and stew smoke sifting through the screens of the cafés; and no wild herds of men cussing and laughing, piling up onto big oil field trucks, waving their dinner boxes back at their women. No fiddle music and yodeling floating out of the pool halls and gambling dens. No gals hustling along the streets in their short skirts and red paint. No dogs fighting in the middle of the streets. No crowds ganged around a pair of little boys banging each other's heads to pieces.

I could look in the dark plate-glass window there and see myself. Hello there, me. What the hell are you walking along so slow for? Who are you? Woody Who? Huh. You've walked along looking at yourself in these windows when they was all lit up with bright lights and hung full of pretty things for pretty women, tough stuff for tough men, fighting clothes for fighting people. And now look. Look, you lonesome outfit. Don't you seem lost flogging along there in that glass window? You thought Okemah never would quit getting better? Hah.

I felt almost as empty and vacant and drifting as the town. I wasn't thinking straight. I didn't want to go back down there and help unload that old truck and that old furniture into that old house. Ol' dead-cat house. Ol' long-gone Main Street. Who's gonna buy what I grow? I don't wanta bum nobody for my nickels. I wanta grow me a garden. But, gosh, who'd eat it? Few people driftin' across th' streets now an' then, but most of them look like they ain't eatin' very much. He's right. That ol' fat man was right. Okemah's gone an' died.

The chickens argued with the turkeys and ducks all along the sides of the road when I walked back down through the old east end toward home. I saw a light in our house that looked about like the whole world was going down with the sun. It would be the same old thing when I got home. Mama would feel worse to know the town was dead, and Roy would feel bad, too. Maybe I wouldn't tell them how Main Street really did look. Maybe I'd walk in and say something funny and try to make them all feel as good as I could. What could I think of funny?

I opened the gate trying to think up something, and when I walked in the front door I hadn't thought of it yet.

I was surprised to see Mama carrying a couple of coffee cups off of a little reading table in the middle of the front room floor, humming one of her songs. I looked all around. Beds all up. Dirt and trash cleaned out. Three straight chairs and the reading table in the front room, and our sofa back against the east wall. Roy must have just said something pretty glad, because he was rearing back in one of the chairs with his foot up on the table, looking awful well pleased on his face.

"Howdy, Mister Sawmill." Roy waved his hand in the air by the lamp. "Well, by God, I got some good news!"

"I'm hungry. What news?" I asked him as I walked past him into the kitchen where Mama was.

"I'll tell you!" Mama was frisking all around over the kitchen. "I'll—"

"I said I'd tell you!" Roy joked and tried to jump up out of his chair, but he bent backwards too far and fell all over the floor. "I'll tell—whoooaaapp!"

The three of us laughed so much for a minute that nobody could talk. But then Mama managed to get her stomach quieted down and she said, "Well, your papa has got a good new job!"

"Papa workin'?"

"For th' State!" Roy was picking up a few things that had fell out of his pockets. "Steady!"

"What?" I asked.

"Bet you couldn't guess if you tried a thousand years!" Mama went back to her work in the kitchen.

"Tell me!" I told them.

"Selling automobile licenses!" Roy said.

And Mama said, "Car tags."

I danced all around the room, singing and swaying my head. "Yay! Hay! Hooray! Really? Fer th' who? Fer th' State? Ever' day? I mean, it ain't no little few-day job?"

Roy acted like he was skipping around with me joking, "Best part is, it gives me a job, too. Writin' on a typewriter! Papa gets so much for each set of tags he sells!"

"Both gonna work? Gosh, ever' kid in Okfuskee County'll be wishin' you was their brother an' papa! Sellin' real car tags? Wheee!"

Mama didn't say anything for a little bit, and Roy and me got quieted down. He took a book from a box on the wall and set down to the table to read by the lamp. "Take my girl to th' show, now," he told us.

"You can take me, too, Mister Smart," Mama said.

"Gosh," I said, "I wuz gittin' tired of jest ol' 'taters 'n' flour gravy. Be glad we c'n have somethin' ta eat better." I took a seat in the middle of the floor. "Deeesssert!"

"I'll see to it that you boys and your papa get plenty of good meals. And with good dessert, too." Mama held her eyes squinted almost shut, picturing the good things she was talking about in the light of the lamp.

"Mama," I asked, "what does it mean when ya got a job fer th' State? Mean ya'll always have work, huh? Git money?"

"It's better than working for some one man." Mama smiled at me like she was feeling a new light coming back.

"Gosh! Will you'n Papa be like cops, er somethin'?"

"No," Roy said over his shoulder at me, "we're just agents. Just auto-license agents, and get anywhere from a half a dollar or more for writing out papers."

"Woody. You look all fussed up." Mama caught sight of my black eye and scratches. "Come over here. Is this blood in your hair?"

I said, "He wuz bigger'n me. It's quit hurtin'." Her hand tangling in with the curls of my hair felt like olden times again.

Roy and me kept quiet, him soaking up what was in the book, and me soaking up a game I was playing on the floor. I heard Mama say, "Woody, have you got that box of matches again?"

"Yes'um. Jist playin' with 'em."

"What are you playing?"

"War."

"I thought you were too big to play little games like that. You're twelve years old."

"Ya don't git too old ta play war."

"You can just have a war, then, with something else." Mama got down on the floor putting my rows of matches back in the box. "So matches are your soldiers, huh?"

"Fire soldiers." I helped her to pick them up.

"Isn't that another match lying in yonder on the front room floor?" Mama was putting the matches on their shelf and pointing back into the front room.

"I don't see none. Where 'bouts?"

I got down on my hands and knees looking around over the cracks and splinters on the boards in the floor. Mama put her hand on the back of my head and pushed my nose down close to the floor. She got down on her knees and I jerked loose and rolled over laughing. "I don't see no match."

"In that crack there? Now do you see?" She picked the match out of the crack and held it up. "See that, Fire Bug?"

"Ha! I seen it all th' time!"

"Old mean Woody. Mean to his mama. Teasing me because I'm so nervous about matches. Hhmmm. Little Woodshaver, maybe you don't know, maybe your little eyes haven't seen. Maybe you don't even halfway guess the misery that goes through my mind every time I hold a match in my hand."

"Hadn' oughtta be skeerd."

Mama got up with the match in her hand. She struck the match on the floor and held it up between her eyes and mine, and it lit up both of our thoughts and reflected in both of our minds, and struck a million memories and ten million secrets that fire had turned into ashes between us. "I know," she said. "I'm not afraid. I'm not scared of anybody or anything on the face of this earth. We're not the scared people, Woody!"

Next morning I jumped into my overhalls when the sun shot through the window. I seen a few grasshoppers and butterflies in the yard, birds out there whistling and trying to sneak kisses in our mulberry trees. It looked like a mighty pretty day. I busted out the back door and noticed the whole yard was hanging full of fresh washed, drippy clothes, shirts, sheets, overhalls, dresses. And this made me feel a whole light brighter in the morning, because this was the first time in more than two months that I had seen Mama put out a washing.

"You out of bed, Mister Mattress-Presser?" I heard her scrubbing on the rub board out under the mulberry tree. "Wash your face and hands good and clean, and then go in the kitchen and you'll find some breakfast fixed."

"I'm hungery as a great big alligater! Yom. Yom. Yom." I washed my hands and face and looked around for the eats. "Where's Roy an' Papa at?"

"Selling automobile tags!"

"Oh, gosh, I fergot. Thought I jist drempt that."

"No, you certainly didn't dream it. They're down there on the job now! Hurry and eat!"

"I'm a-gonna go down an' git me a set of tags fer my four big long red racers!"

"You can get me some for my steamboat!" she told me.

"Yacht. Yacht. Some fer my bran'-new airplane, too! Them's good scrammeled eggs!"

"Them is, or them are, or they are?"

"They wuz."

"Now that you've got a good meal under your belt, Mister Farmer," she smiled at me, "you'll find your shovel right there under the house. By the back door. Awaiting your gentle and manly touch."

I took my shovel out near the back fence and sunk it about a foot deep in the ground. That good ground looked so fine to me that I got down on my hands and knees and broke the dirt apart from the roots and little rocks. A worm about six inches long was all bloody and cut in two pieces. Both halves pulled back into the dirt. I got the half that was in the loose clod and held it in my hands. "Ya hadn't oughtta got in th' way of my shovel, worm. I'll coverya up in this here new dirt. Ya'll be all right. Ya'll heal up in a few days, then ya'll be two worms. Ya might think I'm a purty bad feller. But when ya git ta be two worms, why gosh, you'll have another worm ta run around with, an' ya know, talk to, an' stuff like that. I'll pat this dirt down on top of ya good. Too tight under there? Can ya git yer breath? I know it might hurt a little right this minnit, but ya jist wait an' see, when ya git ta be two worms, ya'll like me so good ya'll be a sendin' all th' other worms 'round ta me."

Roy come home at noon bringing some fumigators with him to smoke out the house. "Look at this guy work!" he said to me when he walked through the gate. "You've got the old back yard looking like a fresh-plowed farm!"

"Good dirt! Lotsa worms!"

"I'll say one thing, you've knocked under a pretty big spot of ground for a man your size."

"Hah! I'm workin' outta doors on my farm! Gittin' tough!"

"I made three dollars already this morning. How's that?"

"Three how much?"

"Three dollars."

"Didn't neither. Gosh!"

"What are you goshing about?"

"Be a long time 'fore I make any money on my garden."

"All of you farmers will just make barrels of money if everything goes just right."

"Yeah, I s'pose we will. But I wuz jist thinkin', ya know, mebbe ever'thing won't go jist right."

"If it don't, you can always go down and have a talk with Big Fat Nick the Banker. Just tell him you know me, and he'll hand you a big bundle of money out through the window."

"Well, I wuz rollin' it over in my mind. Ya know, 'course, I'm purty busy these days a-gittin' my land all turned under. Jist don't git much of a chance ta run inta town to th' bank. Mebbe it'd be a lot easier if ya sorta let me have th' money ahead of time, an' then 'course I could always pay ya back when my crop comes in."

"I'm not personally in the money-lending business. It would be against the law for me to lend you money without letting the governor know it."

"Th' gov'ner? Shucks, me 'n' th' gov'ner's always goin' aroun' with our hands in each other's pockits. Big friends."

"Besides, my motor boat is coming in on the train in the morning, and I'll be needing what few thousand I've got in my pockets for gasoline and oil and I'm having them send me a part of the ocean to run my boat on. So I couldn't be letting any money go out."

"No. Don't see how ya could."

"How much would it take to carry you over?"

"Nickel. Dime, mebbe."

And when Roy turned around and went walking across the yard to the back door, I saw a new dime looking up at me out of the fresh dirt.

I was shoveling as hard and fast as I could, trying to finish out my row, when Mama called, "Woody, come on here and eat! You won't be able to once we get this house full of fumigator smoke!"

"And I've got to get back to my job," Roy said.

I was humming and singing when I set down to my plate:

> Well, I gotta brother
> With purty clothes on
> Yes, I gotta brother
> With purty clothes on
> Got an inside job
> In a place up in town
> Where th' purty little girls
> Go walkin' around.

Roy kept on eating and not looking at me. He started singing a little song:

> Well, I gotta little brother
> With overhauls on
> Yes, I've gotta little brother
> With overhauls on
> He's got a job on a farm
> And he works pretty hard
> But he can't make money
> In his own back yard.

"My song's better'n yores!" I argued at him.

"Mine's the best!" he shot back at me.

"Mine!"

"Mine!"

When the fumigators got all lit up and Roy had gone on back to work, Mama took me by my hand and walked me out under the mulberry tree. I set up on the wash bench trying to look back in at the door and see the fireworks. Mama took a shovel from against the tree and started digging where I had left off.

For a few seconds I was looking at the house, then when I looked around and seen her digging in my dirt there was a feeling in me that I had been hunting for the bigger part of my life. A wide-open feeling that she was just like any other boy's mama.

"Come on here. Go to work. Let's see who can turn under the most dirt!"

"Awww. But yer jest a woman. . . ."

"I can shovel more dirt in a minute than you can in an hour, little man! Look at the worms, wouldn't you?"

"Full of 'em."

"That's a sure sign this is good soil."

"Yeah."

"Hurry up! Why, look how far you've dropped behind! I thought you said something about me being a woman!"

"I guess ya had ta be."

"I had to be. I wanted to be—so I could be your mama."

"I guess I wanted ta be yore boy!" And I suppose that when I told her this, I felt just about the closest to this stuff that is called happiness as I have ever struck. She seemed so all right. Common everyday, just like almost any other woman out working with her boy and both of them sweating, getting somewhere, getting something done.

After about half an hour we dropped our shovels on the ground and took a little rest. "How ya feel? Good?" I asked Mama.

"I feel better than I've felt in years. How do you feel?"

"Fine." I watched the fumigator fumes puffing out the cracks of the house.

"Work is a funny thing. It's the best thing in the world. It's the only religion that's worth a pinch of snuff. Good work and good rest."

"We shore been takin' lotsa medicine this mornin', ain't we?"

"We? Medicine?"

"I mean work's makin' us weller."

"Look. Look at the house. You can see the smoke boiling out between the cracks in those old thin walls."

"Yeah, man. Looks like it's on fire!"

Mama didn't say anything back.

"You know somethin', Mama? Papa feels better, an' Roy feels better, an' it makes me even feel better when all of us sees you feel better. Makes me really feel like workin'."

Mama still didn't say anything back. Just set there with her elbow on her knee and her chin in her hand, looking. Thinking. Rolling things over in her mind while the smoke rolled out through the cracks.

"Harder I work now, better I'm gonna like it. Boy, yip, yip, I feel like really workin' hard an' havin' me a big new garden all growed up out here this evenin' when Papa an' Roy comes home. I bet they'd be su'prised ta see me out here pickin' stuff an' sellin' it, an' all."

Mama rubbed a fly or two off of her arm and kept quiet.

"You know how it is, I guess. After all, you're th' only mama we got. We cain't jist go down ta no store an' buy us a new mama. You're th' mama in this whole family."

No answer from Mama. She had her eyes on the house. Looking and opening her eyes wider, and her mouth and face changing into a stare that was still and cold and stiff. I didn't see her move a single part of her face.

Then I saw her raise up to her knees, staring like she was hypnotized at the house with the smoke leaking out of it.

I let the spade drop out of my hand and my heart felt like a cake of ice inside of me. Fire and flames seemed to crawl across the picture screen of my mind, and everything was scorched out, except the sight I was seeing in front of me. I was popping out with smoky sweat and my eyes saw hopes piled like silky pictures on celluloid film curling away into some kind of a fiery hole that turns everything into nothing.

Mama got up and started taking long steps in the direction of the house. I tore out in front of her and tried to hold her back. She was walking with a strength and a power that I had seen her use before in her bad spells, and an ordinary person's strength wasn't any sort of a match for hers. I held out my hands to try to stop her, and she brushed me over against the fence like I was a paper doll she had played with and was now tossing into the wind.

I sailed across the yard, left down the alley, right along a dirt road three blocks, running with every ounce that my lungs could pull and my heart could pound and my blood could give me. A pain hit me low down in the belly, but I speeded up just that much faster. My eyes didn't see the dogs nor the hungry people nor the shabby shacks along the East End Road, nor my nose didn't smell the dead horse rotting in the weeds, nor my feet didn't ache and hurt getting hit against the rocks that had bruised a thousand other kids running near as wild as me down that same old road before. That look. That long-lost, faraway, fiery, smoky glare that cracked in her eyes and reflected on the sweat on her face. That look. That same old look. Houses and barns and vacant lots and trees whizzed past me like I was riding down the road on a runaway motorcycle.

I blammed into Papa's office, knocking people out of my way with their papers saying something about somebody needing some license tags. I shoved across Papa's desk, and puffed and gasped for air, saying, "Run! Quick! Mama!"

Papa and Roy left their typewriters with papers rolled into them and people looking sideways at one another. They busted out the door and met Warren just starting in to buy Grandma some car tags.

"Take that kid back home with you! Keep him tonight!" Papa ran up the street to the truck. Roy yelled back over his shoulder, "Get Grandma! Come back in the morning!"

Warren took me up into the seat of his car and I was screaming, "I wanta go home where Mama is! I don't wanta stay all night with you! You ol' cat-killer!"

And it was cussing and mad that Warren drove me the

seven miles out to Grandma's, and crying and bawling that I walked into their house.

That night at Grandma's I laid awake and watched a hundred moving pictures go through my mind, but I didn't have to make them up, because they was snapping and cracking and flashing all around me. The crickets chirped like they was calling for their lovers, but halfway scared their own voice would cause them to get stepped on. The frogs down around the banks of the pond seemed to laugh. I laid there in a puddle of cold late-summer sweat, and my body cramped in knots and I didn't move an arm or a leg. I rolled my head on my pillow once to look out the night window, and beyond a turtle dove hay meadow I could see a yellow prairie fire that had broke loose across a slope of dry grass, five or six miles away to the south; and I was glad it wasn't to the east, toward home. I guess Grandpa is asleep and getting ready to go to work with Lawrence in the morning, cutting wood on the hill. Warren is asleep, too; I can hear him snoring here beside me, worried mostly about his own self. But I know that in the next bedroom Grandma, too, like me, is laying there with her eyes stinging and her face salty and wet, having crazy dreams that float across the night winds and twist and turn and roll and coil and jump and fight and burn themselves out, like the meadow fire over across the wind yonder, like the dry hay.

Warren drove Grandma and me back to town when morning came. We walked through the yard gate and in at the back door of the old Jim Cain house. Windows smashed and glass laughing in the sun on the floor. Kitchen upside down and dishes and pots and pans slung across the room and floor. Front room, a handful of torn books and old letters, chairs laying over on their sides, and a coal-oil lamp smashed where the oil soaked the wallpaper and then run down the north wall. Little bedroom, both beds full of wild strewn clothes that almost looked like people that had died in their dreams. Warren and me followed Grandma from the bedroom, through the front room, and back into the kitchen. I didn't hear anybody say a single word. The second-handed oil stove was smashed in the corner and the new kerosene smelled strong, soaking in the floors and walls. Charred wallpaper run up the wall behind the stove, some of the boards black and smoked and scorched with flames that had been beat out with a wet gunny sack at my feet.

Roy walked in from the back porch and I noticed that he was all dirty, messy, and needed a shave; his new shirt and pants tore in several places; his hair was in his eyes and his eyes had a beat-down look. He let his eyes drift around the room without looking us in the face, and then he looked at the oil stove and said, "Oil stove exploded. Papa's in the hospital. Pretty bad burns."

" 'S funny," I said, "I was afraid yesterday when ya started ta fumigate th' house. 'Fraid this coal oil would ketch afire. So I took th' oil tank off of th' stove an' set it out in th' back yard under th' mulberry tree. I cain't figger out how it blowed up." I was looking at the oil tank piled in the corner with the oil soaked out across the floor. "Jist cain't see how."

"Shut you mouth!" Roy doubled up both fists and raved back at me, and his eyes blazed wildfire. "You little rat!"

I set down close to the stove against the wall and heard Grandma say, "Where—how is Nora?"

Warren was listening, swallowing hard.

"She's on the westbound passenger train." Roy slid down on the floor beside me and fumbled with a burner on the wreck of a stove. "On her way to the insane asylum."

Nobody said very much.

Away off somewheres we heard a long gone howl of a fast-running train whistling down.

Chapter X

THE JUNKING SACK

❖

With Mama gone, Papa went to West Texas to live with my aunt in Pampa till he could get over his burns. Roy and me hung on for a while and lived in the old Jim Cain house. When daylight come to our house and I woke up out of bed, there wasn't no warm breakfast, and there wasn't a clean bed. It was a dirty house. A house that had old dirty clothes throwed around here and yonder, or a tub of water, soap suds and soppy pants on the bench out in back, that had set there now for two or three weeks, waiting for Roy or me to wash them. I don't know. That house, that old, old, big mulberry tree, those dried-up flowers in the front yard, the kitchen so sour and lonesome—it seemed like everything in the world echoed in there, but you couldn't hear it. You could stand still and cock your ear to one side, but you couldn't hear anything. I know how I felt about it, I only had one feeling toward it: I wanted to get the hell out of it when daytime come and it got light outside.

Then Roy stumbled onto a job at the Okemah Wholesale House. The day we moved out of the Jim Cain house, I helped him haul and store all of our belongings in the hay-loft of the rottenest barn in town. He asked me to come across town and stay with him in his new three-dollar room, but I told him "no," that I wanted to shuck out on my own.

Every day I combed the alleys and the dump grounds with my gunny sack blistering my shoulders, digging like a mole into everybody's trash heaps to see if I couldn't make a little something out of nothing. Ten or fifteen miles walking a day, with my sack weighing up to fifty pounds, to weigh in and sell my load to the city junk man along about sundown.

The refuse heaps and trash piles didn't turn my stomach. I was baptized into ten or fifteen different junking crews by getting splashed, kicked, squirted on, throwed down, heaped over and covered under in every earthly article of garbage and junk known to man. I'd come back to the gang house laughing and scare the kids with wild tales about the half-kids and half-rats, half-coyotes, and half-men.

When I told Roy good-bye I had brought an old quilt and blanket over to the gang-house shack and made it my hotel.

It had rained and turned hot, rained and turned hot, so many times lately that the whole gang house hill simmered and steamed. The weeds turned into a jungle where spiders wolfed the ladybugs and wasps dive-bombed the spiders. A world where the new babies of one came from the dead bodies of others. The sun was hot as fire on the henhouse, and the chicken manure had carried its lice across the hill in the rains. A smothery vapor covered the place with the smell and the poison of cankering wood.

The waters oozed from the hill above and kept the floor of the house soggy and wet. My quilt and blanket soured and molded. I woke up every morning in my bed on the floor, feeling as if the matter that rotted in the night had soaked into my brain and filled my body with a blind fever. The sun, fermenting the dew in the piles of trash, put out some kind of a gas that made me laugh and lay down in the path in the sun and dream about dying and moldering.

When the kids had gone home on these nights, I'd lay on my back on my damp blanket and whirl away to a land of bloody, cutthroat dreams, and fight and wallow in corruption and slime all night, chased and trampled under the feet of demons and monsters, wound up in the coils of a boa constrictor crawling in the city cesspool. I'd wake up bug-eyed. The sun coming up brought the smell from the weeds again, and the vapor from the hill choked me down.

For several mornings now I'd been too weak to hang my blankets out to air and sun while I was junking. My first thought every morning was to crawl out on the side of the hill and lay in the sun in the path. I felt the rays cut through my whole body and I knew the sun was good medicine. One morning I was so crazy and dizzy I crawled to the top of the hill and pulled myself a block to the school grounds. I flopped down on a bench by a fountain. The world was hot and I was cold. Then the world turned cold and I was hot. I used my gunny sack for a pillow. It felt like lightning was cracking through my head. My teeth chattered.

The next thing I knew somebody was shaking my shoulder and saying, "Hey, Woody, wake up! What's the matter?"

I looked up and saw Roy. "Howdy, brother. How come you ta be passin' by here?"

"How come you piled up here sick?" Roy asked me.

"I ain't sick! Little woozie."

"Where are you living these days? Hanging out up at that little old gang house of a night?"

"I be all right."

"What's this old dirty sack under you head?"

"Junkin' sack."

"Still crawling through the dumps, huh? Listen, young sprout, I've got a good room. You know where Mrs. Hutchinson lives over there in that big white two-story house yonder? You go over there. I'll send a doctor up to look you over pretty quick. See you about six o'clock. Get up! Here's the key!"

"I c'n take care of my own self!"

"Listen, brat, I mean brother! Take this key."

"Go onta work!" I got up and pushed Roy down the sidewalk, "Shore, I'll go sleep in yer room. Send me yer good docter! An' go onta work!" I was pushing Roy in the back and laughing at the same time. Then I got so dizzy I caved in, and Roy caught me and held me up, and give me a little shove to get me started off toward his room.

I come to the big two-story white house and clumb the stairs to room number ten. My junking sack was soaking wet with the morning dew, so I struck a match to a gas heating stove and set down in the floor, spreading out the sack to dry. I felt a cold chill crawling over me. I took off my shirt on the floor and let the warmth from the gas heater bake me. It felt so good I stretched out in front of it, put my hands between my knees and shivered a little while, and laid there chilling and wet with dew, getting warm through my overhalls, and thinking about other times I'd been in hard spots and somebody had always come along. Junk was bringing more money. I guess they want brass. Copper's good. Aluminum's what's best. That old junk man's a Jew. Some folks around town don't like Jews 'cause they're Jews, Niggers 'cause they're black; me 'cause I'm a dam little junk boy, but I don't care 'bout all of that. This old floor's good an' warm. What's that? Fire whistle? O God, no! Not a fire whistle! Not no fire whistle! Fire whistles has run me nuts! Fire! Fire! Put it out! Fire!

"Get up! Wake up! Move!" A lady rolled me over out of the way; then she trampled and danced up and down in front of the stove. Smoke all over the place. She drew a pitcher of water from the sink, poured it along in front of the stove, and a big cloud of white smoke shot up and filled the whole room. "Wake up! You'll burn up! You'll blister!"

You'll blister. You'll blister. You will blister. Wait and

see. Hot tar and hot feathers and you'll blister. Kloo Kluxx Klam. Wake up. Wake up an' crawl on your belly.

The lady yelled at me. She took me by the hand and pulled me up off of the floor. I walked to the bed and crawled in between the covers with my overhalls on. "Looks like you'd at least take off your overhauls, boy! What do you mean spreading that old greasy sack out here on the floor in front of this fire, and then going off to sleep any such a way? You ought to have your little hind end blistered!"

You low-down lousy sneakin' Kluck Klucks! Git th' hell outta my house! Ol' ghosty robes! Wound up in a windin' sheet! Windin' sheet! Windin' sheet!

The lady pushed her hair back out of her face and walked to the edge of the bed. "Why, you're having a fever!" She touched her hand to my forehead. "Your face is simply blistered!"

Tar me an' feather me! I hate ya! Hoodlum . . . .

I made a dive for her and missed, and went down to the floor. I scrambled around trying to get up. Everything blacked out. . . .

"Feel better now? This nice cool rag on your forehead?" She smiled and looked into my face like my mama used to look at me a long, long time ago. "It burned a hole or two in my old rug, but you'll have to go out and hunt in the alleys and find you a brand-new gunny sack. Don't worry about my old rug. Do you know when I first bursted into this room and found the smoke and the sack blazing on the floor, and I saw you there asleep on the floor, I wasn't mad. Nooo. Here. Eat this oatmeal. And drink this warm milk down. Good? Sugar enough? I took your overhalls off. You ought to wear some underwear, little tousle-head."

I looked out through the screened window across the old school grounds and thought of a million friends and a million faces, a million brawls and fights, and a whole town full of just as good a people as you'll ever find anywhere. The lady still knelt down at the side of my bed.

She put her hand on my head and said, "Go to sleep?"

"Back of my head. Hurts. Jumps."

"You roll over and lay on your tummy. That's a good boy. I'll rub the back of your head for you. Does this feel good?" She rubbed and petted, and rubbed and petted.

"Is it rainin'?" I snuggled down under the covers deeper.

"Why, no. Why?" She patted the back of my neck.

"I'm all wet an' cold."

"You're dreaming!" She rubbed and petted some more.

"Is this train runnin' away?"

"Go to sleep."

"Ever'thing's funny, ain't it? I c'n hear it rainin'."

"Does this rubbing feel better?" She patted me again.

" 'At's better."

"Quit your talking and go to sleep."

" 'At's better."

"Want anything?"

"Yup."

"What?"

"New junkin' sack."

Chapter XI

BOY IN SEARCH OF SOMETHING

❖

I was thirteen when I went to live with a family of thirteen people in a two-room house. I was going on fifteen when I got me a job shining shoes, washing spittoons, meeting the night trains in a hotel up in town. I was a little past sixteen when I first hit the highway and took a trip down around the Gulf of Mexico, hoeing figs, watering strawberries, picking mustang grapes, helping carpenters and well drillers, cleaning yards, chopping weeds, and moving garbage cans. Then I got tired of being a stranger, so I stuck my thumb in the air again and landed back in the old home town, Okemah.

I found me a job at five dollars a week in a push-button service station. I got a letter twice a week as regular as a clock from Papa out on the Texas plains. I told him everything I thought and he told me everything he was hoping. Then, one day, he wrote that his burns had healed up enough for him to go to work, and he'd got him a job managing a whole block of property in Pampa, Texas.

In three days I was standing in the little office shaking his hand, talking old times, and all about my job with him as general handyman around the property. I was just past my seventeenth birthday.

Pampa was a Texas oil boom town and wilder than a woodchuck. It traveled fast and traveled light. Oil boom towns come that way and they go that way. Houses aren't built to last very long, because the big majority of the working folks will walk into town, work like a horse for a while, put the oil wells in, drill the holes down fifteen thousand feet, bring in the black gushers, case off the hot flow, cap the high pressure, put valves on them, get the oil to flowing steady and easy into the rich people's tanks, and then the field, a big thick forest of drilling rigs, just sets there pumping oil all over the world to run limousines, factories, war machines, and fast trains. There's not much work left to do in the oil fields once the boys have developed it by hard work and hot sweat, and so they move along down the road, as broke, as down and out, as tough, as hard hitting, as hard working, as the day they come to town.

The town was mainly a scattering of little old shacks. They was built to last a few months; built out of old rotten boards, flattened oil barrels, buckets, sheet iron, crates of all kinds, and gunny sacks. Some were lucky enough to have a floor, others just the dusty old dirt. The rent was high on these shacks. A common price was five dollars a week for a three roomer. That meant one room cut three ways.

Women folks worked hard trying to make their little shacks look like something, but with the dry weather, hot sun, high wind, and the dust piling in, they could clean and wipe and mop and scrub their shanty twenty-four hours a day and never get caught up. Their floors always was warped and crooked. The old linoleum rugs had raised six families and put eighteen kids through school. The walls were made out thin boards, one inch thick and covered over with whatever the women could nail on them: old blue wallpaper, wrapping paper from the boxcars along the tracks, once in a while a layer of beaver board painted with whitewash, or some haywire color ranging from deep-sea blue through all of the midnight blues to a blazing red that would drive a Jersey bull crazy. Each family usually nailed together some sort of a chair or bench out of junk materials and left it in the house when they moved away, so that after an even thirty-five cents worth of hand-made wash benches, or an old chair, or table had been left behind, the landlord hired a sign painter to write the word "Furnished" on the "For Rent" sign.

Lots of folks in the oil fields come in from the country. They heard about the high wages and the great number of jobs. The old farm has dried up and blowed away. The chickens are gone dry and the cows have quit laying. The wind has got high and the sky is black with dust. Blow flies are taking the place over, licking off the milk pails, falling into the cream, getting hung up in the molasses. Besides that, they ain't no more work to do on the farm; can't buy no seed for planting, nor feed for the horses and cows.

Hell, I can work. I like to work. Born working. Raised working. Married working. What kind of work do they want done in this oil boom town? If work is what they want done, plowing or digging or carrying something, I can do that. If they want a cellar dug or some dirt moved, I can do that. If they want some rock hauled and some cement shoveled, I can do that. If they want some boards sawed and some nails drove, hell's bells, I can do that. If they want a tank truck drove, I can do that, too, or if they want some steel towers bolted up, give me a day's practice, and I can do that. I could get pretty good at it. And I wouldn't quit. Even if I could, I wouldn't want to.

Hell with this whole dam layout! I'm a-gonna git up an' hump up, an' walk off of this cussed dam place! Farm, toodle-do. Here I come, oil town! Hundred mile down that big wide road.

Papa's new job was the handling of an old ramshackle rooming house, right on the main street, built out of corrugated iron on a framework of two by four scantlings, and cut up into little stalls called rooms. You couldn't hardly lay down to sleep in your room without your head scraping the wall at one end and your feet sticking out in the hall. You could hear what was taking place in the six stalls all around you, and it was a pretty hard matter to keep your mind on your own business for trying to listen in on the rooms on each side of you. The beds made so much racket it sounded like some kind of a factory screaking. But there was a rhythm and a song in the scraping and the oil boom chasers called it "the rusty bedspring blues." I got so good at this particular song that I could rent a flop in a boom-town hotel, and go to my room and just set there and listen a minute, and then guess within three pounds of the other roomers' weight, just by the squeek of the springs.

My dad run one of these houses. He tended to a block of property where girls rented rooms: the girls that follow the booms. They'd come in to look for work, and they'd hit the rooming house so as to set up a home, and straighten out their citizenship papers with the pimps, the McGimps, the other girls, and the old satchels that acted as mothers of the flock. One of Papa's boarders, for instance, was an old lady with gray hair dyed as red as the side of a brick barn, and her name was Old Rose. Only there never was a rose that old. She'd been in all of the booms, Smackover, Arkansas, Cromwell, Oklahoma, Bristow, Drumright, Sand Springs, Bow Legs, and on to East Texas, Kilgore, Longview, Henderson, then west to Burke-Burnett, Wichita Falls, Electra, and farther west, out on the windy plains, around Panhandle, Amarillo, and Pampa. It was a thriving business, boom chasing; and this old rusty sheet-iron rooming house could have been in any of these towns, and so could Old Rose.

Come to think of it, I've been in every one of these

towns. I might of slept in this old rooming house a dozen times around over the country, and it was awful high-priced sleeping. I might of paid out a lot of them sheets of iron. And the girls that stayed here, they might of paid out a truck load or two of them two by fours. The usual price is about five dollars a week. If a girl is working, that is not so much, but if she's out of job, it's a lot of money. She knows that the officers might grab her by the arm any time for "Vag," for it's a jail house offense to be a-loafing in a boom town.

I remember one little girl that come in from the country. She blowed into town one day from some thriving little church community, and she wasn't what you'd call a good-looking girl, but she wasn't ugly. Sort of plump, but she wasn't a bit fat. She'd worked hard at washing milk buckets, doing housework, washing the family's clothes. She could milk an old Jersey cow. Her face and her hands looked like work. Her room in the rooming house wasn't big enough to spank a cat in. She moved in, straightened it up, and gave it a sweeping and a dusting that is headline news in a oil boom town. Then she washed the old faded window curtains, changed the bed and dresser around every way to see how it looked best, and tacked pretty pictures on her wall.

She didn't have any extra clothes with her. I wondered why; something went haywire at home, maybe. Maybe she left home in a hurry. Guess that's what she done. She just thought she'd come into town and go to work in a café or hotel or in somebody's house, and then when she got her first week's pay, she'd get what things she needed, and add to them as she went along. She wasn't a town girl. You could tell that. Everything about her looked like the farm, and the outhouses and barns, and the pastures, and wide-open spaces, and the cattle grazing, and the herds of sheep, or like looking out across the plains and seeing a hard-working cowhand rolling down across the country on a fat bay mare. Some way or another, her way of talking and the words that she knew just didn't seem to connect up with this oil-smeared, gasoline-soaked, whiskey-flavored, wild and fast-moving boom town. No cattle; no milk buckets. Nothing about raising an early garden, or putting on a big-brim straw hat and driving a speckled mare and a black hoss to a hay rake. I guess she was just a little bit lost. The other girls flocked in to see her, walking on high-heel shoes, with a bottle or two of fingernail paint, some cigarets, different flavors of lipstick, and a half a pint of pale corn whiskey. They jabbered and talked a blue streak. They giggled and snickered, and hollered, Oh, Kid, this, and Oh, Kid, that. Everything they said was funny and new, and she would set, listen, soak it all in, but she didn't talk much. She didn't know much to talk about. Didn't smoke, and didn't know how to use that fingernail paint. Hadn't seen the picture show lately. Once in a great while she'd get up and walk across the floor and straighten up something that had got pushed over, or remark that she had to scrape the grease and dirt off of her two-burner hot plate.

When the girls had gone off to their rooms, she'd take a good look around over her room to see if it was neat enough, and if it was she'd sometimes take a little walk down the old dark hall, out into the back yard that stood about ankle deep in junk and garbage. You'd run onto her every once in a while out there. You'd catch her with a handful of old sacks and papers, carrying them in a high north wind out to the alley to put them in the trash box. Sometimes she'd smile at you and say, "I just thought I'd pick up a few of these papers."

She's thinking it's over a week now since I paid my room rent. Wonder what the landlord will do? Wonder if I'd grab the broom and pitch in and sweep out the hall, and go and carry a few buckets of water and mop it, wonder if he'd care? Maybe it'll get under his skin, and he might give me a job of keeping it up.

She'd come to the office where Papa was, and she'd set down and turn through the magazines and papers, looking at all of the pictures. She liked to look at pictures of the mountains. Sometimes she'd look at a picture for two or three minutes. And then she'd say, "I'd like to be there."

She'd stand up and look out the window. The building was just one story. It was all right down on the ground. The sidewalk went past the door, and all of the oil field boys would crowd up and down the street, talking, staggering, in their work clothes, khaki pants and shirts smeared with crude oil, blue overhalls soaked with grease and covered with thick dust, salted and flavored with sweat. They made good money. The drillers drawed as high as twenty-five dollars a day. Boy, that was a lot of money. They wasted most of it. Whooped it off on slot machines and whiskey. Fights broke out every few minutes up and down the street. She could see the mob gang up. She could see a couple of heads bobbing up and down and going around in the middle. Pretty soon everybody would be beating the hound out of everybody else, choked, wet with blood and hot sweat. You could hear them breathing and cussing a block away. Then the fight would bust up and the men would come down the sidewalk, their clothes tore all to pieces, hats lost, hair full of mud and dirt, whiskey broke.

She was new in town, I knew that because she held back a little when a fist fight broke out. She just didn't much want to jump into that crazy river of oil field fist fighters. She might have liked it if she'd known the people better, but she didn't know anybody well enough to call them friend. It was plumb dangerous for a strange girl even to go from one joint to the other looking for a job, so she waited till her money was all gone and her room rent was about two weeks behind. Then she went to a few places and asked for work. They didn't need her. She wasn't experienced. She went back several times. They still didn't need her. She was flat.

She got acquainted with a one-eyed girl. The one-eyed girl introduced her to a truck driver. The truck driver said he might find her a job. He would come in every day from the fields with a yarn about a job that he was trying to get her. The first few days they usually met in the office or hall and he would tell her all about it. But he'd have to wait another day or two to see for sure. The day come along when they didn't happen to meet in the office or hall, so he had to go to her room to tell her about something else that looked like a job for her. He made this a regular habit for about a week and she turned up at the office one day with seven dollars and fifty cents to pay on her rent. This was a big surprise to my dad, so he got curious. In fact he stayed curious. So he thought he would do a little eaves-dropping around over the hotel to see what was going on. One day he saw her go off uptown with the one-eyed girl. In about an hour they come back with their hats in their hands, brushing their hair back out of their eyes, talking and saying that they was awful tired. The one-eyed girl took her down the hall and they went into a room. Papa tiptoed down to the door and looked through the keyhole. He could see everything that was going on. The one-eyed girl took out a teaspoon and put something in it. He knew then what it was. The girl struck a match and held it under the spoon, and heated it real hot. That's one way of fixing a shot of dope—morphine. Sometimes you use a needle, sometimes you sniff it, sometimes you eat it, sometimes you drink it. The main idea seems to be any old way to get it into your system.

He pushed the door open and run in while they was trying to take the dope. He grabbed the works away from the one-eyed girl and bawled both of them out good and proper, telling how terrible it was to get on the stuff. They cried and bawled and talked like a couple of little babies, and swore up and down that neither of them used it regular, they didn't have the habit. They just bought it for fun. They didn't know. The girl from the country never tasted it. She swore that she never would. They all talked and cried some more and promised never to touch the junk again.

But I stayed around there. I noticed how that girl with the one eye would come and go, and come and go, feeling one minute like she was the queen of the whole wide world, all smiles, laughing and joking; and then she'd go and come again, and she'd be all fagged out, tired and footsore, broke, hungry, lonesome, blue, and her eyes sunk way back, her hair tangled. This kept up after Dad took away her morphine apparatus, and after all of her big promises to lay off the stuff. The farm girl never showed the least signs of being on dope, but the truck driver brought a little bottle of whiskey along with him after he got to knowing her better, and through the partition I heard them drinking.

Mister truck driver ate his meals in a little greasy wall restaurant right next door. He introduced her to the boss of the joint, a man with TB, about six foot four inches tall, skinny and humped as a spider. He had studied to be a preacher, read most of the books on the subject, and was bootlegging liquor in his eating place.

He gave the girl a job in the kitchen of this place, where she done all of her work, his work, and run over two or three swampers and helpers trying to keep the place from falling down, and all of the boards on the roof, and all of the meals cooked and served. It was so hot I don't see how she stood it. I more or less went into and out of these places because Papa was looking after them. Personally, I never have been able to figure out how anybody ate, slept, or lived around in this whole firetrap.

He give her one dollar a day to hang around there. He didn't call it a job, so he didn't have to pay her much. But he said if she wanted to hang around, he'd pitch her a dollar every night just to show her that his heart was on the right side.

The whole rooming house had been added onto a little at a time by moving old odd shacks onto the lot, till it had about fifty stalls. None of them were ever painted. Like a bunch of match-boxes strung along; and some of them housed whole families with gangs of kids, and others sheltered several men in one room where there was fifteen or twenty cots in a one-bed space, dirty, beg-buggy, slick, slimy, and otherwise not fit to live in or around.

It was my job to show folks to their rooms, and show the rooms to the people, and try to convince them that they was really rooms. One day when I was out bungling around with a mattress and a set of rusty bed springs, I chanced to hear a couple having more or less of a two-cylinder celebration in one of the rooms. I knew that the room was supposed to be vacant. Nobody was registered in there. The door was shut and the thumb-latch was throwed. I had a sneaking idea of what was up.

Through a knothole in the shack, I saw a half a pint of hot whiskey setting up on the old dirty dresser, and it was about eighty-nine percent drunk up. The bed didn't have a sheet on it, or any kind of covers, just the bare mattress. It was a faded pink mixed with a running brownish green, trimmed around with a bed-bug tan color soaked into the cloth. The TB boss of the little café and bootleg store was setting on the side of the bed with the country girl. Both of them had had a few out of the bottle. He was talking to her, and what he said had been said too often before by other men like him to put into quotes. You've had lots of trouble lately, haven't you? You look kinda sad. Even when you smile or laugh, it stays in your eyes. It never goes away. I've noticed it a lot since you've been around me lately. You're a good girl. I've read lots of books and studied about people. I know.

She said she liked to work.

He told her that she had a pretty face.

You got pretty eyes, even if they are sad. They're blue. Sad and blue.

She said she wasn't feeling so bad now since she had a job.

He said he wished that he could pay her more than a dollar. He said she made a good hand. He didn't feel like working very hard. It was too hot for him in his condition with the low roof.

I could hear him breathe and could hear the rattling in his lungs. His face was pale and when he rubbed his hand over his chin the red blood would show through his skin. He said, I feel better when I got you around.

She said that she was going to buy a few little things.

Where do your folks live at? Must have run away from home once. Tell me what caused it.

Her family lived thirty-five miles away in Mobeetie. Thirty-five or forty miles. She never did know just how far. Times got hard. And the farm gets awful lonesome when the sun comes up or when it goes down. A family argument got started and she got mad at her folks. So she bought a bus ticket. Hit the oil fields. Heard lots about oil fields. Said they paid good wages and always was needing somebody to work in them.

You've got a job right where you are. Just as long as you want it. I know you'll learn as you keep working. I don't think my dollar is entirely wasted. This fall is going to be good, and you'll know my business better, and I'll pay you better. We'll get an old man to be dishwasher. It's too much for you when business get rushing.

Her hand was resting on the mattress and he looked down at it and said, It looks nice and clean, and I don't want the strong lye soap and the hot dishwater to make it all red and dry the skin out. Cause it to chap. Break open. Bleed. He put his hand on hers and give it a good friendly squeeze. He rubbed real slow up and down her arm with the back of his hand just barely touching her skin, and they stopped talking. Then he took her hand and folded his fingers between hers and pulled her hand from the mattress and took the weight from her arm in such a way that she fell back across the bed. He held her hand and he bent over and kissed her. And then he kissed her again. They kept their mouths together for a long time. He rolled over against her, and she rolled up against him. She had good firm muscles on her shoulders and her back, and he felt each one of them, going from one to the other. Her green café uniform was fresh washed and ironed so that it shined where the light struck it, and where it curved to fit her body. Several times he rubbed across the belt that tied in a big bow knot above her hips and he pulled the sash and the knot came loose. The uniform started coming open a little at the front and by the touch of his hand he laid it half open almost without her knowing about it. His hands was long and his fingers was slim and he'd turned the pages of lots of books, and he took the first two long fingers of his right hand and caught the thickness of the uniform between them, and with a twist of his wrist he turned the rest of the dress back. He played and felt of both of her breasts, his fingers walking from first one and then the other like some kind of a big white spider. His TB caused him to make a loud spitty noise when he breathed in and out, and he was breathing faster all of the time.

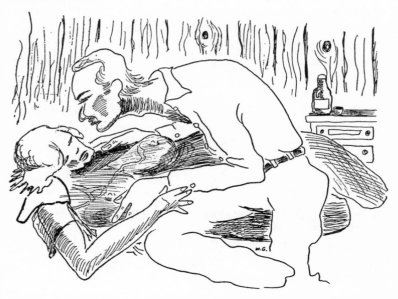

I heard the sound of somebody's feet walking down the old boardwalk, and I took a quick glance down and out of the door, and saw somebody's shadow coming. I was standing on the steel frame of an iron folding cot, and I jumped down from my lookout for a minute. It was my dad. He said he had to go to the bank and for me to come and watch the office. There was a couple there to look at a room and the room had to be fixed up before they moved in. Needed linens. I stood there for about ten seconds not saying a thing. My dad looked sort of funny at me. I didn't let on. Just stood there straining my ears through that wall, and wondering what I was a-missing. But, shucks, I knew. Yeah, I knew, it was just exactly like all of the rest of them, and I wasn't a-missing out on nothing.

About thirty minutes later and along about dark, after the couple had been well rented and well roomed, and the linens had been put on for them, I took a flying high dive back out to the old board wall and knothole and climbed up and took a last look. But they had left. Nothing left to tell the tale but the prints of her hips sunk 'way down deep in the mattress.

I'll never feel as funny as the day I walked into the office and found Papa behind the flowery curtain, setting on the edge of the bed holding his face in his hands.

"Matter?" I asked him.

His finger pointed to the top of the dresser, and I found a check made out to me for a dollar and fifty cents.

At first I grinned and said, "Guess mebbe it's some o' my oil money a-rollin' in."

My blood turned to cold slush oil when my eyes saw on the corner of the check the name and address of the Insane Asylum in Norman, Oklahoma.

I set down by the side of Papa and put my arm around him.

The letter said that Nora B. Guthrie had died some days ago. Her death was a natural death. Because she only knew my address in Okemah, they were sending me the balance of her cash account.

Papa was wiping his eyes red with his knuckles, trying to quit crying. I patted him on the back and held the check down between my knees, reading it again.

I walked over across the tracks, uptown to the bank, not wanting to cash the check in our neighborhood. The man in the bank window could tell by my face that I was nervous and scared, and everybody standing in line was anxious for me to move on out of their way. I seen their hands full of checks, pink, tan, yellow and blue ones. My face turned a pale and sickly color, and my throat was just a wadding of dry cotton, and my eyes got hazy, and my whole life went through my head. It took every muscle in my body to pick up that dollar bill and fifty-cent piece. Somewhere on the outskirts of town, a high whining fire whistle seemed to be blowing.

I got a job selling root beer. It was just a big barrel with a coil running around inside of it, and it cost you a nickel for me to pull the handle, unless you was a personal friend of mine, in which case I'd draw you off a mug free.

Prohibition was on and folks seemed like they were dry. The first day that I was there, the boss come around and said, "Oh, here's your day's pay. We pay every day here, because we may have to close up any day. Business is rushing and good right now, but nobody can tell.

"Another thing I want to show you is about this little door right down here under the counter. You see this little door? Well, you push this trigger right here, just like that, and then you see the door comes open. Then you see inside. There's some little shelves. On these little shelves, as I suppose you see, are some little bottles. These little bottles are two ounces. They are fifty cents a bottle. They are a patented medicine, I think, and it's called Jamaica Ginger, or plain Jake—a mixture of ginger and alcohol. The alcohol is about ninety-nine percent. So now, in case anybody comes in with their thumbnail busted or ankle sprung, or is snake bit, or has got ancestors, or the hoof and mouth disease, or is otherwise sick and has got fifty cents cash money on him, get the fifty cents and then reach down here and give him one of these little bottles of Jake. Be sure to put the money in the register."

While I worked there only about a month, I saved up four

dollars, and to boot I got an inside view of what the human race was drinking.

You couldn't tell any more about the rot-gut called whiskey than you could about the Jake. It was just about as poison. Lots of people fell over dead and was found scattered here and yonder with different kinds of whiskey poisoning. I hated prohibition on that account. I hated it because it was killing people, paralyzing them, and causing them to die like flies. I've seen men set around and squeeze that old pink canned heat through an old dirty rag, get the alcohol drained out of it, and then drink it down. The papers carried tales about the men that drunk radiator alcohol and died from rust poisoning. Others came down with the beer head. That's where your head starts swelling up and it just don't quit. Usually you take the beer head from drinking home brew that ain't made right, or is fermented in old rusty cans, like garbage cans, oil drums, gasoline barrels, and slop buckets. It caused some of the people to die. They even had a kind of beer called Old Chock that was made by throwing everything under the sun into an old barrel, adding the yeast and sugar and water to it, and letting her go. Biscuit heels, corn-bread scraps, potato leavings, and all sorts of table scraps went into this beer. It is a whitish, milky, slicky-looking bunch of crap. But especially down in Oklahoma I've seen men drive fifteen miles out in the country just to get a hold of a few bottles of it. The name Chock come from the Choctaw Indians. I guess they just naturally wanted to celebrate some way or another, and thought a little drink would fire them up so's they'd break loose, forget their worries, and have a good time.

When I was behind the counter, men would come in and purchase bay rum, and I'd get a look into their puffy, red-speckled faces, and their bleary, batty eyes, that looked but didn't see, and that went shut, but never slept, that closed, but never rested, and dreamed but never arrived at a conclusion. I would see a man come in and buy a bottle of rubbing alcohol, and then buy a bottle of coke and go out and mix it half and half, hold his breath, wheeze for a few seconds, and then waddle on away.

One day my curiosity licked me. I said that I was going to taste a bottle of that Jake for myself. Man ought to be interested. I drawed up about a half a mug of root beer. It was cold and nice, and I popped the little stopper out of one of the Jake bottles, and poured the Jake into the root beer. When that Jake hit that beer, it commenced to cook it, and there was seven civil wars and two revolutions broke out inside of that mug. The beer was trying to tame the Jake down and the Jake was trying to eat the beer up. They sizzled and boiled and sounded about like bacon frying. The Jake was chasing the little bubbles and the little bubbles was chasing the Jake, and the beer spun like a whirlpool in a big swift river. It went around and around so fast that it made a little funnel right in the middle. I waited about twenty minutes for it to settle down. Finally it was about the color of a new tan saddle, and about as quiet as it would get. So I bent over it and stuck my ear down over the mug. It was spewing and crackling like a machine gun, but I thought I'd best to drink it before it turned into a waterspout or a dust storm. I took it up and took it down, and it was hot and dry and gingery and spicy, and cloudy, and smooth, and windy and cold, and threatening rain or snow. I took another big swallow and my shirt come unbuttoned and my insides burnt like I was pouring myself full of home-made soapy dishwater. I drank it all down, and when I woke up I was out of a job.

And then a couple of months wheeled past, and I found myself walking all around with my head down, still out of a job, and asking other folks why they had their heads down. But most people was tough, and they still kept their heads up.

I wanted to be my own boss. Have my own job of work whatever it was, and be on my own hook. I walked the streets in the drift of the dust and wondered where was I bound for, where was I going, what was I going to do? My whole life turned into one big question mark. And I was the only living person that could answer it. I went to the town library and scratched around in the books. I carried them home by the dozens and by the armloads, on any subject, I didn't care which. I wanted to look into everything a little bit, and pick out something, something that would turn me into a human being of some kind—free to work for my own self, and free to work for everybody.

My head was mixed up. I looked into every kind of an "ology," "osis," "itis," and "ism" there was. It seemed like it all turned to nothing.

I read the first chapter in a big leather law book. But, no, I didn't want to memorize all of them laws. So I got the bug that I wanted to be a preacher and yell from the street corners as loud as the law allows. But that faded away.

Then I wanted to be a doctor. A lot of folks were sick and I wanted to do something to make them well. I went up to the town library and carried home a big book about all kinds of germs, varmints, cells, and plasms.

Them plasms are humdingers.

They ain't got much shape to brag about, but they can really get around. Some of them, I forgot what bunch it is, just take a notion to go somewhere, and so they start out turning wagon-wheels and handsprings till they get there. And every time they turn a cartwheel they come up a different shape. Some of them they call amebas. They're made out of a jelly that really ain't nothing to speak of. It's about as near to nothing as you could get without fading plumb out. You can see right through these here amebas. But they don't care. They just want to turn handsprings around in your drinking water, and a few flip-flops in your blood.

One day I was unusually lucky. I run onto a hole of the very rottenest and oldest water you ever saw. I took the water up to the doctor's office and he lighted up his microscope for me. He was an old doctor, there around town for a long time, long enough not to have many customers. Since his office was usually empty, he would let me use his microscope. One particular drop of extra live and rotten water was stagnant and full of a green scum. Under the microscope, the scum looked like long green stems of sugar cane. They were long and tangled, and you could see animules of every kind out in there running around.

One was a little black gent. He was double tough. He was a hard fighter and a fast traveler. This little dark-complected gent was coming down across the country, and so I took out after him, just sailing along above him and watching him. He had to fight three or four times in one of his days. I don't know how long he calls a day. But there isn't a minute that he's free to fold up his hands, close his eyes, and dream. He circles the block and he looks all around. Some kind of a white bug meets him. They both square off, and look the other one over. They circle each other and watch. They lick their chops and smack their lips. The lips may be on the side or back or around under their belly somewhere, but wherever they are, they are lips, and so they smack them. They measure their blows. The white one tries a light left hook, not intending to down the black one, but just to get the distance marked. He sticks out his left again, and taps the air twice. The black has got both arms moving like a clock. The white puts out a long arm that stretches twice its ordinary length. The dark one is buffaloed. He looks for an umpire. Is this in the rules? The white grabs the black by the neck with the long arm and then by stretching his other one out he frails the black's knob good and hard; but the black is solid and somehow the blows ain't fatal. He throws his shoulders into a hump that hides his chin. He is taking the licks, but they are hurting. It looks bad for Mister Black, but he's got his eye skint under that hump, and he hasn't had a chance yet to turn loose and fight. He doesn't like this arm-stretching. Don't know what to do. He can't get in close enough to match blows with the long-armed boxer, but he isn't out by a long shot.

The long-arm holds him with one hand and keeps on jabbing him with the other in such a way that it turns the black one about. He lets himself drift with the weight of the blows and he keeps his hands and arms limber and relaxed, but holds them up.

All at once it happens. The black spins on his toe, round and round; he spins in close with so much speed that his arms stick out whirling like a propellor. He gets inside the long reach of the white. He sticks out his arms stiff, and the rights and the lefts crack the white so fast that he thinks he's been lightning struck. He pulls his long arms back in. He tries to use them when they are pulled in short, but finds he is too clumsy. His outlook changes. He wants to wire his Congressman, but it looks bad. He catches three hundred and forty-five more hard lefts and rights. He lets his body go limp so as to drift with the blows, but the little black boxer circles his whole body, spinning and whirling, frailing every inch of the way around. The pale one loosens up, a mass of plasm. He makes one wild stab at the black that is peppering him with dynamite. He throws both of his clumsy arms high into the air, and exposes his head, chest, and diaphragm. The black is the king now. He wants to play with his groceries. He spins the white around slow like, and the white goes into a last coma. The black spot fondles him carefully, finding his face, his eyes, and his throat, and rips his throat open before his jelly can jell. He sticks there for a little while sucking the warm life out of the pale carcass. When he gets full, he spins fast, spins away from his kill, and comes walking in Fifth Avenue fashion down toward another patch of the same green cane.

Now in the canebrakes there lives some sort of an animule that is neither here nor there. I mean he isn't white and he isn't black. He's a middle brown. I run onto him just by accident while I was flying over the most stagnant part of the water, and he looked like a hard worker. The other little black speck was skipping through the morning dew, full of pep, and just had had a good warm meal and everything. He wasn't exactly looking where he was going. He thought he'd just won a battle. He was whistling and singing, and when he got within earshot of the cane patch, why the cane-patch dweller spotted him. The speck in the cane patch hadn't caught his breakfast as yet that day, and he commenced to vibrating like a little electric motor when he saw the other one cavorting in the cane. The brown one in the cane patch was at home there. He grabbed hold of a good solid stalk of cane and waited. When the other one trotted by, he reached out and grabbed him by the coat collar, yanked him bodily into the patch, and the two of them made the heavy cane leaves rattle for forty acres around. This was a real fight.

At first, the little black one was doing pretty well for hisself. He had two arms stuck out and was spinning and dodging and hitting hard and fast; in and out, quick as electricity shocking, he'd sock the boy in the canebrakes. He won the first two rounds hands down, but he wasn't at home in the cane. He tripped and stumbled around over the stalks, and he would get his two big strong arms all tangled up in the cane, and would have to come to a complete rest, untangle himself, and start out spinning all over again. This seemed to make him mighty tired.

The other one was some bigger and he didn't work very hard at first. He just weaved around a little. He had about forty hands, short and sharp like hooks, but not very deadly. He used them sort of two or three at a time and never wore his self out. When two arms would get tired, why, he'd just turn around a few notches, grab some kind of a new handhold on the cane, and fight with a brand-new set of arms and fists. He didn't smoke hump cigarets. He had good wind. He was at home in the brush. He just, so to say, let Mister Black Speck fight and fan the air till he was so tired he couldn't go any more. When he stopped, the bigger boy set in on him with all forty arms and fists. He whim-whammed him. He dynamited his face, torpedoed his heart, and beat the little black fellow into a pulp. He took him gently and sweetly in the hug of his forty arms, and sucked the blood out of him, along with the blood that the black one had just lately sucked out of somebody else. Then when he had his fill, he chunked the dead body over among the tall cane stalks, walked his way slowly into the patch, coiled up and went off to sleep. His belly was full. He was lazy. He'd won because he'd been hungry.

For the next few months I took a spell of spending all of the money I could rake and scrape for brushes, hunks of canvas, and all kinds of oil paints. Whole days would go by and I wouldn't know where they'd went. I put my whole mind and every single thought to the business of painting pictures, mostly people.

I made copies of Whistler's "Mother," "The Song of the Lark," "The Angelus," and lots of babies and boys and dogs, snow and green trees, birds singing on all kinds of limbs, and pictures of the dust across the oil fields and wheat country. I made a couple of dozen heads of Christ, and the cops that killed Him.

Things was starting to stack up in my head and I just felt like I was going out of my wits if I didn't find some way of saying what I was thinking. The world didn't mean any more than a smear to me if I couldn't find ways of putting it down on something. I painted cheap signs and pictures on store windows, warehouses, barns and hotels, hock shops, funeral parlors and blacksmith shops, and I spent the money I made for more tubes of oil colors. "I'll make 'em good an' tough," I said to myself, "so's they'll last a thousand years."

But canvas is too high priced, and so is paint and costly oils, and brushes that you've got to chase a camel or a seal or a Russian red sable forty miles to get.

An uncle of mine taught me to play the guitar and I got to going out a couple of nights a week to the cow ranches around to play for the square dances. I made up new words to old tunes and sung them everywhere I'd go. I had to give my pictures away to get anybody to hang them on their wall, but for singing a song, or a few songs at a country dance, they paid me as high as three dollars a night. A picture—you buy it once, and it bothers you for forty years; but with a song, you sing it out, and it soaks in people's ears and they all jump up and down and sing it with you, and then when you quit singing it, it's gone, and you get a job singing it again. On top of that, you can sing out what you think. You can tell tales of all kinds to put your idea across to the other fellow.

And there on the Texas plains right in the dead center of the dust bowl, with the oil boom over and the wheat blowed out and the hard-working people just stumbling about, bothered with mortgages, debts, bills, sickness, worries of every blowing kind, I seen there was plenty to make up songs about.

Some people liked me, hated me, walked with me, walked over me, jeered me, cheered me, rooted me and hooted me, and before long I was invited in and booted out of every public place of entertainment in that country. But I decided that songs was a music and a language of all tongues.

I never did make up many songs about the cow trails or the moon skipping through the sky, but at first it was funny songs of what all's wrong, and how it turned out good or bad. Then I got a little braver and made up songs telling what I thought was wrong and how to make it right, songs that said what everybody in that country was thinking.

And this has held me ever since.

Chapter XII

TROUBLE BUSTING

❖

My dad married a mail-order wife. She come to Pampa from Los Angeles, and after two or three wedding celebrations most of the relatives went on back to their farms, and Papa and his new wife, Betty Jane, settled down in a shack in a tourist court.

She put an ad in the paper and started telling fortunes. Her trade started out pretty slow at first, then it grew so fast that the customers overflowed her shack.

Oil field dying out, the boom chasers trickled out down the road in long strings of high-loaded cars. The dust crawled down from the north and the banks pushed the farmers off their land. The big flat lakes dried away and left hollow places across the plains full of this hard, dry, crackled, gumbo mud. There isn't a healthier country than West Texas when it wants to be, but when the dust kept whistling down the line blacker and more of it, there was plenty of everything sick, and mad, and mean, and worried.

People hunted for some kind of an answer. The banker didn't give it to them. The sheriff never told anybody the answer. The chamber of commerce was trying to make more money, and they was too busy to tell people the answer to their troubles. So the people asked the preacher, and still didn't learn much where to go or what to do. They even come to the door of the fortune teller.

I was about twenty-four years old at this time and living

233

in a worse shack than Betty Jane and Papa. It had cost me twenty-five dollars on the payment plan a few months before. Oil workers don't build mansions when they open up a new boom town. The work peters out. The workers bundle up and cripple off down the same old road they hit town on. Their shacks are left. Dirty, filthy, and all shot to pieces, and warped, and humped, swaying in every direction like a herd of cattle hit with a plague, these little shacks lean around over the plains.

"Your name Guthrie?" A tough-looking man had just knocked so hard on my door that the whole little house shook. "I'm lookin' for Guthrie!"

"Yessir, my name, all right." I looked out the door. "Come in?"

"No! I won't come in! I've been spending most of my time for the last few months going around to people of your kind. Trying to get some decent advice!" He shook his hands in the wind and preached at me like he was fixing to pass the plate. "I ain't goin' to pay out another red cent! Four bits here. A dollar there. Two bits yonder. It keeps me broke!"

"Mighty bad shape ta be in."

"I'll come in! I'll set myself down! If you can tell me what I want to know, you'll get fifty cents! If you don't, I won't give you a penny! I'm worried!"

"Come on in."

"Okay. I'll sit right here on this chair and listen. But I'm not going to tell you one single word why I'm here. You've got to tell me! Now, Mister Trouble Buster, let's see you strut your stuff!"

"Dust's gittin' purty bad out there."

"Start talkin'!"

"You 'fraid of that dust?"

"I'm not th' least bit afraid of that dust."

"You must not have an outside job, then. You're not no farmer. You ain't no oil field roustabout. If you had a store of any kind, you'd be afraid that dust was drivin' all of yer customers away. So. You know, Mister, you've got the wrong Guthrie."

"Keep talking!"

"My dad married a fortune teller, but I never did claim ta be one, but, I'd like ta just see if I c'n tell ya what ya come here for, an' what ya wanta know."

"Four bits in it if you do."

"You're a inside man. You work in a oil refinery. Good payin' job."

"Right. How did you know?"

"Well, these farmers an' ordinary workin' people aroun' here ain't got enuff money ta throw off four bits here, an a dollar there fer a fortune teller. So yore work is high class. Yer mighty serious about yer work. Ya really take a pride in yer machinery. Ya like to work. Ya like ta see th' most turned out in th' shortest time. Always thinkin' about inventin' somethin' new ta make machinery run better an' faster. Ya tinker with this, even when yer off of yer job an' at home."

"Seventy-five cents. Keep talking."

"That new invention you've got is gonna make ya some money one of these here days. There's a big concern already on yer trail. Wantin' ta buy it. They'll try ta steal it cheap as they can. Don't trust anybody but yer wife with th' secret. She's waitin' out there in yer car. Ya gotta lotta faith in yer own self, an' in her, too. That's mighty good. Keep on with yer inventin'. Keep workin' all time. Ya won't git what ya want outta this big company fer yer invention, but ya'll git enuff ta put ya up in shape ta where ya c'n keep up yer work."

"Make it an even dollar. Go on."

"Yer mind is full of inventions, an' th' world's full of folks that needs 'em bad. Ya jest gotta keep yer mind all clear, like a farm, so's more inventions c'n grow up there. Th' only way ya c'n do this is ta help out th' pore workin' folks all ya can."

"Here's the dollar. What next?"

"That's all. Jest think over what I told ya. Good-bye."

"You are the only fortune teller that I've found that don't claim to tell anything, and tells everything!"

"I don't claim ta be no mind reader. I don't make no charge fer jest talkin'."

"You're just modest. I consider that dollar well spent. Yes, well spent. And I've got lots of friends all over these oil fields. I'll tell all of them to come down here and talk to you! Good-day!"

So there it was. I stood there looking at both sides of the dollar bill, the picture on the gray side, and the big building on the green side. The first dollar I'd made in over a week. Just a man mixed up in his head. Smart guy, too. Hard worker.

The gravels knocked splinters off of the side of the house. And the dust blew and the wind come down. In a couple of days the dollar was almost gone.

Somebody knocked at my front door. I got up and said, "Hello" to three ladies. "Come in, ladies."

"We ain't got no money ner no time to waste neither!"

"This lady has a awful funny thing wrong with her. She can't talk. Lost her voice. And she can't swallow any water. Hasn't had a drink of water in almost a week. We took her to several doctors. They don't know what to do about it. She's just starving."

"But—ladies—I ain't no doctor."

"Some fortune tellers can heal things like this. It's the gift of healing. There are seven gifts—healing, prophecy, faith, wisdom, tongues, interpretation of tongues, and discerning of spirits. You've just got to help her! Poor thing. She can't just die away!"

"Set down right here in this here chair," I told the lady. "Do you have faith that you'll git cured?"

She smiled and choked trying to talk, and nodded her head yes.

"Do you b'lieve yer mind is th' boss of yer whole body?"

She nodded yes at me again.

"You b'lieve yer mind is boss over yer nerves? All yer muscles? Back? Legs? Arms? Your neck?"

She nodded her head again.

I walked to the water bucket and took the dipper and poured a glassful. I handed it to her and said, "Yore husban' wants you ta talk to 'im, don't he? An' yore kids, ta boot? No two ways about it! You say you ain't got no money fer a doctor?"

She shook her head no.

"You'd better quit this monkey bizness, then, an' swig this water down you! Drink it! Drink it! Then tell me how good it feels ta be able ta talk ag'in!"

She held the glass in her fingers, and I could see the skin was so dry it was wrinkling and cracking. She looked around and smiled at me and the other two ladies.

She turned the glass up and drunk the water down.

We all held our mouths open and didn't breathe a breath.

"G-g-l-l-o-o-dd."

"It's what?"

"Good. Water. Water. Good."

"You ladies g'wan back home an' spend th' next three er four days carryin' buckets of good clear fresh drinkin' water ta this lady. Have a water-drinkin' contest. Talk about ever'thing. You don't owe me nuthin'."

And so there ain't no tellin' where the wind will blow or

what will come up out of the weeds. This was the start of one of the best, worst, funniest and saddest parts of my whole life. They thought I was a mind reader. I didn't claim to be, so some of them called me a fortune teller and a healer. But I never claimed to be different from you or anybody else. Does the truth help to heal you when you hear it? Does a clear mind make a sick body well? Sometimes. Sometimes nervous spells cause people to be sick, and worry causes the nervous spells. Yes, I could talk. Did that make them get well? What are words, anyway? If you tell a lie with words, you cause all kinds of people to get sick. If you tell people the real truth, they get together and they get well. Was that it?

I remember a German rancher that would come to my house every time the stock market went up a penny or down a penny. He would ask me, "Vat do de spirits sez aboudt my fadder's cattles?"

"Spirits ain't got nuthin' ta do with yer father's cattle," I would tell him. "What you call spirits ain't nuthin'— nuthin' but th' thoughts ya think in yer head."

"My fadder iss dead. Vat hass he got to tell me aboudt raising and selling his cattles?" he would say.

"Yer father would like fer ya ta do jist what he did fer forty-five years out here on these plains, Mister. Raise 'em young, buy 'em cheap, feed 'em good, an' sell 'em high!" I'd tell him.

He woke me up at all hours of the night. He traveled more than twenty-five miles to my place. And not a week rolled past but what he made the trip and asked the same old question.

An engineer on the Rock Island Railroad spur that runs from Shamrock up north to Pampa used to ride along in his engine and look out at some new oil land. He wanted me to shut my eyes and see a vision for him. "Where had I ought to buy oil land?"

"I see an old oil field, with black oily derricks. It's good oil land because it's an old proven field, an' it's still per-ducin'. In th' middle of this field of black derricks, I see a white derrick, painted with silver paint an' shinin' in th' sun."

"I see that same derrick every day when I pass that field on my run! I've been wondering if I should try to buy some land around that field."

"I see a lot of oil under this land, because this derrick is in th' middle of a whole big forest of black oily rigs. When ya buy yer new oil land, buy it as close to that center derrick as ya can. But don't pay too much fer th' deal."

"You've helped me to solve my whole problem!" he told me as he got up. "You've took a big load off of my mind. How did you know about this silver rig in this bunch of old oily ones?"

And I said, "You're an engineer on this Shamrock spur line, ain't ya? I just guessed that you'd been savin' yer money ta buy—well, some land that ya seen ever' day on yer run. I know this oil field awful well, an' it looks awful purty from a boxcar door—an' I s'pose it looks awful purty from up in an engine cab—'long toward quittin' time, when yer thinkin' 'bout gettin' home to yer wife an' family, an' tryin' ta think of how ta invest yer money so's it'll bring yer folks th' most good. I wuz jist guessin' an' talkin'—I don't know, really, where you'd oughtta buy yer oil land."

"Here's a dollar. I think you saved me several thousand."

"How's that?"

"You told me something I'd never thought of: to buy my land closest to the middle of the biggest field. But an acre of that land would take my life's earnings. And while you had your eyes closed there, talking, I felt afraid to spend my money away off on some new wildcat land that didn't have any oil derricks on it; and so I just got to thinking, maybe the best hole I could put my money in would be the Postal Savings Window of the United States Government. You earned this dollar, take it." And then he walked away and I never did see him any more.

A little girl six years old had big running sores all over her scalp. Her mama took her to the doctor and he treated her for over six months. The sores still stayed. The barber cut her hair all off like a convict on a chain gang. The mother finally brought her over to my place and told me, "Jist wanta see what'cher a-doin' over here."

"Do ya keep 'er head good an' clean?" I asked the lady.

"Yeh. But she bawls an' squawls an' throws wall-eyed fits when she has ta go ta school!" her mama said.

"The old mean kids make fun of me because my head looks like an old jailbird," the little girl told us.

"Take th' white of an egg in a saucer an' rub it into 'er head good ever' night. Let it soak in all night. Then ya can wash 'er head with clear water ever' mornin' 'fore she goes off ta school. Ya won't even hafta bring 'er back over here no more ta see me. Ya'll have a purtier head of hair than any of them old mean teasin' kids."

"How long'll it take?" the little girl asked.

"Ya'll have it by th' day school ends," I told her.

"That'll be nice, won't it?" Her Mama looked at both of us.

"But you—ya quit yer scarin' this girl! Ya quit makin' 'er play by her self. Quit makin' 'er stay inside th' house when all of th' other kids is out whoopin' an' runnin'," I told the mother.

"How'd you know this?" she asked me.

"Quit makin' 'er wear that old dirty hat all of th' time," I kept on. "Quit scrubbin' 'er head with that old strong lye soap! Give it a little rest, it'll heal of its own accord."

"How come you so smart, mister?" The little girl laughed and took hold of my hand. "My mama does everything just like you said."

"Shut yer mouth! Yer talkin' boutcher Ma, ya know!"

"I knowed all of this, because I can look at yer Mama's hands, and tell that she makes her own lye soap. I know she keeps ya in th' house too much, 'cause ya haven't been gittin' no sunshine on yer head. I know you'll have a big long set of purty curls by th' last day of school. Good-bye. Come to see me with yer curls!"

I watched the little girl skip twenty or thirty feet ahead as they went down the road toward shacktown.

The little shack was swaying in the dust one dark winter night, and a man of two hundred and ninety pounds banged in at the door, and brought the weather in with him. "I don't know if you know it or not," he talked in a low, soft voice, "but you're looking at an insane man."

"Off yer coat, havva seat." Then I happened to notice that he wasn't wearing any coat, but several shirts, sweaters, ducking jumpers, and two or three pairs of overhauls. He more than filled the north half of my little room.

"I'm really insane." He watched me like a hawk watching a chicken. I set down in my chair and listened to him. "Really."

"So am I," I told him.

"I've already been to the insane asylum twice."

"Ya'll soon be a-runnin' that place."

"I wasn't crazy when they sent me there, but they kept me shot full of some kind of crap! Run me out of my wits! Made my nerves and muscles go wild. I beat up a couple

of guards out in the pea patch and run off. Now I'm here. I reckin they'll git me purty quick. I see news reels in my head."

"News reels?"

"Yes. They get started and I see them going all of the time. It's like sitting all alone in a big dark theater. I see lots of them and have seen them ever since I was a kid. Farm. Mama always told me I was crazy. I guess I always was. Only trouble with these news reels is—they never stop."

"What's th' news lately?"

"Everybody's going to leave this country. Boom is over. Wheat blowing out. Dust storms getting darker and darker. Everybody running and shooting and killing. Everybody fighting everybody else. These little old shacks like this, they're bad, no good for nobody. Lots of kids sick. Old folks. They won't need us working stiffs around this oil field. People will have to hit the road in all of this bad, bad weather. Everything like that."

"Ain't nuthin' wrong with your head!"

"Don't you think all of us ought to get together and do something about all of this? I see stuff like that in this news reel, too. You know, the way everybody ought to do— something about it."

"Need you fer Mayor 'round this town."

"I see all kinds of shapes and designs in my head, too. All kinds you could ever think of. They bust into my head like a big flying snowstorm, and every one of those shapes means something. How to fix a road better. How to fix up a whole oil field better. How to make work easier. Even how to build these big oil refineries."

"Who was it said you was crazy?"

"Officers. Folks. They threw me in that jail about a hundred times apiece."

"Oughtta been jist th' other way 'round."

"No. I guess I needed it. I'm awful bad to drink and fight on the streets. Guys tease me and I light in and beat the hell out of them; cops jump in to get me, and I throw them around. Always something haywire."

"Work all time?"

"No, work a few days, and then lay off a few weeks. Always owing somebody something."

"I guess this town is jist naturally dryin' up an' blowin' away. You need some kind of steady work."

"Did you paint these pictures of Christ up here on the wall?" He looked around the room and his eyes stayed on each picture for a long time. " 'Song of the Lark.' Good copy."

I said yes, I painted them.

"I always did think maybe I'd like to paint some of this stuff I see in my head. I wish you would teach me a little of what you know. That'd be a good kind of work for me. I could travel and paint pictures in saloons."

I got up and rustled through an orange crate full of old paints and brushes, and wrapped up a good bunch in an old shirt. "Here, go paint."

And so Heavy Chandler took the paints and went home. During the next month he lost over sixty pounds. Every day he made a trip to my house. He carried a new picture painted on slats and boards from apple crates, old hunks of cardboard, and plywood, and I was surprised to see how good he got. Wild blinding snow scenes. Log cabins smoking in the hills. Mountain rivers banging down through green valleys. Desert sands and dreary bones. Cactus. The tumbleweed drifting—rolling through life. Good pictures. He bucked wind, rain, sleet, and terrible bad dust storms to get there. And every day I would ask him if he'd been drunk, and he'd tell me yes or no. He smiled out of his face and eyes one day and said, "I slept good all this week. First solid sleep I've had in six years. The news reel still runs, but I know how to turn it off and on now when I want to. I feel just as sane as the next one."

Then one day he didn't show up. The deputy sheriff drove down to the shack and told me they had Heavy locked up in the jail house for being drunk. "Boy, that was some fight," the officer told me. "Six deputies and Heavy. God, he slung deputy sheriffs all over the south side of town! Nobody could get him inside that patrol car. It was worse than a circus tent full of wild men! Then I says to Heavy, 'Heavy, do you know Woody Guthrie?' Heavy—he puffed and blowed and said, 'Yes.' Then I took him by the arm and says, 'Heavy, Woody wouldn't want you to beat up on all of these deputies, would he, if he knew about it?' And then old Heavy says to me, 'No—where did you find out about Woody Guthrie?' And I says, 'Oh, he's a real good friend of mine!' And, sir, you know, Old Heavy calmed down, tamed right down, got just as sober and nice as anybody in about a minute flat, and smiled out of the side of his eyes and says, 'Take me an' lock me up, Mister Jailer. If you're a friend of Woody's, then you're a friend of mine!' "

"Whattaya s'pose they'll do with Heavy up there in jail?" I asked the deputy.

"Well, 'course you know Heavy was an escaped inmate from the insane asylum, didn't you?"

"Yeah—but—"

"Oh, sure, sure, we knew it, too. We knew where he was all of the time. We knew we could pick him up any minute we wanted him. But we hoped he would get better and come out of it. I don't know what happened to Heavy. But something funny. He got just as sane as you or me or anybody else. Then he was learning how to paint or some dam thing, somebody said, I don't know very much about it. But he's on the train now, headed back down to Wichita Falls."

"Did Heavy tell you to tell me anything?"

"Oh, yes. That is why I made the trip down here. Almost forgot. He told me to tell you that he just wishes to God that you could tell all of those thirty-five hundred inmates down there what you told him. I don't know what it was you told him."

"Naww. I don't reckin ya do," I told the officer; "I don't

guess you know. Well, anyway, thanks. See ya again. 'Bye."

And the car drove away with the deputy. And I went back in and fell down across my bed, rubbing the coat of fine dust on the quilt, and thinking about the message that old Heavy had sent me. And I never did see him any more after that.

Several hundred asked me, "Where can I go to get a job of work?" Farmers heard about me and asked, "Is this dust th' end of th' world?" Business people asked me, "Everybody is on the move, and I've lost everything I ever had; what'll happen next?" A boom town dance-hall chaser barged in on me and asked me, "I'm tryin' to learn how to play th' fiddle; do you think I can get to be elected Sheriff?"

All kinds of cars were parked around my little old shack. People lost. People sick. People wondering. People hungry. People wanting work. People trying to get together and do something.

A bunch of ten, twenty oil field workers and farmers filled the whole room and stood around most of my front yard. Their leader asked me, "What do you think about this feller, Hitler, an' Mussolini? Are they out to kill off all of th' Jews an' niggers?"

I told them, "Hitler an' Mussolini is out ta make a chain-gang slave outta you, outta me, an' outta ever'body else! An' kill ever'body that gits in their road! Try ta make us hate each other on accounta what Goddam color our skin is! Bible says ta love yer neighbor! Don't say any certain color!"

The bunch milled around, talking and arguing. And the leader talked up and told me, "This old world's in a bad condition! Comin' to a mighty bad end!"

"Mebbe th' old one is," I yelled at the whole bunch, "but a new one's in th' mail!"

"This Spanish war's a sign," he kept raving on. "This is th' final battle! Battle of Armagaddeon! This dust, blowin' so thick ya cain't breathe, cain't see th' sky, that's th' scourge over th' face of th' earth! Men too greedy for land an' for money an' for th' power to make slaves out of his feller men! Man has cursed th' very land itself!"

"Now you tell us somethin', Mister Fortune Teller!"

"Hell yes, that's what we come here for! Tell us a vision 'bout all of this stuff!"

I walked out through the door past five or six big husky guys dressed in all kinds of work clothes, whittling, playing with warts on their hands, chewing tobacco, rolling smokes. Everybody in the room walked out in the yard. I stood there on an old rotten board step, and everybody hooted and laughed and cracked some kind of a joke. And then somebody else said, "Tell our fortune."

I looked down at the ground and said, "Well sir, men, I ain't no fortune teller. No more than you are. But I'll tell ya what I see in my own head. Then ya can call it any name ya like."

Everybody stood as still as a bunch of mice.

"We gotta all git together an' find out some way ta build this country up. Make all of this here dust quit blowin'. We gotta find a job an' put ever' single livin' one of us ta work. Better houses 'stead of these here little old sickly shacks. Better carbon-black plants. Better oil refineries. Gotta build up more big oil fields. Pipe lines runnin' from here plumb ta Pittsburgh, Chicago, an' New York. Oil an' gas fer fact'ries ever'where. Gotta keep an' eye peeled on ever' single inch of this whole country an' see to it that none of Hitler's Goddam stooges don't lay a hand on it."

"How we gonna do all of this? Just walk to John D. an' tell 'm we're ready to go to work?" The whole bunch laughed and started milling around again.

"You ain't no prophet!" one big boy yelled. "Hell, any of us coulda say that same thing! You're a dam fake!"

"An' you're a Goddam fool!" I hollered out at him. "I told ya I didn't claim ta be nothin' fancy! Yer own dam head's jist as good as mine! Hell, yes!"

The mob of men snickered and fussed amongst their selves, and made motions with their hands like a baseball umpire saying "out." They shuffled around on their feet, and then broke up into little bunches and started to drift out of the yard. All talking. Above them, the big boy yelled back at me, "Look out who're you're callin' a fool, there, bud!"

"Men! Hey! Listen! I know we all see this same thing— like news reels in our mind. Alla th' work that needs ta be done—better highways, better buildin's, better houses. Ever'thing needs ta be fixed up better! But, Goddamit, I ain't no master mind! All I know is we gotta git together an' stick together! This country won't ever git much better as long as it's dog eat dog, ever' man fer his own self, an' ta hell with th' rest of th' world. We gotta all git together, dam it all, an' make somebody give us a job somewhere doin' somethin'!"

But the whole crowd walked off down toward Main Street, laughing and talking and throwing their hands. I leaned back up against the side of the shack and watched the gravel and dust cutting down the last of the hollyhocks.

"News reels in my head," I was looking and thinking to myself, and I was thinking of old Heavy gone. "News reels in my head. By God, mebbe we all gotta learn how ta see them there news reels in our heads. Mebbe so."

Chapter XIII

OFF TO CALIFORNIA

◆

I rolled my sign-painting brushes up inside an old shirt and stuck them down in my rear pants pocket. On the floor of the shack I was reading a letter and thinking to myself. It said:

"... when Texas is so dusty and bad, California is so green and pretty. You must be twenty-five by now, Woody. I know I can get you a job here in Sonora. Why don't you come? Your aunt Laura."

Yes, I'll go, I was thinking. This is a right nice day for hittin' th' road. 'Bout three o'clock in th' afternoon.

I pulled the crooked door shut as best I could, and walked one block south to the main highway leading west. I turned west and walked along a few blocks, across a railroad track, past a carbon-block warehouse. "Good old Pampa. I hit here in 1926. Worked my tail off 'round this here town. But it didn't give me anything. Town had growed up, strung itself all out across these plains. Just a little old low-built cattle town to start with; jumped up big when the oil boom hit. Now eleven years later it had up and died."

A three- or four-ton beer truck blowed its air brakes and I heard the driver talking, "By God! I thought that looked like you, Woody! Where ya headin'? Amarilla? Hustlin' signs?" We got off to a jumpy start while he was spitting out his window.

"Cal'fornia," I said. "Hustlin' outta this dam dust!"

249

"Fer piece down th' road, ain't it?"

"Enda this dam highway! Ain't a-lookin' back!"

"Aww, ain'tcha gonna take one more good look at good ol' Pampa?"

I looked out my window and seen it go by. It was just shacks all along this side of town, tired and lonesome-looking, and lots of us wasn't needed here no more. Oil derricks running up to the city limits on three sides; silvery refineries that first smelled good, then bad; and off along the rim of the horizon, the big carbon-black plants throwing smoke worse than ten volcanoes, the fine black powder covering the iron grass and the early green wheat that pushes up just in time to kiss this March wind. Oil cars and stock cars lined up like herds of cattle. Sun so clear and so bright that I felt like I was leaving one of the prettiest and ugliest spots I'd ever seen. "They tell me this town has fell down ta somethin' like sixteen thousan' people," I said.

"She's really goin' with th' dust!" the driver told me. Then we hit another railroad crossing that jarred him into saying, "I seen th' day when there was more folks than that goin' to th' picture shows! She's really shrivelin' up!"

"I ain't much a-likin' th' looks o' that bad-lookin' cloud a-hangin' off ta th' north yonder," I told him.

"Bad time uv year fer them right blue northers! Come up awful fast sometimes. Any money on ya?"

"Nope."

"How ya aimin' ta eat?"

"Signs."

"How's it come ya ain't packin' yer music box with ya?"

"Hocked it last week."

"How ya gon'ta paint signs in a dam blue norther with th' temperture hangin' plumb out th' bottom? Here. Fer's I go."

"This'll gimme a good start at least. Mucha 'blige!" I

slammed the door and backed off onto the gravel and watched the truck leave the main highway, bounce over a rough bridge, and head north across a cow pasture. The driver hadn't said good-bye or anything. I thought that was funny. That's a bad cloud. Five miles back to town, though. No use of me thinking about going back. What the hell's this thing stuck here in my shirt pocket? I be dam. Well, I be dam. A greenback dollar bill. No wonder he just chewed his gum. Truck drivers can do a hell of a lot of talking sometimes without even saying a word.

I walked on down the highway buckling into the wind. It got so hard I had to really duck my head and push. Yes. I know this old flat country up here on the caprock plains. Gumbo mud. Hard crust sod. Iron grass for tough cattle and hard-hitting cowboys that work for the ranchers. These old houses that sweep with the country and look like they're crying in the dust. I know who's in there. I know. I've stuck my head in a million. Drove tractors, cleaned plows and harrows, greased discs and pulled the tumbleweeds out from under the machinery. That wind is getting harder. Whoooooo! The wind along the oily weeds sounded like a truck climbing a mountain in second gear. Every step I took to the west, the wind pushed me back harder from the north, like it was trying to tell me, for God's sake, boy, go to the south country, be smart, go where they sleep out every night. Don't split this blue blizzard west, because the country gets higher, and flatter, and windier, and dustier, and you'll get colder and colder. But I thought, somewhere west there's more room. Maybe the west country needs me out there. It's so big and I'm so little. It needs me to help fill it up and I need it to grow up in. I've got to keep bucking this wind, even if it gets colder.

The storm poured in over the wheat country, and the powdery snow was like talcum, or dried paste, blowing along with the grinding bits of dust. The snow was dry. The dust was cold. The sky was dark and the wind was changing the whole world into an awful funny-looking, whistling and whining place. Flat fields and grazing lands got smothery and close. It was about three more miles on to the little town of Kings Mill.

I walked about two of the miles in the blowing storm and got a ride with a truck load of worried cattle, and a bundled-up driver, smoking loose tobacco that blew as wild as the dust and the snow, and stung like acid when it lit in my eyes. We hollered the usual hollers back and forth at each other during the last mile that I rode with him. He said that he was turning north off of the main road at Kings Mill. I said, Let me out at the post office and I'll stand around in there by the stove and try to get another ride.

In the general store, I bought a nickel's worth of postal cards and wrote all five of them back to the folks in Pampa, saying, "Greetings from the Land of Sunshine and just plenty of Good Fresh Air. Having wonderful tour. Yrs. trly. Wdy."

Pretty soon another cattle man offered me a ride on to the next cattle town. He smoked a pipe which had took up more of his time in the last twenty years than wife, kids, or his cow ranching. He told me, "This old Panhandle country can be one mighty nice place when it's purty, but hell on wheels when she gits riled up!" His truck was governed down to fifteen or twenty miles an hour. It was a windy, brittle hour before we crept the fifteen miles from Kings Mill over to White Deer. I was so cold when we got there that I couldn't hardly get out of the truck. The flying heat from the engine had kept me a degree or two above freezing, but stepping out into that wind head-on was worse. I walked another mile or two on down the side of the road and, as long as I walked, kept fairly loose and limber. A time or two I stopped alongside the concrete, and stood and waited with my head ducked into the wind—and it seemed like none of the drivers could see me. When I started to walk some more, I noticed that the muscles in the upper part of my legs were drawn up, and hurt every time I took a step, and that it took me a few hundred yards' walking to get full control over them. This scared me so much that I decided to keep walking or else.

After three or four miles had went under my feet, a big new model Lincoln Zephyr stopped, and I got in the back seat. I saw two people in the front seat. They asked me a few silly questions. I mean they were good questions, but I only gave them silly answers. Why was I out on the highways at any such a time as this? I was just there. Where was I going? I was going to California. What for? Oh, just to see if I couldn't do a little better.

They let me out on the streets of Amarillo, sixty miles away from Pampa. I walked through town, and it got colder. Tumbleweeds, loose gravel, and dirt and beaten snow crawled along the streets and vacant lots, and the dust rolled in on a high wind, and fell on down across the upper plains. I got across town and waited on a bend for a ride. After an hour, I hadn't got one. I didn't want to walk any more down the road to keep warm, because it was getting dark, and nobody could see anything out there on a night like that. I walked twenty-five or thirty blocks back to the main part of Amarillo. A sign on a board said, Population, 50,000, Welcome. I went into a picture show to get warm and bought a hot sack of good, salty popcorn. I figured on staying in the cheap show all I could, but they didn't stay open after midnight in Amarillo, so I was back on the streets pretty soon, just sort of walking up and down, looking at the jewelry and duds in the windows. I got a nickel sack of smoking, and tried rolling a cigaret on every part of Polk Street, and the wind blew the sack away, a whiff at a time. I remember how funny it was. If I did succeed in getting one rolled and licked down and into my mouth, I'd strike up all of the matches in the country trying to get it lit; and as quick as I got it lit, the wind would blow so hard on the lighted end that it would burn up like a Roman candle, too fast to get a good draw off, and in the meantime throwing flaked-off red-hot ashes all over my coat.

I went down to the railroad yards, and asked about the freights. The boys were hanging out in two or three all-night coffee joints, and there was no lead as to where you could get a free flop. I spent my last four-bit piece on a little two-by-four room, and slept in a good warm bed. If it had cockroaches, alligators or snapping turtles in it, I was too sleepy to stay awake and argue with them.

I hit the streets next morning in a bluster of gray, smoky-looking snow that had managed to get a toehold during the night. It covered the whole country, and the highway was there somewhere—if you could only find it. This side of Clovis, fifteen or twenty miles, I met an A Model Ford with three young boys in it. They stopped and let me in. I rode with them toward New Mexico all day long. When they came to the state line, they acted funny, talking and whispering among themselves, and wondering if the cops at the port of entry would notice anything odd about us. I heard them say that the car was borrowed, no ownership papers, bill of sale, driver's license—just borrowed off of the streets. We talked it over. Decided just to act as blank as possible, and trust to our luck that we could get across. We drove over the line. The cops waved us past. The sign read: Trucks and Busses Stop For Inspection. Tourists Welcome to New Mexico.

The three boys were wearing old patched overhalls and khaki work pants and shirts that looked like they'd stand a couple or three good washings without coming any too clean. I looked at their hair, and it was dry, wind-blown, gritty, and full of the dust out of the storm, and not any certain wave or color—just the color of the whole country. I had seen thousands of men that looked just the same way, and could usually tell by the color of the dirt where they were from. I guessed these boys to be from the oil-field country back up around Borger, and asked them if that was a good guess. They said that we could ride together better if we asked each other less questions.

We rolled along, slow, boiling up the higher country, and cooling off coasting down—until we hit the mountains on this side of Alamagordo. We stopped once or twice to let the engine cool off. Finally we hit the top of the mountain ridge, and traveled along a high, straight road that stuck to the middle part of a flat, covered on both sides by evergreen pine, tall, thin-bodied, and straight as an arrow, branching out, about thirty or forty feet up the trunk; and the undergrowth was mostly a mixture of brown scrubby oak, and here and yonder, bunches of green, tough cedar. The air was so light that it made our heads feel funny. We laughed and joked about how it felt.

I noticed that the driver was speeding up and then throwing the clutch in, letting the car slip into neutral, and coasting as far as he could. I mentioned this to the driver, and he said that he was running on his last teacupful of gas, and it was twenty-five miles to the next town. I kept quiet from then on, doing just what the other three were, just gulping and thinking.

For five or six miles we held our breath. We were four guys out, trying to get somewhere in the world, and the roar of that little engine, rattly, knocky and fumy as it was, had a good sound to our ears. It was the only motor we had. We wanted more than anything else in the world to hear it purr along, and we didn't care how people laughed as they went around us, and throwed their clouds of red dust back into our faces. Just take us into town, little motor, and we'll get you some more gas.

A mile or two of up-grade, and the tank was empty. The driver throwed the clutch in, shifted her into neutral, and kept wheeling. The speed read, thirty, twenty, fifteen— and then fell down to five, three, four, three, four, five, seven, ten, fifteen, twenty-five, and we all yelled and hollered as loud and as long as our guts could pump air.

Hooopeee! Made 'er! Over the Goddam hump! Yippeee! It's all down hill from here to Alamagordo! To hell with the oil companies! For the next half an hour we won't be needing you, John D.! We laughed and told all kinds of good jokes going down the piny-covered mountain—some of the best, wildest, prettiest fresh-smelling country you could ever hope to find. And it was a free ride for us. Twenty miles of coasting.

At the bottom we found Alamagordo, a nice little town scattered along a trickling creek or two that chases down from out of the mountains around. There you see the tall, gray-looking cottonwood sticking along the watered places. Brown adobe shacks and houses of sun-dried brick, covered over with plaster and homemade stucco of every color. The adobe houses of the Mexican workers have stood there, some of them, for sixty, seventy-five, and over a hundred years, flat. And the workers, a lot of them, the same way.

On the north side of town we coasted into a homey-looking service station.

The man finally got around to coming out. One of the boys said, "We want to swap you a good wrench for five gallons of gas, worth twice that much. Good shape. Runs true, holds tight, good teeth, never been broke."

The service man took a long, interested, hungry look at the wrench. Good tool. No junky wrench. He was really wanting to make the swap.

"Got as much as fifty cents cash money?" he asked.

"No . . ." the boy answered him. Both forgot all about everything, keeping quiet for a whole minute or more, and turning the wrench over and over. One boy slid out of the door and walked through the shop toward the men's rest room.

"Two bits cash . . .?" the mechanic asked without looking up.

"No . . . no cash . . ." the boy told him.

"Okay . . . get your gas cap off; I'll swap with you boys just to show you that my heart is in the right place."

The gas cap was turned, laid up on a fender, and the gas man held the long brass nozzle down in the empty hole, and listened to the five gallons flow into the tank; and the five gallons sounded lonesome and sad, and the trade was made.

"Okay, Mister, you got the best of this deal. But that's what you're in business for, I reckon; thanks," a boy said, and the old starter turned over a few wheels that were gradually getting toothless, and the motor went over quick, slow, and then a blue cloud of engine smoke puffed up under the floorboards, and the good smell of burning oil told you that you weren't quite walking—yet. Everybody heaved a sigh of relief. The man stood with his good costly wrench in his hands, pitching it up and down, and smiling a little—nodding as we drove away.

My eyes fell for a short minute away from the healthy countryside, and my gaze came upon an old tire tool on the floor of the car, a flat rusty tire iron, an old pump—and a nice wrench, almost exactly like the one that we'd just traded for gas; and I remembered the boy that went to the rest room.

Uptown in Alamagordo, we stopped at the high, west end of the main street. It was dinner time, but no money. Everybody was hungry and that went without asking. I told the boys that I'd get out and hustle the town for some quick signs, signs to paint on windows which I could paint in thirty minutes or an hour, and we'd surely get enough to buy some day-old bakery goods and milk to take out on the side of the road and eat. I felt like I owed them something for my fare. I felt full of pep, rested and relieved, now that there were five gallons of gas splashing around inside of our tank. They agreed to let me hustle for a quick job, but it must not take too long.

I jumped out in a big rush, and started off down the street. I heard one of them holler, "Meet you right here at this spot in an hour and no later."

I yelled back, "Okie doke! Hour! No later." And I walked down through the town. I peeled my eyes for an old sign that needed repainting, or a new one to put on. I stuck my head into ten or fifteen places and got a job at a shoe store, putting a picture of a man's shoe, a lady's shoe, and: Shoe Rapairing Guaranteed. Cowboy Boots a Specialty.

I had left my brushes in the seat of the car, so I made a hard run up the main street. I got to the spot, puffing, grinning, and blowing like a little horse, and looked around—but no boys, and no car.

I trotted up and down the main street again, thinking that they might have decided to come on down to where I was. But there wasn't the old Model A that I'd learned to know and admire, not for being a champion at anything but as a car that really tried. It was gone. So were my pardners. So were all of my paint brushes. Just a little rag wound around some old brushes, but they were Russian Red Sable, the best that money could buy, and about twenty bucks of hard-earned money to me. They were my meal ticket.

Pulling from Alamagordo over to Las Cruces was one of the hardest times I'd ever had. The valley highway turned into a dry, bare stretch of low-lying foothills, too little to be mountains, and too hilly to be flat desert. The hills fooled me completely. Running out from the high mountains, they looked small and easy to walk over, but the highway bent and curled around and got lost a half a dozen times on each little hill. You could see the road ahead shining like a string of tinfoil flattened out, and then you'd lose sight of it again and walk for hours and hours, and more hours, and without ever coming to the part that you'd been looking at ahead for so long.

I was always a big hand to walk along and look at the things along the side of the road. Too curious to stand and wait for a ride. Too nervous to set down and rest. Too struck with the traveling fever to wait. While the other long strings of hitch-hikers was taking it easy in the shade back in the town, I'd be tugging and walking myself to death over the curves, wondering what was just around the next bend; walking to see some distant object, which turned out to be just a big rock, or knoll, from which you could see and wonder about other distant objects. Blisters on your feet, shoes hot as a horse's hide. Still tearing along. I covered about fifteen miles of country, and finally got so tired that I walked out to one side of the road, laid down in the sun, and went off to sleep. I woke up every time a car slid down the highway, and listened to the hot tires sing off a song, and wondered if I didn't miss a good, easy, cool ride all of the way into California. I couldn't rest.

Back on the road, I hung a ride to Las Cruces and was told that you couldn't catch a freight there till the next day. I didn't want to lay over, so I lit out walking toward Deming. Deming was the only town within a hundred miles where you could catch one of them fast ones setting long enough to get on it. I walked a long stretch on the way to Deming. It must have been close to twenty miles. I walked until past midnight. A farmer drove up and stopped and said that he would carry me ten miles. I took him up, and that put me within about fifteen miles of Deming. Next morning I was walking a couple of hours before sunup, and along about ten o'clock, got a ride with a whole truck-load of hitch-hikers. Most every man on the truck was going to catch a freight at Deming. We found a whole bunch walking around the yards and streets in Deming waiting to snag out. Deming is a good town and a going town, but it's a good town to keep quiet in. Us free riders said it was best not to go around spouting off at your mouth too much, or the cops would pull you in just to show the taxpayers that they are earning their salaries.

The train out of Deming was a fast one. I got to Tucson without doing anything much, without even eating for a couple of days.

In the yards at Tucson, I didn't know where to go or what to do. The train rolled in with us after midnight. The cars all banged, and the brake shoes set down tight, and everything wheeled to a standstill.

I was hanging onto her, because she was a red-hot one, and had been fast so far, and other trains had given her the right-of-way. I didn't want to get off now, just for a cup of coffee or something. Besides, I didn't have the nickel. I crawled down in a reefer hole—a hole in the top of a fruit car where ice is packed—and smoked the makings with two men whose faces I hadn't seen.

It was cold there in Tucson that night. We laid low for about a couple of hours. After a while, a dark head and shoulders could be seen in the square hole, set against the bright, icy moonlight night. Whoever it was, said, "Boys, you c'n come on out—we're ditched on a siding. She ain't gonna take these cars on no further."

"Ya mean we lost our train?"

"Yeah, we just missed 'er, that's all."

And as the head and shoulders went out of sight above us, you could hear men scrambling down the sides, hanging onto the shiny iron ladders, and falling out by the tens and dozens all up and down the cinder track.

"Ditched. . . ."

"Shore'n hell. . . ."

"Coulda got'er if we'd of knowed it in time. I had this happen to me before, right here in Tucson."

"Tucson's a bitch, boys, Tucson's a bitch."

"Why?"

"Oh—just is. Hell, I don't know why!"

"Just another town, ain't it?"

" 'Tain't no town, 'tain't no city. Not fer guys like you an' me. You'll find out soon enough. . . ."

"What's funny about Tucson?"

Men ganged around the black cars, and talked in low, grumbling voices that seemed to be as rough as they sounded honest. Cigarets flared in the dark. A little lantern started coming down the tracks toward where we were ganged around talking. Flashlights flittered along the ground, and you could see the funny shadows of the walking feet and legs of men, and the underparts of the brake drums, air hoses, and couplings of the big, fast cars.

"Checkers."

"Car knockers."

"Boys—scatter out!"

"Beat it!"

"And—remember—take an old 'bo's word for it, and stay th' hell out of the city limits of Tucson."

"What kind of a dam town is this, anyhow?"

"Tucson—she's a rich man's bitch, that's what she is, and nothin' else but."

Morning. Men are scattered and gone. A hundred men and more, rolled in on that train last night, and it was cold. Now it's come morning, and men seem to be gone. They've learned how to keep out of the way. They've learned how to meet and talk about their hard traveling, and smoke each other's snipes in the moonlight, or boil a pot of coffee among the weeds like rabbits—hundreds of them, and when the sun comes out bright, they seem to be gone.

Looking out across a low place, growing with the first sprigs of something green and good to eat, I saw the men, and I knew who they were, and what they were doing. They were knocking on doors, talking to housewives, offering to work to earn a little piece of bread and meat, or some cold biscuits, or potatoes and bread and a slice of strong onion; something to stick to your ribs till you could get on down the line to where you knew people, where you had friends who would put you up till you could try to find some work. I felt a funny feeling come over me standing there.

I had always played music, painted signs, and managed to do some kind of work to get a hold of a piece of money, with which I could walk in to town legal, and buy anything I wanted to eat or drink. I'd always felt that satisfied feeling of hearing a coin jingle across the counter, or at least, doing some kind of work to pay for my meals. I'd missed whole days without a meal. But I'd been pretty proud about bumming. I still hoped that I could find some kind of short job to earn me something to eat. This was the longest I had ever gone without anything to eat. More than two whole days and nights.

This was a strange town, with a funny feeling hanging over it, a feeling like there were lots of people in it—the Mexican workers, and the white workers, and the travelers of all skins and colors of eyes, caught hungry, hunting for some kind of work to do. I was too proud to go out like the other men and knock at the doors.

I kept getting weaker and emptier. I got so nervous that I commenced shaking, and couldn't hold myself still. I could smell a piece of bacon or corncake frying at a half a mile away. The very thought of fruit made me lick my hot lips. I kept shaking and looking blanker and blanker. My brain didn't work as good as usual. I couldn't think. Just got into a stupor of some kind, and sat there on the main line of the fast railroad, forgetting about even being there . . . and thinking of homes, with ice boxes, cook stoves, tables, hot meals, cold lunches, with hot coffee, ice-cold beer, home-made wine—and friends and relatives. And I swore to pay more attention to the hungry people that I would meet from there on down the line.

Pretty soon, a wiry-looking man came walking up across the low green patch, with a brown paper sack wadded up under his arm. He walked in my direction until he was about fifteen feet away, and I could see the brown stain of good-tasting grease soaking through his sack. I even sniffed, and stuck my nose up in the air, and swung my head in his direction as he got closer; and I could smell, by real instinct, the good homemade bread, onion, and salty pork that was in the sack. He sat down not more than fifty feet away, under the heavy squared timbers of the under-rigging of a water tank, and opened his sack and ate his meal, with me looking on.

He finished it slowly, taking his good easy time. He licked the ends of his fingers, and turned his head sideways to keep from spilling any of the drippings.

After he'd cleaned the sack out, he wadded it up properly, and threw it over his shoulder. I wondered if there was any crumbs in it. When he left, I says to myself, I'll go and open it up and eat the crumbs. They'll put me on to the next town.

The man walked over to where I sat and said, "What the hell are you doing settin' here on the main line . . .?"

"Waitin' fer a train," I said.

"You don't want one on top of you, do you?" he asked me.

"Nope," I says, "but I don't see none coming. . . ."

"How could you with your back to it?"

"Back?"

"Hell, yes, I seen guys end up like 'burger meat for just such carelessness as that. . . ."

"Pretty mornin'," I said to him.

"You hungry?" he asked me.

"Mister, I'm just as empty as one of them automobile cars there, headed back East to Detroit."

"How long you been this way?"

"More than two days."

"You're a dam fool. . . . Hit any houses for grub?"

"No—don't know which a way to strike out."

"Hell, you are a dam fool, for sure."

"I guess so."

"Guess, hell, I know so." He turned his eyes toward the better section of town. "Don't go up in the fine part of town to try to work for a meal. You'll starve to death, and they'll throw you in jail just for dying on the streets. But see them little shacks and houses over yonder? That's where the railroad workers live. You'll get a feed at the first house you go to, that is, if you're honest, willing to work for it, and ain't afraid to tell it just like it is."

I nodded my head up and down, but I was listening.

Before he quit talking, one of the last things that he said, was, "I been on the bum like this for a long time. I could have split my sack of eats with you right here, but you wouldn't have got any good out of it that way. Wouldn't learn you a dam thing. I had to learn it the hard way. I went to the rich part of town, and I learnt what it was like; and then I went to the working folks' end of town and seen

what it was like. And now it's up to you to go out for yourself and get you some grub when your belly's empty."

I thanked him two or three times, and we sat for a minute
or two not saying much. Just looking around. And then
he got up sort of slow and easy, and wishing me good luck,
he walked away down the side of the rails.

I don't quite know what was going on inside my head.
I got up in a little while and looked around. First, to the
north of me, then to the south of me; and, if I'd been using
what you call horse sense, I would have gone to the north
toward the shacks that belong to the railroad and farm
workers. But a curious feeling was fermenting in me, and
my brain wasn't operating on what you'd call pure sanity.
I looked in the direction that my good sense told me to go,
and started walking in the direction that would lead me to
even less to eat, drink, less of a job of work, less friends
and more hard walking and sweating, that is, in the direction of the so-called "good" part of town, where the
"moneyed" folks live.

The time of day must have been pretty close to nine
o'clock. There were signs of people rustling around, moving and working, over around the shack town; but, in the
part of town that I was going toward, there was a dead lull
of heavy sleep and morning dreams.

You could look ahead and see a steeple sticking up out
of the trees. It comes up from a quiet little church house.
A badly painted sign, crackling from the desert heat and
crisp nights, says something about the Brethren, and so,
feeling like a Brethren, you walk over and size the place up.
There in the morning sun so early, the yellow and brown
leaves are wiggling on the splattered sidewalk, like humping
worms measuring off their humps, and the sun is speckling
the driveway that takes you to the minister's door. Under
the trees it gets colder and shadier till you come to the back

door, and climbing three rotted steps, knock a little knock. Nothing happens. While you're listening through all of the rooms and floors and halls of the old house, everything gets so quiet that the soft Whoo Whoo of a switch engine back down in the yards seems to jar you. Finally, after a minute or two of waiting, threatening to walk off, thinking of the noise that your feet would make smashing the beans and seeds that had fallen from the locust trees on to the driveway, you decide to stick at the door, and knock again.

You hear somebody walking inside the house. It sounds padded, and quiet, and far away. Like a leather-footed mountain lion walking in a cave. And then it swishes through the kitchen, across the cold linoleum, and a door clicks open, and a maid walks out onto the back porch, scooting along in a blue-checkered house dress and tan apron, with a big pocket poked full of dust rags of various kinds, a little tam jerked down over her ear, and her hair jumping out into the morning breeze. She walks up to the screen door, but doesn't open it.

"Ah—er—good morning, lady," you say to her.

She says to you, "What do you want?"

You say back to her, "Why, you see, I'm hunting for a job of work."

"Yeah?"

"Yes, I'm wondering if you've got a job of work that I could do to earn a bite to eat, little snack of some kind. Grass cut. Scrape leaves. Trim some hedge. Anything like that."

"Listen, young man," she tells you, straining her words through the minister's screen, "there's a dozen of you people that come around here every day knocking on this door. I don't want to make you feel bad, or anything like that, but if the minister starts out to feed one of you, you'll go off and tell a dozen others about it, and then they'll all be down here wanting something to eat. You better get on out away from here, before you wake him up, or he'll tell you worst than I'm telling you."

"Yes'm. Thank you, ma'am." And you're off down the driveway and on the scent of another steeple.

I walked past another church. This one is made out of sandy-looking rocks, slowly but surely wearing away, and going out of style. There are two houses, one on each side, so I stood there for a minute wondering which one belongs to the minister. It was a tough choice. But, on closer looks, I saw that one house was sleepier than the other one, and I went to the sleepy one. I was right. It belonged to the minister. I knocked at the back door. A mean-tempered cat ran out from under the back porch and scampered through a naked hedge. Here nothing happened. For five minutes I knocked; still nobody woke up. So feeling ashamed of myself for even being there, I tiptoed out on to the swaying sidewalk and sneaked off across town.

Then I come to a business street. Stores just stretching and yawning, but not wide awake. I moseyed along looking in at the glass windows, warm duds too high in price, and hot, sugary-smelling bakery goods piled up for the delivery man.

A big cop, walking along behind me for half a block, looking over my shoulder, finding out what I was up to. When I turned around, he was smiling at me.

He said, "Good morning."

I said the same back to him.

He asked me, "Going to work?"

"Naw, just looking for work. Like to find a job, and hang around this town for a while."

He looked over my head, and down the street as an early morning driver ran a stop sign, and told me, "No work around here this time of the year."

"I'm generally pretty lucky at gittin' me a job. I'm a good clerk, grocery store, drug store—paint signs to boot."

He talked out into thin air, and says, "You'll starve to death around here. Or make the can."

"Can?"

"That's what I said, can."

"You mean, git in trouble?"

He nodded his head, yes. He meant trouble.

"What kinda trouble? I'm a good hand ta keep outta trouble," I went on to say.

"Listen, boy, when you're not working in this town, you're already in trouble, see? And there ain't no work for you, see? So you're in trouble already." He nodded at a barber jingling his keys at a door.

I decided that the best play I could make was to cut loose from the copper, and go on about my door knocking. So I acted like I was going somewhere. I asked him, "Say, what time of the day is it, by the way?" I tried to crowd a serious look onto my face.

He blowed some foggy breath out past a cigaret hanging limber on his lip, and looked everywhere, except at me and said, "Time for you to get going. Get off of these streets."

I kept quiet.

"Merchants gonna be coming down to open up their stores in about a minute, and they don't want to think that I let a bird like you hang around on the streets all night. Get going. Don't even look back."

And he watched me walk away, each of us knowing just about why the other one acted like he did.

Rounding a warm corner, I met a man, that, to all looks, was a traveler suffering from lack of funds. His clothes had been riding the freights, and I was pretty certain that he was riding with them. Floppy hat, greasy through the headband. A crop of whiskers just about right for getting into jail. He was on his way out of town.

I said, "Howdy. Good-morning."

"What'd the dick say to you?" He got right to the main subject.

"He was telling me how to clear Tucson of myself in five minutes flat," I told the man.

"Tough sonsaguns here, them flatfeet. Rich place. Big tourists get sick and come here for to lay around," he said, spitting off of the sidewalk, out into the street. "Mighty tough town." He talked slow and friendly, and looked at me most of the time, ducking his head, a little bit ashamed of the way he looked. "I was doing all right till I hung a high ball. Engine pulled out and left my car settin' here." Then he nodded a quick nod and ran his eyes over his dirty clothes, two shirts, wadded down inside a tough pair of whipcord cotton pants, and said, "That's how come me to be so dam filthy. Couldn't find a clean hole to ride in."

"Hell," I said, "man, you ain't half as bad off as I am as far as dirt goes. Look at me." And I looked down at my own clothes.

For the first time I stood there and thought to myself just what a funny-looking thing I was—that is, to other people walking along the streets.

He turned around, took off his hat and ran his hand through his straight hair, making it lay down on his head; he moved over a foot or two, and looked at his reflection in the big plate-glass window of a store.

Then he said, "They got a County Garden here that's a dude." His voice was sandy and broken up in little pieces. Lots of things went through your mind when he talked— wheat stems and empty cotton stalks, burnt corn, and eroded farm land. The sound was as quiet as a change in the weather, and yet, it was as strong as he needed. If I was a soldier, I would fight quicker for his talking to me, than for the cop. As I followed his talk, he added, "I been out on that pea patch a couple of shots; I know."

I told him that I'd been hitting the preachers up for a meal.

He said, "That ain't a very smart trick; quickest way to jail's by messing around the nice parts. Oughtta get out on the edge of town. That's best."

The sun was warm on the corner, and Tucson's nice houses jumped up pretty and clean, pale colors of pink and yellow. "Mighty purty sight to see. Make anybody want to come out here to live, wouldn't it?" he asked me.

"Looks like it would," I told him. We both stood and soaked our systems full of the whole thing. Yes, it is a sight to see the early morning sun get warm in Tucson.

" 'Tain't fer fellers like me'n you, though," he said.

"Just something pretty to look at," I said to him. "At least, we know it's here, towns like this to live in, and the only thing we got to do is to learn how to do some kind of work, you know, to make a living here," I said, watching the blue shadows chase around the buildings, under the trees, and fall over the adobe fences that were like regular walls around some of the buildings.

"Hot sun's good for sick folks. Lungers. TB. Consumptives come here all shot to hell, half dead from no sunshine 'er fresh air; hang around here for a few months, takin' it easy, an', by God, leave out of here as sound and well as the day they crippled in," he told me.

I cut in on him and said, "You mean, as well as they ever was. You don't mean they go out as well as the day they come in sick."

He shuffled his feet and laughed at his mistake. " 'At's right, I meant to say that. I meant to say, too, that you can come in here with a little piece of money that you saved up, 'er sold your farm or place of business to get a holt of, an' it don't last till the sun can get up good." He was smiling and moving his head.

I asked him how about the broke people that was lungers.

He said that they hung around on the outsides of the town, and lived as cheap as they could, and worked around in the crops, panned gold, or any old thing to make a living, in order to hang around the place till they could get healed up. Thousands of folks with their lungs shot all to the devil. Every other person, he told me, was a case of some kind of TB.

"Lots of different brands of lungers, huh?" I asked him.

"Hell's bells, thousand different kinds of it. Mostly 'cording to where 'bouts you ketch it, like in a mine, or a cement factory, or saw mill. Dust TB, chemical TB from paint factories, rosin TB from the saw mills."

"Boy howdy, that's hell, ain't it?" I asked him.

"If they is a hell," he told me, "I reckon that's it. To be down with some kind of a trouble, disease, that you get while you're workin', an' it fixes you to where you cain't work no more." He looked down at the ground, ran his hands down into his pockets, and I guessed that he, hisself, was a lunger.

"Yeah, I can see just how it is. Kinda messes a person up all th' way around. But, hell, you don't look so bad off to me; you can still put out plenty of work, I bet; that is, if you could find some to do." I tried to make him feel a little better.

He cleared his throat as quiet as he could, but there was the old give-away, the little dry rattle, like the ticking of a worn-out clock.

He rolled himself a smoke, and from his sack I rolled one. We both lit up from the same match, and blew smoke in the air. He thought to himself for a minute, and didn't say a word. I didn't know whether to talk any more about it or not. There is something in most men that don't like petting or pity.

What he said to me next took care of the whole thing. " 'Tain't so terr'ble a thing. I keep quiet about it mostly on account of I don't want nobody looking at me, or treating me like I was a dying calf, or an old wore-out horse with a broke leg. All I aim to do is to stay out here in this high, dry country—stay out of doors all I can, and get all the work I can. I'll come out from under it."

I could have stood there and talked to this man for a half a day, but my stomach just wasn't willing to wait much longer; and the two of us being in Tucson together would have been a matter of explaining more things to more cops. We wished each other good luck, and shook hands, and he said, "Well, maybe we'll both be millionaires' sons next time that we run onto each other. Hope so, anyhow."

The last glimpse I got of him was when I turned around for a minute, and looked back down his direction. He was walking along with his hands in his pockets, head ducked a little, and kicking in the dust with the toe of his shoe. I couldn't help but think, how friendly most people are that have all of the hard luck.

There was one more church that I had to make, the biggest one in town. A big mission, cathedral, or something. It was a great big, pretty building, with a tower, and lots of fancy rock carving on the high places. Heavy vines clumb around, holding onto the rough face of the rocks, and since it was a fairly new church, everything was just getting off to a good start.

Not familiar with the rules, I didn't know just how to go about things. I seen a young lady dressed in a sad, black robe, so I walked down a mis-matched stone walk and asked her if there was any kind of work around the place that a man could do to earn a meal.

She brushed the robe back out of her face and seemed to be a very polite and friendly person. She talked quiet and seemed to feel very sorry for me since I was so hungry.

"I just sort of heard people talkin' up in town there, an' they said that you folks would always give a stranger a chance to work fer a meal, you know, just sorta on th' road to California. . . ." I was too hungry to quit talking.

Then she took a few steps and walked up onto a low rock porch. "Sit down here where it is cooler," she told me, "and I'll go and find the Sister. She'll be able to help you, I'm sure." She was a nice-looking lady.

Before she could walk away, I felt like I'd ought to say something else, so I said, "Mighty cool porch ya got here."

She turned around, just touching her hand to a doorknob that led somewhere through a garden. We both smiled without making any noise.

She stayed gone about ten minutes. The ten minutes went pretty slow and hungry.

Sister Rosa (I will call her that for a name) appeared, to my surprise, not through the door where the first lady had gone, but through a cluster of tough vines that swung close to a little arched gate cutting through a stone wall. She was a little bit older. She was just as nice, and she listened to me while I told her why I was there. "I tried lots of other places, and this is sort of a last chance."

"I see! Well, I know that, on certain days, we have made it a practice to fix hot meals for the transient workers. Now, unless I am badly mistaken, we are not prepared to give meals out today; and I'm not just exactly certain when it will be free-ration day again. I know that you are sincere in your coming here, and I can plainly see that you are not one of the kind that travels through the country eating free meals when you can get work. I will take the responsibility onto my shoulders, and go and find Father Francisco for you, tell him your whole predicament, and let the judgment of the matter be up to him. As far as all of the sisters and nuns are concerned, we love to prepare the meals when the proper authority is given to us. I, personally, pray that Father Francisco will understand the great faith shown by your presence here, and that he will be led to extend to you the very fullest courtesy and helping hand." And Sister Rosa walked in through the same door that the first lady had walked in at.

I set there and waited ten more minutes, getting a good bit more anxious to get a meal inside of me, and I counted the leaves on a couple of waving vines. Then counted them over again according to dark green or pale green. I was just getting ready to count them according to light green, dark yellow green, and dark green, when the first young lady stepped around through a door at my back, and tapped me on the shoulder and said that if I would go around to the front door, main entrance, Father Francisco would meet me there, and we would discuss the matter until we arrived at some definite conclusion.

I got up shaking like the leaves and held onto the wall like the vines till I got myself under way, and then I walked pretty straight to the main gate.

I knocked on the door, and in about three minutes the door swung open, and there was an old man with white hair, a keen shaved face, and a clean, stiff white collar that fit him right up around his neck. He was friendly and warm. He wore a black suit of clothes which was made out of good material. He said, "How do you do?"

I stuck out my hand to shake, grabbed his and squeezed as friendly as I knew how and said, "Mister Sanfrancisco,

Frizsansco, Frisco, I'm glad to know you! Guthrie's my name. Texas. Panhandle country. Cattle. You know. Oil boom. That's what—fine day."

In a deep, quiet-sounding voice that somehow matched in with the halls of the church, he said that it was a fine day, and that he was very glad to meet me. I assured him again that I was glad to meet him, but would be somewhat gladder if I could also work for a meal. "Two days. No eats," I told him.

And then, soft and friendly as ever, his eyes shining out from the dark hall, his voice spoke up again and said, "Son, I have been in this service all of my life. I have seen to it that thousands of men just like you got to work for a meal. But, right at this moment, there is no kind of work to do here, no kind of work at all; and therefore, it would be just a case of pure charity. Charity here is like charity every-where; it helps for a moment, and then it helps no more. It is part of our policy to be charitable, for to give is better than to receive. You seem still to retain a good measure of your pride and dignity. You do not beg outright for food, but you offer to do hard labor in order to earn your meal. That is the best spirit in this world. To work for yourself is to help others, and to help others is to help yourself. But you have asked a certain question; and I must answer that question in your own words to satisfy your own thinking. You asked if there is work that you can do to earn a meal. My answer is this: There is no work around here that you can do, and therefore, you cannot earn a meal. And, as for charity, God knows, we live on charity ourselves."

The big, heavy door closed without making even a slight sound.

I walked a half a mile trembling past the yards, down to the shacks of the railroad workers, the Mexicanos, the

Negroes, and the whites, and knocked on the first door. It was a little brown wooden house, costing, all together, less than one single rock in the church. A lady opened the door. She said that she didn't have anything for me to do; she acted crabby and fussy, chewing the rag, and talking sour to herself. She went back in the house again, still talking.

"Young men, old men, all kinds of men; walking, walking, all of the time walking, piling off of the freights, making a run across my tomato garden, and knocking on my door; men out gallivantin' around over the country; be better off if you'd of stayed at home; young boys taking all kinds of crazy chances, going hungry, thirsty, getting all dirty and ugly, ruining your clothes, maybe getting run over and killed by a truck or a train—who knows? Yes. Yes. Yes. Don't you dare run away, young nitwit. I'm a fixing you a plate of the best I got. Which is all I got. Blame fools." (Mumbling) "Ought to be at home with your family; that's where you'd ought to be. Here." (Opening the door again, coming out on the porch.) "Here, eat this. It'll at least stick to your ribs. You look like an old hungry hound dog. I'd be ashamed to ever let the world beat me down any such a way. Here. Eat every bite of this. I'll go and fix you a glass of good milk. Crazy world these days. Everybody's cutting loose and hitting the road."

Down the street, I stopped at another house. I walked up to the front door, and knocked. I could hear somebody moving around on the inside, but nobody come to the door. After a few more knocks, and five minutes of waiting, a little woman opened the door back a ways, took a peek out, but wouldn't open up all of the way.

She looked me over good. It was so dark in her house that I couldn't tell much about her. Just some messed-up hair, and her hand on the door. It was clean, and reddish, like she'd been in the dishwater, or putting out some clothes. Mexican or white, you couldn't tell which. She asked me in a whisper, "What, what do you want?"

"Lady, I'm headin' ta California lookin' fer work. I just wondered if you had a job of work of some kind that a man could do to earn a lunch. Sack with somethin' in it ta carry along."

She gave me the feeling that she was afraid of something. "No, I haven't any kind of work. Sshhh. Don't talk so loud. And I haven't got anything in the house—that is—anything fit to pack for you to eat."

"I just got a meal off of th' lady down th' street here, an' just thought maybe—you know, thought maybe a little sack of somethin' might come in purty handy after a day or two out on the desert—any old thing. Not very hard ta please," I told her.

"My husband is sleeping. Don't talk so loud. I'm a little ashamed of what I've got left over here. Pretty poor when you need a good meal. But, if you're not too particular about it, you're welcome to take it with you. Wait here a minute."

I stood there looking back up across the tomato patch to the railroad yards. A switch engine was trotting loose cars up and down the track and I knew that our freight was making up.

She stuck her hand out through an old green screen door, and said, "Sshhh," and I tried to whisper "thank you," but she just kept motioning, nodding her head.

I was wearing a black slip-over sweater and I pulled the loose neck open, and pushed the sack down into the bosom. She'd put something good and warm from the warming-oven into the sack, because already I could feel the good hot feeling against my belly.

Trains were limbering up their big whistles, and there was a long string of cars made up and raring to step. A hundred and ten cars meant pretty certain that she was a hot one with the right-of-way to the next division.

A tired-looking Negro boy trotted down the cinders, looking at the new train to spot him a reefer car to crawl into. He seen that he had a spare second or two, and he stopped alongside of me.

"Ketchin' 'er out?" I asked him.

"Yeah. I'm switchin' ovah pretty fas'. Jes' got in. Didn' even have no time ta hustle me up a feed. I guess I c'n eat when I gets to wheah I'm headed." His pale khaki work clothes were soaked with salty sweat. Loose coal soot, oil smoke, and colored dust was smeared all over him. He made a quick trip over to a clear puddle of water and laid flat of his belly to suck up all of the water he could hold. He blowed out his breath, and came back wiping his face with a bandana handkerchief as dirty as the railroad itself, and then the handkerchief being cool and wet, he tied it around his forehead, with a hard knot on the back of his head. He looked up at me, and shook his head sideways and said, "Keeps th' sweat from runnin' down so bad."

It was an old hobo trick. I knew it, but didn't have any kind of a handkerchief. The heat of the day was getting to be pretty hard to take. I asked him, "When's th' last time ya had anything ta eat?"

"El Paso," he told me. "Coupl'a days back."

My hand didn't ask me anything about it, but it was okay with me anyhow, and I slid the sack out of my sweater and handed it over to him. Still warm. I knew just about how good it felt when he got his hands on that warm greasy sack. He bit into a peanut-butter sandwich together with a hunk of salty pork between two slices of bread. He looked toward the water hole again, but the train jarred the cars a few feet, and we both made for the side of the high yellow cars.

We got split up a few yards, and had to hang separate cars, and I thought maybe he wouldn't make it. I looked down from the top of mine, and saw him trotting easy along the ground, jumping an iron switchpost or two, and holding his sandwich and sack in both hands. He crammed the sandwich down into the sack, rolled the top edge of the sack over a couple of twists, and stuck the sack into his teeth, letting both of his hands free to use to climb up the side of the car. On the top, he crawled along the blistered tin roof until he set facing me, me on the end of my car, and him on the end of his. It was getting windier as the train got her speed up, and we waved our hats "good-bye and good luck and Lord bless you" to the old town of Tucson.

I looked at the lids of my two reefer holes, and both was down so tight that you couldn't budge them with a team of horses. I looked over at my partner again, and seen that he'd got his lid open. He braced the heavy lid open, using the lock-bar for a wedge, so that it couldn't fly shut in the high wind. I seen him crawl down inside, examine the ice hole, and then he stuck his head out, and motioned for me to come on over and ride. I got up and jumped the space between the two cars, and clumb down out of the hot winds; and he finished his lunch without saying a word in the wind.

Our car was an easy rider. No flat wheels to speak of. This is not true of many cars on an empty train, because loaded, a train rides smoother than when empty. Before long, a couple of other riders stuck their heads down into the hole and hollered, "Anybody down in this hole?"

We yelled back, "Two! Room fer two more! Throw yer stuff down! C'mon down!"

A bundle hit the floor, and with it come an old blue serge

coat, from a good suit of clothes, no doubt, during one of the earlier wars. Then one man clumb through each of the holes, and grabbed the coarse net of wire that lined the ice compartment. They settled down into a good position for riding and looked around.

"Howdy. I'm Jack."

The Negro boy nodded his head, "Wheeler." He put the last bite into his mouth, swallowed it down, and said, "Plenty dry."

The second stranger struck a match to relight a spitty cigaret, and mumbled, "Schwartz, my name. Goddam this bull tobaccer!"

The country outside, I knew, was pretty, sunny and clear, with patches of green farming country sticking like moss along the sandy banks of the little dry desert creeks. Yes, and I would like to climb out on top and take a look at it. I told the other three men, "Believe I'll roll me one of them fags, if ya don't mind, an' then git out on top an' watch th' tourists go past."

The owner of the tobacco handed me the sweaty little sack, and I licked one together. Lighting it up, I thanked him, and then I clumb up on top, and soaked up the scenery by ten million square miles. The fast whistling train put up a pretty stiff wind. It caused my cigaret to burn up like a flare of some kind, and then a wild current tore the paper from around the tobacco, and it flew in a million directions, including my own face. Fighting with the cigaret, I tilted my head in the wrong direction, and my hat sailed fifty feet up into the air, rolled out across the sand, and hung on a sticker bush. That was the last I seen of it.

One of the men down in the hole hollered out, "Havin' quite a time up there, ain't you, mister?"

"Quite a blow, quite a blow!" I yelled back into the hole.

"Seein' much up there?" another one asked me.

"Yeah, I see enuff sunshine an' fresh air ta cure all th' trouble in th' world!" I told them.

"How fast we travelin'?"

"I'd jedge about forty or forty-five."

The land changed from a farming country into a weather-beaten, crumbling, and wasted stretch, with gully washes traveling in every way, brownish, hot rocks piled into canyons, and low humps topped with irony weeds and long-eared rabbits loping like army mules to get away from the red-hot train. The hills were deep bright colors, reddish sand, yellow clays, and always, to the distance, there stood up the high, flat-top cliffs, breaking again into the washing, drifting, windy face of the desert. We followed a highway, and once in a while a car coasted past, full of people going somewhere, and we'd wave and yell at one another.

"Must be th' first time you ever crossed this country," the colored boy hollered up at me.

"Yeah, it is." I blinked my eyes to try to wash the powdery dust out of them. "First time."

"I been over this road so many times I ought to tell the conductor how to go," he said. "We'll be headin' down through the low country before very long. You'll run a hundred miles below sea level and look up all at once, and see snow on the mountains and then you'll start over the hump right up to the snow. And you'll freeze yourself coming up out of all of this heat."

"Mighty funny thing."

"You can stay down in this hole and keep pretty warm. If all of us huddle up and cuddle up and put our hands in each others' pockets, our heat'll keep us from freezing."

The coal dust and the heat finally got too tough for me, so I clumb down. The low pounding of the wheels under us, and the swaying and quivering of the train, got so tiresome that we drifted right off to sleep, and covered the miles that would put us across the California line. Night got dark, and we got closer together to keep warm.

There is a little railroad station just east of Yuma where you stop to take on water. It is still at desert altitude, so you climb down and start walking around to limber up a little. The moon here is the fullest and brightest that you ever saw. The medium-size palm plants and fern-looking trees are waving real easy in the moonlight, and the brush on the face of the desert throws black shapes and shadows out across the sand. The sand looks as smooth as a slick pool of crude oil, and shines up yellow and white all around. The clear-cut cactus shapes, the brush, and the silky sand makes one of the prettiest pictures that you ever hope to see.

All of the riders, seeing how pretty the night was, walked, trotted, stretched their legs and arms around, moved their shoulders, and took exercise to get their blood to running right again. Matches flare up as the boys light their smokes, and I could get a quick look at their sunburnt, windburnt faces. Flop hats, caps, or just bareheaded, they looked like the pioneers that got to knowing the feel and the smell of the roots and leaves across the early days of the desert, and it makes me want to sort of hang around there.

Voices talked and said everything.

"Hello."

"Match on yuh?"

"Yeah—shorts on that smoke."

"Headin'?"

" 'Frisco—ship out if I can."

"How's crops in South California?"

"Crops—or cops?"

"Crops. Celery. Fruit. Avacados."

"Work's easy ta git a holt of, but money's hard as hell."

"Hell, Nelly, I wuz borned a-workin', an' I ain't quit yit!"

"Workin', er lookin' fer work?"

There was a big mixture of people here. I could hear the fast accents of men from the big Eastern joints. You heard the slow, easy-going voices of Southern swamp dwellers, and the people from the Southern hills and mountains. Then another one would talk up, and it would be the dry, nosy twang of the folks from the flat wheat plains; or the dialect of people that come from other countries, whose parents talked another tongue. Then you would hear the slow, outdoor voices of the men from Arizona, riding a short hop to get a job, see a girl, or to throw a little celebration. There was the deep, thick voices of two or three Negroes. It sounded mighty good to my ears.

All at once the men hushed up. Somebody nudged somebody else, and said, "Quiet."

Then everybody ducked their heads, turned around and whispered, "Scatter out. Lay low. Hey! You! Git rid of that cigaret! Bulls a-comin'!"

Three men, dressed in hard-wearing railroad suits, walked up to us before we could get gone.

Flashing bright lanterns and flashlights on us, we heard them holler, "Hey! What's goin' on here?"

We didn't say anything back.

"Where you birds headed for?"

Still silence.

"What's wrong? Buncha dam dumb-dumbs? Can't none of you men say nuthin'?" The three men carried guns where it was plain to see, and hard to overlook. Their hands resting on the butts, shuffling their lights around in their hands. They rounded us up. The desert is a good place to look at, but not so easy to hide on. One or two men ducked between cars. A dozen or so stepped out across the desert, and slid down out of sight behind little bushes. The cops herded the rest of us into a crowd.

Men kept scattering, taking a chance of going against the cops' orders to "halt." The few that stood still were asked several questions. "Where yuh headed?"

"Yuma."

"That'll be th' price of a ticket to Yuma. Step right into the office there and buy your ticket—hurry up."

"Hell, fellers, you know I ain't got th' price of no ticket; I wouldn't be ridin' this freight if I had th' money fer a ticket."

"Search 'im."

Each man was shook down, jackets, jumpers, coats, britches and suspenders, pants legs, shoes. As the searching went on, most of us managed to make a quick run for it, and get away from the bulls. Trotting around the end of the train, thinking that we'd give them the dodge, we run head-on into their spotlights, and was face to face with them. We stopped and stood still. One by one, they went through our pockets looking for money. If they found any money, whatever it was, the man was herded into the little house to buy a ticket as far down the line as his money would carry him. Lots of the boys had a few bucks on them. They felt pretty silly, with nothing to eat on, being pushed into buying "tickets" to some town they said they were heading for.

"Find anything on you?" a man asked me.

"Huh uh." I didn't have any for them to find.

"Listen, see that old boy right in front of you? Pinch 'im. Make 'im listen to what I'm tellin' him. Ppsssst!"

I punched the man right in front of me. He waited a minute, and then looked around sideways. "Listen," I said to him.

The other rider commenced to talk, "I just found out"—

then he went down into a whisper "that this train is gonna pull out. Gonna try ta ditch us. When I holler, we're all gonna make a break an' swing 'er. This is a hell of a place to get ditched."

We shook our heads. We all kept extra still, and passed the word along.

Then the train moved backwards a foot or two—and the racket roared all out across the desert—jarring itself into the notion of traveling again, and all at once the man at my side hollered as loud as the high-ball whistle itself, "Go, boy!"

His voice rung out across the cactus.

"Jack rabbit, run!"

Men jumped out from everywhere, from between the cars they'd been hanging onto, and out from behind the clumps of cactus weeds, and the cops, nervous, and looking in every direction, stuttered, yelled, and cussed and snorted, but when the moon looked down at the train steaming out, it saw all of us sticking on the sides, and on the top, waving, cussing, and thumbing our noses back in the faces of the "ticket" sellers.

Then it got morning. A cold draft of wind was sucking in around the sides of the reefer lid. I'd asked the boys during the night how about closing the lid all of the way down. They told me that you had to keep it wedged open a little with the handle of the lock, to keep from getting locked inside. We stuck close together, using each other for sofas and pillows, and hoped for the sun to get warmer.

I asked them, "Wonder how heavy that big ol' lid is, anyhow?"

"Weighs close to a hunderd pound," the Negro boy said. He was piled in the corner, stretched out, and his whole body was shaking with the movement of the train.

"Be a hell of a note if a feller wuz ta git up there, an' start ta climb out, an' that big lid wuz ta fly down an' ketch his head," another fellow said. He screwed his face up just thinking about it.

"I knew a boy that lost a arm that way."

"I know a boy that used ta travel around on these dam freights," I said, "harvestin', an' ramblin' around; an' he was shipped back to his folks in about a hundred pieces. I seen his face. Wheel had run right across it, from his ear, across his mouth, over to his other ear. And I don't know, but every day, ridin' these rattlers, I ketch myself thinkin' about that boy."

" 'Bout as bad a thing as I can think of, is th' two boys they found starved to death, locked up inside of one of these here ice cars. Figgered they'd been in there dead 'bout a week or two when they found 'em. One of 'em wasn't more'n twelve or thirteen years old. Jist a little squirt. They crawled in through the main door, an' pulled it to. First thing they knew, a brakeman come along, locked th' door, dropped a bolt in th' lock, an' there they was. Nobody even knew where they's from, or nuthin'. Just as well been one of your folks or mine." He shook his head, thinking.

The heat got worse as the train sailed along. "Git out on top, an' you c'n see Old Mexico," somebody said.

"Might as well ta git yer money's worth," I told him, and in a minute I'd scrambled up the wire net again, and pushed the heavy lid back. The wind was getting hotter. I could feel the dry, burning sting that let me know that I was getting a windburn. I peeled off my sweater, and shirt, and dropped them onto the hot sheet iron, and hooked my arm around an iron brace, and laid stretched out flat of my back, getting a good Mexican border sunburn along with my Uncle Sam windburn. I get dark awful quick in the sun and wind. My skin likes it, and so do I.

The Negro boy clumb up and set down beside me. His greasy cap whipped in the wind, but he held the bill tight, and it didn't blow off. He turned the cap around backwards, bill down the back of his neck, and there was no more danger of losing it. "Some country!" he told me, rolling his eyes across the sand, cactus, and crooked little bushes. "I guess every part of th' country's good for somethin', if you c'n jist only find out what!"

"Yeah," I said, "Wonder what this is good for?"

"Rabbits, rattlesnakes, gila monsters, tarantulars, childs of the earth, scorpions, lizards, coyotes, wild cats, bob cats, grasshoppers, beetles, bugs, bears, bulls, buffaloes, beef," he said.

"All of that out there?" I asked him.

"No, I was jist runnin' off at th' mouth," he laughed. I knew that he had learned a lot about the country somewhere, and guessed that he'd beat this trail more times than one. He moved his shoulders and squared his self on top of the train. I saw big strong muscles and heavy blood vessels, and tough, calloused palms of his hands; and I knew that for the most part he was an honest working man.

"Lookit that ol' rabbit go!" I poked him in the ribs, and pointed across a ditch.

"Rascal really moves!" he said, keeping up with the jack.

"Watch 'im pick up speed," I said.

"Sonofa bitch. See him clear dat fence?" He shook his head, and smiled a little bit.

Three or four more rabbits began showing their ears above the black weeds. Big grayish brown ears lolling along as loose and limber as could be.

"Whole dam family's out!" he told me.

"Looks like it! Ma an' pa an' th' whole fam damly!" I said. "Purty outfits, ain't they? Rabbits."

He eyed the herd and nodded his head. He was a deep-thinking man. I knew just about what he was thinking about, too.

"How come you ta come out on top ta ride?" I asked my friend.

"The men packing the tobacco didn't much like me."

"Why not?"

"Oh, I dunno. Said somebody had ta go."

"How'd it come up?" I asked him.

"Well, I sort of asked him for a cigaret, and he said that he wasn't panhandlin' for nickels to get tobacco for boys like me. I don't want to have no trouble."

"Boys like you?"

"Yeah, I dunno. Difference 'tween you an' me. He'd let you have tobacco, 'cause you an' him's th' same color."

"What in th' Goddam hell has that got ta do with ridin' together?" I asked him.

"He said it was gettin' pretty hot down in th' hatch, you know, said ever'body was sweatin' a lot. He told me th' further away from each other that we stay th' better we're gonna get along, but I knew what he meant by it."

"Wuz that all?"

"Yeah."

"This is one hell of a place ta go ta bringin' up that kinda dam talk," I said.

The train drew into El Centro, and stopped and filled her belly, panting and sweating. The riders could be seen hitting the ground for a walk and a stretch.

Schwartz, the man with the sack of smoking, come out of his hole, grumbling and cussing under his breath. "Worst Goddam hole on the train, and I had to get caught down in it all night!" he told me, climbing past me on his way to the ground.

"Best ridin' car on th' rail," I said. I was right, too.

"It's th' worst in my book, boy," Schwartz said.

The fourth man from our end of the car crawled out and dropped down to the cinders. All during the ride, he hadn't mentioned his name. He was a smiling man, even walking along by his self. When he walked up behind us, he heard Schwartz say something else about how bad our riding hole was, and he said in a friendly way, " 'Bout th' easiest riding car I've hung in a many a day."

"Like hell it is," Schwartz spoke up, stopping, and looking the fellow in the face. The man looked down mostly at Schwartz's feet and listened to see what Schwartz would say next. Then Schwartz went on talking at the mouth, "It might ride easy, but th' Goddam thing stinks—see?"

"Stinks?" The man looked at him funny.

"I said stink, didn't I?" Schwartz ran his hand down in his pocket. This is a pretty bad thing to do amongst strangers, talking in this tone of voice and running your hand in your pocket. "You don't have to be afraid, Stranger, I ain't got no barlow knife," Schwartz told him.

And then the other man looked along the cinders and smiled and said, "Listen, mister, I wouldn't be the least bit afraid of a whole car load of fellows just like you, with a knife in each pocket and two in each hand."

"Tough about it, huh?" Schwartz frowned the best he could.

"Ain't nothing tough about me, sort of—but I don't make a practice of bein' afraid of you nor anybody else." He settled his self a little more solid on his feet.

It looked like a good fist fight was coming off. Schwartz looked around, up and down the track. "I bet you a dollar that most of the fellows riding this train feel just about like I do about riding in a hole with a dam nigger!"

The Negro boy made a walk toward Schwartz. The smiling man stepped in between them. The Negro said,

"Nobody don't hafta take my part, I can take up for myself. Ain't nobody gonna call me—"

"Take it easy, Wheeler, take it easy," the other man said. "This guy wants something to happen. Just likes to hear his guts crawl."

I took the Negro boy by the arm, and we walked along talking it over. "Nobody else thinks like that goof. Hell, let 'im go an' find another car. Let 'im go. They'll run him out of every hole on th' train. Don't worry. Ya cain't help what ya cain't help."

"You know, that's right," Wheeler told me.

He pulled his arm away from me, and straightened his button-up sweater a little. We turned around and looked back at our friend and Schwartz. Just like you would shoo a fly or a chicken down the road, our friend was waving his arms, and shooing Schwartz along. We could hear him awful faint, yelling, "Go on, you old bastard! Get your gripey ass out of here! And if you so much as even open your trap to make trouble for anybody riding this train, I'll ram my fist down your throat!" It was a funny thing. I felt a little sorry for the old boy, but he needed somebody to teach him a lesson, and evidently he was in the hands of a pretty good teacher.

We waited till the dust had settled again, and then our teacher friend trotted up to where we stood. He was waving at bunches of men, and laughing deep down in his lungs.

"That's that, I reckon," he was saying when he got up to us.

The colored boy said, "I'm gonna run over acrost th' highway an' buy a package of smokes. Be back in a minute—" He left us and ran like a desert rabbit.

There was a faucet dripping water beside a yellow railroad building. We stopped and drank all we could hold.

Washed our hands and faces, and combed our heads. There was a long line of men waiting to use the water. While we walked away, holding our faces to the slight breath of air that was moving across the yards, he asked me, "Say your name was?"

I said, "Woody."

"Mine's Brown. Glad ta meet you, Woody. You know I've run onto this skin trouble before." He walked along on the cinders.

"Skin trouble. That's a dam good name for it." I walked along beside him.

"Hard to cure it after it gets started, too. I was born and raised in a country that's got all kinds of diseases, and this skin trouble is the worst one of the lot," he told me.

"Bad," I answered him.

"I got sick and tired of that kind of stuff when I was just a kid growing up at home. You know. God, I had hell with some of my folks about things like that. But, seems like, little at a time, I'd sort of convince them, you know; lots of folks I never could convince. They're kinda like the old bellyache fellow, they cause a lot of trouble to a hundred people, and then to a thousand people, all on account of just some silly, crazy notion. Like you can help what color you are. Goddamit all. Goddamit all. Why don't they spend that same amount of time and trouble doing something good, like painting their Goddam barns, or building some new roads?"

The four-time whistle blew, and the train bounced back a little. That was our sign. Guys walked and ran along the side of the cars, mumbling and talking, swinging onto their iron ladders, and mounting the top of the string. Wheeler hadn't come back with the cigarets. I went over the top, and when I got set down, I commenced yanking my shirt off again, being a big hand for sunshine. I felt it burning my hide. The train was going too fast now for anybody to catch it. If Wheeler was on the ground, he's just naturally going to have a little stay over in El Centro. I looked over the other edge of the car, and saw his head coming over the rim, and I saw that he was smiling. Smoke flew like a rain cloud from a new tailor-made cigaret in his mouth. He scooted over beside me, and flipped ashes into the breeze.

"You get anything to eat?" he said.

I said, "No," that I hadn't got anything.

He reached under his sweater and under his belt and pulled out a brown paper sack, wet, dripping with ice water, and held it up to me and said, "Cold pop. I brung a couple. Wait. Here's something to gnaw on with it," and he handed me a milk candy bar.

"Candy's meal," I told him.

"Sure is; last you all day. That was my last four bits."

"Four bits more'n I got," I joked.

We chewed and drank and talked very little then for a long time. Wheeler said that he was turning the train back to the railroad company at Indio. That's the town coming up.

"I know just where to go," Wheeler told me, when the train come to a quick stop. "Don't you worry 'bout me, boy." Then before I could talk, he went on saying, "Now listen, I know this track. See? Now, don't you hang on 'er till she gets to Los Angeles, but you leave 'er up here at Colton. You'll be just about fifty miles from L.A. If you stay on till you come to L.A., them big dicks'll throw you so far back in that Lincoln Heights jail, you never will see daylight again. So remember, get off at Colton, hitch on in to Pasadena, and head out north through Burbank, San Fernando, and stay right on that 99 to Turlock." Wheeler was climbing over the side. He stuck out his hand and we shook.

I said, "Good luck, boy, take it easy, but take it."

He said, "Same to you, boy, and I always take it easy, and I always take it!"

Then he stood still for a few seconds, bending his body over the edge of the car, and looked at me and said, "Been good to know you!"

Indio to Edom, rich farm lands. Edom to Banning, with the trees popping up everywhere. Banning to Beaumont, with the fruit hanging all over the trees, and groceries all over the ground, and people all over everything. Beaumont to Redlands, the world turned into such a thick green garden of fruits and vegetables that I didn't know if I was dreaming or not. Coming out of the dustbowl, the colors so bright and smells so thick all around, that it seemed almost too good to be true.

Redlands to Colton. A railroad and farming town, full of people that are wheeling and dealing. Hitch-hikers are standing around thicker than citizens. The 99 looks friendly, heading west to the coast. I'll see the Pacific Ocean, go swimming, and flop on the beach. I'll go down to Chinatown and look around. I'll see the Mexican section. I'll see the whole works. But, no, I don't know. Los Angeles is too big for me. I'm too little for Los Angeles. I'll duck Los Angeles and go north by Pasadena, out through Burbank, like Wheeler told me. I'm against the law, they tell me.

Sign says: "Fruit, see, but don't pick it." Another one reads: "Fruit—beat it." Another one: "Trespassers prosecuted. Keep Out. Get away from Here."

Fruit is on the ground, and it looks like the trees have been just too glad to grow it, and give it to you. The tree likes to grow and you like to eat it; and there is a sign between you and the tree saying: "Beware The Mean Dog's Master."

Fruit is rotting on the ground all around me. Just what in the hell has gone wrong here, anyhow? I'm not a very smart man. Maybe it ought to be this way, with the crops laying all around over the ground. Maybe they couldn't get no pickers just when they wanted them, and they just let the fruit go to the bad. There's enough here on the ground to feed every hungry kid from Maine to Florida, and from there to Seattle.

A Twenty-nine Ford coupé stops and a Japanese boy gives me a ride. He is friendly, and tells me all about the country, the crops and vineyards.

"All you have got to do out in this country is to just pour water around some roots, and yell, 'Grapes!' and next morning the leaves are full grown, and the grapes are hanging in big bunches, all nice and ready to pick!"

The little car traveled right along. A haze was running around the trees, and the colors were different than any that I'd ever seen in my life. The knotty little oak and iron brush that I'd been used to seeing rolling with the Oklahoma hills and looking smoky in the hollers, had been home to my eyes for a long time. My eyes had got sort of used to Oklahoma's beat-up look, but here, with this sight of fertile, rich, damp, sweet soil that smelled like the dew of a jungle, I was learning to love another, greener, part of life. I've tried to keep loving it ever since I first seen it.

The Japanese boy said, "Which way do you plan to go through Los Angeles?"

"Pasadena? That how ya say it? Then north through Burbank, out that a-way!"

"If you want to stay with me, you'll be right in the middle of Los Angeles, but you'll be on a big main highway full of trucks and cars out of town. Road forks here. Make up your mind quick."

"Keep a-drivin'," I said, craning my neck back to watch

the Pasadena road disappear under the palm trees to the north of us.

We rounded a few hills and knolls, curving in our little jitney, and all at once, coming over a high place, the lights of Los Angeles jumped up, running from north to south as far as I could see, and hanging around on the hills and mountains just as if it was level ground. Red and green neon flickering for eats, sleeps, sprees, salvation, money made, lent, blowed, spent. There was an electric sign for dirty clothes, clean clothes, honky tonky tonks, no clothes, floor shows, gyp-joints, furniture in and out of homes. The fog was trying to get a headlock on the houses along the high places. Patches of damp clouds whiffed along the paving in crazy, disorganized little bunches, hunting some more clouds to work with. Los Angeles was lost in its own pretty lights and trying to hold out against the big fog that rolls in from that ocean, and the people that roll in just as reckless, and rambling, from the country as big as the ocean back East.

It was about seven or eight o'clock when I shook hands with my Japanese friend, and we wished each other luck. I got out on the pavement at the Mission Plaza, a block from everything in the world, and listened to the rumbling of people and smoking of cars pouring fumes out across the streets and alleys.

"Hungry?" the boy asked me.

"Pretty empty. Just about like an old empty tub," I laughed at him. If he'd offered me a nickel or a dime, I would of took it, I'd of spent it on a bus to get the hell out of that town. I was empty. But not starved yet, and more than something to eat, I felt like I wanted to get outside of the city limits.

"Good luck! Sorry I haven't any money on me!" he hollered as he circled and wheeled away into the big traffic.

I walked along a rough, paved street. To my left, the slummy old houses ran up a steep hill, and tried to pretend that they were keeping families of people in out of the wind and the weather. To my right there was the noise of the grinding, banging, clanging, and swishing of the dirty railroad yards. Behind me, south, the big middle of Los Angeles, chasing hamburgers. Ahead of me, north, the highway ached on, blinking its red and green eyes and groaning under the heavy load of traffic that it had to carry. Trains hooted in the low yards close under my right elbow, and scared me out of my wits.

"How'd ya git outta this town?" I asked a copper.

He looked me over good, and said, "Just follow your nose, boy. You can read signs. Just keep traveling!"

I walked along the east side of the yards. There was lots of little restaurants beside the road, where the tourists, truck drivers, and railroaders dropped in for a meal. Hot coffee steamed up from the cups along the counters, and the smell of meat frying leaked out through the doors. It was a cold night. Drops of steamy moisture formed on the windows, and it blurred out the sight of the people eating and drinking.

I stopped into a little, sawed-off place, and the only person in sight, away back, was an old Chinaman. He looked up at me with his gray beard, but didn't say a single word.

I stood there a minute, enjoying the warmth. Then I walked back to where he was, and asked him, "Have ya got anything left over that a man could do some work for?"

He set right still, reading his paper, and then looked up and said, "I work. Hard all day. Every day. I got big bunch people to feed. We eat things left over. We do work."

"No job?" I asked him.

"No job. We do job. Self."

I hit the breeze again and tried two or three other places

along the road. Finally, I found an old gray-headed couple humped up in front of a loop-legged radio, listening to some of the hollering being done by a lady name Amy Semple Temple, or something like that. I woke the old pair up out of their sermon on hell fire and hot women, and asked them if they had some work to do for a meal. They told me to grab some scalding hot water and mop the place down. After three times over the floors, tables, kitchen, and dishes, I was wrapping myself around a big chicken dinner, with all of the trimmings.

The old lady handed me a lunch and said, "Here's something extra to take with you—don't let John know about it."

And as I walked out the door again, listening to the whistle of the trains getting ready to whang out, John walked over and handed me a quarter and said, "Here's somethin' ta he'p ye on down th' road. Don't let th' ol' lady know."

A man dressed in an engineer's cap and striped overhalls told me that a train was making up right at that point, and would pull out along about four in the morning. It was now about midnight, so I dropped into a coffee joint and took an hour sipping at a cup. I bought a pint of pretty fair red port wine with the change, and stayed behind a signboard, drinking wine to keep warm.

A Mexican boy walked up on me and said, "Pretty cold iss it not? Do you want a smoke?"

I lit up one of his cigarets, and slipped him the remains of the wine jug. He took about half of the leavings, and looked at me between gulps, "Ahhhh! Warms you up, no?"

"Kill it. I done had my tankful," I told him, and heard the bubbles play a little song that quit when the wine was all downed.

"Time's she gittin' ta be? Know?" I said to him.

"Four o'clock or after," he said.

"When does that Frenso freight run?" I asked him.

"Right now," he said.

I ran out into the yards, jumping dark rails, heavy switches, and darting among the blind cars. A string of black ones were moving backwards in the wrong direction. I mounted the side and went over the top, and down the other side, and took a risk on scrambling between another string at the hitch. I could just barely see, it was so dark. The cars were so blended into the night. But, all at once, I looked up within about a foot of my face, and saw a blur, and a light, and a blur, and a light, and I knew that here was one going my way. I watched the light come along between the cars, and finally spotted an open top car, which was easier to see; and grabbed the ladder, and jumped over into a load of heavy cast-iron machinery. I laid down in the end of the car, and rested.

The train pulled along slow for a while. I ducked as close up behind the head end of the car as I could to break the wind. Pretty soon the old string got the kinks jerked out of her, and whistled through a lot of little towns. Then we hit a good fifty for about an hour, and started up some pretty tough grade. It got colder higher up. The fog turned into a drizzle, and the drizzle into a slow rain.

I imagined a million things bouncing along in the dark. A quick tap of the air brakes to slow the train down, and the hundred tons of heavy machinery would shift its weight all over me. I felt so soft and little. I had felt so tough and big just a few minutes ago.

The lonesome whip of the wind sounded even more lonesome when the big engine joined in on the whistling. The wheels hummed a song, and the weather got colder. We started gaining altitude almost like an airplane. I pulled myself up into a little ball and shook till my bones ached all over. The weather didn't pay any more attention to my clothes than if I didn't have them on. My muscles drew up into hard, leathery strings that hurt. I kept a little warmer by remembering people I'd known, how they looked, faces and all, and all about the warm desert, and cactus and sunshine growing everywhere; picturing in my mind something friendly and free, something to sort of blot out the wind and the freezing train.

On a big slope, that went direct into Bakersfield, we stopped on a siding to let the mail go by. I got off and walked ten or fifteen cars down the track, creaking like an eighty-year-old rocking chair. I had to walk slow along the steep cinder bank, gradually getting the use of myself back again.

I was past the train when the engineer turned the brakes loose, give her the gun, and started off.

I'd never seen a train start up this fast before. Most trains take a little time chugging, getting the load swung into motion. But, setting on this long straight slope, she just lit out. Running along the side, I just barely managed to catch it. I had to take a different car as mine was somewhere down the line. In a few minutes the train was making forty miles an hour, then fifty, then sixty, down across the strip of country where the mountains meet the desert south of Bakersfield. The wind blew and the morning was frosty and cold. Between the two cars, it was freezing. I managed to mount to the top, and pull a reefer lid open. I looked in, and saw the hole was filled with fine chips of new ice.

I held on with all of my strength, and crawled over and opened up another lid. It was packed with chipped ice, too. I was too near froze to try the jump from one car to the next, so I crawled down the ladder between two cars—sort of a wind-break—and held on.

My hands froze stiff around the handle of the ladder, but they were getting too cold and weak to hold on much longer. I listened below to five or six hundred railroad wheels, clipping the rails through the morning frost, and felt the windy ice from the refrigerator car that I was hanging onto. The fingers of one hand slipped from around the handle. I spent twenty minutes or so trying to fish an old rag out of my pocket. Finally I got it wound around my hands and, by blowing my breath inside the cloth for a few minutes, seemed to be getting them a little warmer.

The weather gained on me, though, and my breath turned into thick frosty ice all over my handkerchief, and my hands started freezing worse than ever. My finger slid loose again, and I remembered the tales of the railroaders, people found along the tracks, no way of telling who they were.

If I missed my hold here, one thing was sure, I'd never know what hit me, and I'd never slide my feet under that good eating table full of hot square meals at the big marble house of my rich aunt.

The sun looked warmer as it came up, but the desert is cold when it is clear early in the morning, and the train fanned such a breeze that the sun didn't make much difference.

That was the closest to the 6x3 that I've ever been. My mind ran back to millions of things—my whole life was brought up to date, and all of the people I knew, and all that they meant to me. And, no doubt, my line of politics took on quite a change right then and there, even though I didn't know I was getting educated at the time.

The last twenty miles into the Bakersfield yards was the hardest work, and worst pain, that I ever run onto; that is, of this particular brand. There are pains and work of different sorts, but this was a job that my life depended on, and I didn't have even one ounce to say about it. I was just a little animal of some kind swinging on for my life, and the pain was not being able to do anything about it.

I left the train long before it stopped, and hit the ground running and stumbling. My legs worked more like toys than like my real ones. But the sun was warm in Bakersfield, and I drank all of the good water I could soak up from a faucet outside, and walked over to an old shack that was out of use in the yards, and keeled over on the cinders in the sun. I woke up several hours later, and my train had gone on without me.

Two men said that another train was due out in a few minutes, so I kept an eye run along the tracks, and caught it when it pulled out. The sun was warm now, and there were fifty men lined up along the top of the train, smoking, talking, waving at the folks in cars on the highway, and keeping quiet.

Bakersfield on into Fresno. Just this side of Fresno, the men piled off and walked through the yards, planning to meet the train again when it come out the north end. We took off by ones and twos and tried to get hold of something to eat. Some of the men had a few nickels, some a dollar or two hid on them, and others made the alleys knocking on the back doors of bakeries, greasy-spoon joints, vegetable stands. The meal added up to a couple or three bites apiece, after we'd all pitched ours in. It was something to fill your guts.

I saw a sign tacked up in the Fresno yards that said: Free Meal & Nights Lodging. Rescue Mission.

Men looked at the sign and asked us, "Anybody here need ta be rescued?"

"From what?" somebody hollered.

"All ya got ta do is ta go down there an' kneel down an' say yer prayers, an' ya git a free meal an' a flop!" somebody explained.

"Yeah? Prayers? Which one o' youse boys knows any

t'ing about any prayers?" an Eastern-sounding man yelled out.

"I'd do it, if I wuz just hungery 'nuff! I'd say 'em some prayers!"

"I don't hafta do no prayin' ta get fed!" a hard looker laughed out. He was poking a raw onion whole into his mouth, tears trickling down his jaws.

"Oh, I don't know," a quieter man answered him, "I sometimes believe in prayin'. Lots of folks believes in prayin' before they go out to work, an' others pray before they go out to fight. An' even if you don't believe in a God up on a cloud, still, prayin's a pretty good way to get your mind cleared up, or to get the nerve that it takes to do anything. People pray because it makes them think serious about things, and, God or no God, it's all that most of them know how to do." He was a friendly man with whitish hair, and his easy temper sounded in his voice. It was a thinking voice.

" 'Course," a big Swede told us, "we justa kid along. These monkeys dun't mean about halfa what they say. Now, like, you take me, Swede, I prayed long time ago. Usta believe in it strong. Then, whoof, an' a lot of other things happen that knock my prop out frum under me, make me a railroad bum, an'—I just forget how ta pray an' go church."

A guy that talked more and faster said, "I think it's dam crooks that cause folks like us to be down and out and hungry, worried about finding jobs, worried about our folks, and them a-worrying about us."

"Last two or three years, I been sorta thinkin' 'long them lines—an' it looks like I keep believin' in somethin'; I don't know exactly, but it's in me, an' in you, an' in ever' dam one of us." This talker was a young man with a smooth face, thick hair that was bushy, and a fairly honest look somewhere about him. "An' if we c'n jist find out how ta make good use of it, we'll find out who's causin' us alla th' trouble in th' world, like this Hitler rat, an' git ridda them, an' then not let anybody be outta work, or beat down an' wonderin' where their next meal's a comin' from, by God, with alla these crops an' orchards bubblin' up around here!"

"If God was ta do what's right," a heavy man said, "he'd give all of these here peaches an' cherries, an' oranges, an' grapes, an' stuff to eat, to th' folks that are hungry. An' for a hungry man to pray an' try to tell God how to run his business, looks sort of backwards, plumb silly to me. Hell, a man's got two hands an' a mind of his own, an' feet an' legs to take him where he wants to go; an' if he sees something wrong with the world, he'd ought to get a lot of people together, an' look up in th' air an' say, Hey, up there, God, I'm—I mean, we're goin' to fix this!"

Then I put my three cents worth in, saying, "I believe that when ya pray, you're tryin' ta get yer thinkin' straight, tryin' ta see what's wrong with th' world, an' who's ta blame fer it. Part of it is crooks, crooked laws, an' jist dam greedy people, people that's afraid of this an' afraid of that. Part of it's all of this, an' part of it's jist dam shore our own fault."

"Hell, from what you say, you think we're to blame for everybody here being on the freights?" This young traveler reared his head back and laughed to himself, chewing a mouthful of sticky bread.

"I dunno, fellers, just to be right real frank with you. But it's our own fault, all right, hell yes. It's our own personal fault if we don't talk up, 'er speak out, 'er somethin'—I ain't any too clear on it."

An old white-headed man spoke close to me and said, "Well, boys, I was on the bum, I suppose, before any of you was born into this world." Everybody looked around mostly because he was talking so quiet, interrupting his eating. "All of this talking about what's up in the sky, or down in hell, for that matter, isn't half as important as what's right here, right now, right in front of your eyes. Things are tough. Folks broke. Kids hungry. Sick. Everything. And people has just got to have more faith in one another, believe in each other. There's a spirit of some kind we've all got. That's got to draw us all together."

Heads nodded. Faces watched the old man. He didn't say any more. Toothless for years, he was a little bit slow finishing up his piece of old bread.

Chapter XIV

THE HOUSE ON THE HILL

❖

"Hey! Hey! Train's pullin' out in about ten minnits! This a way! Ever'body!"

We got rolling again. The high peaks of the Sierra Nevada Mountains jumped up their heads in the east. Snow patches white in the sun. There was the green valley of the San Joaquin River, rich, good-smelling; hay meadows waving with thick, juicy feed that is life; people working, walking bending down, carrying heavy loads. Cars from farms waited at the cross-roads, some loaded down with wooden crates, and boxes, and some with tall tin cans of cow's milk. The air was as sweet as could be, and like the faint smell of blossom honey.

Before long we hit a heavy rain. A lot of us crawled into an empty car. Wet and yelling, we hollered and sung till the sun went down, and it got wetter and dark. New riders swung into our car. We curled up on strips of tough brown wrapping paper, pulling it over us like blankets, and using our sweaters and coats for pillows.

Somebody pulled the doors shut, and we rambled on through the night. When I woke up again, the train had stopped, and everything was in a wild hustle and a bustle. Guys shaking me, and saying in my ear, "Hey! Wake up! Tough town! Boy! This is far's she goes!"

"Tough bulls! Gotta git th' hell outta here. C'mon, wake up."

I rousted myself out, pulling my wet sweater over my head. The rain was falling heavy as about twenty-five or thirty of us ganged up in front of a Chinese bean joint; and when a certain big, black patrol car wheeled around a corner, and shot its bright spotlight into our faces, we brushed our clothing, straightened our hats and neck ties, and in order to act like legal citizens, we marched into the Chinaman's bean joint.

Inside, it was warm. The joint contained seven warped stools. And two level-headed Chinese proprietors. "Chili bean! Two chili bean! Seven chili bean!" I heard one say through the hole in the wall to the cook in the back. And from the kitchen, "Me gotcha! All chili bean!"

I was going through the process, not only of starving, but also of being too hot and too cold about fifty times in the last forty-eight hours. I felt dizzy and empty and sick. The peppery smell of the hot chili and beans made me feel worse.

I waited about an hour and a half, until ten minutes before the Chinaman locked the door, and then I said, "Say, friend, will you gimme a bowl of yer chili an' beans fer this green sweater? Good sweater."

"You let me slee sletee."

"Okay—here—feel. Part of it's all wool."

"Chili bean you want this sletee for?"

"Yeah. Cuppa coffee, too."

"Price. You go up."

"Okay. No coffee."

"No. No chili bean."

"Good sweater," I told him.

"Okay. You keep. You see, I got plentee sletee. You think good sletee, you keep sletee. Me keep chili bean."

I set there on the stool, hating to go out into the cold night and leave that good warm stove. I made a start for the

door, and went past three men finishing off their first or
second bowl of chili and beans. The last man was a long,
tall, irony-looking Negro. He kept eating as I walked past,
never turned his face toward me, but told me, "Let me see
yo' sweatah. Heah's yo' dime. Lay th' sweatah down theah
on th' stool. Bettah hurry an' ordah yo' chili. Joint'll shut
down heah in a minute."

I dropped the sweater in a roll on the stool, and parked
myself on the next stool, and a bowl of red-hot, extra hot,
double hot chili beans slid down the counter and under my
nose.

It was long about two o'clock when I stepped out onto
the sidewalk, and the rain was getting harder, meaner, and
colder, and blowing stiffer down the line. A friendly looking cop, wearing a warm overcoat, walked around the corner. Three or four of the boys stood along under the porch,
so as to keep out of the drift of the rain. The cop said,
"Howdy, howdy, boys. Time to call it a night." He smiled
like a man doing an awful good job.

"What time yuh got?" a Southern boy asked him, dripping wet.

"Bed time."

"Oh."

"Say, mister," I said to him, "listen, we're jist a bunch
of guys on th' road, tryin' ta git somewhere where ther's a
job of work of some kind. Come in on that there freight.
Rainin', an' we ain't got no place ta sleep in outta th'
weather. I wuz jist wonderin' if you'd let us sleep here in
yer jail house—jist fer tonight."

"You might," he said, smiling, tickling all of the boys.

"Where's yer jail at?" I asked him.

"It's over across town," he answered.

Then I said, "Reckon ya could put us up?"

And he said, "I certainly can."

"Boy, man, you're a pretty good feller. We're ready, ain't we, guys?"

"I'm ready."

"Git inside out of this bad night."

"Me, too."

The same answer came from everybody.

"Then, see," I said to the cop, "if anything happens, they'd, you'd know it wuzn't us done it."

And then he looked at us like a politician making a speech, and said, "You boys know what'd happen if you went over there to that jail to sleep tonight?"

We said, "Huh uh." "No." "What?"

"Well, they'd let you in, all right, not for just one night, but for thirty nights and thirty days. Give you an awful good chance to rest up out on the County Farm, and dry your clothes by a steam radiator every night. They'd like you men so much, they'd just refuse to let you go. Just keep you for company over there." He had a cold, sour smile across his face by now.

"Let's go, fella." Somebody back of me jerked my arm.

Without talking back, I savvied, and walked away. Most of the men had left. Only six or eight of us in a little bunch. "Where we gonna sleep, anybody know?" I asked them.

"Just keep quiet and follow us."

The cop walked away around the corner.

"And don't ever let a smiling cop fool yuh," a voice in back of me told us. "That wasn't no real smile. Tell by his face an' his eyes."

"Okay, I learnt somethin' new," I said. "But where are we gonna sleep at?"

"We gotta good warm bed, don't you worry. Main thing is just to walk, an' don't talk."

Across a boggy road, rutty, and full of mudholes, over a sharp barb-wire fence, through a splashing patch of weeds that soaked our clothes with cold water, down some crunching cinders, we followed the shiny rails again in the rain about a half a mile. This led us to a little green shack, built low to the ground like a doghouse. We piled in at a square window, and lit on a pile of sand.

"Godamighty!"

"Boy, howdy!"

"Ain't this fine?"

"Warmer'n hell."

"Lemme dig a hole. I wanta dig a hole, an' jist bury myself. I ain't no live man. I'm dead. I been dead a long, long time. I'm gonna jist dig me a grave, an' crawl off in it, an' pull my sand in on top of me. Gonna sleep like old Rip Van Twinkle, twenty, thirty, or fifty dam years. An' when I wake up, I want things ta be changed around better. When I wake up in th' mornin'—" And I was tired and wet, covering up in the sand, talking. I drifted off to sleep. Loose and limber, I felt everything in the world just slipping out from under me and fading away. I woke up before long with my feet burning and stinging. Everything was sailing and mixed up backwards, but when they got straight I saw a man in a black suit bending over me with a big heavy club. He was beating the bottoms of my feet.

"You birds get up, and get your ass out of here! Get up, Goddam you!"

There were three men in black suits, and the black Western hats that told you so plain that you was dealing with a railroad deputy.

They had come in through a little narrow door and were herding us out the same. "Get out of here, and don't you come back! If you show your head back in this sandhouse, you'll go to the judge! Ninety days on that pea farm would do you loafers good!"

Grabbing shoes, hats, little dirty bundles, the migratory workers were chased out of their bed of clean sand. Back outside, the rain was keeping up, and in the V-shaped beam of the spotlights from the patrol car you could see that even the rain was having trouble.

"Git on outta town there!" "Keep travelin'!" "Don't you even look back!" "Start walkin'!" We heard low, grumbling voices coming from the car behind us. Heard, too, the quiet motor start up and the gears shifted as the car rolled along back of us. It followed us about a half a mile, rain and mud. It drove us across a cow pasture.

From the car, one of the watchmen yelled, "Don't you show up in Tracy again tonight! You'll be dam good an' sorry if you do! Keep walking!"

The car lights cut a wide, rippling circle in the dark, and we knew that they had turned around and went back to town. The roar of their exhaust purred and died away.

We'd marched out across the cow pasture, smiling and yelling, "Hep! Hep! Whattaya say, men? Hep! Hep! Hep!"

Now we stood in the rain and cackled like chickens, absolutely lost and buffaloed. Never before had I had anything quite so dam silly happen to me. Our clothes were on crooked and twisted; shoes full of mud and gravel. Hair soaking wet, and water running down our faces. It was a funny sight to see human beings in any such a shape. Wet as we could get, dirty and muddy as the ground, we danced up and down through puddles, ran around in wide circles and laughed our heads off. There is a stage of hard luck that turns into fun, and a stage of poverty that turns into pride, and a place in laughing that turns into fight.

"Okay. Hey, fellers! C'mere. Tell ya what we're gonna do. We're a-gonna all git together, see, an' go walkin' right back into town, an' go back to sleep in that sandhouse ag'in. What say? Who's with me?" a tall, slippery, stoop-shouldered boy was telling us.

"Me!"

"Me."

"Same fer me!"

"Whatever you guys does, I'll stick."

"Hell, I c'n give that carload of bulls a machine gun apiece, an' whip th' whole outfit with my bare hands!" an older man said.

"But, no. We don't aim ta cause no trouble. Ain't gonna be no fightin'."

"I'd just like to get one good poke at that fat belly."

"Get that outta your head, mister."

Just walking back toward town, talking.

"Hey. How many of us here?"

"Two. Four. Six. Eight."

"Mebbe we'd better split up in twos. Too plain to see a whole big bunch. We'll go into town by pairs. If you make it back to the old blacksmith shop right there by the old Chinese bean joint, whistle once, real long. This way, if two gets caught, the rest'll get away."

"What'll we do if we get caught an' run in jail?"

"Whistle twice, real short," and under his breath he showed us how to whistle.

"Can everybody here whistle?"

"I can."

Four of us said yes. So one whistler and one expert listener was put into each pair.

"Now, remember, if you see the patrol car's gonna ketch yuh, stop before it gits yuh, an' whistle twice, real short an' sweet."

"Okay. First pair take that street yonder. Second pair, drop over a block. Third couple, down the paved highway; and us, last pair, will walk back down this same cow trail that we got run out of town on. Remember, don't start no trouble with them coppers. Loaded dice, boys; you cain't win. Just got to try to outsmart 'em a little."

Back through the slick mud, walking different ways, we cussed and laughed. In a few minutes, there came a long, low whistle, and we knew the first pair had made it to the blacksmith shop. Then, in a minute or so, another long one. We came in third, and I let out a whistle that was one of California's best. The last pair walked in and we stood under the wide eaves of the shop, watching the water drip off of the roof, missing our noses by about three inches. We had to stand up straight against the wall to stay out of the rain.

The sandhouse was just across the street and up a few steps.

"Lay low."

"Duck."

"Car."

"Hey! Ho! Got us ag'in!"

The new model black sedan coasted down a side street, out over in our direction real quick, and turned two spots on us. We held our hands up to keep the lights from blinding us. Nobody moved. We thought maybe they'd made a mistake. But, as the car rolled up to within about fifty feet of us, we knew that we were caught, and got ready to be cussed out, and took to the can.

A deputy opened his front door, turned off one spotlight, and shot his good flashlight into our faces. One at a time, he looked us over. We blinked back at him, like a herd of young deer, but nobody was to say afraid.

"Come here, you—" he said in a hard, imitation voice.

The light was in my face. I thought it was shining in everybody's, so I didn't move.

"Hey, mister. Come over here, please." He was a big heavy man, and his voice had a nice clank to it, like cocking back the hammer of a rifle.

I shook the light out of my eyes and said, "Who?"

"You."

I turned around to the men with me and told them loud enough for the cops to hear it, "Be right back, fellers."

I heard the patrol man turn around to the other cops and kid them about something, and as I walked up they were all laughing and saying, "Yeah. He's th' one. He's one. One of them things."

The radio in the car was turned on a Hollywood station, and a lady's voice was singing, telling what all of the pretty girls were thinking about the war situation.

"I'm a what?" I asked the cop.

"You know, one of them 'things.' "

"Well, boys, ya got me there. I don't even know what one of them 'things' is."

"We know what you are."

"Well," I scratched my head in the rain, "maybe you're smarter than I am; 'cause I never did know jist what I am."

"We do."

"Yeah?"

"Yeah."

"What am I then?"

"One of them labor boys."

"Labor?"

"Yeah, labor."

"I think I know what labor is—" I smiled a little.

"What is it?"

"Labor's work."

"Maybe, you're one of them trouble causers."

"Listen, fellers, I jist rolled inta this town from Oklahoma, I mean Texas, an' I'm on my way to Sonora to stay with my relatives."

"Relatives?"

"Yeah," I said. "Aunt. Cousins. Whole bunch. Well off."

"You're going to stay in Sonora when you get there, aren't you?" A different, higher-sounding voice wheezed out from the back seat.

"I'm gonna settle down up there in them mountains, an' try ta go ta work."

"Kinda work, sonny?"

"Painter. Signs. Pictures. Houses. Anything needs paintin'."

"So you don't go around causing trouble, then?"

"I'm runnin' inta a right smart of it. I don't always cause it."

"You don't like trouble, do you, mister painter?"

"Oh, I ain't so 'fraid no more. Sorta broke in by this time."

"Ever talk to anybody about working?"

"Train loads of 'em. That's what ever'body's talkin' 'bout, an' ridin' in all of this bad weather for. Shore, we ain'ta 'fraid of work. We ain't panhandlers, ner stemwinders, jest a bunch of guys out tryin' ta do th' best we can, an' had a little streak of hard luck, that's all."

"Ever talk to the boys about wages?"

"Wages? Oh, I talk to ever'body about somethin'. Religion. Weather. Picture shows. Girls. Wages."

"Well, mister painter, it's been good to get acquainted with you. It seems like you are looking for work and anxious to get on up the road toward Sonora. We'll show you the road and see that you get out onto the main highway."

"Boy, that'll be mighty fine."

"Yes. We try to treat an honest working man right when he comes through our little town here, either by accident or on purpose. We're just a little, what you'd call, 'cautious,' you understand, because there is trouble going around, and you never know who's causing it, until you ask. We will have to ask you to get out in front of this car and start walking down this highway. And don't look back—"

All of the cops were laughing and joking as their car drove along behind me. I heard a lot of lousy jokes. I walked with my head ducked into the rain, and heard cars of other people pass. They yelled smart cracks at me in the rain.

After about a mile, they yelled for me to halt. I stopped and didn't even turn around. "You run a lot of risk tonight, breaking our orders."

"Muddy out there!"

"You know, we tried to treat you nice. Turned you loose. Gave you a chance. Then you broke orders."

"Yeah, I guess I did."

"What made you do it?"

"Well, ta be right, real truthful with you guys, we got pastures just about like these back in Oklahoma, but we let the cows go out there and eat. If people wants to go out there in the cow pasture, we let them go, but if it's rainin' an' a cold night like this, we don't drive or herd anybody out there."

Cop said, "Keep travelin'."

I said, "I wuz born travelin'. Good-bye!"

The car and the lights whirled around in the road, and the tail light and the radio music blacked out down the road in the rain.

I walked a few steps and seen it was too rainy and bad to see in the fog, so I went to thinking about some kind of a place to lay down out of the weather and go to sleep. I walked up to the headstones of a long cement bridge that bent across a running river. And down under the bridge I found a couple of dozen other people curled up, grinding their teeth in the mist and already dreaming. The ground was loose dirt and was awful cold and damp, but not wet or muddy, as the rain couldn't hit us under the concrete. I seen men paired up snoring together, some rolled in newspapers and brown wrapping paper, others in a chilled blanket, one or two here and yonder all snoozed up in some mighty warm-looking bedrolls. And for a minute, I thought, I'm a dam fool not to carry my own bedroll; but then again, in the hot daytime a heavy bedroll is clumsy, no good, and in the way, and besides, people won't give you a ride if you're lugging an old dirty bundle. So here in the moisture of the wind whiffing under the bridge, I scanned around for something to use for a mattress, for a pillow, and for a virgin wool blanket. I found a soaked piece of wrapping paper which I shook the water off of, and spread on the dirt for my easy-rider mattress; but I didn't find a pillow, nor anything to use as a blanket. I drew my muscles down into just a little pile of meat and bones, and shivered on the paper for about an hour. My breath swishing, and teeth hitting together, woke a big square-built man up off his bedroll. He listened at me for a minute, and then asked me, "Don't you know your shiverin's keepin' everybody awake?" I said, "Y-y-y-es-s-s, I sup-p-p-pose it is; I ain't gettin' no sleep, on account of it." Then he said, "You sound like a snare drum rattlin' that paper; c'mon over here an' den up with me."

I rolled across the ground and peeled off my wet clothes, my gobby shoes, and stacked them up in a pile; and then he turned his wool blankets back and said, "Hurry, jump in before the covers get wet!" I was still shivering and shaking so hard it jerked my whole body into kinks, and cramped me all over so that I couldn't move my lips to say a word. I scooted my feet down inside and then pulled the itchy covers all up over my head.

"You feel like a bucket of cold frogs," the man told me. "Where've you been?"

I kept on shaking, without saying a word.

"Cops walk you?" he asked me. And I just nodded my head with my back to him.

"I'm not minding this weather very much; I'm on my way to where it will be a hell of a lot colder than this. I don't know about the cops, but, I'll be in Vancouver by this time next week; and I know it'll freeze the horns off of a brass bulldog up there. Lumberjack. Timber. I guess you're too cold to talk much, huh?" And his last words blotted and soaked out across the swampy river bottom and faded away somewhere in the fog horn and red and green lights on a little boat that pounded down the waters.

It was hard for me to walk next morning early on account of my legs being drawn like torn leather. My thighs felt like the gristle was tore loose from my bones, and my knees ached and jittered in the joints. I shook hands with the lumberjack and we went our opposite ways. I never did get a real close look at him in the clouds; and when he walked away, his head and shoulders just sort of swum away in the fog of the morning. I had made another friend I couldn't see. And I walked along thinking, Well, now, I don't know if I'll ever see that man again or not, but I'll see a lot of men a lot of places and I'll wonder if that could be him.

Before long the sun and the fog had fought and flounced around so long on the river banks the highway run along that it didn't seem like there was enough room in the trees and reeds and canebrakes for the sun or the clouds, either one, to really win out; so the clouds from the ground got mad and raised up off of the earth to grab a-hold of the sunrays, and fight it out higher up in the air. I caught a ride on a truckload of grape stakes and heard a hard-looking truck driver cuss the narrow, bad roads that cause you to get killed so quick; and then found myself wheeling along with a deaf farmer for an hour or two, an Italian grape grower in debt all of the time, a couple of cowboys trying to beat their way to a new rodeo; and before the day was wore very slick, I was walking down the streets of Sonora, the queen of the gold towns, in the upper foothills of the Sierra Nevada Mountains.

Sonora's crooked, narrow streets bent and run about as wild as some of the prospectors and their burros, and I thought as I pushed my way along the tight alleys called streets, that maybe the whole town had been laid out by just following the tracks of a runaway prospector. Little houses poking their bellies out over the curbs and sidewalks, and streets so steep I had to throw myself in low gear to pull them. Down again so steep, I figured, that most of Sonora's citizens come and went by way of parachutes. Creeks and rocky rivers guggling along under the streets, where the gambling dives and dram joints flush their mistakes down the drains, where, on down the creek a-ways, the waters are panned by hungry gold-bugs.

I walked along with my address in my hand, seeing herds of cowboys, miners, timber men, and hard-working, pioneer-looking women and kids from the mountains around; and saw, too, the fake cowboys, the drug-store calibre, blazing shirts of all bright colors along the streets, and crippling along bowlegged in boots never meant to be worn on the hard concrete. And the honest working people stand along in bunches and laugh under their breath when the fake dudes buckle past.

In the smell of the high pines and the ripple of the nugget creeks, Sonora, an old town now, is rated as California's second richest person. Pasadena is first, and looks it, but what fools you in Sonora is that it looks like one of the poorest. I walked up the main street loaded to the brim with horses, hay, children playing, jallopy cars of the ranchers and working folks around, buggies of the Indians, wagons loaded with groceries for grubstake, town cars, limousines, sporty jobs, the big V-16's and the V-Twelves.

The main street crooks pretty sharp right in the business end, and crooks another time or two trying to get out of the first crook. The street is so narrow that people sneeze on the right-hand side and apologize to the ones on the left.

I asked a fireman asleep on a bench, "Could you tell me where 'bouts this address is?"

He disturbed, without scaring, a fly on his eyelid, and told me, "It's that big rock house right yonder up that hill. No danger of missing it, it covers the whole hill."

I thanked him and started walking up a three-block flight of rock steps thinking, Boy, I'm as dirty an' ragged an' messed up as one feller can git. Knees outta my britches. My face needs about a half a dozen shaves. Hands all smeary. Coal dust an' soot all over me. I don't know if I'd even know myself in a lookin'-glass. Shirt all tore to hell, an' my shoes stinkin' with sweat. That's a hell of a big rock house up there. Musta took a mighty lot of work ta build it. I'd go back down in town to a fillin' station an' wash an' clean up, but gosh, I'm so empty an' hungry, so tremblin' weak, I don't know, I couldn't pull it back up these long steps again. I'll go on up.

A black iron fence and a cedar hedge fenced the whole yard off. I stood at the gate with the letter in my hand, looking up and down, back down at the town and the people, and then through the irons at the mansion. I wiped the sweat off of my face on the arm of my shirt, and unlocked the gate and walked through. Wide green grass lawn that made me think of golf courses I'd caddied on. Mowed and petted and smoothed and kept, the yard had a look like it had just got back from a barber shop. The whiff of the scrub cedar and middle-size pine, on top of the flowers that jumped up all around, made it smell good and healthy, like a home for crippled children. But the whole place was so still and so hushed and quiet, that I was thinking maybe everybody was gone off somewhere. When I walked the rock walk a little more, the whole house got plainer to see: gray native stones from the hills around, flagstone porches and sandrock columns holding up the roof; windows so high and wide that the sun got lost trying to find a way to shine through all of them big thick drapes and curtains. Iron braces in the windows built to keep the nice, good, healthy sunshine out for a long, long time. Big double doors with iron cross braces, handles like the entrance to a funeral parlor, locks bigger and stouter than any jail I'd ever slept in.

I'll walk quieter now, because this porch makes a lot of noise, and a little noise, I bet, would scare all of these trees and flowers to death. This place is so quiet. I hope I don't scare nobody when I knock on this door. How in the dickens do you operate this knocker, anyhow? Oh. Pick it up. Let it just fall. It knocks. Gosh. Reckon it'll bring any watchdogs out on me? Hope not. Dern. I don't know. I'm just thinking. This old rambling's pretty bad in some places, but, I don't know, I never did see it get this quiet and this lonesome.

Reckon I rung that door knocker right? Guess I did. Things so still here on this porch, I can hear my blood run, and my thoughts grazing around in my head.

The door opened back.

My breath went away in the tips of the pines where the cones hang on as long as they can, and then fall down to the ground to get covered up in the loose dirt and some day make a new tree.

"How do you do," a man said.

"Ah, yeah, good day." I was gulping for air.

"May I do something for you?"

"Me? No. Nope. I wuz jist lookin' fer a certain party by this name." I handed him the envelope.

He was wearing a nice suit of clothes. An old man, thin-faced, and straight shoulders, gray hair, white cuffs, black tie. The air from the house sifted past him on its way out the door, and there was a smell that made me know that the air had been hemmed up inside that house for a long time. Hemmed up. Walled in. Covered away from the moon and out of the reach of the sun. Cut away from the drift of the leaves and the wash of the waters. Hid out from the going and the coming of the people, cut loose from the thoughts of the crowds on the streets. Lazy in there, sleepy in there, cool and pale and shady in there, dark and dreary in the book case there, and the wind under the beds hadn't been disturbed in twenty-three years. I know, I know, I'm on the right hill, but I'm at the wrong house. This wasn't what I hung that boxcar for, nor hugged that iron ladder for, nor bellied down on top of that high rolling freight train for. The train was laughing and cussing and alive with human people. The cops was alive and pushing me down the road in the rain. The bridge was alive with friends under it. The river was alive and arguing with the fog and the fog was wrestling the wind and boxing the sun.

I remember a frog they found in Okemah, once when they tore the old bank building down. He'd been sealed up in solid concrete for thirty-two years, and had almost turned to jelly. Jelly. Blubbery. Soft and oozy. Slicky and wiggly. I don't want to turn to no jelly. My belly is hard from hard traveling, and I want more than anything else for my belly to stay hard and stay wound up tight and stay alive.

"Yes. You are at the right house. This is the place you are looking for." The little butler stood aside and motioned for me to walk in.

"I—er—ah—think, mebbe I made a mistake—"

"Oh, no." He was talking just about the nicest I'd ever

heard anybody talk, like maybe he'd been practicing. "This is the place you're looking for."

"I don't—ah—think—I think, maybe I made a little mistake. You know—mistake—"

"I'm positive that you are at the right address."

"Yeah? Well, mister, I shore thank ya; but I'm purty shore." I backed down off of the slate-rock steps, looking down at my feet, then up at the house and the door, and said, "Purty shore, I'm at th' wrong address. Sorry I woke ya, I mean bothered ya. Be seein' ya."

When I stood there on top of the hill and listened to that iron gate snap locked behind me, and looked all down across the roofs and church steeples and chimneys and steep houses of Sonora, I smelled the drift of pine rosin in the air and watched a cloud whiff past me over my head, and I was alive again.

Chapter XV

THE TELEGRAM THAT NEVER CAME

❖

In a bend of the Sacramento is the town of Redding, California. The word had scattered out that twenty-five hundred workers was needed to build the Kenneth Dam, and already eight thousand work hands had come to do the job. Redding was like a wild ant den. A mile to the north in a railroad bend had sprung up another camp, a thriving nest of two thousand people, which we just called by the name of the "jungle." In that summer of 1938, I learned a few little things about the folks in Redding, but a whole lot more, some way, down there by that big jungle where the people lived as close to nature, and as far from everything natural, as human beings can.

I landed in Redding early one morning on a long freight train full of wore-out people. I fell off of the freight with my guitar over my shoulder and asked a guy when the work was going to start. He said it was supposed to get going last month. Telegram hadn't come from Washington yet.

"Last month, hell," another old boy said, over his shoulder. "We've been camped right here up and down this slough for over three months, hearin' it would git started any day now!"

I looked down the train and seen about a hundred men dropping off with their sleeping rolls and bundles of all kinds. The guy I was talking with was a big hard looker with a brown flannel shirt on. He said, "They's that many rollin' in on ever' train that runs!"

325

"Where are all of these here people from?" I asked him.

"Some of them are just louses," he said. "Pimps an' gamblers, whores, an' fakes of all kinds. Yes, but they ain't so many of that kind. You talk around to twenty men an' you'll find out that nineteen of them are just as willing and able to work as anybody, just as good a hand, knows just as much, been all over everywhere tryin' ta git onto some kind of a regular job an' bring his whole family, wife, kids, everything, out here an' settle down."

It was a blistering hot day, and some of the men walked across a vacant lot over to the main street. But the biggest part of them looked too dirty and too beat-down and ragged to spend much time on the streets. They didn't walk into town to sign up at no hotel, not even at a twenty-cent cot house, not even somebody's green grass lawn, but walked out slowly across the little hill to the jungle camp. They asked other people already stranded there, Where's the water hole? Where's there a trash pile of pretty good tin cans for cookin'; where's the fish biting in the river? Any of you folks got a razor you ain't using?

I stood there on a railroad platform looking at my old wore-out shirt. I was thinking, Well now, I don't know, there might be a merchant's daughter around this town that's a little bit afraid of all of these other tough lookers, but now, if I was to go an' rustle me up a couple of dollars an' buy me a clean layout, she might spend a little time talking to me. Makes you feel better when you get all slicked up, walking out onto the streets, cops even nod and smile at you, and with your sleeves rolled up and everything, sun and wind sorta brushing your skin, you feel like a new dollar watch. And you think to yourself, Boy, I hope I can meet her before my clothes get all dirty again. Maybe this little Army and Navy store down the street has got a water hydrant in the rest room; and when I put on my new shirt and pants, maybe I can wash myself up a little. I can pull out my razor and shave while I'm washing, keep an eye skint for the store man, not let him see me. And I'll come walkin' out from that little old store looking like a man that's all bought and paid for.

I heard all kinds of singing and playing through the wide-open doors of the saloons along the street, and dropped in at all of them and tried to draw a hand. I'd play my guitar and sing the longest, oldest, and saddest songs and ballads I knew; I'd nod and smile and say thank you every time somebody dropped a penny or a nickel into my cigar box.

A plump Mexican lady wearing a sweated-out black dress, walked over and dropped three pennies in my box and said, "Now I'm broke. All I'm waiting forr iss thiss beeg dam to start. For somebody to come running down the street saying, 'Work hass opened up! Hiring men! Hiring everybody!' "

I made enough money to run down and buy me the new shirt and pair of pants, but they was all sweat-soaked and covered with loose dust before I had a chance to get in good with the merchant's daughter. I was counting my change on the curb and had twenty some odd cents. A bare-headed Indian with warts along his nose looked over in my hand and said, "Twenty-two cent. Huh. Too much for chili. Not enough for beef stew. Too much for sleeping outside, and not enough for sleeping inside. Too much to be broke and not enough to pay a loafing fine. Too much to eat all by yourself, but not enough to feed some other boomer." And I looked at the money and said, "I reckin one of th' unhandiest dam sums of money a feller c'n have is twenty some-odd cents." So I walked around with it jingling loose in my pockets, out across the street, through a vacant lot, down a cinder dump onto a railroad track, till I come to a little grassy trail that led into the jungle camp.

I followed the trail out over the hill through the sun and the weeds. The camp was bigger than the town itself. People had dragged old car fenders up from the dumps, wired them from the limbs of oak trees a few feet off of the ground and this was a roof for some of them. Others had taken old canvas sacks or wagon sheets, stretched the canvas over little limbs cut so the forks braced each other, and that was a house for those folks. I heard two brothers standing back looking at their house saying, "I ain't lost my hand as a carpenter, yet." "My old eyes can still see to hit a nail."

They'd carried buckets and tin cans out of the heap, flattened them on the ground, then nailed the tin onto crooked boards, and that was a mansion for them. Lots of people, families mostly, had some bedclothes with them, and I could see the old stinky, gummy quilts and blankets hung up like tents, and two or three kids of all ages playing around underneath. There was scatterings of cardboard shacks, where the people had lugged cartons, cases, packing boxes out from town and tacked them into a house. They was easy to build, but the first rain that hit them, they was goners.

Then about every few feet down the jungle hill you'd walk past a shack just sort of made out of everything in general—old strips of asphalt tar paper, double gunny sacks, an old dress, shirt, pair of overhalls, stretched up to cover half a side of a wall; bumpy corrugated iron, cement sacks, orange and apple crates took apart and nailed together with old rusty burnt nails from the cinder piles. Through a little square window on the side of a house, I'd hear bedsprings creaking and people talking. Men played cards, whittled, and women talked about work they'd struck and work they were hunting for. Dirt was the floor of the house, and all kinds and colors of crawling and flying bugs come and went like they were getting paid for it. There were the big green blow-flies, the noisy little street flies, manure and lot flies, caterpillars and gnats from other dam jobs, bed bugs, fleas, and ticks sucking blood, while mosquitoes of all army and navy types, hummers, bombers, fighters, sung some good mosquito songs. In most cases, though, the families didn't even have a roof or shelter, but just got together once or twice every day and, squatting sort of Indian fashion around their fire, spaded a few bites of thickened flour gravy, old bread, or a thin watery stew. Gunny sacks, old clothes, hay and straw, fermenting bedclothes, are usually piled full of kids playing, or grown-ups resting and waiting for the word "work" to come.

The sun's shining through lots of places, other patches pretty shady, and right here at my elbow a couple of families are squatting down on an old slick piece of canvas; three or four quiet men, whittling, breaking grass stems, poking holes in leaves, digging into the hard ground; and the women rocking back and forth laughing out at something somebody'd said. A little baby sucks at a wind-burnt breast that nursed the four other kids that crawl about the fire. Cold rusty cans are their china cups and aluminum ware, and the hot still bucket of river water is as warm and clear as the air around. I watch a lot of little circles waving out from the middle of the water where a measuring worm has dropped from the limb of a tree and flips and flops for his very life. And I see a man with a forked stick reach the forks over into the bucket, smile, and go on talking about the work he's done; and in a moment, when the little worm clamps his feet around the forks of the stick, the man will lift him out, pull him up close to his face and look him over, then tap the stick over the rim of the bucket. When the little worm flips to the ground and goes humping away through the twigs and ashes, the whole bunch of people will smile and say, "Pretty close shave, mister worm. What do you think you are, a parshoot jumper?"

You've seen a million people like this already. Maybe you saw them down on the crowded side of your big city; the back side, that's jammed and packed, the hard section to drive through. Maybe you wondered where so many of them come from, how they eat, stay alive, what good they do, what makes them live like this? These people have had a house and a home just about like your own, settled down and had a job of work just about like you. Then something hit them and they lost all of that. They've been pushed out into the high lonesome highway, and they've gone down it, from coast to coast, from Canada to Mexico, looking for that home again. Now they're looking, for a while, in your town. Ain't much difference between you and them. If you was to walk out into this big tangled jungle camp and stand there with the other two thousand, somebody would just walk up and shake hands with you and ask you, What kind of work do you do, pardner?

Then maybe, farther out on the ragged edge of your town you've seen these people after they've hit the road: the people that are called strangers, the people that follow the sun and the seasons to your country, follow the buds and the early leaves and come when the fruit and crops are ready to gather, and leave when the work is done. What kind of crops? Oil fields, power dams, pipe lines, canals, highways and hard-rock tunnels, skyscrapers, ships, are their crops. These are migrants now. They don't just set along in the sun—they go by the sun, and it lights up the country that they know is theirs.

If you'd go looking for social problems, you'd find just a good friendly bunch of people getting a lot of laughing and talking done, and some of it pretty good sense.

I listened to the talk in the tanglewood of the migratory jungle. "What'll be here to keep these people going," a man with baggy overhalls and a set of stickery whiskers is saying, "when this dam job is over? Nothing? No, mister, you're wrong as hell. What do you think we're putting in this dam for, anyhow? To catch water to irrigate new land, and water all of this desert-looking country here. And when a little drop of water hits the ground anywhere out across here—a crop, a bush, sometimes even a big tall tree comes

jumping out of the dirt. Thousands and thousands of whole families are going to have all the good land they need, and I'm a-going to be on one of them little twenty acres!"

"Water, water," a young man about twenty or so, wearing a pair of handmade cowboy shoes, talks up. "You think water's gonna be th' best part? Well, you're just about half right, friend. Did you ever stop to think that th' most, th' best part of it all is th' electric power this dam's gonna turn out? I can just lay here on this old, rotten jungle hill with all of these half-starved people waiting to go to work, and you know, I don't so much see all of this filth and dirt. But I do see—just try to picture in my head, like—what's gonna be here. Th' big factories makin' all kinds of things from fertilizer to bombin' planes. Power lines, steel towers runnin' out acrost these old clumpy hills—most of all, people at work all of th' time on little farms, and whole bunches and bunches of people at work in th' big new factories."

"It's th' gifts of th' Lord, that's what 'tis." A little nervous man, about half Indian, is pulling up grass stems and talking. "Th' Lord gives you a mind to vision all of this, an' th' power to build it. He gives when He wants to. Then when He wants to, He takes it away—if we don't use it right."

"If we all get together, social like, and build something, say, like a big ship, any kind of a factory, railroad, big dam —that's social work, ain't it?" This is a young man with shell-rimmed glasses, a gray felt hat, blue work shirt with a fountain pen stuck with a notebook in his pocket, and his voice had the sound of books in it when he talked. "That's what 'social' means, me and you and you working on something together and owning it together. What the hell's wrong with this, anybody—speak up! If Jesus Christ was sitting right here, right now, he'd say this very same dam thing. You just ask Jesus how the hell come a couple of thousand of us living out here in this jungle camp like a bunch of wild animals. You just ask Jesus how many million of other folks are living the same way? Sharecroppers down South, big city people that work in factories and live like rats in the slimy slums. You know what Jesus'll say back to you? He'll tell you we all just mortally got to work together, build things together, fix up old things together, clean out old filth together, put up new buildings, schools and churches, banks and factories together, and own everything together. Sure, they'll call it a bad ism. Jesus don't care if you call it socialism or communism, or just me and you."

When night come down, everything got a little stiller, and you could walk around from one bunch of people to the other one and talk about the weather. Although the weather wasn't such an ace-high subject to talk about, because around Redding for nine months hand running the weather don't change (it's hot and dry, hot and dry, and tomorrow it's still going to be hot and dry), you can hear little bunches of folks getting acquainted with each other, saying, "Really hot, ain't it?" "Yeah, dry, too." "Mighty dry."

I run onto a few young people of twelve to twenty-five, mostly kids with their families, who picked the banjo or guitar, and sung songs. Two of these people drew quite a bunch every evening along toward sundown and it always took place just about the same way. An old bed was under a tree in their yard, and a baby boy romped around on it when the shade got cool, because in the early parts of the day the flies and bugs nearly packed him off. So this was his ripping and romping time, and it was the job of his two sisters, one around twelve and the other one around fourteen, to watch him and keep him from falling off onto the ground. Their dad parked his self back on an old car cushion. He throwed his eyes out over the rims of some two-bit specks just about every line or two on his reading matter, and run his Adam's apple up and down; and his wife nearby was singing what all the Lord had done for her, while the right young baby stood up for his first time, and jumped up and down, bouncing toward the edge of the mattress. The old man puckered up his face and sprayed a tree with tobacco juice, and said, "Girls. You girls. Go in the house and get your music box, and set there on the bed and play with the baby, so's he won't fall off."

One of the sisters tuned a string or two, then chorded a little. People walked from all over the camp and gathered, and the kid, mama, and dad, and all of the visitors, kept as still as daylight while the girls sang:

> Takes a worried man to sing a worried song
> Takes a worried man to sing a worried song
> Takes a worried man to sing a worried song
> I'm worried nowwww
> But I won't be worried long.

I heard these two girls from a-ways away where I was leaning back up against an old watering trough. I could hear their words just as plain as day, floating all around in the trees and down across the low places. I hung my guitar up on a stub of a limb, went down and stretched myself out on some dry grass, and listened to the girls for a long time. The baby kicked and bucked like a regular army mule whenever they'd quit their singing; but, as quick as they struck their first note or two on the next song, the kid would throw his wrist in his mouth, the slobbers would drip down onto his sister's lap, and the baby would kick both feet, but easy, keeping pretty good time to the guitar.

I don't know why I didn't tell them I had a guitar up yonder hanging on that tree. I just reared back and soaked in every note and every word of their singing. It was so clear and honest sounding, no Hollywood put-on, no fake wiggling. It was better to me than the loud squalling and bawling you've got to do to make yourself heard in the old mobbed saloons. And, instead of getting you all riled up mentally, morally and sexually—no, it done something a lot better, something that's harder to do, something you need ten times more. It cleared your head up, that's what it done, caused you to fall back and let your draggy bones rest and your muscles go limber like a cat's.

Two little girls were making two thousand working people feel like I felt, rest like I rested. And when I say two thousand, take a look down off across these three little hills. You'll see a hat or two bobbing up above the brush. Somebody is going, somebody is coming, somebody is kneeling down drinking from the spring of water trickling out of the west hill. Five men are shaving before the same crooked hunk of old looking-glass, using tin cans for their water. A woman right up close to you wrings out a tough work shirt, saves the water for four more. You skim your eye out around the south hill, and not less than a hundred women are doing the same thing, washing, wringing, hanging out shirts, taking them down dry to iron. Not a one of them is talking above a whisper, and the one that is whispering almost feels guilty because she knows that ninety-nine out of every hundred are tired, weary, have felt sad, joked and laughed to keep from crying. But these two little girls are telling about all of that trouble, and everybody knows it's helping. These songs say something about our hard traveling, something about our hard luck, our hard get-by, but the songs say we'll come through all of these in pretty good shape, and we'll be all right, we'll work, make ourself useful, if only the telegram to build the dam would come in from Washington.

I thought I could act a little bashful and shy, and not rush the people to get to knowing them, but something inside of me just sort of talked out and said, "Awful good singing. What's your name?"

The two little girls talked slow and quiet but it was not nervous, and it wasn't jittery, just plain. They told me their names.

I said, "I like the way you play that guitar with your

fingers! Sounds soft, and you can hear it a long ways off. All of these three hills was just ringing out with your guitar, and all of these people was listening to you sing."

"I saw them listening," one sister said.

"I saw them too," the other sister said.

"I play with a flat celluloid pick. I've got to be loud, because I play in saloons and, well, I just make it my job to make more noise than they make, and they're sorry for me and give me nickels and pennies."

"I don't like old saloons," one little girl said.

"Me neither," the other little girl said.

I looked over at their daddy, and he sort of looked crossways out my side of his specks, pouched his lips up a little, winked at me, and said, "I'm against bars myself."

His wife talked up louder, "Yes, you're against bars! Right square up against them!"

Both of the sisters looked awful sober and serious at their dad. Everybody in the crowd laughed, and took on a new listening position, leaning back up against trees, squatting on smoky buckets turned upside down, stretched out in the grass, patting down places to lay in the short weeds.

I got up and strolled away and took my guitar down off of the sawed-off limb, and thought while I was walking back to where the crowd was, Boy howdy, old guitar, you been a lot of places, seen a lot of faces, but don't you go to actin' up too wild and reckless, 'cause these little girls and their mama don't like saloons.

I got back to where everybody was, and the two little sisters was singing "Columbus Stockade":

> Way down in Columbus stockade
> Where my gally went back on me;
> Way down in Columbus stockade,
> I'd ruther be back in Tennessee.

"Columbus Stockade" was always one of my first picks, so I let them run along for a little while, twisted my guitar up in tune with theirs, holding my ear down against the sounding box, and when I heard it was in tune with them I started picking out the tune, sort of note for note, letting their guitar play the bass chords and second parts. They both smiled when they heard me because two guitars being played this way is what's called the real article, and millions of little kids are raised on this kind of music. If you think of something new to say, if a cyclone comes, or a flood wrecks the country, or a bus load of school children freeze to death along the road, if a big ship goes down, and an airplane falls in your neighborhood, an outlaw shoots it out with the deputies, or the working people go out to win a war, yes, you'll find a train load of things you can set down and make up a song about. You'll hear people singing your words around over the country, and you'll sing their songs everywhere you travel or everywhere you live; and these are the only kind of songs my head or my memory or my guitar has got any room for.

So these two little girls and me sung together till the crowd had got bigger and it was dark under the trees where the moon couldn't hit us.

> Takes a ten-dollar shoe to fit my feet
> Takes a ten-dollar shoe to fit my feet
> Takes a ten-dollar shoe to fit my feet, Lord God!
> And I ain't a-gonna be treated this a-way!

When the night got late and the men in the saloons in town lost their few pennies playing framed-up poker, they drifted out to sleep the night in the jungle camp. We saw a bunch of twenty-five or thirty of them come running over the rim of the hill from town, yelling, cussing, kicking tin buckets and coffee pots thirty feet, and hollering like panthers.

And when the wild bunch run down the little trail to where we was singing—it was then that the whole drunk mess of them stood there reeling and listening in the dark, and then shushed each other to keep quiet and set down on the ground to listen. Everybody got so still that it almost crackled in the air. Men took seats and leaned their heads back against tree trunks and listened to the lightning bugs turn their lights on and off. And the lightning bugs must of been hushing each other, because the old jungle camp was getting a lot of good rest there listening to the little girls' song drift out across the dark wind.

Chapter XVI

STORMY NIGHT

✦

I set my hat on the back of my head and walked out west from Redding through the Redwood forests along the coast, and strolled from town to town, my guitar slung over my shoulder, and sung along the boweries of forty-two states; Reno Avenue in Oklahoma City, Lower Pike Street in Seattle, the jury table in Santa Fe; the Hooversvilles on the flea-bit rims of your city's garbage dump. I sung in the camps called "Little Mexico," on the dirty edge of California's green pastures. I sung on the gravel barges of the East Coast and along New York's Bowery watching the cops chase the bay-rum drinkers. I curved along the bend of the Gulf of Mexico and sung with the tars and salts in Port Arthur, the oilers and greasers in Texas City, the marijuana smokers in the flop town in Houston. I trailed the fairs and rodeos all over Northern California, Grass Valley, Nevada City; I trailed the apricots and peaches around Marysville and the winy-grape sand hills of Auburn, drinking the good homemade vino from the jugs of friendly grape farmers.

Everywhere I went I throwed my hat down in the floor and sung for my tips.

Sometimes I was lucky and found me a good job. I sung on the radio waves in Los Angeles, and I got a job from Uncle Samuel to come to the valley of the Columbia River and I made up and recorded twenty-six songs about the

Grand Coulee Dam. I made two albums of records called "Dust Bowl Ballads" for the Victor people. I hit the road again and crossed the continent twice by way of highway and freights. Folks heard me on the nationwide radio programs CBS and NBC, and thought I was rich and famous, and I didn't have a nickel to my name, when I was hitting the hard way again.

The months flew fast and the people faster, and one day the coast wind blew me out of San Francisco, through San Jose's wide streets, and over the hump to Los Angeles. Month of December, down along old Fifth and Main, Skid Row, one of the skiddiest of all Skid Rows. God, what a wet and windy night! And the clouds swung low and split up like herds of wild horses in the canyons of the street.

I run onto a guitar-playing partner standing on a bad corner, and he called his self the Cisco Kid. He was a long-

legged guy that walked like he was on a rolling ship, a good singer and yodeler, and had sailed the seas a lot of times, busted labels in a lot of ports, and had really been around in his twenty-six years. He banged on the guitar pretty good, and like me, come rain or sun, or cold or heat, he always walked along with his guitar slung over his shoulder from a leather strap.

We moved along the Skid looking in at the bars and taverns, listening to neon signs sputter and crackle, and on the lookout for a gang of live ones. The old splotchy plate-glass windows looked too dirty for the hard rain ever to wash clean. Old doors and dumps and cubbyholes had a sickly pale color about them, and men and women bosses and workhands humped around inside and talked back and forth to each other. Some soggy-smelling news stands tried to keep their fronts open and sell horse-race tips and sheets to the people ducking head-down in the rain, and pool halls stunk to high heaven with tobacco smoke, spit and piles of dirty men yelling over their bets. Hock-shop windows all piled and hanging full of every article known to man, and hocked there by the men that needed them most; tools, shovels, carpenter kits, paint sets, compasses, brass faucets, plumbers tools, saws, axes, big watches that hadn't run since the last war, and canvas tents and bedrolls taken from the fruit tramps. Coffee joints, slippery stool dives, hash counters with open fronts was lined with men swallowing and chewing and hoping the rain would wash something like a job down along the Skid. The garbage is along the street stones and the curbing, a shale and a slush that washes down the hill from the nicer parts of town, the papers crumpled and rotten, the straw, manure, and silt, that comes down from the high places, like the Cisco Kid and me, and like several thousand other rounders, to land and to clog, and to get caught along the Skid Row.

STORMY NIGHT

This is where the working people come to try to squeeze a little fun and rest out of a buffalo nickel; these three or four blocks of old wobbling flop houses and buildings.

I know you people I see here on the Skid. The hats pulled down over the faces I can't see. You know my name and you call me a guitar busker, a joint hopper, tip canary, kitty-box man.

Movie people, hoss wranglers, dead enders, stew bums; stealers, dealers, sidewalk spielers; con men, sly flies, flat foots, reefer riders; dopers, smokers, boiler stokers; sailors, whalers, bar flies, brass railers; spittoon tuners, fruit-tree pruners; cobbers, spiders, three-way riders; honest people, fakes, vamps and bleeders; saviors, saved, and side-street singers; whore-house hunters, door-bell ringers; footloosers, rod riders, caboosers, outsiders; honky tonk and whiskey setters, tight-wads, spendthrifts, race-horse betters; black-mailers, gin soaks, comers, goers; good girls, bad girls, teasers, whores; buskers, corn huskers, dust bowlers, dust panners; waddlers, toddlers, dose packers, syph carriers; money men, honey men, sad men, funny men; ramblers, gamblers, highway anklers; cowards, brave guys, stools and snitches; nice people, bastards, sonsabitches; fair, square, and honest folks; low, sneaking greedy people; and somewhere, in amongst all of these Skid Row skidders—Cisco and me sung for our chips.

This December night was bad for singing from joint to joint. The rain had washed some of the trash along the streets, but had chased most of the cash customers on home. Our system was to walk into a saloon and ask the regular musicians if they would like to rest a few minutes, and they usually was glad to stretch their legs and grab a coffee or a burger. Then we took their places on the little platform and sung our songs and asked the customers what they would like to hear next. Each joint was good for thirty or forty cents, if things went just right, and we usually hit five or six bars every night. But this was an off night. Men and women filled the booths, talking about Hitler and Japan and the Russian Red Army. A few soldiers and sailors and men in uniform scattered along the bar nodding to longshoremen, and tanker men, and freighter men, and dock workers, and factory men, and talking about the war. Cops ducking in and out of the rain stood around and took a good look to see if there was any trouble cooking.

The Cisco Kid was saying, "It looks like most of these old buildings had ought to be jacked up and a new one run under them." He was on the go from door to door, trying to keep his guitar out of the rain.

"Purty old, all right, some of these flop houses. I think th' Spaniards found 'em here when they first chased th' Indians outta this country." I dodged along behind him.

"Wanta drop in here at th' Ace High?"

I followed him in the door. "It'll be a cinch ta git ta play here. I don't know about makin' any money."

The Ace High crowd looked pretty low. We nodded at Charlie the Chinaman and he nodded back toward the music platform. The whole joint was painted a light funny blue that sort of made your head spin whether you was drinking or not. All kinds of ropes and corks and big fishing nets hung around over the walls and down from the ceiling. Cisco turned a nickel machine around with its face to the wall, while I flipped the strings of his guitar hanging on his back and tuned mine up to his. Then I waved at Charlie the Chinaman and he reached above the bar and turned on the loud speaker. I pulled the mike up to where it would be level with our mouths and we started in singing:

Well, I come here to work, I didn't come to hang around
Yes, I come here to work, I didn't come to hang around
And if I don't find me a woman, I'll just roll on out of town.

"Hey there, slim boy," a fast-talking little bald-headed man wearing a right new suit of gray clothes told us, handing Cisco a phone book at the same time, "turn in here and find me a name and a number to call."

"Which number?" Cisco asked him.

"Just any number," he said; "just read one off. I never could read those phone numbers very good."

I listened to Cisco call out a number. The man handed Cisco a dime and then Cisco and me heard him talking.

"Miss Sue Perfalus? How are you? I'm Mister Upjohn Smith, with the Happy Hearth and Home Roofing Company. I was fixing your next-door neighbor's roof today. While I was on top of her house, I looked over on top of your house. The rainy season is here, you know. Your roof is in a terrible condition. I wouldn't be surprised to see the whole thing go any minute. The water will cause the plaster to fall off your laths and ruin your piano and your furniture. It might fall down and hit you in the face some night while you're in bed. What? Sure? Sure, I'm sure! I got your phone number, didn't I? The price? Oh, I'm afraid it's going to run you somewhere around two hundred dollars. What's that? Oh, I see. You haven't got a roof? Apartment house? Oh, I see. Well, good-bye, lady."

"Wrong number?" I asked him when he hung up.

"No. Here, you take this phone book and try calling me off one." He took the book from Cisco and handed it to me.

"Who is this? Oh, Judge V. A. Grant? Your plaster is falling off your roof. This is the Happy Hearth and Home Roofing Company. Sure? Sure, I'm sure! The plaster might fall on your wife while she's in bed. Sure, I can fix it. That's my business. Price? Oh, it's going to run you right at three hundred dollars. Fine. Come around in the morning? I'll be there with bells on!" He took his phone book and handed me another dime and walked out.

Cisco laughed and said, "People do any dam thing under th' sun these days ta make a livin'! Huckle an' buck!"

"Git ta singin'. There's some live ones comin' in th' door. Boy howdy, this is our first catch tonight. I hope we can git three more dimes out of this Navy bunch. Sail on, sailor boys, sail on! Step up an' give us yer request!"

"Let's sing 'em one first," Cisco told me, "so they'll know it ain't juke-box stuff. What'll we sing? Sailor boys are really wet. Got caught out in the rain."

I nodded and started singing:

> Well, it's rainin' on th' Skid Row
> Stormin' down in Birmin'ham
> Rainin' on th' Skid Row
> Stormin' down in Birmin'ham
> But there ain't no stormy weather
> Gonna stop these boys of Uncle Sam!

"You tell 'em, back there, bud!"
"Let 'er reel! Let 'em ramble!"
"Hey! Hey!"

> Lord, it's stormy on that ocean
> Windy on th' deep blue sea
> Boys, it's stormy on the ocean
> Windy on th' deep blue sea
> I'm gonna bake them Nazis a chicken
> Loaded full of TNT!

"Hey, Bud! I ain't got no money, 'cept just a little here to get me a 'burger an' a beer. I'd give you a dime if I had it. But just keep on singing that song, huh?" A big broad sailor was leaning his head over my guitar, talking.

"He's just now makin' that song up, aren't you, friend?"

346

STORMY NIGHT

I woke up this mornin'
Seen what the papers said
Yes, boys, I woke up this mornin',
Seen what the papers said
Them Japanese had bombed Pearl Harbor
And war had been declared.

I didn't boil myself no coffee
I didn't boil no tea
I didn't boil myself no coffee
I didn't boil no tea
I made a run for that recruitin' office
Uncle Sam, make room for me!

We stopped singing and the whole bunch of sailors got around the platform. They all leaned on the rail and listened.

"You boys ought to sing those two verses first every time," one sailor told us.

"Anybody know the latest news from Pearl Harbor?" I asked them.

They all talked at the same time. "It's worse than we figured." "Japs done a lot of damage." "First I heard it was twelve hundred." "Yeah, but they say now it's closer to fifteen." "I'm just askin' one dam thing, boys, an' that's a Goddam close crack at them Jap bastards!" "Why, th' sneakin' skunk buzzards to hell, anyway, I hope to God that Uncle Sam puts me where I can do those Japs the most damage!"

A lone soldier walked in through the door and yelled, "Well, sailors, I'll be on a troopship the first thing in the morning! And you'll be out there keeping me company! C'mon! Beer's on me!"

"Hi, soldier! Come on back here! Charlie will send us

some beer. Five of us! Oh, seven! Two of th' best Goddam singers you ever did cock your ear at! On your way to camp?"

"Gotta be there in about an hour," the soldier said. "Knock me off a tune! This is my last greenback! Seven dam beers, there, Charlie!" He waved the dollar bill.

Five or six couples walked in the door and took seats in some booths.

A lady waved a handkerchief from a booth and said, "Hey, boys! Sing some more!"

"You jingle a nickel there on th' platform, lady," Cisco told her, "that'll sound like back where I come from!"

A nickel hit the platform. A sailor or two laughed and said, "Sing one about th' war. Got any?"

I scratched my head and told him, "Well, not to brag about. We've scribbled one or two."

"Le's hear 'em."

"Ain't learnt 'em so good yet." I pulled a piece of paper out of my pocket and handed it to one of the men. "You be my music rack. Hold this up in th' light where I can see it. I don't even know if I can read my own writin' or not."

> Our planes will down these buzzards
> Before this war has past,
> For they have fired the first, folks,
> But we will fire the last!

Charlie laughed out from behind the bar, "Plenty quick! Song come fast!"

The people in the booths clapped their hands, and the sailors and soldier boy reached across the rail and slapped us on the shoulders.

"Whew! That's gittin' songs out fast!" The soldier drained his beer glass.

"You guys oughtta move up to th' Circle Bar! You'd

pick up some real tips up there!" A wild-looking cowboy turned around from the bar and told us.

"Keep mouth shut!" Charlie hollered and waved a slick glass. "These boy know Cholly Chinee. Like Cholly Chinee! Girly! Take two beer back to sing man."

"I'd set 'em up again, if I could, guys," the soldier said, "but that was my last lone dollar."

"Cholly!" I yelled. "Did you say two free beers fer us?"

"Yes. I say girly bring. Two free beer," he said.

"Make it seven!" I told him.

"Seven free beer?"

"If ya don't, we're gonna move th' singin' up to th' Circle Bar!" Cisco put in.

"Seven?" Charlie looked up quick. Then he held up his finger and said, "Cholly good man. Cholly bring."

"By God, we gotta treat our soldiers an' sailors like earls an' dukes from here on out," Cisco laughed. We'd both tried that morning to ship aboard a freighter headed for Murmansk. They'd turned us down for some damn health reason and now Cisco and me was hot and crazy and laughing and mad clear through.

"Well, men!" One of the sailors held up his new glass of beer off of Charlie's tray. "I got th' prettiest gal in Los Angeles. Got a good uniform on. Got a free glass of beer. Got some real honest music. Got a great big war to fight. I'm satisfied. I'm ready. So here's to beatin' th' Japs!" He drained his glass at one pull.

"Beat 'em down!" another one said.

"And quick!"

"I'm in!"

"Gimme a ship!"

"I ain't no talker. I'm a fighter! Wow!"

One of the biggest and toughest of the civilian bunch downed a double drink of hard cold liquor and washed it down with a glass of beer, then he stood right in the middle of the floor and said, "Well, people! Soldiers! Sailors! Wimmen an' gals! I'm not physical fit ta be in th' navy er th' army, but I'll promise ya I'll beat th' livin' hell outta ever' Goddam livin' Jap in this town!"

"If you ain't got no more sense than that, big shot, you just better pull your head in your hole and keep it there!" a long, tall sailor yelled back at him. "None of your wild talk in here!"

"Cholly got plentee good friend. Japonee. You say more, Cholly bust bottle. Your head!" The boss was shaking a towel over the bar.

"We no fight Japonee people!" Charlie's waitress talked up at the far end of the bar by the door. "We fight big-shot Japonee crook. Big lie! Big steal! You not got no good sense! Try start Japonee fight here! Me China girl. Plentee Japonee friend!"

The soldier boy walked across the floor with his fists doubled up, shoving his glass empty along the counter, and saying in the tough boy's face, "Beat it, mister. Start walkin'. We ain't fightin' these Japs just because they happen to be Japs."

The big man backed out through the door into a crowd of fifteen or twenty people. He ducked off up the street in the dark.

"Hell!" The soldier walked back through the saloon saying, "That guy won't last a dam week talking that kind of stuff!"

"Far as that goes," Cisco was bending over, talking in my ear, "this Imperial Saloon right next door here is run by a whole family of Japanese folks. I know all of them. Sung in there a hundred times. They always help me to get tips. They're just as good as I am!" He started a song on his guitar.

"Music! Play, boys, play!" The sailors grabbed each other and danced around in the floor, doing the jitterbug, sticking their fingers up in the air, making all sorts of goofy faces, and yelling, "Yippee! Cut th' rug!"

Most of the girls got up out of the booths and walked across the floor smiling and saying, "No two men allowed to dance together in this place tonight." "No sailors are allowed to dance unless it's with an awful pretty girl." And a sailor cracked back when he danced his girl around, "It never was this a-way back home! Yow!"

Somebody else yelled, "I hope it stays this a-way fer th' doorashun! Yeah, man!"

Cisco and me played a whipped-up version of the old One Dime Blues, fast enough to keep up with the jitterbugs. Everybody was wheeling and whirling, waving their hands and shuffling along like a gang of circus clowns dancing in the sawdust.

"Mama, don't treat yore daughter mean!" I joked over the loud speaker.

"Meanest thing that a man most ever seen!" Cisco threw in.

The music rolled from the sound holes of the guitars and floated out through the loud speaker. Everybody at the bar tapped their glasses in time with the music. One man was tapping a nickel against the rim of his beer glass and grinning at his face in the big looking-glass. The joint boomed with music and dancing. Charlie stood behind the bar and smiled like a full moon. Music turned a pretty bad old night outside into a good, friendly, warm shindig on the inside. Sailors bowed their necks and humped their backs and made goo-goo eyes and clown faces. Girls slung their hair through the air and spun like tops. Whoops and hollers. "Spin 'er!" "That sailor ain't no slouch!" "Hold 'er, boy!" "Hey! Hey! I thought I had 'er, but she got away!"

And then just out on the street there came a clattering of glass breaking on the sidewalk. I quit the music and listened. People were running past the door, darting around in big bunches, cussing and hollering.

The girls and the sailors stopped dancing and walked to the door.

"What is it?" I spoke over the microphone.

"Big fight! Looks like!" the fat sailor was saying.

"Let's go see, boys!" another sailor said. He pushed off out the door.

"All time fight. Me not bother." Charlie kept swabbing the bar down with a wet rag. "Me got work."

I slung my guitar across my shoulder and run out the door with Cisco right in after me saying, "Must be a young war!"

A bunch of men that had the looks of being pool-hall gamblers and horse-race bookies stood on the curb across the street hooting and heaving and cussing and pointing. The sailors and working men from our saloon stepped out and walked in front of the Imperial Bar next door. Already plate glass lay at our feet in the dark. Out of all of the milling and loud talking something whizzed over our heads and smashed a second window. Glass flew like chipped ice all around us. A slice cracked one of Cisco's guitar strings, and the music bonged.

"Who throwed that can of corn?" a lady yelled from right at my elbow.

"Was that a can of corn?" I asked her.

"Yes. Two cans," she told me. "Who throwed them two cans of corn, and broke them windows? I've a good notion to bust my parasol over his head when I find out!"

Two men in the middle of the street argued and pushed each other all around.

"You're th' man I want, all right!" the biggest one said.

"You won't want me very long!"

A soldier with a brown overcoat on was pushing the big man back to the curb. I elbowed near and saw it was the same soldier that had just bought us the seven beers. I looked a little closer in the night and seen the face of the big pug-ugly that had said he was going to beat hell out of all of the Japs in Los Angeles.

About ten of his thug friends chewed on old cigars, smoked snipe cigarets, and backed him up with tough talk when he said anything. "We come ta git 'em, an' dam me, we're gonna git 'em! Japs is Japs!" "I'm da guy wot t'rew dat corn, lady, whattaya gonna do wid me?"

"I'll show you, you big bully!" She waved the can in the air to throw it at him, and her man right behind her said, "No, don't. We don't want to start no trouble. What's this all about, anyhow?" He took the can of corn away from her in the air.

"We're at war with them yeller-belly Japs! An' we come down ta git our share of 'em!" A big man with a lost voice was talking on the curb. "We're 'Meric'ns!"

"You ain't nuthin', but th' worst dam scum of th' Skid Row! Two-bit gambler!" A big half-Indian truck driver was trying to push his way across the street to get the man.

"Jap rats!" another tough one said.

"Spies! They tipped off th' Goddam Jap army! These yeller snakes knew to a split second when Pearl Harbor was gonna be blowed up. Git 'em! Jail 'em! Kill 'em!" He started to cross from the other side of the street.

A couple of sailors edged their way toward him saying, "You're not going to hurt anybody, Mister Blowoff!"

"Where is th' cops?" a girl was asking her boy friend.

"I guess they're on th' way," Cisco told her.

"Cops ain'ta gonna put no stop ta us, neither!" one of the mob yelled across at us.

353

"But, brother, we are!" I answered him back.

"You mangy little honky-tonk guitar-playin' sot, I'll come over there an' bust that music box over yore bastardly head!"

"I'll furnish th' guitar, mister," I talked back, "but you'll hafta furnish th' head!"

Everybody squeezed around me and laughed back at the rioters. Cursing flew in the air and fists waved above the crowd in the rain and in the dark. The people on our side of the street formed two or three lines in front of the Imperial's door. Several Japanese men and women stood inside picking up glass from the floor. "That's it, folks," Cisco told everybody, "squeeze together. Stand right where you are. Don't let that crazy mob get through!"

"Wonder why they threw two cans of corn?" I was looking around asking people.

Then I listened across the street and a wild man mounted the running board of a car and hollered out, "Listen, people! I know! Why, just this morning, right here in this neighborhood, a housewife went into a Japanese grocery store. She asked him how much for a can of corn. He told her it was fifteen cents. Then she said that was too much. And so he said when his Goddam country took th' U. S. A. over, that she would be doing the work in the store, and the corn would cost her thirty-five cents! She hit him over the head with that can of corn! Ha! A good patriotic American mother! That's why we smashed that Goddam window with th' cans of corn! Nobody can stop us, men! Go on, fight! Get 'em!"

"Listen, folks," Cisco climbed up on the wheel of a little vegetable cart at our curb. "These little Japanese farmers that you see up and down the country here, and these Japanese people that run the little old cafés and gin joints, they can't help it because they happen to be Japanese. Nine-tenths of them hate their Rising Sun robbers just as much as I do, or you do."

"Lyin' coward! Git down frum dere!" a guy with hairs sticking out from his shirt collar bawled at Cisco.

"Pipe down, brother. I'll take care of you later. But this dam story about the can of corn is a rotten, black and dirty lie! Made up to be used by killers that never hit a day's honest work in their whole life. I know it's a lie, this can-of-corn story, because even two years ago, I heard this same tale, word for word! Somebody right here in our country is spreading all kinds of just such lies to keep us battling against each other!" Cisco said.

"Rave on, you silly galoon!"

"You're righter than hell, boy! Pour it on!"

"You're a sneakin' fifth column sonofabitch! Tryin' ta pertect them skunk Japs agin' native-borned American citizens!"

The crowd started slow across from the other side. We stood there ready to keep them back. The whole air was full of a funny, still feeling, like all of hell's angels was just about to break loose.

Just then an electric train, loaded down with men and railroad tools, pulled past in front of them. The railroad workers hollered a few cracks at the two sides. "What goes on here?" "Gangfight?" "Keep back there, ya'll git run over!" "Listen ta these ratheads bark!"

Cisco dropped down fast off of the hub of the wheel. "Me, I'm going to stand right here," he hollered, "right here on this curb. I just ain't moving."

"I'm with yuh, brother!" A lady walked up with a big black purse and a gallon jug of wine, ready to be broke over somebody's head.

"I ain't a-movin', neither!" A little old skinny man was flipping his belt buckle. "Let 'em come!"

As the last two or three flat cars of men rolled down the street and kept the wild mob back for a minute, I grabbed my guitar up and started singing:

> We will fight together
> We shall not be moved
> We will fight together
> We shall not be moved
> Just like a tree
> That's planted by the water
> We
> Shall not
> Be moved.

"Everybody sing!" Cisco grabbed his guitar and hollered out.

"All together! Sing! Give it all ya got!" I told them.

So as the last car of the train went on down the middle of the street, everybody was singing like church bells ringing up and down the grand canyon of the old Skid Row:

> Just like
> A treeeee
> Standing by
> The waterrr
> We
> Shall not
> Be
> Moooooved!

The whole bunch of thugs made a big run at us sailing cuss words of a million filthy, low-down, ratty kind. Gritting their teeth and biting their cigar butts and frothing at the mouth. Everybody on our side kept singing. They made a dive to bust into our line. Everyone stood there singing as loud and as clear and as rough-sounding as a war factory hammering.

Sailors threw out their chests and sung it out. Soldiers drifted in. Truck drivers laid their heads back and cotton pickers slung their arms along with the cowboys and ranch hands and bartenders from other saloons around.

The rain come down harder and we all got wetter than wharf rats. Our singing hit the mob of rioters like a cyclone tearing into a haystack. They stopped—fell back on their heels like you had poked them in the teeth with a ball bat. Fumbled for words. Spewed between their teeth and rubbed their fingers across their eyes. Scratched their heads and smeared rainwater down across their cheeks. I saw three or four in the front row coming toward us that grinned like monkeys up a grapevine. The bunch backing them up split off and stopped there in the rain for a little bit, then mostly slunk off in twos and threes in different directions. Four or five walked like gorillas and waved their arms and fists in the faces of the soldiers and sailors standing along the curb singing. I thought for a minute that the battle was on, but nobody touched each other.

And then, after some howling and screeching that didn't halfway match with our singing, there whined through the clouds that old familiar siren that tinhorn pimps, horse betters, and gamblers get to knowing so good, the moan of the police patrol wagon a block away. In a second, the toughs bent over and skidded away in between the cars, and got lost in the crowds along the walk, and hit the alleys and disappeared.

A big long black hoodlum wagon drove up and fifteen or twenty big cops fell out with all of the guns and sticks and clubs it would take to win a war. They made a step or two at us, and then stopped and listened to the raindrops and the wind in the sky and the singing echoing around over the old skiddy row. They shook their heads, looked at their address books, flashed searchlights around.

"The chief said this was where the riot was." A cop pointed his flashlight onto his address sheet.

"Jest a buncha people singin'." Another big copper shook his head. "Hhmmmm."

"Sing with us, officer?" Cisco laughed out in the crowd.

"How does it go?" the big chief asked him back.

"Listen."

"Yeah. Dat's it. Tum. Tum. Tum. Tum. Dat's planted by de water, we shall not—be—moved!"

All of the cops stood around smiling and swinging their clubs. They patted their feet and hands. They watched and hummed and they listened.

"Okay! Dat's all!" the head officer told them. "Back on da wagon, men! Back on!"

And when it drove off down the street-car tracks to fade away into the night rain, that old patrol wagon was singing:

> Just like a treeee
> Planted by th' waterrr
> We
> Shall not
> Be
> Mooooved!

Chapter XVII

EXTRY SELECTS

❖

"You look like one of these here pretty boys that tries to get out of all th' hard work you can!" a nice pretty girl, about eighteen, was saying to me as we rode along.

It was about a 1929 sedan, the kind of used car salesmen call lemons. No two wires quite connected like they ought to; there was a gap of daylight between every two moving parts, and every part was moving.

"I got jest as many callouses on my hands as you!" I hollered at her above the racket. "Take a look at th' ends of my fingers!"

She set her eyes on the ends of my guitar fingers. Then she told me, "Well, I reckon I was wrong."

"That's about th' only place ya get stuck pickin' cotton, too!" I told her. I pulled my hand back. I sung a little song and made my old guitar talk about it, too:

> I worked in your farm
> I worked in your town
> My hands is blistered
> From the elbows down
>
> Ride around little doggies
> Ride around them slow
> They're fiery, they're snuffy,
> And rarin' to go.

A middle-size lady in the front seat, with streaks of gray hair sailing in the wind, grinned at her husband beside her and said, "Well, I don't know if that guitar boy back there hits any of th' heavy work or not, but he can dang shore sing about it!"

"Mighty near make work sound like fun, cain't he?" Her husband kept his eyes running along the road ahead, and all I seen of him was just an old slouch hat jammed on the back of his head.

"Long ye been runnin' around playin' an' singin'?" the mama asked me.

"Round about eight years," I said.

"That's a pretty good little spell," she told me. She was watching out the broke window at the scenery jumping past. "California's mortally loaded down with stuff to ride along an' look at, ain't it?"

"Long on climate out here! But still, it costs ya like th' devil ta soak up any of it!" the boy who was driving said.

"All you folks one family?" I asked them.

"All one family. This is me'n my husband, an' these is all th' kids we got left! Four of us now. Used to be eight."

"Where's th' other four?" I asked her. The trees got so thick and green along the river bottom that the leaves blotted out the sunlight.

"They just went," I heard the lady say.

The girl in the back seat with me said, "You know where they go," and she didn't take her eyes off of the loaded orchard all along out through the window. She had gray eyes and her black hair sort of curled down to her shoulders.

"Yeah," I told her, "I know all right."

And just about that time there was a big racket and a tire right under where I was setting went out, Keeeeblam! The car got out of gallop with the trailer and jumped along like a sick frog. I could feel the tire tearing itself to pieces between the iron rim and the pavement, and we all had to hold what we had till everything bounced to a stop.

"Good-bye, little trailer hitch!" The driver boy was talking to his self as he piled out of the front door and trotted around to the back.

"Shot to hell," the papa said.

"Tire ration's on, top of all this," the mama was telling us.

"Rubber's rubber, old 'er new. Uncle Sammy says, 'Gotta save that rubber ta haul soldiers 'n' guns, 'n' cannons." The driver was talking while he wired some old wire around the bolt that kept up the friendship between the car and trailer.

"I'd shore hate to see a soldier ridin' aroun' with a hungry gut, myself." The old man was running a couple of fingers down over his chin and smacking his lips over the fence at the orchard.

"Now, Mister Papa, just tell me, what has this old rotten tire got to do with a hungry soldier?" the girl asked her dad.

"Well, if we could git on down th' country just a little bit further, 'y God, I could pick enuff fruit an' stuff ta feed three er four soldiers, heavy eaters." I seen a light strike fire in the old man's eyes. " 'Bout all I'm good fer, I reckon. I can pick more fruit with both hands over my eyes than most of these new pickers floodin' out here."

"Don't go to braggin'," the old lady told him. "You was th' best blacksmith back in Johnson County, all right, but I ain't seen you break no pickin' records yet. That's one mighty fine-lookin' orchard right in through there. Wonder what it is?"

"Apercots," the girl spoke up.

"Nice even rows," the old man told us; "trees all just 'bout th' same size. Limbs just achin' full wantin' us to come over that old fence an' pick 'em clean. I suppose a soldier wouldn't smack his goozler over a good big hot apercot pie right about now!"

"How we gonna get another tire?" I asked the bunch.
"Anybody got any money in their clothes?"

"Ain't a-packin' nothin' that jingles," one of them said.

" 'Er folds either," another one talked up.

I heard the slick drone of an easy motor oozing down
the line. Before I could center my eyes on it good, there
was a Sssss Swish. And a Zzooommmm—a blue gray sedan
lit up in the sun like a truckload of diamonds sailing past.
The heavy tread on the new tires sung a sad-sounding song
off down the highway.

A truck come angling down the highway, no two wheels
running in the same direction. This truck just wasn't quite
politically clear. But it had a big bunch of men, women,
and kids on it, and stopped on the shoulder just ahead of
us. Five or six people yelled back, but one big raw-boned
lady drowned most of the others out. "Need some help, or
just lost?"

"Both!" the mama of our little bunch hollered back.

"Tire blowed off!"

"Can't you fix it up?" the big lady asked us.

"Not this 'un! It'd take th' Badyear Rubber Outfit three
months to make this thing ever hold air again!" the lady in
our bunch said.

"Tire ration got us!"

"Wanta pick?" the lady asked us.

"Pickin' around here? Where 'bouts? What?"

"We ain't got no time to waste! But if ya wanta work,
foller us! First gate here! Crank up and roll on that bad
tire! Ya cain't hurt it no worse!"

Our bunch piled back into the seats. I was riding right
on top of the bad tire and the girl asked me, "What kind of
a song would you make up now, to sing about this?"

I let out with:

Tell me, mama, is your tread thin as mine?
Hey! Hey! Woman, is your tread thin as mine?
Work and roll, is your tread thin as mine?
Every old tire's gonna blow its side sometime!

"Wheel 'em an' deal 'em!" the driver laughed out.

Say, Lord Godamighty, roll them wheels around!
Hey! Good gal, you gotta roll them wheels around!
Workin' woman, roll your wheels around!
I'll find me a job or roll California down!

"Where 'bouts ye hear that ther song? 'At's a mighty good 'un," the old man asked me from the front seat.

"That ain't even no song. I just made it up," I told him. There was a big orchard passing us up on both sides.

The young girl by me in the back seat said, "Boy, you sure can sing about work, whether you get any done or not."

"Time ya sing six hours or eight or ten, right straight hand runnin', in some of these saloons or places, like I do, you'll say music runs inta work!" I told her.

"Sing that long every night?" she asked.

"General thing. Get started out about eight o'clock, sing till 'bout two or three, sometimes daylight in th' mornin'."

"Make how much?" she asked.

"Dollar, dollar an' a half," I said.

"Just about an orchard day." She glanced out the window at a stinging bee trying to carry a big load of honey and keep up with our car. "Looky! This poor little old bee. He's a havin' a hard time tryin' to fly with too much honey!"

"Looks like even that little old bee's all lined up workin' fer Uncle Sam Deeefense!" her papa said, bending his neck and head around to see the bee.

" 'Tain't deefense!" she told him.

"Deeefense. Beeeefense. Some kind of a fence," the old man said.

She screwed her eyes up a little bit and told him, " 'Tain't deefense. Not no more, it ain't!"

"What is it?"

"War."

"Same thing, war's defense, ain't it?" her papa asked her.

"Not by a dam sight!" the girl talked back at him.

"What's th' diff'rence?"

"If Hitler made a run at me with a big club, an' I took a step backwards to get fixed, that'd be defense," she said.

"So what?"

"Then if I reached and got me a hell of a lot bigger club," she made a grab for the tire pump on the floor, "that'd be changin' my belt line!"

"Yeah?"

"Then when I hauled off an' beat old Hitler plumb into th' ground, that'd be war!"

" 'Y God, 'at's right, sis," the old man backed her up. "Only you don't hafta swing that there pump aroun' so much here in th' car. You don't want to konk none of yer own soldiers out, do you?"

"No." She smiled a little and dropped the pump back down onto the floorboards. "Gotta not hurt none of my own soldiers here."

The mama spit out her front window and said, "Reckon all of us is soldiers these days. Look like th' gate where we turn."

The car turned through a big swinging gate into an orchard of trees set out in a deep sandy land.

"Truck stopped on ahead yonder," I heard the old man say.

People piled down off th' truck bed, men in their overhalls and khaki britches, shirts two or three colors where a new patch had been sewed, and the blue and brownish color sweated out a lot of times. Some tied handkerchiefs around their necks and slipped on their gloves. Tobacco cans flew out and men rolled the makin's. You could see a snuff can shine like it was polished in the sun. Hoppers and bugs and all kinds of critters with wings wheeled through the air, and spider webs ran from tree limbs to the clods of orchard dirt.

The tall lady from the truck jumped on our running board and said, "Keep drivin'. Careful, don't run over none of our pickers. Lucky to get 'em these days to come out in the fields with this gas and rubber cut down like it is." I could see her arm and hand stuck through the window, holding onto the door handle inside. She had fair skin with light freckles and I took her to be a Swedish lady. "See that bunch of cars and trailers through yonder? Pull on ahead!"

The Swedish lady stepped down on the ground and the car stopped. I got out and brushed some of the dust out of my duds, and everybody was standing there waiting for her to tell us something about something.

"You folks pick for a living?"

"Yes'm." Everybody nodded.

"Know about apricots then, I suppose?"

We all nodded that we knew.

"Do you know how we grade the apricots?"

"Grade 'em?"

"No'm."

"I don't reckon."

"Three grades of apricots, you know. Just plain ones. Then, next best are called Selects. Very best, Extra Selects."

"Plain ones."

"Selects."

"Extry Seelects."

We nodded our heads up and down.

"Now, the plain ones ripen last in the warm weather; anybody can pick the plain ones. Pay so much a box. Selects ripen earlier. Better taste, better shape, less of them. You get a little more money for picking them, about twice as much a box as the plain ones."

"Is th' Seelects on now?" the old man in our bunch asked her.

"No," the lady said to us. "Too early. The Extra Selects are on now."

The young girl nodded her head. "Oh, yes ma'm. They're th' very earliest ones, aren't they?" The sun was hitting down in her face and I saw her hair was going to curl up awful pretty when she washed the dirt out in river water.

"First to ripen. Moneyed folks want the very best they can get, and the best is the Extra Selects. Now, here, I'll give you an idea how you pick them, so when the orchard boss gets here in a minute, you'll already know the answers. See those limbs over there?"

"Loaded plumb down."

"Man alive, look at them apercots!"

"Trees got a lot of patience, ain't they?"

"Ooooooooozin' in juice."

"You've got to be able to tell an Extra Select when you run onto one," the Swede lady told us. "Here's one. See? Clear bright color. Nice gold look."

"Makes my mouth run water," the old man said.

"I won't even have time to dip my snuff, I'll be eatin' so many of them there yeller outfits." The old lady was laughing and winking at all of us.

"I'm sure we see what you mean," the young girl told the lady. "We've picked lots of other fruit where they graded them just about the same way. They're pretty, aren't they?"

"One little thing," the lady talked so quiet I had to step

closer to hear, "I'll tell you to save the field boss from tangling horns with you. If he catches you eating the Extra Selects, he takes it out of your day's pay, so don't say I didn't warn you. He's walking over toward us now. You'll make out all right. He's short-handed around here, needs you pretty bad. Don't ever let him back you down. I think he was born tough, and just naturally likes to see everything tough."

"New pickers?" He hollered out about fifty feet before he got to us. He was holding the top wire of a fence, spraddling it, and he was sort of a chunky built, low-set man. You could tell he had to grunt and stretch to make it over the fence. "New hands?"

The mother said, "Well, I ain't so new no more." She smiled at the boss, then she looked down at the deep dirt.

"I mean you're new around here, ain't you?" He was yanking at his belt trying to poke his two or three shirts down inside his pants. Everything about him seemed to be greasy, and bagging down to the ground.

"New here," the mother said. Everybody else was standing there waiting for him or the belt, one or the other, to come out winner. "Just blowed in on a bad tire."

"Know yer Exter Selecks pretty well?"

"We don't fool around with nothin' but the very best," I told him.

"Well, far's that goes, I hope I don't ketch you foolin' around in this orchard when the order comes in."

"Order comes where?" the girl asked him.

"Cann'ry order. Ain't come yet. Due today. Very latest tomorrow. Well, get your stuff all unpacked over yonder under those trees." He was looking at the old car steaming at the mouth. Then he turned around and started walking away.

I took a couple of steps behind him and said, "Say, boss,

I don't think these people quite understand all of this order business. If we're goin' to even eat, we gotta get some work 'cause we ain't got no money. Cain't wait even another day."

He stopped and turned around to me, and told me, "Listen, I don't know who you are, but you drive in here with a bunch of pickers. You wanta work, don't you?" He waved his hands around in the air so much that he worked his shirt out from under his belt again and fought with his britches to try to keep them from falling down. "You don't act like you ever picked an apricot before! Or did you?" He eyed me up and down the front.

"No. I never picked an apricot before, except to eat. I play music for a livin'. I don't have to pick your dam apricots for my livin'! Just these other people. That's their only way of eatin'! They've got a busted tire, mister. This is far as they can get. No work, no eat!" I told him.

"Come on down. Sign up."

"Sign up? Where?" I asked him.

"Store. Can't you see that fillin' station, big as it is? And store?" He was pointing ahead of himself and walking away.

I took several steps alongside of him and then told him, "I'm not with these people, I cain't sign up for them. What is it we got to sign?"

"Register book," he told me. Then he stopped real quick and asked me, "You ain't with these folks? How come?" He was giving me the real combing down with his eyes. "How come you so interested in my business?"

"I was just hitchin'. These people let me ride. I sing in saloons for a livin'," I told him.

"I guess I won't need you to work for me, then. You can take your ukelelaydeehoo and beat it."

"Well, I ain't in no awful big rush," I said to the man. "I thought I might hang around till they get their tire fixed."

Then I turned around and hollered to the people, "Say! Somebody's got to come down to th' store an' sign somethin'!"

"Sign which?" I heard somebody say.

"Register up! Sign somethin' or other!" I told them.

"You better go, honey," I heard the old man say to the young girl. "You got good eyes. See better'n me. An' you write a better hand than yer brother's."

So the girl and me walked along kicking clods apart in under the apricot trees. She was trying to fix her hair back over her ear some way and saying, "I've signed a lot of these register books. Just to keep track of who's working, and how much you've got coming, and all how many's in your family and stuff like that. You can sign up, too."

" 'Fraid I won't," I told her.

"Not going to work?" she asked me.

"Not pickin' apercots."

"I was just thinking how much fun we'd have picking together. We'd get a lot more picked, even if you didn't pick a single apricot."

"How's that? Now?"

"You play your guitar and sing for us out in the orchard, and we'll work just that much easier and better. See, mister singin' man?"

"You know, you're an awful, awful smart girl. You know what I'm gonna do?"

"What?"

"I'm gonna get you a real good job. Best job in th' whole state of California!"

"Movie star?"

"Hell, no. Gov'nor!"

"Me be gov'nor?"

"We can tell everybody that you're gonna win this war quick!"

369

"Lady be gov'nor, hey?"

"Tell ever'body you're gonna take all th' pretty red an' green neon signs an' all th' pretty lit-up nickel phonographs out of th' road houses, an' cat houses, an' joints, an' put 'em around in th' factories an' in th' shops an' in th' fields!"

"What's a cat house?"

"Skip it."

"Home for little cats?"

"Some of 'em ain't so little. Anyway, then, instead of drawin' ever'body from out on th' job down to th' saloon, see, it'd draw ever'body from th' saloon out on to th' job. An' we'd all have such a good time workin' that we'd work 'bout three times harder."

"And win the war! Here's the sign-'em-up store," she said, and I held her hand till she could jump across a puddle of oil on the ground close to the porch. We slammed in through an old screen door. "So dark in here I won't be able to make out where to sign my name. Say, mister boss man, do you hang around this old dark hole much of your time?" she asked the owner.

"How much of my time I spend inside my own place of business is my own affair, little lady. Here. I suppose you can at least write your name!" He growled and his belly ached because he was such an old growler. "Sign th' name of every member of your family an' put a cross by th' ones that'll be pickin'. Right down this list here."

I watched her write the names of all four members of her family. "Four. Used to be eight," she told herself almost, I guessed, by force of habit.

"Who owns your car an' trailer?" the storekeeper asked her.

She looked up at him. "My father. Why?"

"Be needin' some things to cook an' eat, won't you?" He glanced over his specks at her.

"Yes, I guess so."

"Take this security note down to your old man. Tell 'im to sign it an' bring it back an' you're good for twenty-five dollars worth of credit here at th' store. Just a little piece of paper we all sign."

I'd been walking around over the store, taking a look at the price tags. "Eagle Milk, two bits a can?" I asked him. "Goshamighty, never did see Eagle Milk cost more'n eighteen cents, even in all of th' Texas an' Oklahoma oil booms!"

"If you don't want it, leave it on th' shelf!" He cut his eyes over at me.

She let the pencil drop. "Things are so awful high. I just don't quite hardly see how we can even afford to eat anything." She took me by the hand and looked like she was sorry the boss had heard her.

"Me, I wouldn't sign th' dam thing if I starved plum to death," I said to her. "But you folks, 'course, there's your whole family; bad tire; sorta stuck here."

The girl carried the slip back to her folks and we had to shake hands with twenty-five or thirty other people around in the bunch before we got a chance to talk about the credit business. Gray-looking clothes and old floppy sacks and rags everywhere. Broke-down cars and homemade trailers. People smiled and pointed to their own, bragging, "Built 'er jist like I wanted 'er, my own way." "Yes sir, took me right onto six months of hard old pinchin' an' savin' ta git th' money ta throw this'n together." "Our'n looks like th' Los Angeles junk heap headin' down th' highways, but them slick purty cars duck off ta one side ta let us pass!" We'd all laugh when somebody told a good one on their jaloppy or trailer. "Mine wants ta run so fast I gotta keep it loaded fulla rocks ta keep it from jist takin' off like a big bird!"

"I just don't know. I just don't know," the old man was

saying, rubbing his hand around over his face at the same time. "Mama, what do you think, what you got to say about this here Goddern credit?" He looked around for his wife, but she wasn't in the crowd. Then he asked his boy, "I dam me, if I know, what do you think? Run a big risk a-losin' th' whole business." He looked at the rest of his family. "You helped me, you helped me build th' whole works. You got somethin' to say in th' way things is got an' got rid of." Then he asked another man there, "Hay, mister, do you know a dam thing about this dam infernal credit slip?"

"Do I know?" A tall gangling man thumbed his overhall suspenders and told the old man, "See this slip of mine? Just exactly like yours. I advise you not sign nothin' for nobody."

"Much ablige," the old man said. "I wish to hell an' little santypedes I could find my wife! Runs off 'n' hides. Cain't find 'er high ner low! Lory! Lorrry! Where'n th' hell are you hidin' at?" He was calling through his hands.

"Go ahead and sign that thing, Pa." His wife was laying stretched out on an old slice of gray canvas, looking up through the limbs of a wild-looking tree of some kind, talking between the leaves, right on out into the open bright sky. "You know you'll sign it, anyhow. You'll think of ten thousand mean things to say about the store man. You'll think of five thousand things wrong with this orchard here. You'll say there's a blue jillion things wrong with how th' country's run; but you'll sign it. You'll cuss old mister Hitler an' Mussolini and Kaiser Bill an' Father Coffin; an' then you'll think about th' soldiers fightin' Hitler, an' you'll say you just got to pick th' fruit for 'em; an' you'll think about yer own little hungry youngins, an' you'll sign it. . . . If it said bring your left eye an' yer right arm down to that old store when you went to buy somethin', you'd sign it.

I know what's in back of that old head of your'n. Th' whole world's fightin' to keep from bein' hungry. Yore own little family's standin' around with their bellies crawlin'. Hand my man an endelible pencil, somebody. He's goin' to write his name on a slip. Gonna lose all we got here. He's thinkin' 'bout all of them soldiers out yonder shootin' an' he's gonna write his name down on a Comp'ny Credit slip. . . ."

The sun went down on everybody. You could hear the jingle of the four-for-a-nickel knives and forks. "Smells like ever'body's a-eatin' 'bout th' same supper 'roun' here," the father was saying.

"Sow bosom and beans!" The girl laughed at my elbow and her hair touched my face when she took the tin plates away. "But when you've worked real hard and are good and hungry, it smells good, don't it?"

A lady from a car across from our trailer walked over with a tin bucket in each hand and said, "I brung ye these rag buckits, bugs 'n' skeeters, 'n' all kindsa bitin', stingin', 'n' jist arguin' vermits is a gonna make a big land rush f'r this place quick's we light these here lanterns. Ye jist strike a match to these here rags, see, an' push 'em right back down inta th' buckit real tight, an' leave 'em smolder along. Makes a cloud of smoke almost's bad as them fellers thet usta sling tear gas at us 'fore th' war come along an' we quit our strikin'."

"I'm one that's shore glad we quit that strikin'," the mother said, " 'cause just ain't right for one buncha people to up an' quit work, an' another bunch to drive down an' shoot you full of that old tear gas, crops of all kinds a-goin' to waste all around. That's a right friendly lady, ain't she? Just walked off 'fore any of us had a chance to thank her for them buckets."

Her daughter eased around in the dark and I felt her take

a good warm seat beside me on the beer case, and I took her by the hand and said, "Yep siree, you've got an awful honest hard-workin' set of hands on you."

She squeezed mine a little and said, "Could I, do you think, learn how to play the guitar?"

"If ya try, ya would. Want ta take lessons? Shucks, I could show ya th' easy part in a little o' no time."

"You two quit'cher flirtin' an' sing us a song. Happ'n ta know th' Talkin' Blues?"

"I'll teach ya after th' dishes an' stuff's all put away." I was just catching part of what the person talking was saying, "Huh? Th' Talkin' Blues? I know a few verses."

"While you're doing your Talking Blues," the girl told me, "I'll try not to make any noise, but I've just got to put these dishes back into their boxes."

"Okay," I said, then started playing and talking:

> If you wanta get to heaven,
> Let me tell you what to do,
> Just grease your feet in a mutton stew,
> Just slide out of the devil's hand
> And ooze over into the Promised Land!
> Take it easy. An' go greasy.

> Down in the hen house on my knees
> I thought I heard a chicken sneeze;
> Nothin' but a rooster a-sayin' his prayers,
> An' givin' out thanks fer th' hens upstairs.
> Rooster preachin'. Hens a-singin'.
> Little young chickens jest a-hopin'.

> Now I been here an' I been there,
> Rambled aroun' most everywhere,
> Purtiest little gal that I ever did see
> A-walkin' up an' down by th' side of me.
> Mouth wide open. Catchin' flies.
> Knows I'm crazy.

Everybody would snigger and laugh between verses. I played the guitar while several other folks added verses they'd picked up somewhere. A woman with a blue bonnet on held her chin in one hand and fanned the insects of all kinds off her baby asleep at her feet on a old sack; she sung:

> Down in th' holler settin' on a log,
> Hand on my trigger an' my eye on a hog;
> Pulled that trigger, th' gun went 'zip';
> Grabbed mister hog with all of my grip.
>   Cain't eat hog eyes. But I need greasin'.

"Well, this singing is fine and dandy!" The girl talked up at her work with the dishes. "But this isn't getting these dishes clean! Mister guitar picker, come on here, help me carry up a bucket of water from the river!"

As I followed her along I heard somebody in the crowd laugh out, "He shore didn't hafta be coaxed none!"

"You know I never did ask you yer name yet." I was talking and following her along a path under the trees down to the banks of the river. "I s'pose ya got one, ain't ya?"

"Ruth. I already know yours; I'll call you Curley. Lordy, I wonder how deep this water runs along in here. It's pretty and clear. You can almost see the fish swimming around." She waded out barefooted and left her shoes kicked off on the bank. She dipped up two buckets of water and made an awful pretty picture standing there reflecting upside-down with all of the trees and banks. "Pretty cold," she was trying to put her wet feet back into her sandals.

"Dry yer feet 'fore ya put 'em back in yer shoes!" I took the buckets and set them on the ground a few feet from the path, and held her hand while we walked back into the underbrush. We both dropped down on some leaves and I dried her feet one at a time with my handkerchief.

"Feels good to have somebody kneel down and dry my feet!"

"Makes 'em warmer. Yeah. It feels fine."

"But how do you know how it feels, it's me that's getting my feet dried."

"Yeah, but it's me that's doin' th' dryin'."

"My skin is all sunburned and rough-looking. I'm always going without stockings and scratching the hide off on twigs and bushes. They look terrible."

"Look all right to me. You got 'em wet plumb up above yer knees."

"You mind?"

"Naw, I don't mind. Fact, I was just thinkin', I sort of wish you'd waded out deeper."

"Teach me a guitar lesson."

"Right now?"

"Show me something real easy to do."

I put both arms around her and made a pillow with my hand out of the leaves; then I picked up a handful of leaves and dropped them in her hair and said, "This is easy to do." And I kissed her four times and said, "And this is easy, and this is easy, and this, and this." I put my face against her neck and felt her put her arms around mine, felt her cheek warm up and she told me, "Is this your first guitar lesson?"

"This is what you call the first and easy steps."

"You're warm and I'm all cold from wading the water."

"If you had ice-cicles hangin' in yer hair, you'd feel warm ta me."

"Teach me the next lesson."

"Next lesson is mostly learning how ta use yer hands an' fingers. Gettin' th' feel of th' instrument. Gettin' use ta th' strings that're attached."

"Strings attached?"

"A few."

"What?"

"I want me 'n' you ta be tied t'gether, sort of b'long ta one another, an' be like this all th' time. Jest like we are now. An' you c'n be gov'nor."

"Who's Governor?"

"My gov'nor."

"Teach me lessons on the guitar? Buy me penny candy twice a week?"

"Penny candy, twice a week."

"I'm thinking about it."

"You look mighty purty layin' here thinkin' 'bout it."

"And you look good, too. Tell me all about yourself. Tell me all about where you've been. All about your guitar. I'll bet if it could talk it could tell a lot."

"It does talk."

"Guitar talks? What does it say?"

"Said it liked you. A whole big bunch."

"How much?"

"All o' these tree limbs full, an' that river full, an' two buckets over. That enuf?"

"Gosh. Nobody ever did love me that much before!"

"I did, but I jest didn't see ya till now. I been a-lookin' fer you up an' down a lotta roads—jest now locatin' ya. I know. Tell it by lookin' in yer eyes there, all over yer face, even behind yer ears there."

"How does it happen that you've got to play in saloons? I don't like for you to sing in old liquor joints."

"Oh, I dunno, goin' 'crost th' country, ya know, saloons is handy on th' side of th' road, make a nickel er two, an' light out ag'in."

"Going where? Hunting what?"

"This."

"Maybe some day you'll find better places to play, huh?

377

Sing? Oh, like on the stage or radio or something like
that?"

"I like ta go where th' big work jobs are, like buildin'
dams, an' oil fields, an' harvestin' th' crops. Might find a
steady job if you'd push me jest a little."

We were silent for a while.

"No," she said in my ear, "don't look. Don't watch the
sun go down. Don't watch it get dark. Don't tell me any
story about a sheet of paper called a marriage license, no,
don't tell me anything like that, just stay here and don't
make big promises; you're right here right now; tomorrow
you'll be up and gone; I know that; but for now, just say
you'll think about me, and wherever you ramble off to,

when you get tired of rambling, just think about this, huh?"

"Okay." And I heard her heart beat under my ear when I laid my head on her breast. "I'm sorry I ain't no very good talker. Cain't think of much worth sayin' right now. You talk awhile, I'll do th' listenin'."

"Let's both just lay here and listen and think."

Her skin felt warm to the touch of my hands and my fingers combed her hair through the scattered leaves. Her lips were moist like damp earth under the leaves there. She was a warmth and a movement and a life that no man can live good without. I blinked my eyelashes in her ear, but she just smiled and kept her eyes closed like she was dreaming something.

We lugged the buckets of water up to the camp and I was walking behind her, brushing leaves and twigs out of her hair. We poured water and washed pots and pans together, and listened to the others. Pretty good crowd around.

"Hey, mister!" a boy about fifteen was saying above the others, "ever find that indelible pencil you was lookin' for?"

"No, never did. Why? You got one?" The father of our bunch told the boy. "Thank ye."

Then a big fellow, wearing a patched and re-patched shirt with a quick sharp sound in his voice, spoke up, "Say, old man, want me to tell you all there is to know about these slips?"

"Wis't somebody would."

"Okay." He put his foot up on an apple crate and pointed his pipe out into the dark, and while he was talking the only three things that lit up in the night was his pipe, a white button on his shirt, and the light from the fires of the rag-pots shining in his eyes. "You're gonna think it over. This fruit will be set back a week or ten days on account of one dam thing or another. Cannery order. Weather. Market. What the hell. Anyway, you'll sign that credit slip tonight.

You'll take it down in the morning to buy your stuff and go to work. You'll get a bill of goods and find out the crops have been held up a few days. So you'll buy a few more days. You'll buy shy. Skimp. Do without a lot of things you need. Try to keep your bill down." When this fellow talked I looked him over; he was wearing rags, hit hard, stuck down. He kept smoking his pipe and resting his wore-out boot on the box.

"I'd buy light. We'd try ta go easy. Wouldn't we, kids? Mama?" Their papa was holding his yellow slip in his hand on his knee, squatted down cross-legged, and every time he said a word he pointed his indelible pencil around at everybody.

"You'll get about ten days or two weeks behind at the store. Might be a few scattered 'cots to pick, but not half enough to feed and keep your bunch. Then the weather will warm up and force the boss to pick the 'cots. You'll go to work. Make enough to live on while you're working."

"We c'n make that, all right, cain't we, Mama?"

"You'll just barely make enough to keep you going while you work. But you won't make enough to be able to pay the ten days' bill you owe. You'll just be ten days behind the world. Twenty dollars, twenty-five. Ten days! Behind the world!"

The crowd drifted away to bed, everybody going his own way thinking. Ruth and me set on the steps of the trailer and talked for an hour or two.

Early next morning by the rising sun I was bending over washing my face with water out of the filling station hose, thinking I'd get something off of the store boss even if it was just free water. I saw the old man come walking all by his self, slow across the orchard. I was drying my face on the tail of my shirt when he walked up behind me and said, "Ain't you th' guitar man?"

I smiled up at him and said I was.

"Early mornin' sun's right good on a man, ain't it?" he asked me. Then, trying to hold the little yellow slip behind his back so I couldn't see it, he spit over into a little puddle of used oil and said, "I gotta step inside of th' store here a minnit."

I was thinking to myself that old man had come down a hard road, then I heard someone say, "Good-morning, Governor." I turned around and there was Ruth standing behind a little bush on the sunny side of the store.

"What're ya hidin' in th' flower beds about?" I asked her. "Eavesdroppin' on yer old man, huh?"

She was digging four holes with her shoe heels in the dirt of the flower bed, and saying, "No. I don't have to sneak around and eavesdrop on that old man of mine to know what he's going to do. He'll just hand the Company man his credit slip, and won't say much. Maybe how pretty the morning is. I'll tell you a secret if you'll not tell." She got her fourth hole dug and looked around to see if anybody was looking. "I stole four of these big pretty yellow apricots. I had them for breakfast. And now I'm planting them back here by the side of this old store. Grow up some day. Then I can rest easy knowing I paid him back."

I lifted her head up and kissed her and said, "Didja make a wish for each one ya planted?"

She shook her head "yes."

"Any of 'em about you 'n' me?"

"Yes." She patted the ground with her foot where she had planted the fourth seed. "First, I hope you go on with your rambling. Second, I hope you get enough of it, and find out you don't like it. Third, I hope you keep on with your music and singing, because you've got it in you, and you think you're some kind of a preacher or a doctor going around to saloons listening to people's troubles, and you think you can lift their spirits a little, make somebody feel a little better. Fourth, I want to give you this mailing address; it's a family of my kinfolks, they always keep pretty close track of us and send all of our mail."

We stood in the sun out of sight behind a bush and held each other close again, and I kissed her eyelids while she said, "Both of us have been looking for this very thing for a long time. Both of us have thought we found it somewhere before."

"And somethin' happened an' busted it all up. I hoped a lot when I was a kid. Jest fast as one hope got tore up, I had all kindsa fun jest a-hopin' somethin' new. But lately, I guess, my hopin' machine's been a little on th' blink. I think if you loved me much's I love you, we could sleep under a railroad bridge an' be all right."

"You're one kind of a liar."

"Liar?"

"Yes. You've had better things. I can tell. So have I. Ten dozen times. Then they go. You hit the road and stumble around from town to town, and all along, you see pretty farms, pretty cars, pretty people, pretty towns, and you don't think you can ever make enough money with your guitar and singing to have all of this, so you lie, you lie to your ownself, and you say 'Everybody else in the whole world is all haywire, all wrong, I hate their pretty world, because I can't find a hole to break into it!' And every breath you're a liar. Maybe a good guy, and maybe I love you, but still a liar." She put her face on my shoulder.

We sat down out of sight between a tall bush and the side of the store building, and for another hour talked low and thought together.

"Yesterday, last night, I got my handkerchief all wet dryin' yer legs off; now, this mornin' I b'lieve ya got more water in yer eyes th'n there is in th' river down yonder. Feel bad?"

"Oh, no." She tried to smile. "You don't mind me calling you a liar? We all lie some. I lie, too."

"Yeah. I know. I am a liar. I know th' real things I'm a-lookin' fer. Workin'. Makin' money. Buildin' up somethin'. Little house with ever'thing in it. An' you there. I knew what I wanted. But I couldn't have none of it if I didn't find my work. I wanted ta pick out my own kinda work. I'll work like a Goddam dog, but I aim ta pick out my work. I coulda got a job pushin' a truck er a tractor, wheelin' a wheelbarrow, pullin' a cross-cut saw, paintin' signs, er even doin' picture work; but while I was singin' on th' radio in Los Angeles I got more'n fifteen thousan' letters tellin' me ta keep on singin' them good ol' songs, makin' up new ones, tellin' tall tales, jokes, an' singin' ta a whole ocean fulla folks I couldn't see. Letters from guys on ships at sea; letters from farm families, folks that trail around pickin' crops; fact'ry workers all over th' country; desert rats pannin' fer gold; even widders up in Reno there a gettin' on a beeline fer their fourth husban'. People yell, an' laff, an' cry, hug me, kiss me, cuss me, take swings at me, in saloons an' likker joints. An' still, th' big shots that owns them radio stations says I ain't got what folks wants. Ya see, I happ'n ta know. An' I swore a long time ago I'd stick ta my guitar an' my singin'. But most radio stations, they won't let ya sing th' real songs. They want ya ta sing pure ol' bull manure an' nothin' else. So I cain't never git ahold of money an' stuff it'd take ta keep you an' me in a house an' home—so I been a-lyin' ta my own self now fer a good long time, sayin' I didn't want no little house an' alla that.

"But, Ruth, I think I know. I'm hittin' th' road ag'in. Right now. Right this minute. Don't know how far I'll hafta go till I find out where I c'n sing what I want ta sing, an' my brain's hangin' jest as fulla new ideas fer songs as

a tree on a hill full of all colors o'blossoms. I'll sing any-
wheres they'll stand an' listen. An' they'll see to it I don't
starve out. They'll see to it that me an' you c'n be together."

Her lips felt like butterflies lighting on my face.

The people from the trailers and cars walked in twos
and threes, kicking up the morning dust and gathering all
around the store, forty or fifty all told, stomping from one
foot to the other one, whittling or digging under finger
nails with long keen knives. "Man, howdy! Am I just fairly
itchin' to grab that fruit off'n them old heavy limbs!"

"I didn't come out hyere t' Californiooo f'r no Goddam
sunbath!"

"Trot out yore work, mister!"

"Hurry out here, mister orchard boss, read that tellygram
that says for me to exert my manly muscles in th' art of
snatchin' apercots!"

"I done had my ham 'n' eggs, 'n' or'nge joose! My veins
is runnin' fulla vitaphones!"

When one would blast loose with a wisecrack, the whole
crowd would laugh and a little rumble would run through
them like an earthquake.

"Hey! Guitar man!" One old boy seen me and Ruth walk
up from the side of the store. "Could you turn loose of that
purty gal this mornin' long enough to sing us a little song?"

I said I reckoned as to how I could.

"Play us somethin' 'bout all of us standin' 'roun' here
waitin' to go to work!"

So I flipped a few strings to see if the box was in tune,
and I smiled a little at Ruth watching me:

> I work in your orchards of peaches and prunes
> Sleep on the ground 'neath the light of the moon
> On the edge of your city you see us and then
> We come with the dust and we go with the wind.

Green pastures of plenty from dry desert ground
From the Grand Coulee Dam where the waters come down
Every state in this Union us migrants has been
We will work in your fight and we'll fight till we win!

They just kept quiet till I got done. Then every single person seemed like they took a deep breath, started to say something, maybe; but I heard a screen door slam behind me, and when I looked around, I saw Ruth's old dad walk out onto the little porch, and the orchard boss walked out with him. The boss carried a piece of paper in his hand, and he waved it in the air, meaning for all of us to get quiet.

"Quiet, everybody. Listen. Hhhhmmmmm. Won't bother to read all of this order. 'DEAR SIRS: DUE TO COLD WEATHER OF THE PAST THIRTY DAYS, THE APRICOT CROP WILL NOT BE RIPE ENOUGH TO BE SUITABLE FOR CANNING. THERE WILL BE A TEN DAY WAITING PERIOD TO ALLOW THE FRUIT TO MATURE. PICKERS MAY STAND BY AND AWAIT ORDERS, AS THE WEATHER MAY TAKE A WARM CHANGE AND RIPEN THE FRUIT SOONER. USUAL CREDIT SLIPS MAY BE OBTAINED BY MAKING THE PROPER ARRANGEMENTS AT THE COMPANY STORE' . . . . Hhhhmmm. Yes. Anybody want to ask any questions?" He looked out over the bunch.

I believe this was the quietest crowd I was ever in. A kid about fifteen asked his mama, "What're we alla gonna do now, Mama? Jes' be useless?" I heard a little girl not more than nine crying, "Papa, why don't we get in our car 'n' leave this ol' place?" And her daddy told her, "We ain't got no gas, honey. We sent it all to th' soldiers to fight that old mean Hitler man with." Everybody talked so quiet the orchard boss never heard a word. He thought we was all scattering out without a sound, like a herd of lost sheep.

Ruth squeezed my hand.

"Why don't ye come on back down to th' camp an' sing us ten days worth of them there good songs?" Her dad was asking at my back. "We got ten days' credit. Ye'll eat. Stay?"

"Mighty nice of ya." I put my guitar back over my shoulder, then told him, "Guess I'd better hit th' road. Keep goin'. Lookin'. I hope you folks come outta this hard spot."

"I don't mind the spots getting hard!" Ruth leaned up against the gas pump. "War ain't fought with powder puffs." She was blinking her eyes fast.

"I'd kind of like ta stay here, spend some time. I feel like half of me's stayin' an' half of me's goin'. Kinda funny," I told her.

"Remember the four seeds I planted and the four hopes I hoped?" Ruth looked me up and down. "I'm hoping another hope, we can get some work to help win this war."

I shook the old man's hand. Then Ruth's. And as I walked off down the road, the old man hollered out to my back:

"I'm mailin' all my gas 'n' tires on to my son! Drives one of them there *jeeps!*"

Chapter XVIII

CROSSROADS

❖

There was big drops of sweat standing out on my forehead and my fingers didn't feel like they was mine. I was floating in high finances, sixty-five stories above the ground, leaning my elbow on a stiff-looking tablecloth as white as a runaway ghost, and tapping my finger on the side of a big fishbowl. The bowl was full of clear water with a bright red rose as wide as your hand sunk down in the water, which made the rose look bigger and redder and the leaves greener than they actually was. But everything else in the room looked this same way when you looked through the rose bowls of water on the other twenty-five or thirty tables. Each row of tables was in a horseshoe curve, and each curve a little higher than the one below. I was at the lowest. The price of the table for the night was twenty-five dollars.

Sixty-five stories back to the world. Quite a little elevator ride down to where the human race was being run. The name of the place, the Rainbow Room, in the city called New York, in the building called Rockefeller's Center, where the shrimps are boiled in Standard Oil. I was waiting to take an audition to see about getting a job singing there. Classiest joint I'd ever seen. I looked all around at the deep rugs like a grassy lawn, and the wavy drapes bellied back from the windows, and laughed to myself as I heard the other performers crack jokes at the whole works.

"This must be th' ravin' ward, th' way they got things

all padded up." A sissy-looking little man in a long tail coat was waiting for his time to try out.

"I just don't think they mowed th' upholst'ry yet this year," some lady with a accordion folded acrost her lap was whispering.

"An' them tables," I almost laughed, saying, "is jest like this here buildin', th' higher up ya git, th' colder it gits."

The man that had been our guide and got us up there in the first place, walked across the rug with his nose in the air like a trained seal, grinned up at us waiting to take our tryouts, and said, "Sssshhh. Quiet, everybody."

Everybody slumped down and straightened up and set tight and got awful quiet while three or four men, and a lady or two dressed to match the fixtures, walked in through a high arch door from the main terrace and took seats at one of the tables.

"Main boss?" I said behind the back of my hand to the others at our table.

Heads shook up and down, "yes." I noticed that everybody put on a different face, like wax people almost, tilting their heads in the breeze, grinning into the late afternoon sun that fell across the floor, and smiling like they'd never missed a meal. This look is the look that most show folks learn pretty early in the game; they paint it on their faces, or sort of mold it on, so it will always smile like a monkey through his bars, so nobody will know their rent ain't paid up yet, or they ain't had no job this season or last, and that they just finished a sensational, whirlwind run of five flops in a row. The performers looked like rich customers shining in the sun, and the head boss with his table full of middle-size bosses looked like they'd been shot at and missed. Through the water in the rose-bowls everything in the place had an upside-down look; the floor looked like the ceiling and the halls looked like the walls, and the hungry looked like they was rich, and the rich looked like they was hungry.

Finally somebody must of made a motion or give a signal, because a girl in a gunny-sack dress got up and sung a song that told how she was already going on thirteen, and was getting pretty hot under the collar, tired of waiting and afraid of being an old maid, and wanting to be a hillbilly bride. Heads shook up and down and the big boss and middle-size bosses and agents and handlers smiled across the empty tables. I hear somebody whisper, "She's hired."

"Next! Woody Guthrie!" a snazzy-looking gent was saying over the mike.

"Reckin that's me," I was mumbling under my chin, talking to myself, and looking out the window, thinking. I reached in my pocket and spun a thin dime out acrost the tablecloth and watched it whirl around and around, first heads, then tails, and said to myself, "Some difference 'tween that there apercot orchard las' June where th' folks wuz stuck down along th' river bottom, an' this here Rainbow Room on an August afternoon. Gosh, I come a long ways in th' last few months. Ain't made no money ta speak about, but I've stuck my head in a lot of plain an' fancy places. Some good, some just barely fair, an' some awful bad. I wrote up a lot of songs for union folks, sung 'em all over ever'where, wherever folks got together an' talked an' sung, from Madison Square Garden to a Cuban Cigar Makers' tavern in Spanish Harlem an hour later; from th' padded studios of CBS an' NBC to th' wild back country in th' raggedy Ghetto. In some places I was put on display as a freak, and others as a hero, an' in th' tough joints around th' Battery Park, I wuz jes' another shadow blund'rin' along with th' rest. It had been like this here little ol' dime spinnin', a whirl of heads an' tails. I'd liked mostly th' union workers an' th' soldiers an' th' men in fightin' clothes, shootin' clothes, shippin' clothes, or farmin' clothes, 'cause singing with them made me friends with them, an' I felt like I was somehow in on their work. But this coin spinnin', that's my las' dime—an' this Rainbow Room job, well, rumors are it'll pay as much as seventy-five a week, an' seventy-five a week is dam shore seventy-five a week."

"Woody Guthrie!"

"Comin'!" I walked up to the microphone, gulping and trying to think of something to sing about. I was a little blank in the head or something, and no matter how dam hard I tried, I just couldn't think up any kind of a song to sing—just empty.

"What will be your first selection, Mister Guthrie?"

"Little tune, I guess, call'd New York City." And so I forked the announcer out of the way with the wiry end of my guitar handle and made up these words as I sung:

> This Rainbow Room she's mighty fine
> You can spit from here to th' Texas line!
>   In New York City
>   Lord, New York City
>   This is New York City, an' I really gotta know my line!

> This Rainbow Room is up so high
> That John D.'s spirit comes a-driftin' by
>   This is New York City
>   She's New York City
>   I'm in New York City an' I really gotta know my line!

> New York town's on a great big boom
> Got me a-singin' in th' Rainbow Room
>   That's New York City
>   That's New York City
>   She's old New York City
>   Where I really gotta know my line!

I took the tune to church, took it holy roller, shot in a few split notes, oozed in a fake one, come down barrel house, hit off a good old cross-country lonesome note or two, trying to get that old guitar to help me, to talk with me, talk for me, and say what I was thinking, just this one time.

> Well this Rainbow Room's a funny place ta play
> It's a long way's from here to th' U.S.A.
>> An' back ta New York City
>> God! New York City
>> Hey! New York City
>> Where I really gotta know my line!

The microphone man come running out and waved me to a stop, asking me, "Hhhhmmm, where does this particular song end, sir?"

"End?" I looked over at him. "Jest a-gittin' strung out good, mister!"

"The number is most amusing. Exciting. Extremely colorful. But I'm wondering if it would be suited to the customers. Ahemm. To our customers. Just a couple of questions. How do you get out to the microphone and back again?"

"Walk, as a rule."

"That won't do. Let's see you trot in through that arch doorway there, sidestep when you come to that flat platform, prance pretty lively when you go down those three stairs, and then spring up to the microphone on the balls of your feet throwing your weight on the joints of your ankles." And before I could say anything he had run out and trotted back, showing me exactly what he was talking about.

Another one of the bosses from the table at the back wall yelled, "As far as his entrance is concerned, I think we can rehearse it a week or two and get it ironed out!"

"Yes! Of course, his microphoning has got to be tested and lights adjusted to his size, but that can come later. I'm thinking about his make-up. What kind of make-up do you use, young man?" Another boss was talking from his table.

"Ain't been a-usin' none," I talked into the mike. I felt the faraway rattling and rumbling of freight trains and transfer trucks calling to me. I bit my tongue and listened.

"Under the lights, you know, your natural skin would look too pale and too dead. You wouldn't mind putting on some kind of make-up just to liven you up, would you?"

"Naww. Don't 'spose." Why was I thinking one thing in my head and saying something different with my mouth?

"Fine!" A lady nodded her head from the boss's table. "Now, oh yes, now, what kind of a costume shall I get for him?"

"Which?" I said, but nobody heard me.

She folded her hands together under her chin and clicked her wax eyelashes together like loose shingles in a high wind. "I can just imagine a hay wagon piled high with singing field hands, and this carefree character following along in the dust behind the wagon, singing after the day's work is done! That's it. A French peasant garb!"

"Or—no—wait! I see him as a Louisiana swamp dweller, half asleep on the flat top of a gum stump, his feet dangling in the mud, and his gun leaning near his head! Ah! What a follow-up for the gunny-sack girl singing, 'Hillbilly Bride'!" A man losing a wrestling match with a four-bit cigar was arguing with the lady.

"I have it! Listen! I have it!" The lady rose up from her table with a look on her face like she was in a trance of some kind, and she walked over across the carpet to where I was standing, saying, "I have it! Pierrot! We shall dress him in a Pierrot costume! One of those darling clown suits! It will bring out the life and the pep and the giddy humor of his period! Isn't that a simply swell idea?" She folded her hands under her chin again and swayed over against my shoulder as I sidestepped to miss her. "Imagine! What the proper costuming will bring out in these people! Their carefree life! Open skies! The quaint simplicity. Pierrot! Pierrot!" She was dragging me across the floor by the arm, and we left the room with everybody talking at once. Some taking tryouts said, "Gosh! Gon'ta catch on!"

Outside, on a high glass porch of some kind, where wild tangled green things growed all along the floor by the windows, she shoved me down in a leather chair by a plastic table and sighed and puffed like she'd done an honest day's work. "Now, let me see, oh yes, now, my impression of the slight sample of your work is a bit, so to say, incomplete, that is, as far as the cultural traditions represented and the exchange and interrelationships and overlappings of these same cultural patterns are concerned, especially here in America, where we have, well, such a mixing bowl of culture, such a stew-pot of shades and colors. But, nevertheless, I think the clown costume will represent a large portion of the humorous spirit of all of them—and—"

I let my ears bend away from her talking and I let my eyes drift out the window and down sixty-five stories where the town of old New York was standing up living and breathing and cussing and laughing down yonder acrost that long island.

I begun to pace back and forth, keeping my gaze out the window, way down, watching the diapers and underwear blow from fire escapes and clothes lines on the back sides of the buildings; seeing the smoke whip itself into a hazy blur that smeared across the sky and mixed in with all of the other smoke that tried to hide the town. Limp papers whipped and beat upwards, rose into the air and fell head over heels, curving over backwards and sideways, over and over, loose sheets of newspaper with pictures of people and stories of people printed somewhere on them, turning loops in the air. And it was blow little paper, blow! Twist and turn and stay up as long as you can, and when you come down, come down on a pent-house porch, come down easy so's not to hurt your self. Come down and lay there in the rain and the wind and the soot and smoke and the grit that gets in your eyes in the big city—and lay there in the sun and get faded and rotten. But keep on trying to tell your message, and keep on trying to be a picture of a man, because without that story and without that message printed on you there, you wouldn't be much. Remember, it's just maybe, some day, sometime, somebody will pick you up and look at your picture and read your message, and carry you in his pocket, and lay you on his shelf, and burn you in his stove. But he'll have your message in his head and he'll talk it and it'll get around. I'm blowing, and just as wild and whirling as you are, and lots of times I've been picked up, throwed down, and picked up; but my eyes has been my camera taking pictures of the world and my songs has been messages that I tried to scatter across the back sides and along the steps of the fire escapes and on the window sills and through the dark halls.

Still going like a Nineteen Hundred and Ten talking machine, my lady friend had said a whole raft of stuff that I'd not heard a single word of. I'm afraid my ears had been running somewhere down along the streets. I heard her say, "So, the interest manifest by the manager is not at all a personal thing, not at all, not at all; but there is another reason why you are so certain to satisfy the desires of his customers; and I always say, don't you always say, 'What the customer says is what we all have to say'?" Her teeth shined and her eyes snapped different colors. "Don't you?"

"Don't I? What? Oh, 'scuse me jest a minute, huh? Be

right back." I took one good long look all up and down the red leather seats and the plastic tables in the glassed-in room, and grabbed my guitar by the neck and said to a boy in uniform, "Rest room?" And I followed where he pointed, except that when I got within a couple of feet of the sign that said "Men," I took a quick dodge down a little hallway that said "Elevator."

The lady shook her head and nodded with her back turned to me. And I asked the elevator man, "Goin' down? Okay. Groun' floor. Quickest way's too slow!" When we hit bottom I walked out onto the slick marble floor whanging as hard as I could on the guitar and singing:

> Ever' good man gits in hard luck sometime
> Ever' good man gits in hard luck sometime
> > Gits down an' out
> > Dead broke
> > Ain't gotta dime!

I never heard my guitar ring so loud and so long and so clear as it did there in them high-polished marble halls. Every note was ten times as loud, and so was my singing. I filled myself full of free air and sung as loud as the building would stand. I wanted the poodle dogs leading the ladies around to stick up their noses and wonder what in the hell had struck that joint. People had walked hushed up and too nice and quiet through these tiled floors too long. I decided that for this minute, for this one snap of their lives, they'd see a human walking through that place, not singing because he was hired and told what to sing, but just walking through there thinking about the world and singing about it.

She mortally echoed around and glanced across the murals painted on the walls. And folks in herds and family groups stopped looking in the fancy lit-up shop windows along the corridors and listened to me telling the world:

Old John Dee he ain't no friend of mine
Old John Dee he ain't no friend of mine
   I'm a-sayin' Old John Dee shore ain't no friend of mine
   Takes all th' purty wimmen
   An' leaves us men behind!

Little boys and girls trotted up alongside of me, jerking out from their parents' hands, and kept their ears and noses rubbing against my guitar's sounding board. While I was beating the blues chords and not singing, I heard side remarks:

"What is he advertising?"

"Isn't he a card?"

"Quaint."

"A Westerner. Possibly lost in a subway."

"Children! Come back here!"

I heard a cop say, "Cut it! Hey! Yez cain't pull dat stuff in here!" But before he could get at me, I'd whirled through a spinning door and fought my way across some avenues packed with traffic, and was lighting out along some sidewalks and not even paying much attention to where I was heading. A few hours could of went by. Or days. I wasn't noticing. But I was dodging walking people, playing kids, and rusting iron fences, rotting doorsteps, and my head was buzzing, trying to think up some reason why I'd darted out away from the sixty-fifth story of that big high building back yonder. But something in me must of knowed why. Because in a little while I found myself walking along New York's Ninth Avenue, and cutting over another long cement block to come to the waterfront. I seen mothers perched on high rock steps and out along the curbs on cane-bottom chairs, some in the shade, some in the sun, talking, talking, talking. Their gift of the spirit was talking, talking to the mother or to the lady next to them, about the wind, the weather, the curbs, the sidewalks, the rooms, roaches,

bugs, rent, and the landlord, and managing to keep one eye
on all of the hundreds and hundreds of kids playing in the
open street. As I walked along, no matter what they'd been
talking about, I heard them first to one side and then to the
other, saying, "music man!" "Heyyy! Playa for ussa th'
song!" "Hi! Le's hear ya tromp it!" "Would you geeve to us
a museek?" "Play!" "Ser'nade me!" And so, not half caring,
there in the last few patches of the setting sun, I walked
along winding my way through the women and young
boys and girls, and singing:

> What does the deep sea say?
> Tell me, what does the deep sea say?
> Well, it moans and it groans,
> It swells and it foams
> And it rolls on its weary way!

I walked along, the day just leaving out over the tops of
the tall buildings, and sifting through the old scarred chimneys sticking up. Thank the good Lord, everybody, everything ain't all slicked up, and starched and imitation. Thank
God, everybody ain't afraid. Afraid in the skyscrapers, and
afraid in the red tape offices, and afraid in the tick of the
little machine that never explodes, stock market tickers,
that scare how many to death, ticking off deaths, marriages
and divorces, friends and enemies; tickers connected and
plugged in like juke boxes, playing the false and corny
lies that are sung in the wild canyons of Wall Street; songs
wept by the families that lose, songs jingled on the silver
spurs of the men that win. Here on the slummy edges, people are crammed down on the curbs, the sidewalks and the
fireplugs, and cars and trucks and kids and rubber balls
are bouncing through the streets. I was thinking, "This is
what I call bein' borned an' a-livin'; I don't know what I
call that big high building back yonder that I left."

I'd noticed a quiet-faced young Mexican seaman following along behind my shoulder. He was of a small build, almost like a kid, and the sea and the sun had kept his hair oily and his smile smooth. After a block or two we'd got to knowing each other and he'd told me, "My name iss Carlos, call me Carl." Outside of that Carl didn't say much; we just almost knew that we was buddies without making lectures on the subject. So for about an hour I walked along singing, while this man walked beside me, smiling right on down through the wind, not telling me no big tall tale of submarines and torpedoes, no hero stories.

A little girl and boy clattered on roller skates, and told me to sing louder so's they could hear me above the noise. Other kids quit swatting each other and walked along listening. Mamas called in a hundred tongues, "Kids, come back here!" The kids would usually follow along humming and singing with me for about a block, and then stand on the curb when I crossed the street and look for a long time. In each block a new gang formed and herded along, feeling of the wood of the guitar, and getting their hands on the strap, the strings. Older kids tittered and flirted in dark doorways and pushed each other around in front of soda fountains and penny-candy hangouts, and I managed to sing them at least a little snatch, a few words of the songs they'd ask to hear. At times I stopped for a minute and papas and mamas and kids of all ages stood around as quiet as they could, but the whamming and banging of big trucks, busses, vans, and cars made us stand jammed together real tight to be heard.

It got to be night, the kind of summer night that pitches on the wind and dips in the white clouds and makes buildings look like all kinds of freighters creaking along. Dark swarms of us sprawled out along stone steps and iron railings, and I felt that old feeling coming back to me.

When I reached the water front, the song I was singing over and over was:

> It was early in the spring
> Of nineteen forty-two
> She was queen of the seas
> And the wide ocean blue
>
> Her smoke filled the sky
> In that Hudson River's tide
> And she rolled on her side
> When that good ship went down
>
> Oh, the *Normandie* was her name
> And great was her fame
> And great was her shame
> When that good ship went down

Folks joined in like one voice in the dark. I could vision on the screen of fog rolling down a picture of myself sing ing back yonder on the sixty-fifth floor of Rockefeller's Center, singing a couple of songs and ducking back into a dressing room to smoke and play cards for two more hours until the next show, then more smoke and cards until the next show. And I knew that I was glad to be loose from that sentimental and dreamy trash, and gladder to be edging on my way along here singing with the people, singing something with fight and guts and belly laughs and power and dynamite to it.

When Carl touched me on the arm we was throwing on our brakes in the green shiver of a neon sign that said, "Anchor Bar." We stood outside on the curb and he grinned and told me, "This iss a nice place; always a good bunch here." By now we had a whole crew around us waving their heads in the wind, singing:

> Oh, the *Normandie* was her name
> And great was her fame
> And great was her shame
> When that good ship went down

I sung out by myself:

> So remember her sorrow
> And remember her name
> We will all work together
> And she'll soon sail again

All kinds of hats, caps, sweaters, and dresses stood around tapping shoes against the concrete, patting hands, like getting new hope out of old religion; and when my eyes got a plainer look at the crowd, I seen lots of uniforms and sailor caps of all kinds. Light sifted through the open door and big windows of the bar, and hit against our backs and faces.

"More!"

"Sing!"

"Crank up!"

A funny little gang of us there on that curb.

"Where'd ja pick up such songs at?" one lady asked me.

"Ohh," I told her, "jest bummin' aroun', see stuff, make up a little song about it."

"Buy ya a drink if ya want it!" a man said.

"Mister, I'll take ya up in jest a minute! Cain't stop right now ta buy no drink! I'd lose my crowd!"

"What th' hell you doin'?" he said back in the crowd. "Runnin' f'r office with that whang-danger music box?"

"Back in Oklahoma," I kidded him, "I know one Negro boy that blows a mouth organ, an' he's elected our las' four gov'nors!"

There was a little laugh run through the listeners, and

you could see a pile of smoke rising out of our huddle from cigarets and cigars and ocean-going pipes the people was pulling on. In the flare of the smoking, I got looks at their faces, and when I seen how hard and tough they was, I thought I must be in just about the best of company.

A tall man pushed through the rest, with both hands stuck down in his overcoat pockets, and said, "By God an' by Jesus! Howya makin' out?" It was my old friend, Will Geer, an actor playing the lead part of Jeeter Lester in the play, *Tobacco Road*. Will was a big tall cuss, head and shoulders over the most of us, and I rocked considerably when he whopped me down across the back and shoulders with his open hand. "You ol' dog! Howya been?"

"Hi! Will! Dam yer hide! Lay yer head back, boy, an' sing!"

"Go right on. Don't let me stop you." Will's voice had a dry crackle to it that sounded like a stick in the fire. "Mighta knew who 'twas when I saw this big crowd here singin'! Keep it up!"

"Carl, shake han's with Will there."

"Meester Will? I am glad to know you."

"Hey! Ever'body! Here's another frienda mine! Name's Will!"

He stood with his long chin and square jaw set against the dampness of the fog, and folded his hands together and waved them above our heads. Behind him the doorway of the Anchor Bar was filled with three people on their way out, the bartender leading a lady and a man by the arm. She was about fifty, little and slight, leathery skin like wet canvas full of pulling wind, coarse black hair all tangled up with the atmosphere and scenery, and a voice like sand washing back into the ocean, "I don't need your help! I wanta buy another drink!" Then she looked up at the crowd and said, "Cain't insult a lady this-a way!"

"Lady," the bartender was pushing the pair onto the sidewalk, "I know you're a lady, an' we all know you're a lady; but Mayor La Gad-about says no drinks after closin' time, an' it's after closin' time now!"

"Honey, sweet thing," I could hear her husband talking, "don't hurt th' man, don't, he just only works here."

"Who ask'd you f'r advice?" She marched out onto the sidewalk beside us.

"Put'cher coat on! Here, hold still!" He was tip-toeing around her trying to get the coat untangled. First he held it upside down with the sleeves dragging the sidewalk; then he got hold of the sleeves, but he had the lining on the wrong side; and after a couple of minutes, they had one sleeve plumb on, but she was still running her fist through the air feeling for the last sleeve. She had a look on her face like she was searching the waterfront for a man because she knew he had one sleeve of her coat, and he was working in the wind with a serious look in his eye, but always, just about a foot or two south of where she was holding her arm up, fishing.

Will walked over and took her fist and jammed it through the sleeve, and except for some mumbling and grumbling in the crowd nobody laughed. Will lit up some kind of a long cigaret and took the pair by the arms and brought them over to the bunch. "Meet ever'body!" He was smiling and saying, "All of you, here, meet Somebody!"

"Ever'body, gladta knowya!"

"Somebody, hello! Join up!"

"Don' mind gittin' booted outa that joint! We're a-havin' a lot th' bes' time out here!"

"Welcome ta our mists! Wahooo!"

"What yez a-doin'? Sangin'? Oh! Lord Godamighty! I mortully luv ta hear good sangin'! Sang! Make some racket!" The lady was standing at my elbow in the middle of the crowd. We sung our song about the *Normandie* all over again, and her and her man both shook the wax out of their ears in a minute and started singing, and their voices sounded good, like coal being dumped down into a cellar.

I took a look over the heads of the crowd and seen the bartender standing just outside the door talking to a copper, and I knew our singing had cut off about three fourths of his trade for the night, so I started walking with my eyes up toward the stars, and the little mob followed me along, filling the Hudson River's tide and the hulls of the warehouses, the markets, loading buildings, and all of the docks, and all of the ocean, with good husky voices. Some rasping, some gasping, some growling and some rattling with whiskey, rum, beer, gin, tobacco, but singing all the same.

We'd walked for about a block when we heard a tough talker behind us yell, "Hey, sailor!"

We walked a few more steps singing, then it come again. "Hey, sailor!"

"Keep on with th' singin'." A sailor was ducking at my ear saying, "Law says he's got ta yell 'hey sailor' three times!"

"Go on! Sing!" a second sailor said.

"Keep it up!" a third one put in.

Then it was, "*Heyyyy, sailor!*"

And a dead still spell come over our whole gang. The Military Policeman had yelled his third time. The sailors stopped and stood at attention.

"Yessir, Off'cer."

"Go to your stations, sailors!"

"Aye, aye, Off'cer!"

"At once, sailor!"

"Goin', off'cer!"

And the sailors walked away in good order, rubbing their eyes and faces in the night air, shaking their heads clear of tobacco smoke, and the dregs of beer. There in a few steps, they seemed to turn into somebody else, straightening up, fixing each other's shirts, blouses, ties, getting rigging in order. Low talk, laughs, thanks, and pats on the back was about all they give me, but as they slipped off in their different directions for their ships, some French, some British, some American, some Everything Else, I was thinking, There goes th' best fellers I ever seen.

"How'dya like ta be in th' Navy, Carl?" Will said.

"I would like to be in the Navy just fine," Carl said, "but I don't guess I ever can."

"Reason?" I asked Carl.

"I have a leetle something the matter with my lungs. Rosin. TB. I worked on a shingle-saw a few years. I'm in 4-F." His eyes followed the sailors away in the dark, and then he said, "The Navy, yes, it would be fine."

A Military Policeman swung his club around doing tricks and said to us, "Go ahead with y'r party, by God, ya gotta perty dam good song there—'bout that there *Norm'ndie.*"

Another cop turned around and walked away saying, "It's jus' that we gotta git our sailors ta werk on time. Those songs was doin' them men a lot o' good!"

One or two of the bunch that was left took off in different directions and then three or four shook my hand and told me, "Well, we had a dam good time." "Be seein' ya." "Saved us money, too!" And all that was left was me and Carl and Will and the lady and her husband, standing there on the curb, looking out toward the waterfront, out across the big dark mountains moving up and down at their docks, bigger than buildings, more alive than the hills, sloshing at the portholes and water-lines, floating still and quiet, like three women, the living *Queen Elizabeth*, the breathing *Queen Mary*, and the sleeping *Normandie* on her side.

"Fellers game ta go home with me?" the lady asked us. "Got a great, great big bottle, nearly almost half full."

Her husband held his hands in his pockets and shook his head after every word his wife said, his little hat rocking back and forth on his head when he nodded.

"Take us!" Will told her, winking around at us. "I haven't even had a drink tonight!"

We walked along just keeping our eyes on the red glare of her cigaret, first bright, then dull, in the dark. The old hard cobblestones was lit up with the filtered neon light that leaks somehow or other, some strange way, down into all of the big town's dirtiest corners, and shines like million-dollar jewelry, even on the spitty, foggy stones.

I seen the big hump-backs of five or six flat barges loaded full to the brim. Heavy highway gravel. The tie ropes bucking and stretching, the waters lapping and swelling and falling in the river with the up and down of the ocean's roll.

"Fair warnin'!" I heard the lady holler ahead of us. "Walk careful! Don't want hafta waste my time fishin' no land wallopers outa this slimy warsh!"

I followed the others across some narrow planks and I held my breath when I looked down under me at all of the moving, slurping water licking its mouth under my feet. Finally, after crossing over more whitish loads of gravel and rocks, we come to a little two-by-scantling shanty built on the head end of a creaking, heavy barge.

"So this is your homestead, huh?" Will asked her.

"I ain't so graceful out there much on that there solid groun'." She was fumbling with a lock at the door, and walked into the shack saying, "But they ain't a gal in th' show business c'n foller me aroun' over these here river boats!"

She lit the lantern, lit the oil stove, and set a half a gallon coffee pot on the flame. We all found chairs on boxes and big lard cans; then she said, "Why not sing me a song about somethin' perty? While this here coffee's a-comin' ta a boirl? Likker goes a lot longer ways when ya mix it with scaldin' hot coffee."

"I'll make ya up one 'bout yer barge house here. Lemme think."

> My bottle it will soon be empty
> And I myself won't have a dime
> But I've hauled my freight from here to yonder
> A many, and a many, and a many a time

While fishing under her tin-topped cupboard she chanted and sung almost under her breath:

> I pulled this package from here ta Albanyyyyy
> From there ta Uticayyyyy
> From there ta Schenectadyyyyyy
> It's a many, an' a many, an' a many a time
> Ohhh yes
> A many, an' a many, an' a many a time

The only thing that broke up her singing was the coffee pot spewing over the sides and the fire barking at the steam. Then she said, "Never did ask me my name. Dam that stove ta hell, anyhow! Boirl all o' my coffee away!" She grabbed a few cups from nails over the sink and poured one half full in front of every one of us. Then she popped a stopper out of a mean-looking bottle and poured the cups the rest of the way full. "McElroy. That's me! But don't tell me your names," she said to all of us, " 'cause I can't remember names none too good noway. I'll jus' call you Mr. Broadshoulders, an' you there, lemme see, I'll name you Eel Foot! Mister Eel Foot; an' next, you there with th' music doin's, I'll name you—le's see—Curley."

She jammed the red-hot coffee pot down on the table under my nose, and a half a cupful sloshed out like melted lead and soaked the front part of my britches. I jumped to the floor and fought and fanned the spots where the coffee was

scalding me, but she was laughing as loud as the barge would stand it, and yelling, while she downed her hot drink, "Whheeeww! Yipppeee! Flappin' salmon! What's th' matter, Hot Pants? Scorch you?" Her face turned against the lantern light and it was the first time I'd got a real look at her. Weather-whipped and wind-blistered, salt-soaked and frost-bit ten thousand times just like the skim that shines across the humps and the swells of the tidewaters. "Mister Hot Pants! Yah! Yah! Yah!" she laughed while I fanned my legs to cool the hot spots.

Her husband in the deal got up and stumbled ten or fifteen feet through a little partition, heaving like a sick horse, and I heard him fall down across some kind of a couch. I watched her drain her cup into her mouth, and then she stuck out her tongue and made a witchy-looking face out through the window at the moon splashing along on the clouds. Will and Carl and me tipped our cups together, held our breath, shut our eyes, and sloshed our mouths full of the fiery mixture. While she was waiting for us to fall over on the floor, we lit up some smokes, and I sung her another made-up verse:

> I've freighted and barged it from New York and up
> I drunk my hard likker from a blistering cup
> And who was the pride of the brave river boys?
> A lass by the name of Miss McElroy.

"Now ain't that perty? Ain't that a slippery shame?" She only had two teeth in her head, one low and on the left, one high and on the right, but she put a look on her face like she was a Freshman in a girls' school. "You mighty rum-com-a-tootin'! I wuz th' only female she womern up an' down this Goddern slimy warsh! I wuzn't no dam house cat! No flower pot! an' if I wuz jus' twenty-five years younger tonight, I'd give you gents a honest ta God run fer yer marbles!" Then she run the end of her tongue out over her pair of mismated teeth, and tapped the oilcloth of the table, and laughed; and the whole string of barges rocked in the ooze and the bellies of the old rafts pushed against each other, and the waterfront groaned and foamed around the edges.

Songs rippled across the loads of highway rock and dripped off down across the edges, and such songs and such yarns and lies and windy tales as we pulled out of our minds for the next hour or two was never before or since topped by the humans on this planet.

She said she'd had six children, that being pregnant so much had caused her teeth to fall out. Four boys. Three alive. Two girls, both up and gone. She showed us picture post cards of the places one daughter had worked as a taxi-dancer. The other girl lived across the river and come to see her on Sundays. One son used to send picture cards, but he was a merchant seaman, and she hadn't heard from him for over eight months. One son got in jail four or five times for little rackets; then he went out West to work in the mines, and he never wrote much anyhow. Him and his pa was always a-scrappin' when they'd get together, because the old man did believe in being honest as the law allows. They'd of killed each other if the boy hadn'ta left. She was glad he was gone.

"What's this leave you with?" Will asked her.

"Well," she smiled around at all of us just a speck and let her eyes fall away to one side, "let me see. Thirty years o' river freightin', twenty-six years o' married ta th' same man, if ya wanta call 'im a man. This old rotten barge here. Three nice gent visitors, if ya call 'em gentlemen; an' well, a little less th'n a halfa bottle o' perty pore whiskey. Plenty o' hot scaldin' coffee f'r th' nights run, an' ta boot, ta boot, ya might add, I liv'd ta see th' day that by God, I gotta song wrote up about me!"

Will and me excused ourselves and walked out the door. We stood on the edge on the next-door barge, and listened to the water trickle into the Hudson River. The moon was pretty and scared-looking and the clouds chased across the sky like early morning newskids. I could feel a sticky veil of fog settle over the wood and the strings of my guitar, and when I played it, the tone was soft and damp and muffled along the waters. I kept picking off a little tune.

"Been doin' last few days?" Will asked me walking along.

"Awww, nuthin' very much. Singin' 'roun'."

"Chances for any jobs?"

"Yeah, few."

" 'Bouts?"

"Night clubs, mostly."

"Get on?"

"Well, I, ah, that is, er, ah—I hadda big try-out ta day. Rockefeller's Center."

"Rockefeller Center! Wow! Come out all right?"

"I come *out*, all right."

"Walk out on 'em?"

"Goddammit! I jes' had ta walk out, Will! Couldn't take that stuff!"

"Goin' ta keep pullin' them one-man walkouts till you've ruined all of y'r chances here in New York. Better watch y'r step."

"Will, you know me. You know dam good an' well I'd play fer my beans an' cornbread, an' drink branch water, 'er anything else ta play an' sing fer folks that likes it, folks that knows it, an' lives what I'm a singin' 'bout. I'm all screwed up in my head. They try ta tell me if I wanta eat an' stay alive, I gotta sing their dam old phony junk!"

"You'd just naturally explode up in that high society, wouldn't you? But, money's what it takes, Woody."

"Yeah. I know." I was thinking of a girl named Ruth. "Damit all ta hell, anyhow! Mebbe I jest ain't got brains 'nuf in my head ta see that. But after alla th' hard luck I had, Will, I seen money come, an' money go, ever since I was jesta kid, an' I never thought 'bout nuthin' else, 'sides jest passin' out my songs."

"Takes money, boy. You want to make any kind of a name f'r yourself, well, takes all kinds of money. An' if you want to donate to poor folks all over th' country, that takes money."

"Cain't I jest sorta donate my own self, sort of?"

Will grunted. "Can't you go back to the Rainbow Room? Not too late, is it?"

I said, "No, not too late. I guess I could go back. I guess I *could!*"

I looked up at the big tall building. The silence around us seemed to be hollering at me—all right, whatcha gonna do? Come on, runt, make up your mind. This is it! Christ, boy, *this is it!*

A little tugboat throwing smoke plowed out from ahead of us, and I looked at it working in the smeared water like a black bug kicking up dust.

"This barge a-movin'?" I asked Will.

"B'lieve 'tis." He walked a few feet along the back end, made a jump clearing a two-foot gap, and landed back on the McElroy barge. "That barge you're on's gettin' hauled out by that tug! Better throw me y'r guitar! Jump!"

I didn't say anything right then. Will walked alongside where I was moving along and I stalled for a little time, saying, "Looks like it really is a-movin'."

"Jump! Jump quick! I'll catch your guitar! Jump!" He was trotting now at a pretty fair gait. "Jump!"

I set myself down on the hind-end of the moving load of gravel, and lit up a cigaret and blowed the smoke up toward the long, tall Rockefeller Building. Will had a great big grin in his face there by the light of the moon, and he said, "Got any money on ya?"

I flipped a rock into the water and said, "Mornin' comes, I'll feel in my pockets an' see!"

"But, where'll ya be?"

"I dunno."

My old friend was left behind, panting and all out of breath. I drug my thumb down across the strings of the guitar. In the river waters at my feet, I could see the reflection of fire and kids fighting their gang wars and a right young kid up a tree and a mama cat hunting the squeezed-out bodies of her kittens. Clara didn't look burnt and Mama didn't look crazy in that river water, but kind of pretty. I seen the oil on the river and it might have come from somewhere down in my old country, West Texas maybe, Pampa, or Okemah. I seen the Redding jungle camp reflected there too, and the saloons along Skid Row except that they looked awful clean. But mostly I saw a girl in an orchard and how she danced along the mud bank of a river.

Sail on, little barge, heave on, little tug, pound your guts out, work, dig in, plow this river all to hell.

It'll heal over.

Chapter XIX

TRAIN BOUND FOR GLORY

❖

The wind howled all around me. Rain blistered my skin. Beating down against the iron roof of the car, the sheets of rain sounded like some kind of a high-pressure fire hose trying to drill holes. The night was as pitch black as a night can get, and it was only when the bolts of lightning knocked holes in the clouds that you could see the square shape of the train rumbling along in the thunder.

"Jeez!" the kid was laying up as close to me as he could get, talking with his face the other way, "I tink she's slowin' up."

"I'm ready ta stop any old time," I was laying on my side with my left arm around his belly. "I'd like ta git cleaned up 'fore I git ta Chicago."

I listened in the dark and heard somebody yelling, "Hey, you guys! Been asleep?"

"That you, John?" I yelled back at my Negro riding pardner.

"Dis is me, all right! Been asleep?"

"I been about half knocked out!"

"Me, too!" I heard the older kid yell out.

"Youse boids is softies!" the kid I was holding grunted.

"How's yo' music box?"

"Still wrapped up in them shirts! I'm 'fraid ta even think about it!"

"She's clackin' 'er gait! We'll be stoppin' heah in a few minnits!"

"Hope so! Is this purty close to Chicago?" I was yelling loud as I could.

The little kid put in, "Naaa. Dis ain't ennywheres near Chucago. Dis is Freeport. Tink."

"Illinois?" I asked him.

"Yaaa. Illinoy."

"Son, is yore face got as much dirt an' cinders an' coal dust on it as mine's got?"

"How can I tell? I cain't even see yer mug. Too dark."

"I'd give a dollar fer a good smoke."

"Come ta Chi, I'll git youse a smoke from me brudder."

"Wonder if them guys got finished with their fightin' inside th' car?"

"Shucks, man! Dey might of done et each othah up!" John slapped his hand against the back of the kid he was holding.

"I benna listinin' to 'em down through da rooof."

"Shore 'nuff? What're they doin'?"

"Banged aroun' a long time. Cuss'n. Been kinda quiet last few miles."

"Sho' been still! Man, I bet dey jes' natchilly cut one 'nothah ta pieces!"

"I'm jest wonderin' how many we're gonna find that-away when this dam train stops. These is good guys. Just outta work. You know how a feller is."

John oozed along on his belly from the end of the car where he had been riding with his head to the wind. I felt him lay down at my side and hold his arm across my ribs to hang onto a plank in the boardwalk. "Seems like dis heah rain jus' holds alla dis train smoke right down on toppa th' train, don' it? I seen 'em befo'. Take a buncha th' bes' workin' fellas in th' worl'. Let 'em jus' git down an' out. No kinda steady job. Jus' makes ya mean's all hell."

"Me ol' man wuz datta way." I could hear the oldest kid

talking while he crawled up and laid down alongside of the little one. "He was okay, okay. Man gits outta woik, tho', goes off on a Goddam blink. Wuz two diff'rent fellas. I go upstate now an' visit me maw when he ain't around. Slugged me 'bout a month ago. Ain't seen 'em since." His voice sounded slow and dry in the banging and the rain.

"None a ya mushy talk."

"By gosh, little squirt, ya know, I believe that you talk tougher than that whole boxcar fulla railroad rounders."

"Sho' do."

"I say what I t'ink, see!"

"Okay. Whatta yez men a-gonna do? Dere's de air brakes!"

I lifted my head up and looked over the top of my guitar. I saw the crazy red glares from neon lights cutting against the clouds. Bushes and hedges whizzing past with nice warm smears of electric lights from the windows of houses. Spotlights and headlights from other locomotives shot around in the rain. Chug holes and vacant lots standing full of water shined like new money when the lightning cracked. I tried to keep the buckets of water wiped out of my face long enough to see. "Edge of some town."

"Freeport. Ain't I done told yez oncet?" The runty kid snorted rain out of his nose poking his head over the guitar. "I put da bum on alla dese happy homes. Freeport."

All four of us got up on our hands and knees and listened to the screaking and jamming of the brakes against the wheels. A red-hot switch engine pounded past us. Heat flew from the fire box and every single one of us set down and held our hands out to warm a little. The rain was falling harder. Our car was wobbling along like a crippled elephant. Red and green switch lights looked like melted globs of Christmas candy. A purplish white glare was coming from a danger flare stabbed into a cross tie across the yards to the right. To the left there I could make out a lonesome dull red electric light blinking out through the windows of a burger joint. Headlights from fast cars danced along the highway past the chili places. Our train slowed down to a slow crawl, on both sides nothing but dirty strings of every crazy kind of a railroad car.

"Alla dem bright lites up ahead, dat's de highway crossin'. Bull hangout." The little kid was poking me and pointing.

"Shore 'nuf? This a tough town?"

"Worse'n dat."

"Hay, dere, Pee Wee. You'n me'd betta unload." The tall kid kept down on his belly and crawled over the end of the roof. "We left our packs in this open machinery car," he explained to me.

"Wid ya." The little kid slipped along and followed him down the ladder.

I eased along on my hands and knees and looked over the end of the roof between the two cars. "Take it easy." I was holding my breath and watching them slip down the slick ladder. The rain and the clouds made it so dark I couldn't see the ground below him. "Watch out fer them wheels, big shot! All right?"

"Made 'er!" I heard him tell me. Then I saw his head and shoulders drop down into the end of the carload of machinery. Just then a bright streak of light shot up along the car. Both kids kept ducked down out of sight, but a man trotted along on the cinders and kept his flashlight beamed on them.

"Hey! Hey!" I heard him bellering out. He mounted the steps of the low car and shot his light over the edge. "Stand up! Stand up! Stand up there, you! Well! I be Goddamed! Where do you senators think you're going?"

The pair of kids' heads raised up between the machinery and the end of the car. Wet. Dirty with coal soot. Hats gone. Hair tangled. Sheets of rain pouring down on them in the bright glare of the cop's light. They blinked and frowned and wiped their hands across their faces.

"Mornin', Cap'n," the little one saluted.

"Tryin' ta git home," the big one was slipping his canvas pack on his back.

The little one grinned up into the flashlight and said, "Little rainy."

"That's a dam dangerous place to ride! Don't you know wet weather makes these loads skid? Beat it! Skat! Hit th' ground!" He motioned with his light.

Both kids slipped over the wall of the car and I rolled across the roof to the right-hand side and waved my guitar over the side at them. "Hey, want yer shirts back?" I swung down the ladder where the cop couldn't see me and hissed at the kids as they walked along beside our train. "Shirts? Shirts?"

Both kids pulled up their britches, laughed a little, and said, "Naaa!"

I swung there on the ladder for a bit watching the little fellers just sort of fade out. Rain. Smoke. All kinds of clouds. Night just darker than hell. I felt a little funny, I guess. Then they was gone. I pulled myself back up on top of the car and said, "Well, John, there goes our ridin' pardners."

"Sho' gone, all right. You still got dem shirts wrapped 'round yo' music box! Keep it dry?"

"Naw." I patted my guitar on the sides. "Couldn't be wetter. They wanted to give 'em to me, so I just took 'em."

"Little tramps some day."

"Well, one thing they gotta teach soldiers is how ta tramp."

"I sho' wish't I could fine me a good fast job of truck drivin'. I'd sho' as hell quit dis trampin'."

"Quiet! Duck down!"

As we oozed across the highway, a high-power spotlight shot its beams from a black sedan under a street light. The train pulled clear of the highway and then stopped. The sedan rolled up at the side of our car, a low siren sounded like a mean tomcat under a barrel. About a dozen harness cops wheeled the boxcar door wide open. Flashlights played around over the sixty-six men while three or four of the patrol cops crawled in the door.

"Wake up!"

"Okay! Pile out."

"Git movin', you!"

"Yes, sir."

"One at a time!"

"Who're you? Where's your draft card?"

"Whitaker's my name. Blacksmith. Here's my draft number."

"Next! Dam! What's been going on in this car? Civil war? How come everybody all tied up? Wrapped up?"

"Greenleaf is my name. Truck mechanic. Well, see, mister officer, we was havin' a sort of a picnic an' a dance in th' car here. Th' engineer hit his air brakes a little too quick. So quite a bunch of us got throwed down. Bumped our heads up against th' walls. On th' floor. Ah. Right here. My draft card. That's it, ain't it? I cain't see with this rag over me eye."

"I don't believe a word of it! Been some trouble in this car! What was it? Next! You!"

"Here's my card. Dynamite man. Lebeque. I broke my fist all to pieces when I stumbled."

"Draft card, bud! What is this? Car load of drunks? All of you smell like liquor!"

"Picolla. There's my number. Oil field driller. Somebody poured a bottle of wine down my back while I was asleep!"

"Asleep. Yeah! I see they left the chipped glass all over your shirt collar, too! Draft cards, men! Move faster!"

"My name's Mickey the Slick, see! I won't lie to yez! I'm a gambler. Da best. I wear good clothes an' I spent good money! I was lookin' all right, new suit, an' ever'ting. Den sombudy popped me with a quart wine bottle. Cracked my head. Ruint my suit! Here's my number, officer!"

"Whoever cracked this man, I wish to congratulate him! Move on! Fall out the door, there! Line up over there by that patrol car with the rest of them!"

"Tommy Bear. Quarter-breed Indian. Mechanic."

"Hey, Cap! Some of these birds are all beat up! Trouble of some kind! Every single one of them has got a busted ear, or a black eye, or a broken fist, or their clothes ripped dam near off! Been a hell of a fight in this car! About fifty of them!"

"Herd 'em out! All in a bunch!" The captain stuck his head in the door. "March 'em out there under that street light! We'll make 'em talk! Any dead ones?"

"I don't know!" The sarg shot his light around over the car. "I see a few that don't seem to be able to get up!"

"Load 'em out! Git along, you guys! Walk! All of you! Right here under this light! Line 'em up! Finding any dead ones back there?"

"Three or four knocked out! Don't think they're dead! We'll pull them out in this rain and wake them up! Load that one right out through the door. Shake him a little. He looks like he's still flickering. How is this one? His eyes are still batting a little around the edges. Stick his face up to the rain. Bring them other two, boys. Help them along. Shake them good. Looks like they might be salvaged. God, they really must have had a knockdown dragout! Hold them up a little."

"This boid's okay. Rain brought 'im aroun'."

"March him on over yonder to where the captain is. What's the matter with you dam fool men, anyway? Is this all you've got to do? Fight! Beat the hell out of each other! Why, dam me, I didn't think any of you had that much spunk left in you! Why in the hell don't you spend that much energy working? Walk along, there, stud horse! Walk! Here's these four, Cap. That's all of them."

"They look like a bunch of dam corpses!" The captain looked the crowd over. Then he turned toward the boxcar and hollered, "Any more in there? Look for guns an' knives around on th' floor!"

"Here's a pair!" A big tough looker stood up on top of the car behind John and me. "Duckin' outta sight, huh? Git movin' down dat ladder! Now. Watcha got wrapped up dere, mister?"

"This thing?"

"Dat ting. Corpse a some kind?"

"Guitar."

"Aha. Yodel lay dee hoo stuff, eh?"

"My meal ticket."

"Where you headin', black boy?"

"Anywhere I c'n find some work."

"Woik, eh? Where 'bouts is yer shoit?"

"On his guitar."

"Jeez! Christamighty. Do yez think more 'bout dat music box den yer own back?"

"Mah back c'n take it."

"Drop down dere on de groun'. Now git movin'. Over dere where yez see de whole gang 'round dat street light."

I walked along, shaking the water out of my hair.

John said, "Sho' some bad ol' stormy night."

"Here's de pair I caught up on toppa de car, capt'n."

"You two line up. Where's your shirt?"

"Ah done tole him. Dis boy heah got it wrapped 'roun' his music box. Rainin'."

"You tryin' to tell me? It's raining! Men! Did you know that? It's raining! Any of you get wet?"

The sarg was shooting his light in our faces and saying, "Wash some of the blood off of this bloody bunch. What was the trouble, fellows? Who started it all? Who beat up who? Out with it. Talk!"

The last two officers trotted from the boxcar over to the gang. "Here's their artillery," one of them said. He dumped a double handful of knives and the necks of three wine bottles. "No guns."

"No guns?" The captain looked the knives over. "You could cut a man all to pieces with the neck of one of these broken bottles. How many drunks among them?"

"Smell and see."

"I don't think you could tell by smelling, chief. Some bird broke a whole quart over another one's head. Then two or three other jugs got broke over other's heads. Everybody smells like liquor."

We passed by in double file, the cops guiding us, watching us. The sarg looked at one string of draft cards. The big chief looked at another string.

"You two boys. No draft card? It's th' jail if you haven't got 'em. Huh?" the chief said.

"Too young. Sixteen," one boy said.

"Seventeen," the next one nodded.

"All look okay, chief?"

"You, there! What you got wrapped up there—a baby?" The chief asked me.

"Guitar."

"Ohhh. Well. Why not take it out and plunk us offa ditty? Like this. Dum tee dum. Dum tee dum. Tra la la la la!

Yodel layyy dee whooooo! Ha! Ha!" He flumped his coat sleeve and danced around.

"Too wet to play," I told him.

"What th' hell do you bring it out in this stormy weather for, then?" he asked me.

"I didn't order this stormy weather."

"What's this all over you fellows?" the sarg asked us.

"Cement dust," John talked up by my elbow.

"With all of this rain," the chief asked us, "what's gonna happen to all of you?"

I said, "Gonna turn inta statues. You can set us around in yer streets an' parks, so rich ladies can see how purty we are."

"No, men. I ain't holdin' you for nothin'." The chief looked us over. "I could jail you if I wanted to. But I don't know. Vag. Disturbing th' peace. Fighting. Lots of things."

"Riding the freights," the sarg put in.

"Or just bein' here," I said.

"Tell you one thing, by God. I never did see such a dirty, messy, bloody, beat-up bunch of people in my whole life, and I've been a copper for twenty years. I could toss you men in the jug if I wanted to. I don't know. You see, men. . . ."

A big eight-wheel driver locomotive pounded across the road, throwing steam a hundred feet on each side, easing along, ringing its bell, snorting and letting out a four-time toot on its whistle, and drowned out the chief's talking.

"Westbound," John was telling me over my shoulder. "She's sho' a daisy, ain't she?"

"Mighty purty," I told him.

An old gray-headed hobo trotted past us in the dark, swinging his bundle up onto his back, splashing through the mudholes and not even noticing the patrol men. He got a glimpse of all of us guys there under the light and yelled,

"Plenty o' work! Buildin' ships! War's on! Goddam that thunder an' lightnin' to hell! Work, boys, work! I gotta letter right hyere!" He bogged on a few yards past us, waving a white sheet of paper in the dark.

"Work?" One guy broke and trotted in after the old man.

"Job? Where 'bouts?" Another man swung his bundle under his arm and started off.

"Letter?"

"Lemme see it!"

"Where'd he say?"

"Hey! Old man! Wait!"

"Don't let dat stuff fool yez, men. 'Tain't nuttin' but justa dam hobo, wid a dam sheeta paper!"

"Seattle! Seattle!" I heard the old man holler back through the rain. "Work, worrrrrk!"

"Crazy."

"Yuh know, men, they ain't no work out at Seattle. Hell's bells, that's more'n fifteen hundred miles west uv here!"

"Out toward Japan!"

"Th' old man had th' letter right there in his hand!"

"Reckin he's right?"

Three more men tore loose through the dark.

"I know them Seattle people. You cain't beat 'em. Mighty purty women. An', by God, they don't write letters, less they mean what they say!"

"I slep' under ever' bridge in Seattle! That's a workin' town!"

"You men going entirely nuts?" a cop asked us.

"I want as close ta Japan as I kin git!" Another man drifted off in the dark.

"Ah wants a crack at that Horehouse Heato mah own se'f!"

"Pahdon me, mistah poleese. Is dat train headin' to'd

wheah them Japs is fightin'?"

Men sloshed holes of water dry, and bogged off through the spray of wind and rain. Cops stood behind us in the street light, scratching and laughing. I snuffed my nose and squinched my eyes to keep the water from getting me.

"Risin' sun! Wahooo!"

"See ya latah, offisssahh!"

"Rain on, little storm, rain on!"

More men charged after the moving train. It creaked along, the wet enamel flicking the dim light from the telephone pole where the cops stood around. Big iron wheels groaning along on the shiny rails. Slick ladders. Slippery tin roofs, bucking first to one side, then the other, and the black shapes of the men sticking like waterbugs, sucking on like snails, swaying with the cars, everybody mumbling and talking and cracking jokes back at the storm.

"Did Mr. A. Hitler say we was a nation of sissies?"

Four more men sidled off down and caught onto a boxcar right beside me. Six more slushed along behind them. Eight swung up the ladder at their heels. Whole boxcars littered with men talking and going to fight.

"Read that letter, old man! Yippeee!"

Ten more come up the ladder. Twenty behind them.

I told the cop next to me, "Those boys are shore gonna need some music! Let her rain!" And I shinnied up the iron ladder of the next car.

I hunkered down on top of the car, with John setting right beside me.

"Thunder! Let 'er crack!" An older man was waving his arms like a monk praying on top of a mountain.

"Ain't you th' dam guy I split in th' mouth? I'm sorry, man!"

"You broke a wine bottle over my head? We won' break de nex' wine! By God, we'll drink it! Yah!"

Men rolled around and laughed. Rocked back and forth as the train picked up speed. Smoke rolled back down along the tops of the cars, blotting them almost out. I looked back at the dozen cops standing around under the street light.

"Too bad we cain't ride inside!" I was yelling around at the night riders. "Gonna git wetter'n holy hell!"

"Let 'er ripple! What th' hell d'ya want in a war, boy, a big soft ass cushion? Ha! Ha! Ha!"

"Trot me out a ship needs a buildin'!"

"Whooofff!"

I was having a hard time standing up, blinking my eyes to try to get some cinders out. I looked around with my head ducked down into the wind and smoke.

And in that one blink of my one eye I got another look along the train. Men. A mixed-up bunch of blurred shadows and train smoke. Heard about work. Just heard about it.

"I'm da wattah boy!"

I looked down at my elbow.

"How. How'n th' hell come you two on this here train? I thought you was a long time gone!"

"Nawww. Nuttin' like dat," the little runt spit out into the rain. "Nuttin' like dat."

"This train's a-goin' ta Seattle! Fifteen hundred miles!"

"Yeaaaa."

John was riding at my feet, setting down with his bare back to the wind, talking. "Gonna be one mighty bad ol' night, boys. Rainy."

"Yaaaa."

"Stormy."

"So whattt?"

"We're goin' out ta th' West Coast ta build ships an' stuff ta fight them Japs with, if this rain don't wash us out before we get there!"

"Wid ya. Wid ya."

"Hell! We're fightin' a war!"

"Cut de mushy stuff."

I listened back along the train and my ears picked some low singing starting up. I strained in the storm to hear what the song was. The whoof-whoof of the big engine hitting her speed drowned the singing out for a minute, and the rattle and creaking of the cars smothered it under; but as I listened as close as I could, I heard the song coming my way and getting louder, and I joined with the rest of the men singing:

> This train don't carry no smoker,
> Lyin' tongues or two-bit jokers;
> This train is bound for glory
> This train!

Wet wind curled in the drift of the train and cinders stung against my eyelids, and I held them closed and sung out at the top of my voice. Then I opened my eyes just a little slit, and a great big cloud of black engine smoke pushed down over the whole string of cars, like a blanket for the men through the storm.

THE END

For more information about Woody Guthrie and The Woody Guthrie Tribute Fund, write to the Fund at Room 2017, 250 West 57th Street, New York, N.Y., 10019.